OF PRELATES AND PRINCES

OF PRELATES AND PRINCES

A Study of
the Economic and Social Position of
the Tudor Episcopate

FELICITY HEAL

CAMBRIDGE UNIVERSITY PRESS

Cambridge

London   New York   New Rochelle

Melbourne   Sydney

Published by the Press Syndicate of the University of Cambridge
The Pitt Building, Trumpington Street, Cambridge CB2 1RP
32 East 57th Street, New York, NY 10022, USA
296 Beaconsfield Parade, Middle Park, Melbourne 3206, Australia

First published 1980

Printed in Great Britain by The Anchor Press Ltd
and bound by Wm Brendon & Son Ltd
both of Tiptree, Essex

British Library Cataloguing in Publication Data
Heal, Felicity
Of prelates and princes.
I. Title
262'.12   BX5067   79-41791
ISBN 0 521 22950 2

To Geoff and Bridget

CONTENTS

FIGURES

ix

PREFACE

This book has been written from a conviction that the economic and social problems of the Tudor episcopate have not yet been given adequate attention by historians. Since Christopher Hill's seminal work *The Economic Problems of the Church* indicated the importance of this field of Reformation studies, there have been a number of detailed investigations by other scholars, covering particular dioceses or groups of the clergy. But there has been no other attempt to analyse the fortunes of a whole section of the church, and the local studies often remain scattered in unpublished dissertations or individual articles. My own struggles with the diocese of Ely and its bishops persuaded me that there was a need for a more general consideration of the state of the bishops, since understanding the social and economic role of the higher clergy is an important prerequisite to a perception of why they succeeded or failed as spiritual leaders. This volume is therefore intended as a first essay in understanding the circumstances of the episcopate during the disturbed century of the English Reformation. It depends upon the research undertaken by a variety of people during the last fifteen years, as well as on my own extensive quarrying in diocesan and other local record offices.

It was apparent from the inception of my research that questions about the economic behaviour and fortunes of the leaders of the church could not be dissociated from questions about the policies of the crown. Even before 1534 the crown did much to mould and influence the financial arrangements and life-pattern of its higher clergy. Thereafter royal power was all-pervasive and was often the key determinant in establishing the financial well-being or suffering of the bishops. I have therefore linked my analysis of the circumstances of the episcopate to a narrative account of the changes in royal policy which materially influenced its welfare. This has not always made for an easy arrangement of the text, but the basic plan adopted is chronological, a plan designed to emphasise the important role of the prince in the financial affairs of the church.

The Tudor bishop as 'homo economicus' has often had a bad name among historians. From Browne Willis's condemnation of the 'sacrilegious alienations' of some prelates to Christopher Hill's more cautious remarks upon the 'frailties' of others, he has often been seen as weak and ineffective in the exercise of secular power and occasionally noted as downright corrupt. The present narrative tends to err a little in the opposite direction, to seek to explain sympathetically the difficulties of the clerics who lived through these troublesome years and were expected to assume the leadership of a complex church. One cannot live for some years with the embattled Edwardian and Elizabethan prelates without developing some sense of identity with them and a corresponding or even stronger distaste for the rapacity of their lay counterparts. History may have been on the side of the new lay 'possessioners' but their individual behaviour is often a sorry reflection upon the ethical standards of Tudor society. The minority of corrupt, inept or ineffective prelates must not be explained away, but the majority of their colleagues, who had none of these obvious vices, should be evaluated in relation to their own time and to contemporary standards of behaviour as well as by some ideal concept of Christian stewardship.

The book, during its slow conception and gestation, has been much influenced by others. My principal debt is to Professor Geoffrey Elton, who not only introduced me to the study of the Tudor church but has been unfailing in his support and encouragement ever since. Perhaps only his other students will understand how important this support can be. His most recent kindness has been to read the various drafts through which this volume has passed, and his comments have added substantially to the approach of the final work. Particular gratitude is also due to Dr Claire Cross and Mrs Dorothy Owen, who have for some years been unstinting with their time in offering me insights into the history and organisation of the English church. Both have read drafts of this volume for me, and I have profited greatly from their comments. Dr David Loades and Professor Joel Berlatsky were also kind enough to read the sections of the book relevant to their own interests and to save me from a variety of errors with their perceptive remarks. I would also like to thank Dr Christopher Haigh, Dr Rosemary O'Day, Professor Patrick Collinson, Mr Leslie Jenkins, Dr Stephen Lander and Dr Ralph Houlbrooke for suggestions, ideas and discussions which have contributed materially to the final version of this book.

One of the delights of research based upon local sources is that it offers the opportunity to visit county record offices and other local repositories throughout the land. I have benefited from the kindness, patience and knowledge of many county and diocesan archivists during the years in which this volume was in the making. A particular debt of gratitude to Canon Bussby, librarian to the dean and chapter of Winchester, and to Miss Melanie Barber, archivist at Lambeth Palace, must be recorded, as must thanks to Dr William Sheils for his assistance at the Borthwick Institute of Historical Research. I am grateful to Mr and Mrs More-Molyneux for permission to consult some of the Loseley papers still retained at Loseley House. Much of the early research on which this book is based was undertaken while I held a research fellowship at Newnham College, Cambridge from 1970 to 1973, and I would like to thank the Principal and Fellows of the College for all their support during this period.

Miss Alison Boyd performed a very valuable service for me in transcribing the leases of the archbishops of York which survive in the registers of the dean and chapter. She offered me far more detail and insight into the records than I had a right to expect when I applied to her for help. Thanks are also due to Miss Caroline McKenna, who undertook the typing of the last stages of the book. Finally I would like to express gratitude to my husband for his assistance with the tables and statistics and to my mother for offering me much of the domestic support that has made this enterprise possible.

F.H.

Lewes, Sussex
July 1979

ABBREVIATIONS

APC   *Acts of the Privy Council of England*, n.s., ed. J. R. Dasent (1890–1907)
BIHR   *Bulletin of the Institute of Historical Research*
BL   British Library
  Add. MSS.   Additional Manuscripts
  Cott. MSS.   Cottonian Manuscripts
  Harl. MSS.   Harleian Manuscripts
  Lans. MSS.   Lansdowne Manuscripts
Bodl.   Bodleian Library
CCCC   Corpus Christi College, Cambridge
CDC   Canterbury Dean and Chapter Records
CPR   *Calendars of the Patent Rolls*
CStP   *Calendars of the State Papers*
  Dom.   *Domestic*
  For.   *Foreign*
  Ven.   *Venetian*
CUL   Cambridge University Library
CuRO   Cumberland Record Office
DDR   Durham Diocesan Records (Dept of Palaeography, University
    of Durham)
DNB   *Dictionary of National Biography*
DRO   Devon Record Office
Du Boulay   F. Du Boulay, *The Lordship of Canterbury* (1966)
EcHR   *Economic History Review*
EDR   Ely Diocesan Records (Cambridge University Library)
EETS   Early English Text Society
EHR   *English Historical Review*
Hembry   P. Hembry, *The Bishops of Bath and Wells, 1540–1640* (1967)
HeRO   Hereford Record Office
Hill   C. Hill, *Economic Problems of the Church from Archbishop Whitgift to the
    Long Parliament* (Oxford 1956)
HJ   *Historical Journal*
HMC   *Historical Manuscripts Commission Reports*
HRO   Hampshire Record Office

JEH   *Journal of Ecclesiastical History*
LP   *Letters and Papers Foreign and Domestic of the Reign of Henry VIII*, ed. J. S.
    Brewer, J. Gairdner and R. H. Brodie, 21 vols. (1862–1932)
LPL   Lambeth Palace Library
NRO   Norwich Record Office
Parker Correspondence   *The Correspondence of Matthew Parker,* ed. J. Bruce and
                T. Perowne, Parker Society (Cambridge 1853)
PRO   Public Record Office
PROB   Public Record Office – Probate Records of the Prerogative
    Court of Canterbury
SaRO   Salisbury Record Office
SRO   Surrey Record Office (Guildford Muniments Room)
StPDC   St Paul's Cathedral Dean and Chapter Records
TRHS   *Transactions of the Royal Historical Society*
VCH   *Victoria County Histories of England*
VE   *Valor Ecclesiasticus,* ed. J. Caley and J. Hunter, 6 vols. (1810–34)
WiDC   Winchester Dean and Chapter Records
WRO   Worcester Record Office
WSRO   West Sussex Record Office
YDC   York Dean and Chapter Records

1

THE BISHOPS AND THE
PRELUDE TO REFORMATION

I

The Reformation of the sixteenth century brought changes of great importance in the life of northern Europe. The consequences of the new confessions of faith were far-reaching: political and economic patterns of behaviour were altered just as definitely as were the modes of worship. An obvious feature of these changes was the transfer of much of the power and wealth of the old church to the laity. Wherever the authority of the papacy was rejected the symbols of ecclesiastical power, independent jurisdiction and large estates, were likely to be denied the clergy and turned to other uses. The great reformers all advocated a fundamental change in the condition of the priesthood; they all converted the separated, consecrated *sacerdos* into a preaching pastor, called by his congregation to his particular vocation principally for his skill in expounding the Word. Such a man had no need of great possessions, merely of the 'sufficient maintenance' which would guarantee him the freedom to pursue his duties. The residual wealth of the old church should be used for godly purposes – charity, learning and the building of a Christian commonwealth. These ideas took deep root in Protestant Europe: it became part of the common coin of contemporary polemical writings that many of the errors of the Roman church derived from its acceptance of wealth and political power in the century of Constantine. Such ideas were as music to the ears of those princes who saw the wealth and power of the old church as more appropriate for themselves than for the priesthood. A crude lust for wealth cannot, of course, be taken as the sole explanation for the behaviour of the German or Scandinavian princes, but the desire to harness the power of the ecclesiastical establishment, of which wealth was an integral part, does still stand as the key reason for the reception of Lutheran ideas by Gustavus Vasa in Sweden and Christian III in Denmark.

In England, where reformation was initiated from above by a devout Catholic king, the ecclesiastical structure continued to conform more closely to that of Rome than to Wittenberg or Geneva. Yet in practice the position of the clergy was altered almost as fundamentally as in the fully reformed polities. The crown aggregated to itself all control over the church as institution. The most dramatic consequence of this action was the dissolution of the monasteries, undertaken with an efficiency and ruthlessness that demonstrated the strength of the English monarchy. Few Protestant princes could move so swiftly or directly against the clerical establishment. The dissolution also underlined the dependence of the survivors, the secular clergy, upon the goodwill of the crown. Admittedly, the king could not dispense with their services in the way he could with those of the monastic orders, but neither their wealth nor their station within society were immune from his attentions. It was the choice of the monarchy that the English clergy did not conform to the new continental model: they remained instead a curious hybrid, increasingly ministers of the Word but still organised within an essentially Catholic institutional structure.

The mixture inevitably produced tensions and problems, most of all for the leaders of the clergy, the bishops. The very survival of consecrated bishops in a system supposedly Protestant was something of an anomaly. The explanation must lie not only in the convoluted history of the Reformation in England, but in the close interdependence of crown and bishops in the preceding centuries. For the English bishop already had two roles before the Reformation. He was a leader and pastor to his flock, with an especial obligation to supervise the lesser clergy. He was also the servant of the crown: usually a nominee of the king and often engaged in secular administration. In executing these dual roles the bishop helped to maintain and reinforce those ideas of hierarchy and degree, harmony and order, that were so valued by the monarchy. The prelates had been tamed and fitted to their duties to an extent not found elsewhere in northern Europe, even across the border in Scotland, and there was no logical reason for Henry VIII and his successors to abandon so valuable an order. In one sense the break with Rome simplified the obligations of churchmen, for they now served but one master. Yet dependence upon the monarchy brought its own problems: there was the constant need for royal support in the enforcement of religious conformity, and there was the issue of royal control over the revenues and administration of the church. The former problem was created by the diversity of opinion nurtured by doctrinal change and the difficulty of enforcing discipline upon the dissenting minorities. This was compounded in the Elizabethan era by the fact that neither the Catholics nor a vocal section of the puritans accepted that the bishops had any authority. Royal control over revenues raised other issues: the crown could, at one extreme, have chosen to make the prelates salaried officials of the state; at the other, it could have chosen to defend all the rights and powers of the clergy. In practice it steered an erratic course between the two extremes, the former being on the whole too revolutionary for the Tudor polity, the latter unattractive in an age when it had become acceptable to take wealth from the church. Moreover the Reformation encouraged other laymen to look for profit from ecclesiastical wealth, and the crown had to weigh the demands of influential laymen against the needs of a vulnerable clergy.

It is one of the fascinations of the English Reformation that the bishops and cathedral chapters not only survived in this new environment but actually retained much of their wealth and social influence. Despite the events of the mid-seventeenth century, the episcopal principle remained deeply embedded in English society: aristocracy and episcopacy were the twin pillars of the Establishment until the beginning of our own century. Unlike aristocracy, however, episcopacy had to survive not one but two 'crises'.[1] The second in time, that of the Civil War, was evidently the more serious, since it meant the temporary abolition of the order. This study is not concerned with that crisis, nor even with the contribution of Archbishop Laud to its beginnings, but with the difficulties of the preceding century. There is some value in considering the survival of the bishops between the 1530s and 1603 as separate from the Stuart sequel. A chapter was closed with the arrival of James I and with the legislation of his first parliament, which prohibited the alienation or long lease of episcopal lands even to the crown (1 Jac. I c. 3). The year 1603 obviously did not mark the end of the difficulties of the bishops, but it does mark the point at which the fortunes of the order begin to be associated more closely and more consistently with those of the crown than they had been during the Tudor age.

The existence of a crisis for the bishops in the sixteenth century has long been recognised by historians. The Anglican authors of the seventeenth and eighteenth centuries – Bishop Burnet, Browne Willis and John Strype – ascribed most of their problems to the

1. L. Stone, *The Crisis of the Aristocracy 1558–1641* (Oxford 1967).

inconsistent behaviour of the crown and to the machinations of the avaricious lay élite. Recent studies have been more interested in the influence of ideology and economics. Christopher Hill has linked demands upon the church with the growth of puritan sentiment and alternative views on ecclesiastical organisation. Inflation is now recognised as a major enemy for most Tudor landlords, and the bishops were no more exempt from its effects than were the nobility. But, while the general nature of the crisis is widely known, there has been no attempt to trace its course in detail between the Reformation and the end of the century. Such an undertaking involves a twofold analysis: a close investigation of the bishops from their own archives and papers and from the local studies that have been written in recent years, plus a consideration of royal policy and lay attitudes and demands, the 'external dimension' which determined the general fortunes of the bishops. The present study is an attempt to marry these two themes in order to produce a clearer understanding of the episcopate and the nature of its survival under the Tudors. Much still remains to be investigated and discovered, especially in the rich diocesan archives that have not yet found their specialist historians, and it is hoped that this volume will provide stimulus to others to continue the investigation.[2]

It is necessary at the outset to justify the isolation of the bishops as a social and economic group suitable for study. In certain ways their economic and social existence was little differentiated from that of other great landowners. Their estates were managed by similar methods, and their wealth allowed them to consort with the nobility and substantial gentry of the realm. After the 1540s, when the clergy were allowed to marry, the resemblances appear even closer as dynastic considerations became important for the prelates. Nevertheless, the differences between lay and ecclesiastical landlords easily outweigh the similarities. The lands of the church were non-hereditary: like the king the bishop had property only by virtue of his office, but unlike the king he had no hope that the office would descend to his heirs. Moreover, the bishops were clearly separated from their lay compeers: most of the criteria used to identify a different social grouping can be applied here. They were marked out by function,

2. G. Burnet, *History of the Reformation* (Oxford 1829). Browne Willis, *Survey of the Cathedrals* (1742). J. Strype, *Ecclesiastical Memorials* (Oxford 1820–40); *Annals of the Reformation* (Oxford 1820–40). C. Hill, *Economic Problems of the Church from Archbishop Whitgift to the Long Parliament* (Oxford 1956).

manners and dress from the laity, and they had identifiable group interests that could and did bring them into conflict with the rest of the political élite.

It is less easy to claim any sharp division between the bishops and the rest of the 'higher clergy'. Here manners, dress and social mores were almost identical, and there was a constant movement of individuals across the barrier as deans, archdeacons or royal chaplains became bishops. Since land and power accompanied office in the church, it was much easier for individuals to be upwardly mobile there than in the lay hierarchy. The obstacles to promotion often occurred early in a cleric's career rather than at the moment when he reached the senior levels of the church. Once his education and connections had been secured, a priest could as readily aspire to a bishopric as to rich pluralities or a prebend. But this study is not concerned with the mobility of the clergy so much as with the office of bishop. That office was sharply delimited from all others within the church. Not only did the prelates exercise unique powers, they also had the lands and wealth to support their seniority. By very rough analogy they occupied the position of the nobility with gentlemen of varying means clustered beneath them. A few of the 'gentlemen', for example some of the deans, might be richer than the Welsh bishops, but on the whole rank and degree were observed in income as well as organisation. The practical step from the post of dean or archdeacon to that of bishop might not be very dramatic, but the social distance was immense. To become 'My Lord of —' instead of merely 'Mr Dean' always seems to have been an exhilarating feeling even when the fortunes of the episcopate were at their lowest. 'The revenue of the place is small', wrote Thomas Cecil of Peterborough in the 1590s, 'and *but for the title of a bishop* I think few will affect it' (my italics).[3] Many did affect that title, and one of the fascinating aspects of the Reformation is the way in which even the most devout and sincere reformers continued to be attracted by the title of bishop. Despite all the links with the rest of the church, the episcopate was a separate and cohesive social group and can be studied as such, provided that we do not neglect its connections with the rest of the clerical establishment.

3. *HMC, Salisbury MSS.*, v, p. 333.

II

The debate about the validity of the church's owning wealth and exercising secular power is almost as old as the institution itself. The gospel message that poverty is a virtue, especially for the ministry, provided a set of values with which the church constantly had to contend. From the time of Christianity's acceptance by the late Roman Empire those with responsibility for the development of the church argued that the work of Christ could not be furthered without wealth. The wealth was understood to be held in trust for the good of the whole *societas Christiana*, not to be for the benefit of an institution or individual. The councils of the church ruled that property and goods given to the clergy must be conserved and used for godly and charitable ends. Bishops were to play a particularly important role in protecting and using this property correctly. In 787 the Council of Nicaea ordained that 'A bishop has responsibility for all ecclesiastical property, and he must administer it as though God is his overseer. It is not lawful for him to appropriate any part of it to himself, or to give his relatives the things that belong to God.'[4] Throughout the Middle Ages there was a continuing need to protect church property from the laity on the one hand and from the churchmen themselves on the other. The question of whether the wealth was of itself valid was easily thrust into the background. Those who found the concepts of wealth and power deeply distasteful found an outlet for their views in the monastic revivals and in the Franciscan movement. The canonists concentrated upon the idea that the possessions of the church were 'in use' for the effective performance of spiritual duties and for works of charity. 'The Church of God', argued canon 18 of Lateran III, 'as a devoted mother is bound to provide for those in need, both in things that pertain to the body, and those that pertain to the good of the soul.'[5] Bishops needed unusual resources because of the extent of their cures and because they were especially enjoined to be charitable. Paul spoke of bishops as 'maintainers' of hospitality, and in the early church one of their principal functions was that of redistribution to the poor.

One of the common complaints against the prelates was not that they accumulated wealth but that they failed in the work of distribution. As Langland's sharp pen has it, 'At one time Charity con-

4. J. Gilchrist, *The Church and Economic Activity in the Middle Ages* (1969), p. 158.
5. *Ibid.* p. 166.

sorted with great prelates, with Bishops and Archbishops, and shared out Christ's patrimony among the poor. But nowadays Avarice keeps the keys, reserving all the treasure for his kinsmen, his servants and his executors – not to mention the Bishop's own offspring.'[6] This concern for charitable behaviour outlived the Reformation: it was often against the standards of earlier prelates who had given generously to the poor, rather than against the ideal of apostolic poverty, that the Tudor bishops were measured. Laymen lamented that the clergy were greedy and that wealth would be better used by themselves: clerical reformers urged generosity to the poor as an integral part of a caring ministry. Thomas Becon, in particular, pleaded for a continuation of the old ideals: 'For, albeit that hospitality is required in all spiritual ministers, yet in bishops chiefly. A bishop's house without hospitality is as a tavern without wine.'[7] Since even the parochial clergy were supposed to bestow a quarter or third of their income in acts of charity, these expectations were large indeed. Most ecclesiastics examined by the late-medieval writers, as well as by their sixteenth-century successors, inevitably failed to do so much.

The issue of hospitality provides a good example of continuity of attitudes from the medieval period into the age of Reformation. Since much of the lay hostility to clerical wealth and power which we shall encounter in the sixteenth century had these roots in the past, it is necessary to look briefly at the knotty problem of anticlericalism in the Middle Ages. We have been reminded that on the eve of the Reformation anticlericalism was a many-headed hydra, ranging from popular hostility towards the privileged, through demands for the dispossession of bishops and abbots, to those reformers who insisted that only upon the abolition of ecclesiastical privilege could the true renewal of society begin. Perhaps the most common form in the fourteenth and fifteenth centuries combined popular hostility with some measure of hope for social renewal, though the latter often took the form only of a longing to return to some imagined golden age when the spirit of Christianity was more truly observed by the church. Few writers or preachers could resist the temptation to criticise the clergy, but the seriousness of intent varied enormously. In a narrative such as *Reynard the Fox* the rich prelates have their passing mention, since they 'preach and say all other wise than they think and do', but no prolonged moralising is permitted to interrupt the

6. William Langland, *Piers the Ploughman* (1968), p. 186.
7. Thomas Becon, *Early Writings* (Cambridge 1843), p. 24.

tale. Sebastian Brant's *Ship of Fools* often shows the clergy out-follying the laity but draws no further conclusions than that all estates are cast adrift upon the sea of life. Even the more pointed satire of John Skelton seems more bent upon appealing to popular hostility to the mighty than upon well-analysed criticism.

> Bishops, if they may
> Small houses woulde keep,
> Not slumber forth and sleep,
> And essay to creep
> Within the noble walls
> Of the kinges halls,
> To fat their bodies full,
> Their soules lean and dull . . .[8]

This vein of writing upon clerical abuses and pride, sometimes associated with more general mistrust of the mighty, of the folly of ambition and so on, is the easiest to associate, at least by inference, with popular attitudes. It recurs in various forms in many of the mystery and morality plays and even in the occasional romance. It was not at all incompatible with the flourishing lay piety which characterised this period, though the prevalence of cynicism about the 'possessioner' church helps to explain the flow of charitable donations away from the seculars towards the mendicants. The more constructive and serious forms of anticlericalism are largely to be found, as one would expect, within the clerical estate. Langland may be said to stand on the borders of that estate, and his criticism combines overt hostility with the yearning for reform. On the one hand he preserves the story most commonly used in attacks upon the wealthy church: 'When Constantine endowed the Church so generously, and gave it land and vassals, estates and incomes, an angel was heard to cry in the air above the city of Rome, saying: "This day the wealth of the Church is poisoned and those who have Peter's power have drunk venom." ' On the other the whole journey of his dreamer in *Piers Plowman* is towards a salvation that can be achieved only with the aid of the church through the sacraments. Clerical moralists closer to the establishment tempered their words more obviously but could still challenge the values of the contemporary episcopate

---

8. *The History of Reynard the Fox*, ed. N. F. Blake, EETS (1970), p. 60. The English version of the *Ship of Fools* is a loose translation by Alexander Barclay, ed. G. A. Jamieson (Edinburgh 1874). *The Complete Poems of John Skelton*, ed. P. Henderson (1959), p. 253.

in compelling terms. Those two great preachers of the fourteenth century, Thomas Brinton and Archbishop Fitzralph, consistently argued that the bishops failed in their duties of visitation and preaching because they were beguiled by wealth and power, 'for prelates at court do not usually visit their flocks except in the person of the sheep shearers'. The consequence of such neglect must be similar failures from the lower clergy and indifference or hostility from the laity.[9] Men such as Langland, Brinton and Fitzralph had a positive belief in the need for reform, but had not yet found any adequate mode for its expression. They advocated merely a return to the old 'right observance' of duty by every estate: an outer demonstration of inner spiritual renewal within the existing pattern and framework of society.

The humanist writers of the early sixteenth century at least began to recognise that renewal implied external change, that the education of the clergy was an integral part of their advance towards a truly Christian life. But by contrast, their attack upon the structure and hierarchy of the church, upon the commitment of its members to secular office and cares, was often less pointed than that of their predecessors. Even the acerbic Erasmus was less inclined to assail careerist bishops than indolent monks. The prelates did not, of course, escape the wit of Folly. They were reminded of their obligations to act as shepherds to their flocks, obligations so easily forgotten: 'Yet when it comes to pecuniary matters they truly act the part of a bishop to the hilt, overseeing everything – and overlooking nothing.' But there is no doubt that Erasmus pointed to the regulars as the most suitable target for the anticlerical feelings of the laity. Other humanists were even less willing to expose the leaders of the church to the contempt of the generality. When Bishop Fisher did consider the problem of rich prelates his tone was nostalgic rather than explicitly critical or reformist: 'Truly it was a more glorious sight to see St. Paul, which got his living by his own great labour . . . than to behold now the archbishops and bishops in their apparel be it never so rich. In that time there were no chalices of gold, but there were many golden priests . . .'[10]

The reasons for the comparative reticence of the English humanists

9. Langland, *Piers the Ploughman*, p. 193. G. Owst, *Preaching in Medieval England* (Cambridge 1926), p. 253.
10. *The Essential Erasmus*, ed. J. P. Dolan (1964), p. 156. John Fisher, *English Works* (1876), p. 181.

are not far to seek. Most were either clerics themselves or had close links with the hierarchy: they sought the regeneration of church and society through the bishops and were therefore reluctant to expose their weaknesses. The exposure of the folly and ambition of all estates was one thing; specific criticism of the sort found in Brinton's sermons was quite another in the climate of the early sixteenth century. So the clerical humanists concentrated upon the practical work of reformation: the foundation of colleges and schools, the close supervision of the parochial clergy and the improvement of moral discipline. In the years before the Reformation this produced a generation of bishops who answered many of the charges of earlier moralists. Men such as Fisher, Nicholas West, Robert Sherburne, Hugh Oldham and John Longland were often resident in their sees, were energetic as overseers and maintainers and did attempt to instil humanist educational values whenever they had the opportunity. Some of them even preached regularly, though failure to preach was still one of the most obvious omissions of the prelates. In all of this the dilemma of wealth and the jealousy that it aroused among the laity were readily forgotten: wealth was put to sound use, its holders would probably have argued, and was therefore better left in the hands of the church than dispersed among the avaricious men outside.[11]

The caution of the leaders of the church was founded upon real tensions with the laity that cannot have been fully apparent to Brinton or Fitzralph. It was the experience of the early Lollard movement that convinced most prelates that there was a genuine danger of power and wealth being taken from the church and that this danger must be resisted. Not, of course, that the church in England had ever been free of royal intervention. The whole period since the Norman Conquest had been marked by a series of accommodations between church and state on financial matters and rights of dominion. The monarch commanded considerable power over his clerical subjects; by the fourteenth century this included rights to money and services from his tenants and regalian control over lands of a see during a vacancy. The 1279 Statute of Mortmain had secured a royal veto over

11. On the humanist bishops of the early sixteenth century see J. J. Scarisbrick, 'The Conservative Episcopate in England, 1529–35', unpub. Ph.D. thesis, Cambridge University (1956). A. A. Mumford, *Hugh Oldham* (1936). S. J. Lander' 'The Diocese of Chichester, 1508–58: Episcopal Reform under Robert Sherburne and its Aftermath', unpub. Ph.D. thesis, Cambridge Univeristy (1974). F. Heal, 'The Bishops of Ely and their Diocese during the Reformation', unpub. Ph.D. thesis, Cambridge University (1972).

lands which passed into the hands of the clergy, although licences to alienate were granted readily enough, and the measure proved principally a revenue-raising device. The first half of the fourteenth century witnessed the struggle of the crown to claim general taxes from the clergy. This fundamental inroad into clerical privileges was strenuously resisted by convocation, although the bishops, as royal appointees, began to support the crown against the rest of their order from the mid-century onwards. None of these demands upon the clergy extended to their fundamental rights of landholding. The only lands which the crown seized were those of the Templars in 1308 and the possessions of alien priories a century later. Although both acts set some precedent for the future, they were seen as justified by the unusual circumstances of disgrace and war. The money from the alien houses was used to endow new establishments, though Edward II set a clearer example to Henry VIII by using part of the Templars' money to finance his chamber administration between the death of Gaveston and his reconciliation with the earls.[12]

A peculiar conjunction of circumstances in the 1370s helped to bring together for a short time crown demands upon the church, popular anticlericalism and the austere criticism of clerical wealth by the moralists. The conjunction is worth a brief examination for the light which it throws on later ecclesiastical attitudes and for its resemblances to Reformation agitation. The heavy taxation required to finance the French wars had revived the demand that the clergy should pay their taxes alongside the laity. The bishops, having lent support to Edward III in earlier decades, were now prepared to resist the crown again, especially when it was John of Gaunt who was the royal agent. In the Parliament of 1371 two Austin friars offered a theoretical justification for the crown's demands. They argued that a refusal to pay taxes properly required by the government for the defence of the realm was contrary to divine and natural law and that the goods of the clergy could be taken by force in lieu of payment. This theme recurred in the parliamentary sessions of the next two decades: the laity were by no means averse to threatening the clergy with alienations if they failed in their duties as loyal subjects. In 1385 Courtenay, archbishop of Canterbury, refused to sanction a grant of

12. M. Howell, *Regalian Right in Medieval England* (Oxford 1962). M. V. Clarke, *Medieval Representation and Consent* (1936), ch. 3. T. F. T. Plucknett, *Legislation of Edward I* (Oxford 1949), pp. 97–101. M. McKisack, *The Fourteenth Century* (Oxford 1959), p. 292.

a fifteenth and tenth from the clergy which the Commons had demanded as a condition of their own offering.[13] By then the question of taxation had been subsumed into a broader dispute about the relationship of church and state, a dispute that threatened, albeit only for a short time, to shake the foundations of the Catholic church in England.

It was into the dispute upon taxes that John Wycliffe was propelled in the early 1370s to be the scourge of the recalcitrant bishops. Wycliffe's arguments upon lordship and the temporal wealth of the church, part in the first instance of a scholastic examination of the nature of dominion, were presented in London just at the time when feelings ran high against the obstructiveness of the clergy. His impact owed much to this favourable conjunction of circumstances: the ideas themselves were similar to those of some of the friars, especially Augustinian and Franciscan notions upon lordship and grace. Wycliffe distinguished between the righteous and the unrighteous man who claimed dominion. The unrighteous man could not exercise any true lordship, while the righteous had dominion over all things. Thus far he did not diverge significantly from the paths of orthodoxy, but when his work became more specific its potential threat to the 'possessioners' was revealed. Lordship over other men was dependent upon the grace imparted to the individual steward, and if he was found unworthy his authority was no longer legitimate. John of Gaunt was interested in the practical application of these ideas to the clergy who were refusing him support. If they failed in their stewardship, then Wycliffe accorded to the temporal lord the right to deprive them of their property. Refusal to pay war taxation was precisely this sort of failure. The king was a benefactor of the whole church, and since founders and benefactors had the right to expect relief and aid from their endowments, the church was bound to aid the king as part of its stewardship.[14]

The notions which Wycliffe used in his support of Gaunt were therefore valuable to the crown but fairly circumscribed. Freed from

---

13. The statement of the Austins to the Parliament of 1371 is printed in *EHR*, xxxiv (1919), pp. 579–82. Thomas Walsingham, *Historia Anglicana* (1864), ii, pp. 139–40.

14. John Wycliffe, *De Civile Dominio* (1885), i, cc. 1–5, 34; *De Paupertate Christi, Opera Minora* (1913), p. 64. The idea of the privileges of benefactors has, of course, a long ancestry and is connected with the concept of *Eigenkirche*, the rights of a layman over the church of his foundation. Much of the crown's intrusion into the affairs of the church came from this proprietorial notion.

the constraints of the immediate occasion, however, he could attack much more directly the whole of the 'possessioner' church. Here the theory of dominion blended with a much more explicit rejection of wealth as at all legitimate for the clergy. In the third conclusion of *De Paupertate Christi*, for example, he stated bluntly: 'Omnes sacerdotes Christi: pape, cardinales, episcopi, abbates, priores vel eius subditi tenentur sequi Christum in evangelica paupertate.' There is, of course, here something of the common coin of medieval moralising, something of the same tone as that found in *Piers Plowman*. There is also the accepted custom of offering extreme propositions for scholastic dispute. But there is also an earnestness of intent, especially in his later writings, that helped to transmit the ideal of poverty to his followers. The Lollards both insisted on poverty for their own ministers and continued Wycliffe's attack upon the leaders of the church who could not exercise dominion because they were not in a state of grace.[15]

The heresiarch obviously did much to articulate the anticlerical feeling of his age. But the force of his arguments and the zeal of his followers provoked a reaction against heterodox teaching amongst the governing classes as well as in the church. After the papacy's forthright condemnation of his views upon lordship, their implications for lay authority began slowly to dawn upon those who had once supported him. The Peasants' Revolt and the preaching of the early Lollards no doubt helped to produce a clearer perception of the relationship between spiritual and temporal lordship. The conservative attitudes which marked the behaviour of the crown towards the church for most of the fifteenth century are largely the fruit of the traumas of the 1370s and 1380s. The bishops were strongly committed to a policy of assailing heresy and looked to the monarchy to support them. The Lancastrian and Yorkist kings often saw the advantages of such support, especially when it might secure the spiritual sanction of the papacy for their shaky political régimes.[16]

Yet the issue of church wealth was not allowed to die without a struggle. It was still perfectly possible for parliament to feel aggrieved over clerical taxes, or hostile to ecclesiastical wealth, without associating these emotions with a direct attack upon the church. The Lollards played on this contradiction with some skill. In the Parlia-

15. *De Paupertate*, p. 62. H. B. Workman, *John Wyclif: A Study of the English Medieval Church* (Oxford 1926), pp. 297–8.
16. See for example M. E. Aston, *Thomas Arundel* (Oxford 1967).

ment of 1404 there was an attempt to confiscate the temporalities of the clergy for a limited time in order to improve the king's financial position after the wars against Wales and Scotland. Archbishop Arundel vigorously defended the clergy. He claimed that their wealth was inalienable but also argued that they already made a great contribution to the security of the realm. They paid higher taxes than the laity and provided just as many men for the royal host, as well as praying day and night for the success of the armies. This attempt cannot be proved to be Lollard-inspired, but six years later a petition that was definitely connected with the movement was presented in parliament. This was a proposal which had already been presented to Richard II in the 1390s and which offered a practical programme for the alienation of the wealth of the higher clergy. The petitioners claimed that the king could create fifteen earls and fifteen hundred knights, and endow a number of almshouses, from the temporal lands of the church. 'Bishops, abbots, and priors, who are such worldly lords, should live of their spiritual revenues . . .' For the Tudor historian this petition is interesting as the first of a genre that becomes common from the Reformation onwards: suggestions that the lands of the church could be better employed to support the particular concerns of the individual projector. In the context of the early fifteenth century it is of more importance that the petitioners had switched their attention from the crown, which was not receptive to these ideas, to the Commons, where projects for the improvement of royal finance continued to coexist with some anticlerical sympathy. When agitation against clerical power revived again in the early sixteenth century, the Commons were once more in the lead, and it may be only the relative weakness of parliament in the intervening century that leads to the apparent disappearance of lay attacks upon the clergy. The clerical humanists probably had reason for their caution in commenting upon the abuses of the church. The old secular anticlericalism already had strong roots before Henry VIII contemplated his breach with Rome.[17]

17. Walsingham, *Historia Anglicana*, II, pp. 265ff. BL, Cott. MS. Julius B II. The plan is printed in J. Youings, *The Dissolution of the Monasteries* (1972), p. 135. Workman, *John Wyclif*, p. 397, attributes the scheme to the Lollard leader John Purvey and suggests that it was first proposed to Richard II in 1395. For the general demands of the Commons for improvement in royal finances see B. P. Wolffe, *The Crown Lands, 1461–1536* (1970), pp. 24–7.

III

The precedent offered by the events of the late fourteenth century must have been generally available to those most closely involved in the policy decisions of the English Reformation. The crown used the statutes of provisors and praemunire directly, for example, when it was bullying convocation in 1530.[18] The name of Wycliffe was rarely invoked in official circles, since he remained synonymous with a challenge to established authority, but some of the reformers were proud to acknowledge a debt to him. It is much more difficult to demonstrate how the continental reformers influenced English ideas upon the legitimacy of clerical wealth and power. It may well be that there was little specific contact or comparison with other reformed polities until the reign of Edward VI when the full implications of Lutheranism were examined for the first time by the political leadership. Yet already in the 1530s Cromwell and others sympathetic to reform were obviously looking to continental examples. Moreover, it is difficult to imagine the dissolution of the monasteries and the heavy taxation of the clergy imposed by Henry VIII taking place without the stimulus provided by Lutheran Germany.

The two keys to change in those German lands which accepted the Reformation were the doctrine of justification by faith alone and the new attitudes to the prince as Christian magistrate. Solafideism led on towards Luther's belief in the priesthood of all men and overthrew the power of the priesthood as a separate order. The ministry became one among a number of callings. This in turn meant a denial of the assumptions upon which the wealth of the church had been founded. There was now no reason why the cleric should retain land 'in use' for the benefit of the poor and works of charity: every man now had the same responsibility for these activities, and if there was any need to remove this duty from the individual, the state was the obvious agent for distribution. The ministry retained no place within the old feudal hierarchy, and therefore its wealth could not be justified by references to old social or political norms. The minister was now a called man, worthy of his hire as was any good labourer. Ranks within

18. The writ of praemunire never ceased to be used in the intervening period and seems to have been used more regularly under Henry VII, probably with the direct encouragement of the crown. R. Houlbrooke, 'The Decline of Ecclesiastical Jurisdiction under the Tudors', in *Continuity and Change: Personnel and Administration of the Church in England, 1500–1640*, ed. M. R. O'Day and F. Heal (Leicester 1976), pp. 240–1.

the church might in certain circumstances be preserved for the sake of good discipline, but knowledge and experience, rather than gradations of wealth, should provide the main distinctions. To these changes in the role of the parish priest must be added Luther's attack upon monasticism, which emptied the regular orders and left their property at the disposal of the secular authorities. Since the godly magistrate was positively required, as part of his vocation, to supervise and protect the evangelical church, this changed view of the priesthood offered enormous and tempting scope for the exploitation of the property of the old church.

Luther himself advocated that evangelical ministers should be given adequate maintenance and that the other revenues of the church should be used for the education of the clergy and laity and for works of charity. Some of the towns and cities which turned to reform under Luther's guidance succeeded in establishing common chests with exactly these aims in mind. One of the earliest and best-known examples, that of Leisnig, arranged for the transfer of all dues formerly paid to the church into the common chest, from which there was to be a range of disbursements. The most important were the salaries of the minister and chaplain, it being specified that 'with such . . . maintenance they are to be content, and shall in no wise seek or receive anything further from their parishioners'. This was a useful enough arrangement in a small town, or even in one of the imperial free cities where the use of church funds for salaries and works of charity might save the city fathers from having to use their own money to pacify the proletariat. In the principalities, however, the lure of ecclesiastical wealth often proved too strong. The Landgrave Philip of Hesse, for example, consulted his diet in 1527 about the disposal of church goods. A plan was prepared for the establishment of a committee which would allocate 50 per cent of the revenues to the maintenance of the ministry, to education and to charity, while the rest would be used by the prince for the purposes of government. In practice even the 50 per cent designated for general uses was closely controlled by Philip and part seems to have found its way into secular expenditure. Duke Ulrich of Württemberg proceeded by more obviously arbitrary means: he was restored to his territory in 1534 and in the following year seized the property of the church, secularised the monasteries and used most of the proceeds to pay his war debts and finance his government. He used these drastic methods partly because he wished to avoid any dependence upon his estates, and with enough income at his disposal he could manage without even a meeting of the assembly. It is interesting to note that in Württemberg the bishops were not so easily cowed as the monasteries: during the interval after the Schmalkaldic War, when the duchy reverted temporarily to Catholicism, the Protestant higher clergy quietly consolidated their position so that they were able to emerge as a working episcopate with a claim to a place in the counsels of the realm after the final return to the Protestant fold.[19]

Although the developments in Lutheran Germany have some general similarities with those of England, the most interesting parallels are undoubtedly with the Scandinavian lands. Sweden and Denmark began their reformations within a few years of England; they were both relatively centralised kingdoms with a strong monarchical structure that could usefully be reinforced by organising the church for the support and benefit of the prince. But there were also differences from England which dictated the immediate direction of the princes' efforts against the church. Gustavus Vasa was faced in Sweden with the need to overcome the immunity which the clergy enjoyed from taxation: he started from a point which the English monarchy had settled in the fourteenth century. His energy was therefore directed from the first against the secular clergy and the bishops rather than the monasteries. As early as 1524 the Swedish chancellor announced that the church was the whole community of the faithful and that the church's wealth was therefore the people's wealth. Gustavus could not proceed too rapidly in the face of general sympathy for Catholicism, but by 1527 he was strong enough to force the Recess of Västeras upon his reluctant estates. By the provisions of the Recess all bishops were to 'furnish the King with a schedule of their rents and incomes of every kind. From these schedules he shall determine the relative proportions for them to keep and hand over to the Crown.'[20] Property given to the church since 1454 was to revert to its donor – often the crown. This last provision would have been of little significance in England, where the church had almost ceased to increase its landed territory, but the Swedish establishment was still relatively young and continued to be endowed with new lands until the very eve of the Reformation. Gustavus quickly demonstrated his

19. *Martin Luther*, ed. E. G. Rupp and S. Drewery (1970), p. 103. F. L. Carsten, *Princes and Parliaments in Germany* (Oxford 1959), pp. 160, 19ff, 35.
20. M. Roberts, *The Early Vasas* (1968), pp. 62–114. *Documents Illustrative of the Continental Reformation*, ed. B. J. Kidd (1911), p. 235.

B

intention of using the Recess to the full: for example, three of the
bishops consecrated in the following years had to take a new oath
that they would preach and be content with their wages. By the early
1530s the bishops were becoming salaried officials of the state and the
monasteries were meanwhile allowed to wither away as recruiting
was prohibited. The king accepted Lutheran tenets as the theological
basis for his new church, but throughout his reign he showed far more
interest in the power and wealth to be derived from the clergy than
in doctrinal formulae. The justification for his attitude must be sought
in the urgent need of the Swedish monarchy for new sources of
finance in order to increase its power. Gustavus Vasa was one of the
principal architects of royal power in Sweden, and the church was
a key means of financing this construction.

The final movement towards reform was even more abrupt in
Denmark than in Sweden. The succession struggle between Duke
Christian and Christopher, count of Oldenburg, ended in the defeat
of the latter in July 1536. Since Oldenburg had had the support of the
Catholic episcopate, his defeat spelt the doom for the old order.
Frederick I had already in the 1520s won the support of part of the
Catholic nobility for his own reform measures by allowing them to
exploit the lands of the church. Christian III went much further: he
imprisoned the bishops, deprived them of their lands and eventually
abolished the whole order. The estates of the bishops were permanently vested in the crown. Some gesture was made towards learning
and other godly objectives, since episcopal tithes were made available
for the support of the clergy, for the repair of churches and for payment to scholars. In a deliberate break with the past, superintendents
were appointed by the crown in place of the bishops and were paid
salaries by the state. As in Sweden, the monasteries were treated more
gently and allowed to wither away as their inhabitants died.[21] It is
interesting that in both Sweden and Denmark there was later in the
century a slow drift back towards traditional organisation and terminology: 'bishop' superseded the Lutheran 'superintendent' as the
common form of address, for example. However, the events of the
1520s and 1530s in both countries shattered the economic and political
power of the old order and left the leaders of the church with little
influence beyond their powers of spiritual persuasion. This marked
break with the past made it unlikely that any ecclesiastical revival

21. E. H. Dunkley, *The Reformation in Denmark* (1948), pp. 70–85. N. Cragii, *Annales
    Daniae* (Hafniae 1737), add. i, pp. 3ff. Kidd (ed.), pp. 325ff.

in these northern lands could have had the wide repercussions that Arminianism had in England.

In the Scandinavian kingdoms the bishops posed the major threat to the authority of the crown. The monarchies had been too weak in the later Middle Ages to bring the prelates and the church they led under effective control. Monasticism was less of a problem, and since Christianity had taken root comparatively late in the north, the monasteries had not accumulated wealth and lands to the same degree as their English counterparts. William Cecil, writing at the beginning of Elizabeth's reign, praised the Reformation in Denmark specifically because it had deprived the bishops of all their power. But this was long after the dissolution of the monasteries and was anyway said in a letter to the Scottish nobility, who had not been entirely successful in controlling their own prelates.[22] The circumstances of England in the 1530s dictated the priorities of the crown. The bishops were already crown nominees, and the structure of the church over which they presided was relatively well integrated into the English commonwealth. Since they were likely to wish to support the crown, the bishops could play a valuable role in the enforcement of any new settlement, especially in securing the cooperation of the parochial clergy who had to introduce the changes to their congregation. All of this made the bishops much more valuable to the crown than their Scandinavian counterparts and helps to explain why some of the substance of episcopacy survived in England while merely its shadow remained in the northern lands.

22. *CStP For.*, 1558–9, no. 1086.

2

LAND AND SOCIAL AUTHORITY
BEFORE THE REFORMATION

I

The wealth and power of the pre-Reformation episcopate lent force to the criticisms of the friars and Lollards. The bishops were spiritual noblemen and as such were inevitably far removed from any apostolic pattern of ministry. Instead, they were possessed of all the trappings of authority that the church and monarchy could offer. The most essential of their secular adjuncts of power was land, for no nobleman could maintain his place without the income and control over men that land alone afforded. The way in which land had come to the church served to stress the dual role of its leaders. It had come as pious donations and bequests from the Saxon monarchy and nobility and as a reward for feudal service from the Normans. This, of course, simplifies unduly the complex process by which the episcopal estates were acquired, but all the bishoprics had those two elements as the foundation of their possessions.[1] Service to the crown, primarily in the form of the provision of revenue and men for war, continued to be an important duty of the bishops as tenants-in-chief in the early sixteenth century. In this sense, as in their daily management of property, it is difficult to differentiate the spiritual peers from their lay counterparts. The fact that much of the land had originally been given as an act of piety, to aid the church in its work of organising the faithful and of charity, was more easily forgotten in the daily lives of the bishops. Yet it was never wholly neglected, as we shall see in our examination of the endowments and bequests of the early Tudor bench. Many of the humanist bishops acknowledged that their privileges brought responsibilities greater than those imposed upon the laity.

The great period of land accumulation ended for the prelates by the

---

1. On the formation and growth of the episcopal estates see E. Miller, *The Abbey and Bishopric of Ely* (Cambridge 1951); Du Boulay; P. Heath in *VCH, Staffordshire*, III, pp. 15–17.

thirteenth century. The institutional inhibition of the Statute of Mortmain merely confirmed this process. There was little further incentive for the laity to donate lands to the episcopate, and their endowments went instead to the monasteries or later the orders of friars. A few bishops continued to purchase lands to support their sees, but the gains were insignificant in comparison to those of an earlier period. The only group of properties that were acquired late were the London residences, a reflection of the fact that the government was becoming more sedentary and fixed in the capital. Thus the pattern of landholding which we can describe on the eve of the Reformation was already ancient in the eyes of contemporaries. When the commissioners of 1535 returned their information upon the lands and holdings of the church which was brought together to form the *Valor Ecclesiasticus*, they were counting the same number of manors for the bishops as had existed in the mid-fifteenth century, and not many more than those recorded in the earlier survey of the church, the taxation of Pope Nicholas IV of 1291. The prelates could justifiably think of themselves as one of the most stable social and economic groups within the commonwealth.[2]

From the *Valor Ecclesiasticus* it can be estimated that the twenty-one English and Welsh sees, excluding Sodor and Man, held approximately 640 manors in 1535. The manor remained everywhere the basic unit of land and lordship, but its value and significance could range widely. The assessed annual value of these episcopal manors ranged from £1 to over £200; the former probably included no more than a few customary rents and the right to hold court, the latter would have embraced large communities of tenants and substantial tracts of demesne. Despite these wide variations in value, there was usually a direct correlation between the number of manors held and the total revenue of the see. Winchester with seventy-five estates, Canterbury with sixty-six, Durham with sixty-two and Ely with fifty were the four richest sees, all with an income of over £2000 per annum. At the other extreme the poorest bishoprics, Bangor and St Asaph, had only seven and three manors respectively. The manors were scattered throughout the country, though, as fig. 1 shows, they tended to cluster around the cathedral cities. The figure also shows uneven distribution from area to area. Just under 50 per cent of the

2. Plucknett, *Legislation of Edward I*, pp. 97–101. The last large estate to be added to any see was Knole in Kent, given to Canterbury in 1456 by Archbishop Bouchier.

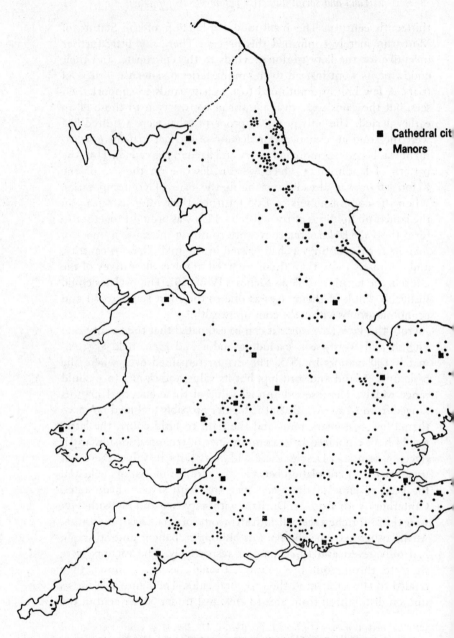

Fig. 1   *Episcopal manors in England and Wales, 1535*

estates were spread across the southern and eastern counties, from Somerset and Dorset in the west to Norfolk and Cambridgeshire in the east. In the remaining thirty-five counties of England and Wales there were only three important concentrations of property: in the Severn valley and the adjoining areas of Hereford and Worcester, in Yorkshire, especially in the North and East Ridings, and in the Durham palatinate. Some counties had scarcely a manor, Lancashire being the most obvious example. In Wales the bishops owned only a few properties around the sea fringes, and the only substantial group of manors was in the extreme south-west, where the castles of St David's give a brooding reminder of the presence of the church. More surprising is the relative shortage of estates in the central counties of England – Buckinghamshire, Bedfordshire, Northamptonshire and Leicestershire.[3]

This pattern of occupation is clearly related to the arrangement of the dioceses. The southern sees were on the whole smaller than those of the north and west and owed their concentration of manors to their early establishment and the patronage of the Saxon kings. Dioceses such as Exeter and York had vast tracts of land under their jurisdiction, and their estates were therefore more scattered. In these large sees the distribution of manors was not normally even: a glance at fig. 1 shows the Exeter lands centred in two areas of Devon, with a thin line extending into Cornwall. It also shows the exclusive focus of York estates in the east and the lack of any in Lancashire, which was under the jurisdiction of the northern archbishop. This uneven distribution explains the emptiness of the central counties, for these were all under the control of the vast see of Lincoln, and most Lincoln manors were near the cathedral city or in Oxfordshire. From the time of the Reformation onwards it is common to find the bishops complaining that their disciplinary work was hampered by this uneven scatter of lands and residences. While the ecclesiastical system had continued without major crises, the fact that the archbishop of York was never resident in Lancashire, or the bishop of St David's in Carmarthen, had hardly mattered, provided that they had reliable deputies. But when the religious settlement was in flux the personal appearance of a leader of the church might have a significant effect on local attitudes and behaviour. Thus the lack of residences in these 'dark corners of the land' was argued to be one of the

3. *VE, passim.*

main reasons for the tenacity of old beliefs, of ignorance and superstition.[4]

Before we can proceed to any estimates of the income of the bishops, it is necessary to ask what precisely an episcopal manor was and what was its importance for the Tudor episcopate. The manor could and did assume a variety of forms. It might be a nucleated estate composed of customary lands and adjacent or intermingled demesne, with the associated rights of lordship and jurisdiction. This 'classic' manorial pattern obtained in many different agricultural areas: to take just three examples, Banwell in Somerset, Terrington in the Norfolk marshland and Alresford in wooded country in Hampshire all followed this general description. From lands of this type the lord received the rents of assize, or customary rents, the payments from the demesne whether rents or produce, the court perquisites and any additional monies that might come from the lease of mills, fisheries, parks or woods. A related estate pattern, especially common in those areas where land had long been enclosed or there were a high percentage of freeholders, was that of a manor with scattered dependent units. These so-called members might be spread over a considerable geographical area and usually consisted of groups of customary and freehold tenants, and demesne being concentrated in one place. Thus Wingham in Kent had eight dependent members but only one central demesne. Most bishoprics also had a few bartons or granges, properties on which sheep-farming was the dominant activity. The bartons were often associated with an ordinary manor, as at Ely, where the barton specialised in pasturing large flocks of sheep on the summer-dry fenlands. In almost all the types so far described there was still a close coherence between the physical reality of the estates and the operation of the manor as a unit of lordship. The bishops seem to have possessed few of those artificial creations which linked diverse parcels of property together merely for the purpose of providing a unit of lordship. When a manor was associated with a town this diversity was often avoided by the division of the estate into a 'burgus' and 'foren' which operated and accounted separately. Of course in the London manors, as in some other towns, the breakdown of the links

4. On the Lincoln bishops and their far-flung diocese see M. Bowker, *The Secular Clergy in the Diocese of Lincoln, 1495–1520* (Cambridge 1967). On Lancashire, C. Haigh, *Reformation and Resistance in Tudor Lancashire* (Cambridge 1975). See also for the situation of Peterborough after the Reformation W. Sheils, 'Some Problems of Government in a New Diocese', in *Continuity and Change*.

between land and lordship was already well advanced. However, it was not until after the Reformation that the bishops began to receive rural manors that were not cohesive units. It was then, for example, that the archbishops of Canterbury found themselves blessed with a property such as Enbroke, composed of three separate tracts of demesne, two unrelated sets of rents of assize, and a rectory.[5]

The tenurial arrangements upon these diverse manors depended upon the customs of the locality rather than upon any peculiarity of episcopal management. Thus, in Kent, Durham and Northumberland freeholders formed an important part of the tenantry, while in much of the south copyhold tenure was the norm. Most bishoprics still had their share of bondmen in the early sixteenth century: manumissions, or the release from bondage, were still being granted at Ely at the beginning of Elizabeth's reign. Tenancy-at-will, rather than by copy of court roll, was common in some sees, but it is not always easy to isolate in the surviving financial records, which usually place all payments of both types under the rents-of-assize heading. The customary tenants and the bishops' officers had their closest contacts through the manorial court. This provided, of course, a centre for regulating the agrarian life of the community, and the lord had the responsibility for adjudicating issues that arose between the tenants in conformity with the established custom of the manor. Normally, however, the main interest of the officers was financial, the levying of the agreed fines for misbehaviour and the securing of the rights of lordship – entry fines, heriots and recognisances. Only a major change in agrarian practice was likely to bring the lord and tenant into a closer relationship and create the circumstances for possible conflict. In the sixteenth century enclosure was the change most likely to occur, and there is evidence from various manors of land being taken into severalty either by agreement among the tenants or sometimes by the initiative of the demesne farmers. Bishop Foxe was charged with making illegal enclosures in Hampshire, but the fault seems to lie with his farmers, as it does in Ely where some of Bishop Goodrich's demesne farmers engaged in a prolonged struggle against the customary tenants of Ely town. The bishops themselves seem to have engaged in enclosure only to extend their parklands: the 1517 investigations revealed, for example, that Bishop Audley had enlarged Colwall park in Herefordshire, and in 1548 a jury at Ely alleged that

---

5. Heal, 'The Bishops of Ely', pp. 205–7. Du Boulay, pp. 56–60. Sixteen manors have been omitted from fig. 1 because of uncertainty about their location.

Bishop West had earlier enclosed an area known as Chettisham Bushes, intending to make a deer park of it.[6]

The importance of the manor to the bishops was not therefore that it offered them influence or control over the agrarian round. The manor was principally a source of income which brought a range of secondary benefits – patronage, comfortable residences and power over men. Income was by this period mainly in cash from the rents, fines and dues of the tenants. Even the demesne, that land which the lord could farm for himself, had been largely surrendered to farmers before and during the fifteenth century. The bishops always seem to have been less committed to direct farming than the settled monastic houses. While the monasteries needed a relatively constant supply of food, and monastic organisation was designed to secure continuity in the administration, the needs of an episcopal household were variable. A percentage of the bishops were permanent absentees from their dioceses, and before the Reformation most of the rest spent part of their time in London, far from their main estates. Moreover, bishops, unlike an institution, were not immortal, and a change of lord might lead to a change of circumstances that made long-term planning for direct farming difficult. This did not, of course, prevent the episcopate from following the general pattern of the thirteenth century and farming intensively both for their own needs and for the market. But it did mean that when the movement towards leasing began in the fourteenth century, the bishops were among the first to divest themselves of much of their entrepreneurial activity. By the beginning of our period they were commonly *rentiers*, at least on the majority of their outlying manors.[7]

Much of the income that derived from the estates was inflexible; that is, it was governed by customary rules which could not be altered unilaterally by the bishop or his officers. Rents of assize were fixed by custom, as were most fines and dues. It was the task of the estate officials to ensure that all sums to which the lord was entitled were collected. The demesne was a different proposition, for it was

6. *The Agrarian History of England and Wales, vol.* IV; *1500–1640*, ed. J. Thirsk (Cambridge 1967), pp. 19–20. *Letters of Richard Fox, 1486–1527*, ed. P. S. and M. H. Allen (Oxford 1928), no. 66. Heal, 'The Bishops of Ely', p. 205. *Registrum Caroli Bothe*, ed. A. T. Bannister, Cantilupe Soc. (1921), p. 61. W. M. Palmer, 'Enclosures at Ely, Downham and Littleport, 1548', *Trans. of the Cambridge and Huntingdonshire Archaeological Soc.*, V (1930–7), 369.

7. E. Miller, *The Abbey of Ely*, pp. 81–3, 110–12. F. Du Boulay, 'A Rentier Economy in the Later Middle Ages: The Archbishopric of Canterbury', *EcHR*, 2nd ser., XVI (1964), 427–38.

under the direct control of the lord and offered, at least in theory, an income which could be adapted and increased to meet new economic circumstances. For this reason, and because it was a valuable source of patronage, the bishops were more likely to be involved in the leasing of the demesne than in most other aspects of estate management. There were three possible forms of lease which could be employed in granting out the demesne. First, the land could be given at will of the lord, with no written indenture, often from year to year only. The main advantage of this was that it ensured that land was not removed from the see for long periods at a time: it was often used on estates that were visited irregularly, so that when the bishop did choose to come into residence, meadows could be taken back into his hands to provide fodder. A few sees, such as Hereford, leased considerable portions of their demesne on tenancies-at-will as late as the 1530s, but on the whole the more secure forms of tenure seem to have been favoured. Both the latter types employed a proper indenture, either issued under the seal of the bishop's surveyor or sealed by the bishop and confirmed by the dean and chapter. Indentures sealed by the surveyor were undoubtedly important in the early sixteenth century but are difficult to study, since few of the relevant records have survived. An exception is a York document dating from the years of Wolsey's episcopate. This offers a list of leases made on thirty-two manors and shows that in eleven of them demesne had been granted by surveyor's seal, while in another thirteen at least part of the lord's land was held by tenants-at-will.[8]

Even the proper indenture sealed by the surveyor was not as secure as it might have been. The common law regarded the bishop and his chapter as one legal entity, and therefore for a lease to have full status in the eyes of the law it had to be sealed by both bodies. This might not be very important on grants made for a short time or those made to local men who were already tenants of the manor. It became important when leases were made for longer periods and when the whole demesne might be leased in one block to a man of some social standing. In these circumstances it was a great benefit to the tenant to have a secure lease covered by the proper seals, and the only reason for the bishops to object to such an arrangement was that it increased the administrative difficulties of making grants. The advantages to the tenants were so clear that Wolsey's officials were able to take fines of between 10 marks and £20 for transferring tenancies-at-will or by

8. *VE*, III, pp. 1–4. PRO, SC 12/17/58.

surveyors' indentures to indentures covered by capitular seal. York may not be the only diocese in which this change was happening, for in almost every diocese that has been studied there is a sharp increase in the number of confirmed leases recorded in the first decades of the sixteenth century. This could be merely evidence of better record-keeping, especially by the chapters from whose act books most of this information is taken, but the change seems too consistent to be attributed to the availability of good scribes. It reflects perhaps the movement towards longer leases which are a feature of this period and the greater need for security created by such grants.

Two features of the demesne lease are particularly important for our understanding of the relationship between the bishop and his land. The first is the way in which the land was divided: whether it was retained in one unit or was split into small parcels. Sees such as Winchester, Hereford, Worcester and Ely favoured the grant of the whole manorial 'site' to one substantial tenant farmer. Ancillary rights such as woodlands, mills and fisheries would usually be separated from the main lease, though the precise arrangements varied markedly from diocese to diocese. At the other extreme was the see of Durham, which had almost all its demesne leased in small parcels. The origins of this system can be seen clearly on a few of the manors which still in the early sixteenth century had demesne tenants holding plots of almost equal value. When these lands had first been leased they had obviously been granted out in portions of the same worth. One of the reasons for this arrangement in the north is suggested by comments in the York document about the regality of Hexhamshire in Northumberland. Here again the tenants all worked small plots, contrary to the practice on most of the rest of the estates, and they were regularly troubled by the depredations of the Scots. In these lands men remained sufficiently important to outweigh considerations of the efficiency of larger farms or the needs of patronage. Elsewhere an intermediate state between one and many farmers is sometimes found: several tenants sharing the manorial site. This could reflect either the conscious choice of the episcopal administration or the consolidation of smaller holdings by the most successful farmers in the community. The latter pattern seems to obtain on the manor of Sharrow, owned by York. There Miles Staveley had managed to get into his possession several leases which had once been separate and distinct and which were still recorded separately in the episcopal accounts. But whatever the original reason for the pattern that we find in the early sixteenth century, there is no doubt that the movement was towards consolidation, to the leasing of large units everywhere but in the extreme north. Large units were more valuable as patronage and also greatly eased the administrative burden of the estate officials. They represented a logical step on the road to complete rentiership, to the withdrawal of the lord from all activity except the issue of the occasional lease and the receipt of the rent of one farmer.[9]

The other feature of the demesne leases which is of particular interest is the length of the grants. Since these leases were in theory needed to supply some of the flexibility in episcopal finances that could not be achieved through the customary rents, it was of particular importance that they should be adaptable and fit the general economic circumstances of the age. There were, of course, considerable variations in the length of leases not only between dioceses but between different types of grant. Certain of the lord's perquisites, notably mills, could be more of a burden than a boon to their occupants, and the terms on which they were demised therefore had to be generous. Either the tenants had to be given considerable security on a long lease or there had to be concessions such as all repairs being paid by the lord. In every grant there must have been individual issues to resolve: how tight a bargain should be driven with an episcopal servant or a man of local influence, what was the condition of the property, whether the tenant was new or of an established family and so on. These nice calculations can rarely be reconstructed by the historian: the best that can be done when examining a range of leases is to divide them according to general type – whole manors or manorial sites, small parcels of land and ancillary rights, and the rectories, which again raise different issues. Before the Reformation the number of appropriated rectories in the bishops' hands was very small, so the data in table 2:1 are confined to temporal property only. The table shows the percentage of grants made for various time-spans in the recorded leases of Ely, York, Worcester, Hereford, Winchester and Salisbury. In all cases except Hereford these are the grants registered in the books of the cathedral chapters and therefore show only the most secure, and probably the longest demesne leases.[10]

9. DDR, HC/M64. PRO, SC 12/17/58.
10. On the cost of mills see the evidence for Durham, where repair charges on these alone were often £30 per annum. DDR, CC 190054–62.

Table 2:1 *Lease lengths from a sample of six bishoprics, 1485–1534*

No. of years	Whole manors and sites		Smaller temporalities	
	Henry VII	Early Henry VIII	Henry VII	Early Henry VIII
0–21	8%	4%	8%	13%
22–40	48%	55%	30%	42%
41–60	26%	23%	19%	15%
61–80	8%	7%	22%	11%
81–98	–	7%	5%	9%
99	10%	4%	16%	9%

Sources: EDR, G/2/3 and CC 95550. YDC, M(2)5 and Wa. WRO, 900/1, 37 (iv) and CC lease transcript vol. WiDC, Ledger I. SaRO, Bpric 460. *Registrum Ricardi Mayhew. Registrum Bothe.*

The table shows that the most favoured length of grant was between twenty-two and forty years, regardless of the type of land being leased. But longer periods were by no means uncommon, especially for the smaller temporalities. The collective figures do not indicate any clear movement towards longer grants over the first fifty years of Tudor rule, but this is somewhat deceptive, for some sees were static or fluctuating while others did experience longer leases. Hereford, for example, adhered to a rigid rule of making all leases for twenty-nine years, and at Worcester there is no evidence that grants were increasing in length. On the other hand, the site leases at Ely and Winchester showed some upward movement by the 1530s. At Canterbury, Warham, like the bishops whose policy is studied in table 2:1, favoured leases made for twenty-five to forty years. This was a marked increase over the fifteenth century, when twenty-one years, or even shorter periods, had been common. The prebendaries of Salisbury were worried that the same phenomenon was apparent there under Bishop Audley. In 1518 Audley wrote to the chapter denying that he had 'made and given assent to divers grants . . . of lands and farms . . . to the hinderance and derogation of my said church'. The dean accepted Audley's assurance and allowed the passage of two contentious leases, but only after their terms had been reduced from sixty to thirty and from forty to twenty-seven years. A longer time-perspective reaching back into the earlier fifteenth century might well reveal a clearer pattern of increasing lease lengths. However, what is important for our purposes is that by the early sixteenth century demesne grants were habitually being made for fairly long periods and that the level of rents from the demesne was therefore being fixed at the beginning of an era of inflation.[11]

Explanations for this pattern of leasing by the bishops and their officers can be found, even if none of them is wholly satisfactory. The grants go far enough back into the fifteenth century to reflect a set of economic circumstances which favoured the tenant rather than the landlord. Reliable farmers who could guarantee rent payments were worth generous indentures. The high cost of labour for the tenant also meant that he needed incentives to take an episcopal lease and to keep the land in good heart. In some cases the bishops may have had specific reasons to be generous: Bishop Sherburne, who was shrewd in the management of his Chichester estates, gave relatively long grants but in return shifted the burden of repair costs from himself to his farmers. Nicholas West at Ely began to share repair charges with his tenants. But in general the bishops seem to have become fixed in a system of grants that had been relevant in the fifteenth century and by the 1530s were so no longer. It was difficult to reverse the longer leases of the previous period: existing tenants had a claim upon the landlord and the expectation that they would be able to renew their farms upon the same terms as before. Long grants were a very useful form of patronage, and the economic situation had not yet changed dramatically enough to indicate permanent inflation or a fall in the real cost of labour. Perhaps more than anything else the continuation of long leases in the years before the Reformation is an indication of the mentality of the bishops and their officers. The officers of Canterbury have been described as above all concerned with the stability of the estates, which they sought to preserve in a state of 'dutiful petrifaction'. The bishops were most interested in a steady flow of rents into their coffers, and most of them had sufficient income to live in considerable comfort. It was therefore easy to allow the renting of the demesne to follow the general pattern that had developed during the two preceding centuries rather than respond to signs of a new economic situation. Even those bishops and administrators who showed initiative and concern about the estates usually hesitated to intervene in the existing demesne arrangements. It was one of the misfortunes of the post-Reformation bishops that their predecessors had not made any attempt to reverse lease lengths at a time when they would have had the power and capacity to do so.[12]

11. Du Boulay, p. 230. SaRO, Bpric 460.
12. Lander, 'The Diocese of Chichester', pp. 5-7. EDR, G/2/3.

Land was primarily a source of money income for the bishops, but it still in modest degree continued to be a source of provisions. The retreat from direct farming for the market left the bishops with home farms with which to supply their households. It is usually difficult to assess the size of these lands retained in hand, and one is often left to argue their existence from gaps in other records. Thus when manors attached to episcopal residences have little or no demesne in lease, it is safe to assume that the land was kept in hand by the bishop. At Winchester there was no demesne in lease at Wolversey, in the cathedral city, and only small amounts at Bishop's Waltham and Farnham, two of the most favoured residences of the early-sixteenth-century bishops. The bishops of Ely kept Somersham and Downham demesnes largely in hand, as the bishops of Bath and Wells did Wells and Banwell. The great manor of Southwell, belonging to York, had three parks for the use of the bishops in 1536 and only one close and a mill in lease on the whole demesne. On the other hand, it cannot be assumed automatically that all bishops retained enough to supply the essential needs of the household. A London survey of 1539 shows that only Fulham had much land out of lease; elsewhere there were only the woodlands and some meadows at Hadham in Hertfordshire. The expenditure accounts examined below suggest that most bishops had to make substantial purchases even of those items which could be produced on their lands. The only necessities that rarely appear, except in accounts made in London, are fodder for animals and fuel. It seems to have been a consistent policy of all the bishops to keep most of their woodlands and parks out of lease and to have meadows or pastures on short grant so that they could readily be used to provision horses.[13]

The demesne in hand was intended in almost all cases for the benefit of the household. Only wood was still sold regularly as a supplement to episcopal income and remained a valuable casual asset for many sees. Other sales were usually of little value, being the by-products of household management or the remains of income paid in kind by the customary tenants. Thus the bishop of Carlisle derived £8 in 1512 from the sale of hides and skins, while in 1533 at Rochester £14 was made from stock and skin sales. The detailed accounts from Exeter under Hugh Oldham show that his steward made between £7 and £46 per annum from sales. One of the largest figures was made as a

13. HRO, Bpric 155648. BL, Lans. MS. 20/73. Hembry, p. 19. BL, Royal MS. 7c/16/134. PRO, SP 1/153.

result of the sale of stock before an extended visit to London by Oldham. Similar figures can be cited for the disposal of grain and stock rents: these were reckoned to be worth £26 to Winchester in 1503 and only £16 to Canterbury in the 1530s. By contrast, wood sales realised £72 for Winchester in 1503 and in several years early in the century exceeded £100. In most of these bishoprics the legislation of 1529, which forbade clerics to farm for the market, was irrelevant. The only example from the 1530s of a man whose demesne organisation seems larger than necessary for the household is Richard Rawlins of St David's. Rawlins died in 1536, and his inventory reveals that he had three manors in hand, on which he reared 16 bullocks and 120 sheep and grew 378 bushels of wheat, barley and oats. This places him on much the same footing as the affluent gentry of Pembrokeshire and, since his household appears modest in other respects, suggests that he was selling part of the product of his farming.[14]

Reasons can readily be found for the curtailment of direct exploitation of the demesne in most sees. Provisions were normally useful only if a bishop resided in his see reasonably regularly, and when there was an absentee the most rational arrangement was to place almost all land in lease. Moreover, even a resident bishop faced the same problems as his farmers: the high cost of labour and the relatively low profit to be made from agriculture. At the end of the fifteenth century the bishops of Carlisle kept land worth £27 in hand, but from this they had to find the wages of two husbandmen and the running costs of the land, so the economic advantage was very limited. Even more telling is the example of Durham where, in the second decade of the sixteenth century, there was a systematic attempt to organise stock-rearing. An instaurer was appointed and cows and sheep were reared for the benefit of the bishops. From 1514 onwards cows were despatched to London accompanied by sheep every other year. The scheme was distinguished from much of the other demesne farming of the bishops by the fact that stock was actually reared and not merely fattened in the parklands and meadows. But if Bishop Ruthal and his advisers hoped for a large profit from this arrangement, they must have been disappointed. The cattle made a modest profit, perhaps £27 in 1514–15, but the sheep were much less beneficial. They proved prone to diseases, and a number were stolen, so that any spare revenue was used to bring the flock up to size once more. The whole

14. CuRO, DRC/2/28. PRO, SC 6/H. VIII/1699. Exeter Cathedral, MS. 3690. HRO, Bpric 155648. *VE*, I, pp. 1–7. *LP*, X, 431.

operation proved more effort than it was worth, and after 1518 the flock was abandoned. Thereafter the bishops of Durham seem to have confined themselves to fattening cattle. It is interesting to note that Ruthal was in London for the duration of the scheme, although he may have initiated it on his visit to the north in 1513, when he found his estates very poorly provisioned. The additional charge and difficulty of walking beasts from County Durham to London may have been the key to the failure of the sheep-rearing arrangements. A bishop in residence might just have found it worth while to continue the plan, though even then the accounts suggest that the benefits would have been marginal.[15]

The see of Durham also offers evidence that the retreat from direct involvement in exploiting the estates was not confined to agriculture. It was in these same years that the bishops turned the operation of their coal-mines over to farmers, presumably because the bishopric no longer wished to engage in the costly and hazardous business of taking coal from the ground. Instead agreements were made with the lessees that the bishops should have the right to a percentage of coal as well as to rent. Even when the episcopal officers were seeking ways of increasing revenue in the early 1520s, the chancellor, William Franklin, did not recommend a return to mining. Instead he urged Wolsey to support the merchants of Gateshead, so that the coal of the Durham field could be exported without passing through the acquisitive hands of the Newcastle merchants: 'If your grace will stick to your liberties (as in conscience your grace is bound to do) the bishopric will be better than it is by 1000 marks a year only in coal and lead.' Durham was the only see with mineral resources on this scale, but there is no reason to suppose that the pattern of behaviour of the bishop and his officials would have been different elsewhere. Economic circumstances and the situation of the bishops simply did not justify sustained effort to exploit resources when the work could equally well be done by a farmer who bore the risks as well as the profits of the enterprise.[16]

15. CuRO, DRC/29. P. Horton, 'Administrative, Social and Economic Structure of the Durham Bishopric Estates, 1500–1640', unpub. M.Litt. thesis, Durham University (1975), pp. 135–7.
16. Horton, 'Durham Bishopric Estates', pp. 50–1. *VCH, Durham*, II, p. 325.

II

Land as a source of patronage was inextricably linked to the management of the demesne, which has already been discussed. Whenever one tenant was selected to lease a piece of land, the bishop inevitably became his patron and 'good lord'. Where the traditions of feudalism remained alive, especially in the northern dioceses, this could still be a meaningful relationship, one which served to decide political loyalties. But even in a county such as Durham these bonds were weakening more quickly for the bishops than for the lay nobility. The bishops were crown nominees, were in occupation of their office for only a limited period of time and were often absent. In these circumstances the personal loyalty of the tenants to their patron was less instinctive than was that of a tenant of the Percys or Nevilles. Elsewhere patronage had already come to mean the favouring of a select few men rather than the protection of a large group of clients who were connected to the bishop by virtue of their tenures. These selective favours are not always easily discernible: we do not know in the pre-Reformation period whether there was competition to become episcopal tenants or what sort of men attracted the support of the bishops. However, there are two groups who can be predicted to have attracted their patronage: the politically influential and their own relatives. Relatives certainly benefited from episcopal favour: at Ely, Bishop West gave two major eighty-year leases to his nephew, Thomas Megges, and earlier Bishop Alcock had given one for ninety-nine years to his relative Robert Rowdon. These grants are much longer than was normal for Ely at this time. Both Morton as archbishop of Canterbury and his successor, Warham, leased out lands to their families: Warham made at least one grant to his brother for ninety-nine years. Thomas Langton established one of his relatives, another Thomas, with lands and office in the Soke at Winchester. Examples could be multiplied, although not every prelate had the need or desire to support his family: none of Foxe's leases suggest this sort of concern, nor do those of Richard Mayhew and Charles Booth at Hereford.[17]

Surprisingly few episcopal leases can, with confidence, be attributed to the relationships formed at the centre of government. In the dioceses studied only one really obtrudes: in 1508 Thomas Brandon,

17. On the difference between the bishops and lay nobility as lords see M. R. James, *Family, Lineage and Civil Society* (Oxford 1974). EDR, CC 95550, p. 44; G/2/3. fo. 108. *HMC, 9th Report*, pp. 120–1. WiDC, Ledger Book II, fo. 37v.

the father of Charles, was given a grant of the demesne meadows of Southwark, which belonged to Winchester, for ninety years. Two other leases of about the same date suggest some measure of political influence. Richard Empson was given a Worcestershire lease in 1507, and a year later Humphrey Savage also acquired one. The case of Worcester is rather exceptional, for throughout this period it was occupied by absentee Italian bishops. This meant that the prelate could have little direct control even over patronage and leases, and much of the initiative in organising the diocese was left to John Hornigold, the receiver-general and surveyor. It may be that he felt the need for the protection of the mighty far more than a bishop would have done. The role of the bishop in patronising local families is a more important topic, for in those counties where concentrations of episcopal property existed, these tenancies could make the fortunes of a yeoman or minor-gentry family. To take just two examples: the Abington family, which played a considerable part in the affairs of Worcestershire under Elizabeth, derived much of their wealth from the lease of Bromyard, which they held from the beginning of the century. At Ely the Stewards, who were one of the few gentry families in the Isle in the later sixteenth century, had built their position from the chapter and episcopal leases they had been granted from the 1530s onwards.[18]

The powers of the bishops as patrons extended to office as well as land, and office might be even more attractive to those who aspired to political influence or already possessed it. Many of the offices under the prelates involved, of course, considerable expertise and regular involvement in the affairs of the sees. The receivers, auditors and surveyors all had to devote much time to their offices, as did the stewards of the individual courts. Such offices might be used as support for members of the episcopal family, but they did not offer as much scope for patronage as those which could be exercised by deputy or which entailed few duties. The most interesting of the latter category were the keeperships of parks and the stewardships. Game and parks could actually be maintained by quite lowly officials, but the nobility and gentry prized the offices for their fees and fringe benefits. The hunting facilities of the greatest episcopal estates were open to the keepers, and many of the parks and chases provided outstanding sport, as Henry VIII was to discover. In some sees the

18. WiDC, Ledger Book II, fo. 33v. WRO, CC lease transcript vol. *Registrum Ricardi Mayhew*, ed. A. T. Bannister, Cantilupe Soc. (1920), p. 73. EDR, CC 95550, p. 46.

number of keeperships actually increased in the early sixteenth century. At Winchester in 1503 there was only one master for all parks and chases; by 1531 Wolsey had managed to create six offices, and two were held by men no less weighty than Lord Montacute and Lord Lisle. Sir Thomas More, hardly an ardent hunter, was keeper of the bishop of Ely's parks at Hatfield, and he was succeeded in the office by Sir Anthony Denny. Not all custodians of game possessed quite this degree of political influence, but the gentry and nobility were consistently favoured for the position in every bishopric that has been studied.[19]

The situation of the steward, or high steward as he was called in some bishoprics, was a little different. Although the specialisation of episcopal administration had curtailed his functions, he still remained the principal officer of the see. The steward still had control of the manorial courts and all other courts of the episcopal liberty: he was also responsible for leading the tenants when they were summoned to do royal service. Even when much of the judicial activity had been removed from his shoulders by more specialised deputies, the office remained an important one. It offered that lordship over men that the nobility and gentry valued more than the bishops. In 1536 Shaxton, bishop of Salisbury, commented that one of his stewards, Henry Norris, had always given his fees to his servant, 'but the leading of men, whenever it took place, was what he regarded'. This could have its dangers for the government even in the sixteenth century: Walter Blount suggested to Cromwell in 1534 that disaffected nobles might try to retain men under the guise of acting as stewards to the spirituality. The real risk was perhaps more subtle than this; it was that a local family might use the stewardship of a bishopric as a means of increasing its dominance and hold over its own area. Thus the Courtenay family gained an almost hereditary right to the Exeter stewardship, as did the Paulet family to that of Bath and Wells. In these cases the bishops had already lost the initiative for choosing a powerful servant and ally before the Reformation. But Exeter and Bath seem to be the exceptions: elsewhere the bishops retained the power to select their own men. The range of their choice is interesting. Some continued to look to men of modest social standing who could discharge the actual duties of holding courts – Richard Nix at Norwich appointed William At Mere, a clerk; Foxe at Winchester appointed

19. HRO, Bpric 155648. SRO, LM/927/3. EDR, G/1/7, fo. 43. PRO, Land Rev. Misc. Book 216.

William Frost. Others selected local gentlemen, such as Nicholas Pointz, one of the Worcester stewards. A few already followed the pattern that was to become common later in the century of having as steward a man close to the centre of power; Reginald Bray was Foxe's choice in his first years at Winchester, Charles Brandon controlled some of the Lincoln courts in the 1530s, and Edmund Audley selected as his steward William Compton, groom of the stool, and one of those closest to the king.[20]

The office of steward linked together two major aspects of the bishop's temporal authority: land and liberties. For beyond the key unit of income, the manor, lay the liberties over which the prelates had judicial influence. The nature of their authority varied considerably. At one extreme was the most famous of English liberties, the Durham palatinate. Within the county of Durham the bishops had almost vice-regal powers: until 1536 they appointed the only chief justice, and it was their writ, not that of the king, that ran within its borders. The practical control by the monarch was far greater than these formal arrangements would suggest, but the Durham bishops did have unique opportunities to exercise lordship in all its forms. For example, they had a far wider claim to the feudal rights of wardship and marriage than any of their fellows on the bench, and such rights brought not only fiscal advantage but the opportunity to influence social patterns in the county. The liberty which the bishops of Ely enjoyed in the Isle was in some respects an echo of that of Durham: they were also allowed to appoint a chief justice and to exclude the sheriff of Cambridgeshire, although writs ran in the king's name. It may be that informally the Ely prelates held more power by virtue of their liberty than did their northern colleagues, for there were few gentry families in the Isle to check their wishes. In Durham there were always the Nevilles as an alternative focus for local loyalties.[21]

Other liberties and franchises did not cover such large areas of the country. They merely derived from the old seigneuralties – from rights of jurisdiction and feudal control over those estates which had been sub-enfeoffed by earlier bishops or from special grants that had been made by the crown. In most sees they continued to produce a

20. *LP*, x, 986; vii, 1495. A. J. Rowse, *Tudor Cornwall* (1941), p. 142. Hembry, pp. 46–8. NRO, Epis. est/15, 1/6, 1/7. *VE*, iii, p. 217. HRO, Bpric 155648. *VE*, iv, p. 2. PRO, e 101/519/33.
21. G. T. Lapsley, *The County Palatine of Durham* (New York 1900). Heal, 'The Bishops of Ely', pp. 297ff. James, *Family, Lineage*, pp. 30ff.

modest revenue from fines and escheats: for example, the archbishop of Canterbury derived a profit of between £30 and £40 from his liberty courts in the years before the Reformation. They also offered the opportunity to control the wardships and marriages of the enfeoffed tenants. But the liberty was probably valued most for the symbolic authority that it conferred upon the bishop. The very right of holding courts beyond the normal manorial ones was evidence of high status within one's own locality, and even on the eve of the Reformation the bishops and their officers were still zealous in defending their liberties. In 1512 William Smith considered it worth while to bring an action in the exchequer against the escheator of Nottinghamshire because some cattle had been seized wrongly within the episcopal liberty. Hugh Oldham of Exeter and Richard Foxe of Winchester both exerted themselves personally in defence of their liberties, especially when there was any risk of lay encroachment. In some ways these disputes are perhaps the forerunners of Reformation conflicts: the bishops taking their stand upon the principle that nothing must be alienated from the church, the laity seeking to nibble at the edge of clerical privileges if they could do so without opposition.[22]

Land and liberties were therefore a form both of income and of local authority. Land was also a form of status display, and the bishops were as concerned as the magnates to demonstrate this. The residences which they built upon their lands were intended for their convenience to allow them easy access to various parts of their dioceses and staging-posts on the journey to and from London. In addition they were a focus for the political and social life of their localities, where hospitality and patronage were dispensed, ecclesiastical business transacted and the political problems of the area discussed. The buildings therefore had to be suitable for these tasks and sufficiently impressive to overawe the ordinary citizen and win the commendation of the gentry. Although the bishops had almost stopped acquiring new manors by the fifteenth century, they continued to build new houses and palaces until the very eve of the Reformation. Old houses, including some of the castles, were still used, but most underwent extensive modernisation to suit the standards of the new age. Thus Durham Castle was slowly rebuilt from within by a succession of bishops, Bishop's Waltham in Hampshire had a new wing added to

22. Du Boulay, pp. 312–16. Mumford, *Hugh Oldham*, p. 100. PRO, Exchequer of Pleas, 1 H. VIII, m. 9; 3 H. VIII, m. 15v.

it, and fortified houses at Lamphey and St David's belonging to the bishop of St David's were refurbished. The more settled conditions of the early Tudor period encouraged the bishops, like the laity, to move out from most of their remaining castles and concentrate instead upon the building of unfortified manors and hunting-lodges. The greatest of these builders was undoubtedly Cardinal Morton, archbishop of Canterbury from 1486 to 1500. While still bishop of Ely he ordered the construction of what is now the Old Palace at Hatfield. At Canterbury he rebuilt Otford, added the magnificent gateway to Lambeth Palace, extended Croydon and undertook major work at Knole and the palace at Canterbury. Leland, the topographer, adds that he built 'a great piece of the house of Maidstone. He builded Alington Park. He made great building at Charing. He made almost the whole house at Ford.' Indeed, Morton seems to have been as obsessed with building projects as Cardinal Wolsey, and the great losses which Canterbury experienced in the 1530s become more explicable when the quality and variety of its new property are recognised. Others echoed Morton on more modest scale: Smith of Lincoln extended Buckden manor and almost rebuilt Liddington, Sherburne at Chichester enlarged Aldingbourne and Selsey and restored the manor of Cakeham which had been ruined in the thirteenth century.[23]

Even those bishops who were not possessed by the fever for improvement usually maintained four or five dwellings for their regular use. There would be several country residences, a palace in the cathedral city and a London home. Most of the London houses were located in the Strand, on the south bank of the Thames or in Holborn. It requires an effort of imagination to see the England through which John Leland rode dominated by monastic houses and the properties of the bishops rather than by the country homes of the nobility. Yet it is to the residences of the clergy that Leland constantly recurs. In Yorkshire and Durham he described seven houses belonging to the bishop of Durham, and even so he missed Stockton, which was in regular use for much of the sixteenth century. At Bishop Auckland he waxed quite lyrical about the palace, where there was a great hall with 'divers pillars of black marble, speckled with white, and [an]

23. *DNB*, Morton. *The Itinerary of John Leland in or about the Years 1535–1543*, ed. L. T. Smith (1907–10), IV, p. 62. *Letters of Fox*, pp. 20–1. *VCH, Rutland*, II, p. 188. *VCH, Sussex*, III, pp. 148, 217. For a detailed examination of episcopal palaces see P. Hembry, 'Episcopal Palaces, 1535–1660', in *Wealth and Power in Tudor England*, ed. E. W. Ives, J. J. Scarisbrick and R. J. Knecht (1978).

exceeding fair great chamber'. Durham was one of the richest English sees, but the pattern was not very different at Salisbury. There Leland described five houses and omitted any reference to another that existed at Pottern. The best was still the castle of Sherborne, which had been refurbished so that 'there be few pieces of work in England of the antiquity of this that standeth so whole and so well-couched'. The houses were often associated with impressive parks and chases: the topographer described one of the Durham parks which had a circumference of twelve to fourteen miles and was particularly impressed by the three parks attached to the archbishop of York's house at Southwell.[24]

While most of the bishops felt obliged to maintain several large residences, there is already some evidence that some sought to limit their profusion of houses. As more and more of the demesnes were placed in lease it became less convenient to maintain outlying manors, and there was an incentive to complete the conversion of the estate into cash by leasing the house or letting it fall into disrepair. It might then become a condition of the new tenant's lease that he must accommodate the auditor and steward on their regular rounds; no doubt this was the only use to which some of the manors had been put in the preceding period. Leland records the decay of some houses which probably predated the Reformation. The bishops of Hereford had a 'fair manor house' all in ruins at Ross and another at Ledbury. Bishop Shaxton of Salisbury had pulled down the manor of Woodford which had been in decay. When one turns to the actual itineraries of some of the pre-Reformation bishops it becomes clear that they favoured only two or three houses, the rest being left empty for much of the time. In the year 1516 Nicholas West of Ely moved from London via Hatfield to his Huntingdonshire estate of Somersham. Thence he travelled to Ely on his first visit to the cathedral city. April found him in Wisbech investigating the serious flooding of the fenland; then he returned to London. Much of the summer and autumn was passed at Somersham, presumably enjoying the hunting, although he spent a few weeks in autumn in the cathedral city. By Christmas he was back at Somersham again. Hugh Oldham moved in a similar pattern between his London residence and his favoured country estates. In 1509, for example, he began the year at Exeter and

---

24. *The Itinerary of John Leland*, I, pp. 52, 66, 68, 69–73, 109, 154, 261, 267; IV, p. 18; V, p. 79. The parks were often well stocked, as witness for example the 600 deer that the bishops of London had at Clacton in 1539. PRO, SP 1/153.

then retired to Bishop Clyst, where he spent most of the spring. During this time he went briefly to Exeter on several occasions, presumably to transact diocesan business. In June he went up to London, but by August he was back in Crewkerne in Somerset. However, this was an unusually busy year, since Henry VIII had just succeeded to the throne, and during the autumn Oldham was forced to go up to London again.[25]

Many other bishops undoubtedly used their manors in the same way as West and Oldham, living for choice on one or two country estates but making reasonably regular visits to their cathedral towns and of course to London. There were others who were not even this close to their lands, whose preoccupation with government allowed no time for the affairs of their sees. Thus Foxe apparently spoke the truth when he said that he had never entered the dioceses of Exeter and Bath and Wells when he had held them: it was only after he had been on the bench for almost thirty years that he took up residence in his diocese of Winchester. Wolsey was shocked by the bareness of his northern palaces when he was forced to retire to the diocese of York after his disgrace. He had rarely used any of his episcopal homes except York Place in Whitehall and Esher, which belonged to Winchester. Then there were the Welsh bishops, very few of whom were Welshmen. They showed little relish for living beyond the Marches, and it is noticeable that at St Asaph, Bangor and Llandaff most of the manors were being leased in their entirety before this became common practice in England. A third group of absentees were the foreign bishops: between 1485 and the 1530s six of them held English office and two sees had prolonged periods under their sway. At Worcester three Italians succeeded one another between 1498 and 1533, and at Bath the see was held by Hadrian de Castello between 1504 and 1518. The involvement of this last group with their bishoprics was obviously minimal, but otherwise one cannot always equate nonresidence with neglect of local affairs. The political bishops might be preoccupied with other affairs, but they drew at least a part of their power from their wealth and local standing and as a result could not afford to ignore the organisation of their lands and revenues.[26]

---

25. *Registrum Bothe*, p. 144. WiDC, Ledger Book i, fo. 136. YDC, Wa, fo. 51. *The Itinerary of John Leland*, v, p. 184. EDR, G/1/7. *LP*, ii, i, 1733. Exeter Cathedral, MS. 3690.
26. *Letters of Fox*, p. 93. *LP*, iv, iii, 6344.

III

Our discussion of the function of land therefore leads on to the further question: how close was the personal involvement of the bishop in the care of his property which offered him so much wealth and social authority? In one sense there was little need for his direct intervention; every see had its administrative machinery, its hierarchy of officers who could care for all aspects of the organisation. When a bishop was a permanent absentee, as were the Italians, or Cardinal Bainbridge after he departed for the Roman court, the administration continued to function in his see in the normal way – rents were collected, leases granted and courts held. The officers of order, that is, the auditor, steward and surveyor, checked the activities of the officers of charge, that is, the receivers. Since the revenue-collection system was designed to minimise fraud, it could run relatively smoothly without any direct intervention by the bishop. But total absenteeism and lack of concern by the lord were inevitably likely to breed inefficiency and bureaucratic inertia in the running of the estates. Without personal support the officials were less able to resist intrusion upon the lord's rights, especially if they came from powerful laymen. They might also be tempted to look to their own concerns rather than those of the see. The receiver-general of the bishops of Worcester, John Hornigold, was certainly taking advantage of the absence of his masters to secure his own position. During his tenure of office he arranged that three leases should be granted to him, in each case for the unusually long term of ninety-nine years.[27]

It therefore behoved a bishop to devote some attention to his territories, even if he could not often reside on them. The best means of protecting his interests was to appoint estate officials whom he could trust and from whom he could gain regular information about the state of his lands. In most bishoprics this meant that the receiver-general, surveyor and auditor should be carefully chosen, for it was these officials who held the prime responsibility for the regular control of the property of the bishop. Occasionally the titles might vary: at Durham it was the chancellor who was at the heart of the administration, at Winchester the receiver was known as treasurer of Wolvesey. In some sees the financial administration was less centralised than others: at Chichester, for example, there was no general receiver until after 1529, when George Rose was appointed general

27. WRO, CC lease transcript vol.

bailiff and all other bailiffs were ordered to bring their accounts to him 'so that all shall run in the name of the general bailiff'. At Canterbury and York much of the arrangement for revenue-collection and expenditure remained in the hands of local receivers because the size and complexity of the estates made this the most satisfactory means of organisation. Nevertheless there was in all bishoprics a small core of officials concerned with the central control of the lord's receipts and of the lands from which they came. Together they would form part of the estate council which met to consider the general care of the lands and to advise the bishop. Evidence for the existence of such a council survives at York, Durham, Winchester, London, Exeter and Hereford.[28]

Although there was in all dioceses a well-established hierarchy of officials, the bishops were not normally constrained to depend upon the advice of the holder of a particular office. They obviously endeavoured to insert their own candidates into all major positions and were usually successful in so doing, since office-holding for life was not so common as it became later in the century. Within the major offices a prelate might choose to make his most trusted adviser the receiver or surveyor or auditor or might even turn for assistance to someone outside this circle. Thus at Durham under Bishop Ruthal, his brother was trusted with important business for the see although he held no high office. It was often the case that the bishop depended upon a relative to maintain his interests and supervise the estates. Thomas Clerk, the brother of the bishop, was receiver-general at Bath and Wells in the 1520s, and William Capon occupied the same office for his brother at Bangor. Nicholas West made his nephew, Thomas Megges, auditor at Ely, and Henry Standish did the same for his relative Thomas at St Asaph. This nepotism was obviously based upon the sound principle that the family were likely to protect their own interests; and men such as Clerk and Megges certainly showed vigour, if not always discretion, in their support of the bishops. When relatives were not available or were considered unsuitable by the prelates, clerics sometimes supplied their place. The Durham chancellors before the Reformation were all clerics, and Nix of Norwich continued to surround himself with clerks until the time of his death. It is, however, difficult to offer any generalisations about whom a

28. *The Acts of the Dean and Chapter of the Cathedral Church of Chichester, 1472–1544*, ed. W. D. Peckham, Sussex Record Soc. LII (1951–2), p. 23. PRO, SC 12/17/58, fo. 14. *LP*, VI, ii, 5111 (iii). *Registrum Bothe*, p. 52. DRO, Russell Papers, G2/27.

bishop might trust and look to for advice. At Winchester Bishop Foxe clearly reposed most of his confidence in two laymen who were his steward and surveyor. The steward, William Frost, he described as 'a sad, substantial, faithful man, and well learned in the law' and his correspondence and will suggest that Frost was a close friend. Between them Frost and William Pound seem to have presided over much of the estate management of this large see, seeking the support of the bishop only when a difficult or delicate situation arose such as an intrusion upon the liberties.[29]

At Durham the consistent pattern of absenteeism among the early sixteenth-century bishops meant that it was necessary to delegate authority even more formally. The chancellors were given wide powers over the estates and formed the main channel of communication between the diocese and the prelates. Since most of the bishops were deeply involved in national politics, they relied upon the judgement of their local officials to an unusual degree. Men such as William Franklin, who was Ruthal's chancellor and receiver-general, and William Strangways, who was Wolsey's agent in the north, did more than ensure the smooth running of the administration. They suggested new projects to their masters: we have already noted Franklin's advice upon the export of coal, and it was probably Strangways who encouraged Wolsey to exploit the lead-mines of the see. They also undertook tasks of some political sensitivity: Franklin continued on behalf of both Ruthal and Wolsey the struggle against Lord Lumley, who was asserting a hereditary claim to the forestership of Weardale. Since the bishops themselves were in some measure acting as royal agents in seeking to establish effective political control over the powerful laity of this northern region, the chancellors were in a very exposed situation. They and the bishops had on occasion to yield to the power of local interests, but the surviving records suggest that they pursued the advantage of the see with skill and pertinacity.[30]

Such devotion to duty was normally achieved by close supervision from the bishops as well as by the careful choice of men. Even when great trust was reposed in a particular official, it was obviously wise to maintain a regular correspondence with him, to demand information and to issue orders when necessary. Very few remembrances from bishops to their officials survive, but those that do cover a

29. *LP*, III, i, 440. Hembry, p. 55. *VE*, IV, p. 415. EDR, D/7/3. *VE*, IV, p. 433. NRO, Epis. EST/15, 1/6. *Letters of Fox*, pp. 112–13.
30. Horton, 'Durham Bishopric Estates', pp. 27ff. James, *Family, Lineage*, pp. 44–5.

sufficient range of sees to suggest that they must have been a common form of communication. Bishop Voysey of Exeter, a man not usually noted for his devotion to his see, evidently maintained a regular correspondence with his officers. In one such letter he urged them to be careful in taking fines and showed a detailed knowledge of which tenants had defaulted in their payments on his Devon manors. Wolsey's council at York kept their master, or rather his officials in London, well informed upon the tenants of the see and were given advice in return upon the best way to extract profit for the cardinal. Bishop Audley, who was an occasional resident, was given full details of local affairs both by his officials and by the dean and chapter of Salisbury, who seem to have taken an unusually close interest in the episcopal estates.[31]

The most sustained evidence for this interplay between bishop and officials comes, once again, from Durham. Letters survive from every bishop of the early Tudor period showing the combination of involvement in the affairs of the see and dependence upon the capacity and initiative of the local officials. Three specific examples will serve to distinguish the nature and limitation of this involvement under three different bishops. The first comes from the period when Foxe was in charge of the see. He chose to take the bailiwicks of Auckland, Darlington and Gateshead out of farm and to appoint keepers to them instead. There was a dual purpose in so doing: his officers would be able to control the bailiwicks better and realise a higher profit from them, and the keepers, who had served the bishop in the siege of Norham, would be rewarded. The prior and chapter of Durham objected to this arrangement, since it meant an increase in the number of officers feed by the bishopric, but Foxe was adamant. In this case he presumably derived his detailed information about the losses of the farms from his local advisers but was determined to have his way because of his obligations as a patron. The second example shows a bishop less in command of the situation. William Senhouse was the only one of the Durham prelates of this period not to hold high political office, and his letter 'to Mr. Chamber, my chancellor' suggests little administrative expertise. He needed £1200 for the payment towards the restitution of his temporalities due at Whitsuntide 1503 but had received only £471. He urged his chancellor to consider 'my charges that I have viz for my temporalities and my bulls . . .' and

31. DRO, Russell Papers, G2/27. PRO, SC 12/17/58. SaRO, Bpric 460.

referred the whole matter to his discretion. But this dependence is not unique to Senhouse: in financial matters the officers of the see tended to reign supreme because only they presided over the receipt of monies. When patronage or the appointment of officers was involved, the bishop was better able to exercise his own judgement and authority.[32]

The third Durham example is particularly interesting because it does show the bishop taking a direct initiative in financial matters. In 1528 Wolsey issued a series of orders to his local agents William Strangways and Richard Bellysis. They were to levy all arrears due to the see, to discover those who were liable to be made wards of the bishop and to sell existing wardships at the best possible price. In addition they were to survey the coal- and lead-mines and let them to the advantage of the see, to lease the Norham fisheries to the men of Berwick for £120 and to establish a works for the refining of lead with sea coals. Here indeed was a comprehensive programme of improvement, one which indicated that a high degree of trust was being reposed in the officials of the see but that the results had to be discernible by the cardinal. The programme was undoubtedly too ambitious, and its results help to indicate some of the constraints under which the diocesan officials laboured. Strangways and his colleague claimed considerable success with wardships and other feudal dues, and they leased the Norham fisheries. However, the metalworks proved very trying: the workers were difficult to control and the technical problems of refining meant that little was achieved. As for the arrears, William Franklin wrote to Cromwell pointing out that his master had obviously not understood the local situation, for there had been a series of bad harvests and it had not been possible even to levy the arrears from the last year of Ruthal's episcopate. Thus an absentee could expect too much of his agents, both of their capacity to supervise the direct exploitation of the estates and of their ability to produce a high income in difficult circumstances. Even in a well-organised bishopric such as Durham an absentee could easily misjudge the local situation and suffer from a shortage of information upon which to take sound decisions.[33]

The ambitious demands that Wolsey made upon his deputies cannot readily be paralleled in other cases. Few of the prelates apparently

32. *Historiae Dunelmensis Scriptores Tres*, ed. J. Raine, Surtees Soc. IX (1839), app. cccv–cccviii, cccxii.
33. *LP*, VI, ii, 4416, 5111 (iii and iv).

contemplated entrepreneurial activity such as the melting of lead, and even the exploitation of feudal revenues seems to have been rare. Robert Sherburne at Chichester is one of the other bishops known to have taken a close interest in the improvement of his estates and revenue, but he concentrated his energies upon raising rents and reorganising his leases. Bishop Nix of Norwich also kept a close watch over his income: he specialised in keeping his leases short and driving hard bargains with his tenants. When the fee farm of the borough of Bishop's Lynn had to be renewed, the bishop engaged in person in tough negotiations with the townsmen, and it took three years to reach a satisfactory compromise. Even when the bishops did not have 'improvement' in mind, many of them gave close attention to their leases and fee farms. The demesne leases meant patronage as well as wealth and were a measure of the authority which the bishop could exercise within his own locality. It was therefore of the utmost importance that he should be seen to be in control of leases. 'I require you', wrote Longland to the Lincoln chapter in 1532, 'that you suffer not my chapter seals to pass any of my prebends or lands unless you have any especial letter from me for the same.' When Bishop Audley was challenged by his chapter about the length of his grants, or Bishop Foxe by his about his creation of new offices, they refused to alter the arrangements they had made with the new tenants and patentees. To have done so would have been tantamount to admitting that they could not manage their own property, and such a loss of face could have damaged their influence over local affairs. The bishop still had to retain the attributes of a 'good lord': to be generous in his use of patronage, bountiful in his personal behaviour and powerful in his own locality.[34]

The importance of good lordship and the relative stability of the economic situation in the early years of the sixteenth century may explain why few of the bishops followed the example of Wolsey and Sherburne and sought to increase their incomes. They and their officers were more concerned with the careful use of existing resources than with new devices and schemes. But it would probably be a mistake to attribute this conservatism to the fact that the bishops were churchmen and therefore generous landlords. Cautious conservation was the hallmark of most large landowners in the early sixteenth

---

34. Lander, 'The Diocese of Chichester', pp. 105ff. King's Lynn Municipal Records Entry Book 3, fos. 120v, 135, 156. *Chapter Acts of the Cathedral Church of St. Mary of Lincoln*, ed. R. E. Cole, Lincoln Record Soc. XII (1915), p. 157.

century and was an attitude engendered partly by the nature of estate administration, by the concern above all for the honesty of officers. It was to take at least half a century of inflation to persuade the majority of the lay nobility to adopt a more flexible estate policy, and the bishops therefore merely shared the values of their peers in the handling of their lands. The leading prelates also had incomes large enough to offer them little incentive towards vigorous exploitation of their lands. The most powerful among them held office under the crown, and if they sought spectacular financial rewards they, like their lay successors, were more likely to find them at court and in government than in the patient development of their lands. Only Wolsey's gargantuan appetite for wealth drove him onwards to the more aggressive estate policy which his officers were urged to pursue both at Durham and York.[35]

35. *The Agrarian History of England and Wales*, IV, pp. 686–7.

3

THE REVENUES OF THE BISHOPS
AND THE *VALOR ECCLESIASTICUS*

I

The possessions of the early Tudor bishops were valuable as sources of patronage and offered lordship over men. But above all they provided incumbents with the income necessary to support the dignity and charge of sitting upon the episcopal bench. The temporalities were only one part of that income, which also included spiritual dues, and some prelates had the additional benefit of 'foreign receipts' from the profits of office. For a few of the really powerful clerical servants of Henry VII and Henry VIII, such as John Morton, Thomas Ruthal and of course the voracious Wolsey, the last-mentioned were probably more important than the swelling acres of their sees as forms of revenue. Most of their colleagues, however, found their principal security and profit in their lands and their ecclesiastical office, which were often the reward for earlier service to the state. Any discussion of episcopal income must therefore be first and foremost concerned with the value of the estates, of those manors and lordships which were encountered in the preceding chapter.

Revenue derived from land has the additional advantage that it was regularly recorded in complex series of accounts and that enough of these have survived to form the basis of reasonable estimates of value. The great survey of ecclesiastical properties made in 1535, the *Valor Ecclesiasticus*, also provides an apparently comprehensive picture of the receipts of the bishops' estates at the beginning of the Reformation. Unfortunately, the figures to be gleaned from these sources all too often give only the illusion of accuracy and comparability. The pitfalls which greet any student of medieval accounts are notoriously legion. The most obvious is that the bailiffs and receivers-general who prepared them were concerned, not with profit and loss, but with their obligation to perform their duties honestly. The account was a check upon this, prepared under the headings of charge (that is, all the sums that were the responsibility of the particular collector of revenue) and discharge (that is, the way in which he met his obligations). Since this form of record was not designed primarily as a means of recording the lord's total income, it is necessary to be very circumspect in employing the accounts as a guide to revenue. In practice the records can usually be persuaded to yield at least three different pieces of income information. They may indicate the gross anticipated receipts, after the deduction of accumulated arrears but before any allowances had been made for local costs, illeviable fines, decayed rents and so on. They may also reveal the anticipated receipts of the receiver-general or other central financial officer, after the deduction of these costs but before any central disbursements. Finally, they may give the sums of money actually delivered over to the bishops after the payment of all fixed costs: these last figures also included any arrears paid during the financial year.[1] None of the three types of information is ideal as a guide to income, and not all accounts can be made to yield all three. Valuations, such as the great 1535 survey, obviously say nothing about actual net income, while many of the accounts of the receivers-general do not have details of gross anticipated receipts. Since receivers' accounts will be our most common source of information in this survey, figures have been confined, as far as possible, to the second and third types of information, gross receipts anticipated at the centre of the episcopal organisation and the so-called liveries made to the treasurer's chest or elsewhere. Even so, there is not sufficient uniformity in the categories of accounts or in the detail with which they were recorded or in the purpose of their collection to offer more than general orders of magnitude for the income of all bishoprics at any moment in time. Only in the few sees with good series of accounts – Durham, Winchester and Exeter before the Reformation and Durham, Winchester and London in the later part of the century – is it possible to be relatively precise about the movement of income over time. In these sees one can trace with some accuracy the differences between anticipated and actual income and the appearance or disappearance of particular sources of revenue.[2]

1. See C. Ross and T. B. Pugh, 'Materials for the Study of Baronial Incomes in Fifteenth-Century England', *EcHR*, 2nd ser., VI (1953), 185–95; A. Simpson, *The Wealth of the Gentry, 1540–1640* (Cambridge 1963), ch. 1.
2. At Winchester the continuation of the Pipe Roll series is virtually complete. Durham has several series including the books of Great Receipt, discussed in detail in Horton, 'Durham Bishopric Estates', Exeter has the series of rolls for Oldham's episcopate. Exeter Cathedral, MS. 3690. For details of London see G. Alexander, 'Victim or Spendthrift? The Bishop of London and his Income in the Sixteenth Century', in *Wealth and Power in Tudor England*.

Any estimates of episcopal income must therefore be made with extreme caution and hedged with qualifications. Nevertheless, the weight of evidence is sufficient to ensure that the attempt is worth while, especially as the rich details of the *Valor Ecclesiasticus* make the task simpler for the bishops than for their lay peers. The *Valor* has been described as the great 'geld' book of the English church. It was prepared at the instigation of Cromwell by groups of local commissioners working in each diocese, and the majority of men responsible for its preparation were also those engaged in other aspects of Tudor local government, notably the J.P.s. Very few clerics were among those appointed to estimate clerical wealth, though the bishops were in all cases named in their own sees. The orders to the commissioners make it abundantly clear what was required. In the case of the bishoprics they were to enquire into the full yearly value of the estates and into the receipts from spiritual dues. Details were to be obtained by examining the bishops' financial officers and by studying the accounts of the preceding few years. Certain deductions were permitted to meet the regular fees of the bailiffs, auditors, stewards and so on and to pay pensions. Less specific guidance was given upon how this information should be presented to the government: the only requirement was that it should be entered in a 'fair book after the auditors' fashion'. This last instruction was given widely different interpretations. The Hampshire commissioners gave only the gross and net totals for the temporalities and spiritualities of the bishopric of Winchester. At the other extreme the Canterbury and Lincoln sees were described in the sort of detail normally found in bailiffs' accounts. The commissioners for St David's felt that Welsh sees were so special that they prefaced their return with a discussion of the various forms of tenure that obtained in South Wales. In most bishoprics the details recorded fell between these extremes: individual manors were listed, with perhaps the main heads of income recorded, but no further information. Returns survive for all sees except York, and even this gap can in some measure be made good by using the detailed valuation prepared for the royal visitation of the subsequent year.[3]

Historians have already given much serious thought to the *Valor* and its accuracy, but only in relation to the monasteries. There are

---

3. A. Savine, 'English Monasteries on the Eve of the Dissolution', in *Oxford Studies in Social and Legal History*, vol. I, ed. P. Vinogradoff (Oxford 1909), p. 88. PRO, E 36/114; SC 11/roll 766. The detailed returns for Ely are not at the PRO, but survive in a copy in Bodl., Tanner MS. 141, fos. 74ff. For a transcription see Heal, 'The Bishops of Ely', app. IV.

some *a priori* grounds for assuming that such a vast undertaking, which had to be completed within a few months at a time when many of the commissioners were also engaged in other business for the government, would be riddled with omissions and inaccuracies. In the case of the monasteries there certainly were some mistakes, especially in Lancashire, but most commentators have been impressed by the thoroughness and general accuracy of the work. The weakness of the monastic surveys seems to have been that the commissioners regularly underassessed the value of the demesne retained to serve the household, for this was less readily checked in written accounts than were the rents and customary payments.[4] The bishops depended less upon the demesne than most monasteries and were not so well placed to conceal anything from their fellow commissioners. It behoved them to make a show of honesty and industry as men entrusted by the government with the delicate task of assessing their own income for the purpose of taxation. On 30 June 1535, Archbishop Lee of York assured Cromwell that he had not spared himself and that the clear sum at which he was to be taxed was more than he ever received in his archiepiscopal coffers. Stephen Gardiner of Winchester was even more emphatic. 'You shall see', he wrote to Cromwell, 'in the valuation of my bishopric a goodly portion but whereof I shall not receive now very little above the one half to mine own use. I am in some men's judgements too strait in charging myself, but I will have mine own will therein . . .' Such protestations must of course be treated with caution, but at least it seems true that the prelates were careful to list all their properties and to furnish accurate information upon their receipts from rents and farms.[5]

One glimpse into the way in which the figures for the bishoprics were prepared is offered by documents from Exeter. Among the episcopal papers is a valuation for 1535 which is clearly a draft of the details prepared for the *Valor*. The figures for the spiritualities in the two lists are almost identical. On the other hand, the temporalities were listed in the draft as worth £1497, while in the final printed version they are taxed at £1433. Almost every manor was altered slightly and reduced in value in the final assessment, most by only a few pounds, but two by as much as £20. There is no direct evidence of why the reductions were made, but a reasonable inference might

4. Savine, 'English Monasteries', pp. 1–267. C. Haigh, *The Last Days of the Lancashire Monasteries and the Pilgrimage of Grace* (Manchester 1969), pp. 32–8.
5. *LP*, VIII, 952. *Letters of Stephen Gardiner*, ed. J. A. Muller (Cambridge 1933), p. 64.

Table 3:1 *Net taxable income of the English bishoprics from the 'Valor Ecclesiasticus', 1535*

Winchester	£3885	3s.	$3\frac{3}{8}$d.
Canterbury	£3223	18s.	$7\frac{1}{8}$d.
Durham	£2821	1s.	$5\frac{1}{4}$d.
Ely	£2134	18s.	5d.
York	£2035	13s.	7d.
Lincoln	£1962	17s.	$4\frac{1}{2}$d.
Bath and Wells	£1843	14s.	$5\frac{1}{4}$d.
Exeter	£1566	13s.	$6\frac{1}{2}$d.
Salisbury	£1367	12s.	8d.
London	£1119	8s.	0d.
Worcester	£1049	17s.	$3\frac{3}{4}$d.
Norwich	£978	19s.	$4\frac{1}{2}$d.
Hereford	£768	10s.	$10\frac{7}{8}$d.
Coventry and Lichfield	£703	5s.	$2\frac{5}{8}$d.
Chichester	£677	1s.	3d.
Carlisle	£541	4s.	$11\frac{1}{2}$d.
St David's	£457	2s.	$10\frac{3}{4}$d.
Rochester	£411	0s.	$11\frac{3}{4}$d.
St Asaph	£187	11s.	6d.
Llandaff	£154	14s.	1d.
Bangor	£131	16s.	$3\frac{1}{2}$d.

be that the first set of figures were those prepared for the commissioners from the episcopal accounts, which then became the subject of bargaining between the bishop and his fellows. Variable items of income such as fines and receipts from wood sales probably left sufficient scope for the bishop to make this sort of adjustment if he could convince the rest of the commissioners. A similar, and much better documented, process occurred in 1559 when commissions were issued to value some of the episcopal estates prior to their exchange with property of the crown. Then the bishops managed to enhance the valuation of some of their manors in negotiations with the commissioners.[6]

The figures that were finally used for taxing the English prelates are given in table 3:1. They include both temporal and spiritual income but allow for the deduction of certain fixed costs such as fees and pensions. The net taxable total for the twenty-one English and Welsh sees (excluding Sodor and Man) was £28,022. The gross value of the temporalities was approximately £26,100, that of the spiritualities £3450. Spiritual dues and rectories therefore yielded the bishops under 12 per cent of their income according to the commissioners,

6. DRO, 382/ER 3. F. Heal, 'The Bishops and the Act of Exchange of 1559', *HJ*, XVII (1974), 239–40.

although the figure for the temporalities includes a few appropriated rectories which have not been separated from their accompanying manors. There are interesting problems associated with the spiritualities, to which we must return, but it is evident that the estates produced the preponderant part of episcopal income and that it is important to assess how accurate were the estimates of the *Valor* in this area. Students of the monasteries are fortunate in being able to compare the information given in the great survey with the dissolution returns prepared a few years later. For the episcopate one is compelled to depend upon surviving accounts, accounts which were themselves one of the bases for the assessments of the commissioners. It is therefore not surprising to find in table 3:2 that there is a close resemblance between the income figures available for various sees during the decade 1526–35 and the estimates of the *Valor*. Only three of the examples given have percentage income differences higher than ∓12 per cent from the *Valor*. But it is interesting that most of these

Table 3:2 *The episcopal temporalities: a comparison of the 'Valor Ecclesiasticus' and other accounts, 1526–35*

	Valor Ecclesiasticus (Gross valuation minus local fees)	Episcopal accounts			Percentage difference between Valor Ecc. and gross receivers' receipts
		Year	Gross receivers' receipts	Livery	
Winchester	£3888	1531	£3977	£2927	2.3
Durham	£3023	1527	£3741	£2769	23.7
		1531	£3582		18.5
York	£1832[a]	1532	£1616	£1660	−11.8
Exeter	£1442	1527	£1591	£1587	11.0
		1535	£1497		4.5
London	£1181	1527	£997	£966	−1.5
Salisbury (Wilts. and Berks. only)	£752	1534	£726	£691	−3.5
Worcester	£980	1535	£975	£213	−0.5
Norwich	£767	1535	£787	£629	2.6
Hereford	£718	1534	£787	£629	−4.2
Coventry and Lichfield	£652	1534	£817	£675	25.3
Chichester	£590	1535	£590	–	0.0
Rochester	£281	1533	£286	£278	1.8

[a]This figure is from the royal visitation of 1536, excluding Battersea and Wandsworth to make the figure comparable with that for 1532.

differences show that the accounts suggest a higher gross revenue than the survey. Even if we exclude the higher of the two figures for Durham and Exeter, so that there is one comparison for each see, the average for the accounts is 3.5 per cent higher. These are, of course, totals for a particular year and therefore are not so representative as the valuation. However, where series of figures are available they seem to confirm the pattern suggested by the table. At Winchester in these years the temporalities normally produced around £4000, and at Durham the figure fluctuated between £3500 and £3700.[7]

A detailed examination of the accounts and the *Valor* suggests that it was in the estimation of casual income that the commissioners often went astray. The receipts from the manorial courts, for example, varied considerably from year to year, and it must have been relatively easy for the episcopal officials to argue that they should not be assessed too highly. The Hereford courts were reckoned to be worth £47 in 1535, but two years later they produced £86 for the bishops. At Worcester in the very year when court income was assessed at £15 it yielded £29, while the bishops of Coventry and Lichfield, who were supposed to receive only £5, had in 1524 gained £32 from amercements alone. There may be more than just undervaluation by the officers involved here: manorial jurisdiction was in decline, and the court perquisites, especially fines and amercements, may have suffered as a result. Canterbury certainly gained more from its courts in the mid-fifteenth century than it did at the time of the *Valor*. On some Winchester manors with large groups of customary tenants such as Meon and Bishop Stoke, court revenues were declining from the 1520s onwards, a situation only arrested by the rise in the value of entry fines after the middle of the century. It is possible, therefore, that this change in value was taken into account when the survey was prepared, and it is certainly the case that many of the court receipts of the mid-Tudor years were no higher than those which the *Valor* gives.[8]

7. *VE, passim*. SRO, LM 927/3. DDR, Bpric CC 220201/2, 186690. PRO, SC H. VIII/ 4412. DRO, Chanter 1072; 382/ER 3. Guildhall, MS. 10123/3. SRO, LM/1895. PRO, SC 6/H. VIII/4035. NRO, EP, EST/15/1/7. PRO, SC 11/roll 840. *LP*, VII, 1203. WSRO, Ep. VI/4/1/fos. 70ff. PRO, SC 6/H. VIII/1699. The very low livery found for Worcester in table 3:2 is probably unusual. C. Dyer found that in the early sixteenth century in that diocese the bishops were able to raise 90 per cent of their receipts from the current year's income. Dyer, 'A Redistribution of Incomes in Fifteenth-Century England', *Past and Present*, XXXIX (1968), 31.

8. PRO, SC 6/H. VIII/1511; H. VIII/4035; SC 11/roll 840. Du Boulay, p. 316. HRO, Ecc. II/BW 125–37; Ecc. II/box 88/159493.

The sale of wood and stock and the exploitation of minerals were also awkward items to estimate. Wood sales were a particularly delicate topic, since the bishops were entitled to sell redundant trees but not to deplete the capital stock of great timber. In practice, even before the Reformation, it was tempting to exploit the woodlands and to evade the responsibility of giving proper care to a resource which was very slow to mature. Moreover, the bishops knew that if they did not take the trees the crown was likely to do so when their sees were vacant. At precisely the time that the commissioners were preparing their reports, John Hilsey, the bishop-elect of Rochester, discovered that crown agents were busy in his woods and that soon 'nothing [would] be left.' In these circumstances the rather low figures for wood sales given in the *Valor* must be taken as a minimum, as a discouragement to spoil, rather than as a realistic calculation of what an acquisitive bishop might gain. Two isolated examples may help to demonstrate the point: Bath and Wells was estimated to make £18 per annum from wood sales, but in 1519 it had made £49, and Worcester raised £35 from sales in the very year when the commissioners were marking it down at £12. Once again these individual instances can be compared with more consistent underassessment in a see such as Durham. There in 1535 it was calculated that revenues from woods and mines were worth £364, while the accounts show that these casualties almost always realised over £400 and that in good years the figure might rise to over £500.[9]

Woods and court perquisites, although difficult to value, were always faithfully recorded in the great survey. It is less clear that two other sources of income from land – the profits of the demesne and entry fines on leasehold property – were adequately estimated. The profits of land kept in hand by the bishops were calculated in terms of rental value rather than of their yield in kind. This much at least is clear from the detailed returns for Lincoln: lands in Thame, Wooburn, Liddington, Buckden and Nettleton were in the lord's hands and had an estimated value of £12. 13s. 4d. Elsewhere the returns rarely specify figures of this sort, although both Canterbury and Hereford had some lands held on a year-to-year basis which could have formed part of the demesne kept available for the bishops. We have already seen that direct farming by the prelates was no longer a major part of their estate organisation but that they still retained

9. *LP*, IX, 69. SRO, LM/375. PRO, SC 6/H. VIII/4035. DDR, Bpric CC 190217, 189840, 186691, 220201/2.

enough pasture to maintain flocks and herds for the use of the household, and no serious attempt seems to have been made to include
these in the valuation.[10]

If the status of the bishops' agrarian operations is open to question,
that of the entry fines is shrouded in mystery. The fines paid by the
customary tenants were a matter for the manorial courts and were
normally recorded as part of their receipts. However, entry fines
upon the demesne placed in lease were never the concern of the
courts, nor were they listed by the various receivers. Just occasionally
a receiver-general might note these fines under the heading 'foreign
receipts', but otherwise the accounts are so silent on these items that
one is disposed to wonder if fines were taken for most leases. Two
reasons for supposing that they were are that the beneficial lease of
its very nature usually implied some prior payment to compensate
for changes in the value of land, and that it was by this period the
normal practice of the crown and many of the monasteries to take
fines. It is unlikely that the sums taken for entry and renewal fines
were particularly large: on the crown and monastic estates between
one and two years' rental was the most common figure. The few
scraps of evidence suggest that much the same was true on the episcopal lands. On the Exeter manors of Crediton and Morchard tenants
leasing small parcels of demesne in the early sixteenth century paid
sums which varied from under one year's rent to around two years'.
When a survey of London estates was prepared in 1539 Clacton park
was being rented for £4 per annum at a fine of £5, Wickham demesnes
were let out for £22 at a fine of £20 and Bishop's Stortford had been
leased and fined at £40, though the surveyor believed that the fine
could be increased to £50 upon renewal. Some estates were still being
leased without initial payment: Ralph Morice, the secretary to
Archbishop Cranmer, noted the generosity of his master in putting
out some of the Hertfordshire manors to farm and 'taking no manner
of fine for them'. The tone of his comment suggests that by the 1530s
such behaviour was the exception rather than the rule.[11]

The most interesting feature of these entry and renewal fines is that
they were regarded as part of the 'personal' income of the bishop,
rather than as part of the landed revenue of the see. This circumstance
which was in the first instance probably the product of the accounting

10. *VE*, IV, pp. 1–7; I, pp. 1–7.
11. DRO, Russell Papers, A1/7. PRO, SP 1/153. *Narratives of the Reformation*, ed. J. G.
Nichols, Camden Soc. LXXVII (1859), p. 260.

conventions of the episcopal estates, proved very useful to the prelates when the crown became interested in exploiting their wealth
more fully. The *Valor Ecclesiasticus* made no estimate of the value of
entry fines, because they were already a submerged source of profit
and one which was perhaps not yet regarded as very important. The
yield to a particular bishop depended, of course, upon the number
of estates he held and the length of leases already in operation. Hugh
Oldham, bishop of Exeter at the beginning of the reign of Henry
VIII, managed to raise £30–40 in some years from his fines but in
other years nothing at all. Wolsey's officials at York managed to raise
£80 from fines in one year, but this was only done by combining
renewal payments with the sums offered by tenants to gain greater
security by having their leases reissued under the chapter seal. It
seems unlikely, therefore, that the profit to be made from fines
was of major importance to the bishops at this period; their significance still lay in the future, when they provided some escape
from the fixed-value rents and farms in the years of inflation and
insecurity.[12]

The *Valor Ecclesiasticus* has some omissions and sometimes offers an
underassessment of episcopal income from land. Nevertheless it is
important not to exaggerate these deficiences. In most sees rents and
farms formed at least 85 per cent of the temporal revenue, and these
were recorded with accuracy. An average of about 8 per cent of
income came from woods, court profits and other casualties, and the
rest from a miscellany of lordships, feudal dues, tolls and so on. The
items which are not included or are underassessed would probably
not have amounted to more than 5 per cent of gross income in most
sees and, indeed, would not even have been this important in bishoprics with small estates such as Rochester, Carlisle or those in Wales.
As the number of properties increased, so did the opportunities to
gain from the casualties. At Winchester, for example, the bishops
were able to take recognisances from their tenants upon their entry
to the see: these payments were worth £498 to Richard Foxe in 1503.
The same charge levied at Carlisle would have raised no more than
£25. It can therefore be said that the *Valor* offers a better insight into
the revenues of the poor sees than of the wealthy ones, for the latter
had many more opportunities to exploit their situation. But it is a
sufficiently good record of the temporal income of all bishoprics

12. Exeter Cathedral, ms. 3690. PRO, sc 12/17/58.

to form the point of departure for our analysis and a standard of comparison for later income assessments.[13]

Unfortunately, a point of departure in the mid-1530s is less than ideal for a study which seeks to include the early years of the Tudor period. Can the *Valor* be used as evidence for the revenues of the bishops as far back as 1485? The size of the episcopal estates certainly remained almost constant during this era: there were a few modest purchases by men such as Robert Sherburne of Chichester to add to existing manors, but these were of negligible importance in relation to the total land stock of the prelates. Rents also tended to be static, though in urban areas and especially in London they crept upwards in the late fifteenth century. A change in the nature of a lease or the appearance of a few more tenants-at-will upon the fringes of a manor might make the difference of a few pounds in gross income, but on the whole rents remained the same even when grants were renewed. The general revival in the fortunes of landowners and the increased demand for land that occurred in the early sixteenth century had some effect upon the actual, as opposed to the anticipated, income of the bishops. Bailiffs' accounts for the 1520s show fewer 'decayed rents', that is, rents which could not be collected because of the absence or poverty of tenants, than they had earlier done, although this improvement was not felt universally. In Durham, for example, the land market was slow to recover, and decayed rents and arrears remained major problems until later in the century.[14] Table 3:3 gives details of some episcopal accounts between 1488 and 1523; most show a general similarity to the estimates of the 1530s, but are a little lower than these and than the figures given in table 3:2.[15]

Such improvements in income as there were could come from the strict enforcement of rights and from efficient administration as well as from the general change in the fortunes of landowners. Bishop

---

13. In the five sees which are best recorded, Lincoln, Hereford, Canterbury, Exeter, and Coventry and Lichfield, casualties were just over 8 per cent of temporal income. Lawrence Stone has suggested that by the beginning of Elizabeth's reign all casualties on the estates of the nobility, including the profits of direct farming and fines, might have been 20 per cent of gross rental. Stone, *Crisis of the Aristocracy*, p. 141. HRO, Bpric 155648.
14. Du Boulay, p. 226. WRO, Bpric CC 009176/92496, 92505. Dyer, 'A Redistribution on Incomes', p. 32. Horton, 'Durham Bishopric Estates', pp. 112–15.
15. HRO, Bpric 155648. DDR, CC 190217. SRO, LM/375. PRO, SC 6/H. VIII/1981–2; SC 6/1140/27. Exeter Cathedral, MS. 3690. WRO, Bpric CC 009176/92500; CC 900177/92505. NRO, Epis. EST/15, 1/6. PRO, SC 6/H. VIII/7154. WSRO, Ep./4/1. CuRO, DRC/2/16; DRC/2/24. BL, Harl. MS. roll AA/27.

Table 3:3 *The episcopal temporalities: accounts, 1488–1523*

| | | Episcopal accounts | | |
| | | Gross receivers' | | *Valor Eccle-* |
	Year	receipts	Livery	*siasticus*
Winchester	1503	£4202		£3888
Durham	1514	£3233	£2436	£3023
Bath and Wells	1520	£1651	£2609[a]	£1900
Lincoln	1511	£1230	£1122	£1438
	1515	£1241		
London	1515	£1015	£1135	£1181
	1518	£1132	£1166	
Exeter	1509	£1259		£1442
	1516	£1448		
Worcester	1512	£910	£542	£980
	1522	£941	£794	
Norwich	1523	£694	£556	£767
Coventry and Lichfield	1522	£623	£73	£652
Chichester	1522	£580	–	£590
Carlisle	1488	£146	–	£149
(excl. Horncastle)	1511	£152	–	
Rochester	1521	£262	£264	£281

[a]This high figure is in fact the payment to the bishop of two years' rent (1519 and 1520).

Sherburne gave very close attention to his estates, following the example of his master Henry VII in annotating and signing his own accounts. He kept a strict check upon his rights of lordship, saved repair costs by burdening his tenants and raised rents when it was possible. As a result he increased the ordinary revenue of the see by about £55 per annum, an important sum in a relatively poor bishopric. Bishop Audley of Salisbury claimed to have increased his annual income by £60, though in the absence of accounts this is difficult to corroborate. Another prelate who certainly did increase his receipt was Hugh Oldham, for whom a unique series of informal accounts survive at Exeter. These show that the temporal revenues of the see ranged between £1259 and £1566 during his episcopate, with a median point of £1429, which is remarkably close to the *Valor* figure of £1442. In his first five years in office only once did his income exceed £1400, but thereafter it only once fell below that figure. On average he gained about £60 in the later years of his occupation of the see. Other bishoprics which show an apparent increase in regular income during the early sixteenth century, such as Lincoln and Norwich, may well also

owe the improvement to the efficiency of the individuals who controlled them. Bishop Nix of Norwich was certainly deeply interested
in the management of his property and in the accumulation of the
wealth that derived from it.[16]

The great Cromwellian survey therefore stands at the end of a
period when there were few dramatic increases in the temporal
revenues of the bishoprics but when economic circumstances and
the energy of certain prelates combined to produce some slow
improvement in some places. Since the effects of inflation were as
yet little felt by the landowning élite, these improvements presumably
meant an increase in real wealth for the prelates. At the same time
the *Valor* seems to reflect a decline in the benefit which they derived
from the other part of their office, their spiritual jurisdiction. The
spiritualities, as has already been mentioned, produced only about
£3450 in 1535. They included pensions payable to the bishops, the
revenues of rectories appropriated to the use of their households and
the fees and payments due for the proper discharge of episcopal
functions. The most important of this last group were the procurations and synodals, the former payable at the triennial visitation of
the bishopric. The dues also included some share in the fees from
probate, the issue of licences and institutions.[17] In a large see such as
Lincoln the spiritual dues could be a major item of revenue: the
commissioners assessed them as worth £584 out of a total of £1962.
Elsewhere only the poorest sees were very dependent upon non-
manorial income: the Welsh bishoprics (excluding St David's),
Rochester and Carlisle looked to rectories, pensions and procurations
to supply more than a quarter of their revenue. The commissioners
had little apparent trouble in assessing the value of the rectories and
pensions. The churches were usually wholly in lease, and the pensions
were of the same value year after year. The sums due at visitation were
also relatively easy to estimate: the fixed charges were merely divided
by three in order to discover the annual value.[18]

16. Lander, 'The Diocese of Chichester', p. 110. SaRO, Bpric 460. Exeter Cathedral,
    MS. 3690. See below, p. 70.
17. Probate of wills, and the fees arising therefrom, was not always the prerogative
    of the bishop. The archbishops had established claims to certain categories of
    wills, and others were governed by agreements between bishops and arch-
    deacons. C. J. Kitching, 'The Prerogative Court of Canterbury from Warham
    to Whitgift', in *Continuity and Change*, pp. 191–214. M. Bowker, 'The Commons'
    Supplication against the Ordinaries', *TRHS*, 5th ser., XXI (1971), 61–7.
18. In some sees, e.g. Rochester and Hereford, one conveniently located rectory
    was kept out of lease and the tithe produce was used in the household.

The predominantly lay commssioners seem to have found the task of calculating spiritual dues less to their liking than the investigation of lands. Only a few dioceses have their spiritualities recorded with the care that was lavished upon the manors. At Durham, Salisbury and London there was no attempt to list even the procurations. In several other dioceses no distinction was drawn between the visitation fees and the rest of the casualties, so that it is difficult to be sure that everything was included. When other dues were listed separately they were rarely assigned a high value: fairly typical is the £14 recorded for Hereford, though there are a few exceptions such as Exeter, whose casual dues were said to be worth £81. This is surprising at a time when the Reformation Parliament had attacked the church for the extortionate level of its fees. Only at Carlisle and Lincoln did the commissioners bother to itemise the spiritual dues in a way that suggests careful investigation. At Carlisle probate was said to be worth only £6 and vacant churches £2, and if receipts were really this small it could explain the apparent lack of concern of the investigators. It may be, however, that the indifference to fees derives from the immediate situation in which the *Valor* was prepared. Parliament had won its victory over the church courts, or rather the monarchy had done so with the vocal support of parliament, and Cromwell had assumed much of the spiritual jurisdiction of the bishops by virtue of his new office as vicegerent in spirituals. The rights, and hence the income, of the bishops were in an uneasy limbo as the commissioners prepared their returns.[19]

It is therefore less useful to compare earlier spiritual income with the *Valor* than to undertake the same exercise for the temporalities. Nevertheless, the few details which do survive are an interesting addition to our knowledge of the position of the first Tudor generations. The only continuous record of spiritual income comes from the accounts of Hugh Oldham. They show that his receipts ranged from £124 to £315 per annum, the large variation being explained by the triennial visitations. The median for non-visitation years was £150; for visitation years, £288. This compares with a 1535 estimate of £113. Other individual accounts tell much the same tale. At Carlisle in 1510 spiritualities, excluding rectories and tithes, produced £141, of which £50 was a subsidy from the clergy. Even if this is excluded the remainder is still much higher than the *Valor* figure of £46. A Lincoln

19. There is no information at all upon the London spiritualities. *VE*, II, p. 289; III, p. 1; V, p. 273.

receiver-general's account for 1514 shows that testamentary jurisdiction was worth £131, as compared with the later estimate of £32.
The same was true at Coventry and Lichfield, where in 1522 probate
and vacant churches produced £57 rather than the £13 later indicated.
Only at Chichester did the value of the spiritualities before the
Reformation seem to bear much relation to the *Valor*: there in 1522
they were said to be worth £66 as compared to £41. The only accounts
extant for 1534–5, on the other hand, seem to corroborate the estimates of the commissioners: the registrar's office at Hereford actually
produced £2 less than the assessment, and the Chichester casualties
yielded £20 as compared with £13. The conclusion to be drawn from
these scattered figures must surely be that spiritual jurisdiction was
considerably more valuable to the bishops before the Reformation
than in 1535. After the 1530s scarcely any accounts for the spiritualities
survive, which may well indicate their decreasing value to the bishops
as well as the vagaries of record-keeping.[20]

II

The *Valor Ecclesiasticus* proves a very important guide to the revenues
of the English sees. But the income of the bishops cannot be identified
solely with the profits they derived from ecclesiastical office. Most of
the men who reached the bench under Henry VII and Henry VIII had
behind them long years of service to state and church. A minority
continued to stand close to the centre of government after their
promotion and could, if they so chose, enjoy all the financial advantages of political power. An even smaller group may have been able
to depend upon their family connections to increase their revenues,
although even those of noble or gentle birth were usually younger
sons and therefore not likely to inherit large estates. Some attempt to
estimate these additional revenues is important to our understanding
of the wealth and status of the early Tudor bishops.

The profits of office are of course most difficult and elusive to trace.
A few of the major offices under the crown carried reasonable salaries:
the chancellor and the lord treasurer were both paid £365 per annum,
and Cuthbert Tunstal received the same sum as custodian of the
privy seal.[21] But it was not the salaries that offered the main financial

20. Exeter Cathedral, MS. 3690. CuRO, DRC/2/23. PRO, SC 6/H. VIII/1983; SC
    6/H. VIII/7154. WSRO, Ep. VI/4/1. *LP*, VII, 1203.
21. *LP*, II, i, p. 876. PRO, E 179/69/12.

reward to those bishops who were close to the centre of government. Rather it was their opportunities for patronage, for fees and for sinecures. Wolsey, offers, of course, the extreme example of the benefits to be derived from political power. A proper estimate of his annual income would require a separate study, but it can never, after 1518, have been much less than £7000. In 1519 the Venetian ambassador Giustiniani reckoned he received yearly 42,000 ducats, or about £9500, and in 1531 his successor, Falier, reported his ordinary revenues, excluding gifts and pensions, at £35,000. If this last figure were true it would mean that Wolsey was deriving £12,000 a year from his activities as lord chancellor and as legate. This sounds excessive, but even if one assumes that only £4000–5000 could have come from these sources, the cardinal was still left with an income that dwarfed all others in church and state.[22] Yet he was not alone in receiving large sums from his political activities. William Warham, who was hardly a grasping churchman, was said in 1521 to have an income of £5443 net, which suggests that his offices were worth little less than the archbishopric itself. And Thomas Ruthal, secretary to Henry VIII and bishop of Durham, must have been receiving a goodly sum more than the £3500 that his see was worth, if Bishop Godwin's tale of his death is to be believed. According to the story, Ruthal was asked to prepare a particular on the state of the kingdom, which he duly did, binding the manuscript in elegant vellum. At the same time he drew up a full inventory of his own wealth, but made the mistake of providing it with a similar cover. In error he handed Wolsey the inventory, which showed that his property 'amounted to an infinite treasure, no less than £100,000'. The cardinal in turn showed it to the king, so that he might know where 'at any time to command a great mass of money', and Ruthal was so overcome with embarrassment that he died of the shock. Enough is known of Ruthal's activities to indicate that he was interested in accumulating wealth: he bought wardships, petitioned for crown leases and was one of those who lent considerable sums of money to the nobility. These should all have helped to swell his revenues, although it is difficult to believe that he was quite so successful as Godwin suggested.[23]

There are few others who can be compared with Warham or Ruthal,

22. *CStP Ven.*, 1509–19, p. 560; 1527–33, p. 300. For some discussion of Wolsey's income see A. F. Pollard, *Wolsey* (1965), pp. 320–5.
23. W. G. Hoskins, *The Age of Plunder* (1976), p. 31. F. Godwin, *A Catalogue of the Bishops of England* (1601), pp. 530–1.

John Morton, archbishop of Canterbury and lord chancellor from 1486 to 1500, and Richard Foxe, keeper of the privy seal under Henry VII and Henry VIII, must have had similar opportunities for profit. It may well be that Morton at least took advantage of his situation, for his great building programme can scarcely have been financed from the receipts of the archbishopric alone. In the next rank were a group of men to whom office still offered some benefits, though not as great as those already mentioned. John Alcock, Oliver King, Hugh Oldham, Henry Deane, Christopher Bainbridge and Cuthbert Tunstal all held positions of potential advantage under the crown. But royal favour did not lead automatically to an increase in income. Henry Deane, who became lord chancellor on Morton's death, found that any benefits from the office were outweighed by the high costs of his rapid promotion from Salisbury to London and thence to Canterbury. The role of ambassador was one of the less attractive ones that were often given to churchmen. It was notoriously difficult to make much profit from a temporary embassy: indeed, the usual problem was to extract adequate living allowance from the government rather than to find new wealth. Thus Nicholas West was left at the end of an embassy to France with no resources with which to pay for the bulls needed to confirm his promotion to the see of Ely. Elevation to the episcopate must have constituted the main financial reward for many of these lesser servants of the crown. In some cases this final advancement amounted to a retirement gift, a reward for services already rendered. For example, the generation of bishops who immediately preceded the Reformation had in many instances shed their earlier, secular careers. Only five of the English members of the bench were still regularly involved in diplomacy and other government business.[24]

A prudent bishop did not necessarily have to continue in secular office in order to improve his income. For some, the years before promotion had been an opportunity to accumulate land or other assets. The length of some of these earlier careers is suggested by the age at first consecration for those bishops whose dates of birth are recorded. Under Henry VII the average age of elevation to the bench was forty-nine years, under Henry VIII until 1533, forty-six years.[25]

24. *DNB*, Henry Deane. His will (PROB, 11/13/21) suggests that he had very little left to bequeath. Scarisbrick, 'The Conservative Episcopate', pp. 64–6. Apart from Wolsey they were Clerk, Tunstal, Gardiner and Lee.
25. Any estimate of the birth date of most of the Tudor bishops must be treated with caution, especially for this early period. The sample here is confined to

A good example is that of Robert Sherburne, who attained the see of St David's in 1505 and was translated to Chichester three years later. Until his removal to Chichester he had performed a number of services for the government of Henry VII, including holding the secretaryship for four years and acting as ambassador in Scotland and to the papal court. Thereafter his involvement in national politics decreased and disappeared almost completely after the death of his old master. He then devoted his attention to both the spiritual and financial well-being of his diocese and, as we have already seen, increased its ordinary income by his reforms. Yet his receipts were greater than those of the bishopric alone: accounts from the later years of his episcopate suggest he had an annual revenue of about £1200, of which only two-thirds can have come from Chichester. Sherburne seems to have added the profits of his earlier career to the money he was able to save from his estates and to have made land purchases and money loans to increase his current income.[26]

Robert Sherburne's accounts are unique among those surviving for the early sixteenth century since they show details of all his receipts, not merely current revenues from his see. Elsewhere one is forced to guess that a successful early career or continuing government service enriched a bishop. The most that can be done is to estimate some maximum figure – some calculation of the percentage of early-Tudor prelates whose biographies suggest that they had opportunities to benefit from non-ecclesiastical office. Among the fifty-four English-born bishops consecrated or translated between 1485 and 1530, thirteen held major office under the crown, and a further fifteen had some prolonged involvement with government either before or after their promotion. Rather more than half therefore had the possibility of augmenting their income from these sources: if the Welsh are excluded (since few of them performed significant royal service), the figure rises to about two-thirds.[27]

Many of the episcopal bench probably followed a pattern similar to that of Sherburne. They accumulated wealth from their earlier careers and from the surplus of their bishoprics. The problem then

---

twelve bishops under Henry VII and eight under Henry VIII whose ages can be estimated to within three years.

26. *DNB*, Sherburne. Lander, 'The Diocese of Chichester', p. 117. BL, Add. MS. 34317, fos. 65–101.

27. *DNB*. No doubt some family wealth should also be added to these figures. For example, James Stanley, son of the earl of Derby, was left £500 by his father (PROB, 11/14/19).

was how best to invest this money, which was eventually to be used either for the endowment of colleges, schools and chantries or for the bishop's family. Land, the form of investment most favoured by contemporaries, had only a limited attraction for the higher clergy. The estates which they already held presented sufficient administrative difficulties, and their officers could not readily be diverted to care for property not under the jurisdiction of the see. Manors were therefore often purchased with a specific purpose in mind and held for a relatively short time. William Smith, bishop of Lincoln and co-founder of Brasenose, bought lands specifically for the endowment of his college, as did Richard Foxe for Corpus Christi. Sherburne's estates, though held for rather longer, were intended for the support of the cathedral and were conveyed to the dean and chapter before his death. Only when a bishop had dynastic ambitions did manors become a really attractive form of investment: John Morton, for example, left estates in Kent, Dorset and Essex to his nephews. But few others followed his lead: most preferred to reward their relatives with demesne leases and grants of office, or at death to remember them with a gift of plate.[28]

Plate was the most common form of investment, offering as it did the possibility of reconversion into cash if necessary, the pleasures of ostentatious display and an invaluable form of gift or benefaction. Giustiniani reckoned that Wolsey always had a sideboard of plate worth 25,000 ducats, or almost £6000, and a total stock of silver worth 150,000 ducats. No other bishop rivalled this, but the few surviving inventories suggest that large accumulations were common. Nicholas West held $5060\frac{1}{4}$ ounces of silver and silver gilt, which was far more than the monasteries of Ely or Ramsey had to surrender at the dissolution. Even Nix, who was burdened by a large fine in his last years, still had $1634\frac{3}{4}$ ounces of plate when he died in 1536. The episcopal wills which record any detail tell much the same story; most bequests consisted of plate, and the list of individual items to be given was often very lengthy. Oliver King gave his cathedral of Wells an elaborate set of silver-gilt pieces, including two large candelabra and an image of St George on the condition that his soul be remembered among the benefactors. Foxe left a variety of ornate pieces to friends

28. PRO, SC 6/H. VIII/1982. *Letters of Richard Fox*, pp. 84–5. PROB, 11/10/10. On the other hand, enough bishops purchased land to win the disapproval of an old-fashioned moralist such as Edmund Dudley: *The Tree of Commonwealth* (Cambridge 1948), p. 42.

and dependants and the residue to his successor, Wolsey, provided that he demanded no dilapidations from his executors. Plate therefore had the important virtue of flexibility: like cash, it could be used for a variety of ends, while at the same time it could provide visual pleasure and the evidence of social power.[29]

However, elegant silver candelabra or series of gilt bowls and spoons did nothing to increase the capital of the prelates. This may have been done by another form of investment common among the bishops – the making of loans. There is an abundance of evidence that the prelates made loans for varying periods of time to men of all sorts and conditions. It is the details of the agreements behind these loans that are missing, especially details of the interest taken. No doubt many of the sums paid out would have entailed no return upon capital: monies given to fellow clergy, to servants and dependants, to influential nobles or gentlemen, and above all to the crown probably fell into this category. When Bishop Oldham lent £20 'to Lady Masten by Mr. Henshawe against her husband's month mind', it is more likely that he did so in friendship to support the widow than with any view to profit. Nevertheless, so many of the bishops whose financial affairs we can still study made extensive loans that it seems likely that they did so partly with financial advantage in mind. Some of the most acute financiers among the pre-Reformation bishops were involved in the loan business: Robert Sherburne, Charles Booth of Hereford, Hugh Oldham and the grasping Thomas Ruthal all had extensive networks of debtors. Oldham's accounts preserve a particularly valuable list of those who owed him money. His largest debtor was Henry, earl of Wiltshire, who had been lent £100 and was very slow in repaying any of the principal. One or two grants had been made through merchant intermediaries, such as the grant of £40 to two London merchants to the use of Lord de la Warr. Examples such as this suggest that on occasion the resources of the prelates were being used to supplement those of the London capital market, and it would be very surprising if some interest were not involved. Other debtors of Oldham's included local clergy and some servants, and agreements with them may well not have been on the same commercial footing as those with the mercantile community.[30]

29. *CStP Ven.*, 1509–19, p. 560. PRO, sp 1/76/fos. 207–22v; sp 1/101/p. 62. *HMC, Wells*, ii, p. 176. *Letters of Richard Fox*, p. 167.
30. Exeter Cathedral, ms. 3690. Lander, 'The Diocese of Chichester', p. 215. PRO, sp 1/104/fo. 288. *LP*, iii, i, 1285.

Hugh Oldham loaned money, but the totals involved suggest that he was not a serious financier. In 1511 the sum of the debts owing to him was only £260, and even a good return upon all these grants would not have made a great difference to his income. Richard Nix of Norwich was a very different proposition: at his death in 1536 £3067 was owing to him from men of all kinds. They included a number of clerics such as Stephen Gardiner, the archdeacon of Norwich and the prior of Holy Trinity, Norwich. They had probably sought the help of the bishop with their initial payments to the crown and the papacy upon their promotion. Many of the other large debtors were local gentlemen or aldermen of Norwich. It may be that Nix was satisfied with the knowledge that he had some control and influence over these men as a result of his loans, but the wealth which he had accumulated during his lifetime suggests that he had also demanded more tangible benefits. His greatest outstanding debt was £400 that had been given to the use of a London merchant, John Maynard, and was repayable over five years. This once again has the marks of a full commercial transaction. Nix had a particular reputation as a financier, but some of his contemporaries such as Sherburne and Ruthal also had a wide range of debtors and may have rivalled him.[31]

The only positive evidence that interest was sometimes taken upon loans by the bishops comes from the monasteries. Individual prelates sometimes gave sums to the monasteries for long periods of time; interest was paid on the money, but the capital was repaid very slowly. Most of the loans discussed above, however, were intended for re-payment within a few years. Only two of those who still owed Nix money in 1536 had been given their loans in the 1520s, and even the five years allowed to Maynard appears to have been unusual. It could be that in these circumstances the security that was offered against the loan was more important than interest and that the bishops were willing to foreclose if the money was not forthcoming. The whole subject of the clergy as financiers in the early Tudor period is one which would repay detailed study. Meanwhile we must just hazard the supposition that the bishops derived some benefits from their role as money-lenders, benefits which may have made a marked difference to the financial situation of a few such as Nix and Ruthal.[32]

There were few other forms of investment available to tempt the bishops, but two minor ones should be mentioned. The first is the

31. PRO, SP 1/101/p. 62.
32. D. Knowles, *The Religious Orders in England*, vol. III (Cambridge 1959), p. 257.

purchase of wards. Henry VII's accounts provide details of several purchases involving the bishops. The bishop of London paid £300 for the care of one Hamden, and the bishop of Carlisle produced 300 marks for the wardship of Edmund Thwaites. The bishop of Ely found the wardship of young Curwen cheaper to obtain, for he had to pay over only £100. In these instances the prelates were usually associated with one or two other men, and it may be that their function was to provide the capital while the active care of the ward was left to others. The management of the property of a ward seems to have attracted the bishops only when they had some personal reason for their interest. For example, Cranmer undertook the care of a child of a friend and dependant, and later in the century ward-ships were occasionally purchased by the bishops to provide a suitable marriage for their children. Another possible form of investment, until it was prohibited by the legislation of 1529, was the purchase of leases. Ruthal was one of those who held several properties on lease from the crown, but he seems to have been unusual. A few prelates leased lands which adjoined either their own estates or those of their sees, but this form of occupation seems to have attracted them even less than outright purchase.[33]

The figures given from the *Valor Ecclesiasticus* show a great range and diversity in episcopal income. The bishops of Winchester were taxed at a figure almost thirty times as great as that for the bishops of Bangor. Even though the holders of these two offices were allied, were members of the same estate and had the same claim to a voice in convocation and parliament, they were as sharply differentiated by wealth as were a duke and a middling gentleman. Much of the subsequent evidence that has been examined tends to reinforce this sense of difference. The richest sees owned the most extensive estates: they could therefore depend upon more casualties, more additional resources, than could the Welsh bishoprics or Rochester. Their great lands offered a broader command over men and more opportunities for the exercise of patronage. And wealth also called to wealth: the sees of Winchester, Canterbury, Durham, York and Ely were usually given as the reward for outstanding service to the crown. Men such as Foxe, Wolsey and Henry Deane might begin their episcopal careers in sees of middling income, but they all climbed rapidly towards the glittering prizes of the church. If they were not given to royal servants such posts usually went instead to clerics of high social status: James

33. PRO, E 101, 414/16/fo. 211v; 415/3/fos. 206, 211. *LP*, I, 3842.

Stanley became bishop of Ely because he was a son of the earl of Derby, and Thomas Savage may have been helped to the archbishopric of York by his relationship to the important Savage family of Cheshire. Nevertheless, affluence did not depend only upon access to the richest sees or the most important government appointments. Nix and Sherburne acquired wealth by the careful husbanding of their resources and by good fortune, for they were able to live undisturbed in their benefices for many years. They were therefore more prosperous than those who did not live long enough to compensate for the costs of mobility, such as Henry Deane or William Senhouse of Durham.[34]

The revenues and wealth of the senior bishops justified their formal rank within the hierarchy of the realm. The archbishop of Canterbury took precedence over all the lay peers: only Wolsey stood higher by virtue of his legatine office. William Warham had an income very similar to that of the greatest peers. The duke of Buckingham may just have overtopped him with more than £6000 a year, but after 1521 Warham could be compared only with the earl of Northumberland, who had a clear income of *c.* £4000, or with the Howard family. The rest of the bishops were placed in rank below the dukes, marquises and earls but above the baronage, which also seems fairly consonant with their economic standing. The subsidy assessments of 1523 show that the median income for the peerage was £801; by 1534 this had increased to £921. Median income for the bishops, using the 1535 survey, was £1050. It is difficult to place great reliance upon the assessment figures, since there were always incentives to provide too low an estimate, but the margin of error would have to be very great to make the peers as a group richer than the bishops. Only the poorer Welsh prelates had incomes which more closely resembled those of the gentry than of the peerage. In 1523 a group of the court knights were assessed as receiving between £50 and £1100 per annum, with a median point of £225. Feodary surveys for early Henry VIII, which are a better guide to actual revenue than the subsidy assessments, show all knights recorded to have a median income of £204. Even the Welsh bishops had the advantage of living in an area where the laity were not particularly affluent: within their own locality they must have possessed wealth and influence comparable to that of the greater gentry.[35]

34. *DNB*, Stanley and Savage.
35. *LP*, III, i, 1288. J. M. Bean, *The Estates of the Percy Family, 1416–1537* (Oxford 1958).

The bishops were therefore peers of the realm, both by formal right and by right of wealth and political power. Yet it is interesting to note how little correlation there was between their economic rewards and their responsibilities within the church as spiritual leaders. The endowments of the various sees were the result of a series of royal and individual acts of generosity which paid scarcely any regard to the size of a particular see or the burdens of a particular prelate. Thus London, probably the most important bishopric after the two arch-bishoprics, had revenues which were only a little more valuable than the median of all sees. On the other hand, Ely, which was one of the smallest of dioceses, was the fourth in the whole kingdom in terms of wealth. The diocese of Winchester was no more burdensome than half a dozen others, and yet its bishops were the richest of all, because of the donations of the Anglo-Saxon kings. Durham was given its great endowments and its palatine status as a bulwark against the Scots, not for any spiritual reason. Until the Reformation this lack of connection between wealth and pastoral responsibility remained unquestioned. Only in the 1530s did the reformers begin to demand that the riches of the bishops should reflect the degree of their spiritual cares. Some of those who suggested to Cromwell that the wealth of the church should be trimmed advocated that the archbishops and the bishop of London should be left with more income than the rest of the prelates in recognition of the onerous nature of their duties. But even after the great changes of the mid-Tudor decades this view seems to have found favour only with a minority: the alternative notion that lands and wealth were necessary to uphold the place of the spiritual peers in the social structure proved more acceptable to crown and bishops alike.[36]

p. 140. H. Miller, 'Subsidy Assessments of the Peerage in the Sixteenth Century' *BIHR*, XXVIII (1955), 15–34. J. Cornwall, 'The Early Tudor Gentry', *EcHR*, 2nd ser., XVII (1965), 456–75.

36. See below, ch. 5.

4

EXPENDITURE AND CONSPICUOUS CONSUMPTION

Just as the bishops had their ample revenues as a reward for services rendered, so they were expected to expend them in a manner appropriate to their high office in church and state. That traditional moralist Edmund Dudley urged that they could do so merely by keeping to the obligations enjoined by the canon law. This required that they should divide their disposable income into three parts, 'one part thereof for their own living in good household and hospitality, the second in deeds of charity and alms to the poor folk, and specially within their Dioceses and cures . . . and the third part thereof for the reparations and the building of their churches and mansions'.[1] Such an arrangement should have left little scope for the forms of expenditure of which Dudley disapproved, the purchase of land for their heirs or 'for marriages of their kinsfolks'. The tripartite division which won his praise was no doubt a valuable point of reference, a standard against which the bishops might judge themselves, but it took little account of the realities of their situation. The first obligation, to keep good household and hospitality, covers only a part of their secular charges. They had to discharge the duties both of a good lord and an obedient subject, the latter including some of their most burdensome and least predictable financial commitments in the form of taxation and the furnishing of men for war. The need to maintain their station and fulfil the expectations of secular society tended to preoccupy the bishops during their lifetime, while their discharge of the second duty, to be charitable, was largely reserved for some grand gesture in their declining years or at death. This in turn was partly because charity was no longer only the generalised giving to the poor suggested by Dudley's comment: it was often directed towards specific projects, especially the improvement of education, which required substantial capital endowment. Such projects could in turn become enmeshed with a more 'private' use of revenue when the bishop established a chantry as part of a charitable foundation. Dudley himself recognised the importance of this connection, for in

1. Dudley, *Tree of Commonwealth*, pp. 42–3.

a later passage he urged the prelates to foster learning and to spend a part of their income upon scholars, 'for a better chantry shall you never found'.[2]

Charitable foundations, elegant chantries and large mansions all bore witness to the spending-power of the Tudor prelates. But it was their households and trains that above all impressed or alarmed commentators, depending upon their convictions. The magnificent Wolsey is said to have kept 1000 men in his household at the height of his power, and many were men of some substance, for 430 of them were liable for subsidy payments in 1522. He travelled accompanied by a regal train of gentlemen. Others merely kept large establishments: when a group of the bishops were bidden to attend upon the king at the Field of Cloth of Gold in 1520, Warham of Canterbury took seventy servants, Foxe was allowed fifty-six and the other five took forty-four each. Wolsey, on this occasion, was allowed 300 servants, which gives some notion of the disparity between him and his fellow clerics. Yet several of the other prelates had households of at least a hundred men. Richard Foxe in his declining years at Winchester was said to have had about two hundred servants and Nicholas West had a hundred men in livery at Ely. A detailed list of Thomas Ruthal's household shows that he kept eighty-one servants, including such peripheral figures as a permanent vestment-maker and a 'yeoman of the tents'. In addition he may have feed other gentlemen to ride in his train upon formal occasions. The reformer George Joye described in scandalised tones the pomp that surrounded Stephen Gardiner during his early years at Winchester. He rode 'with his gentlemen bare headed, chained with gold, before and after him', and he had many a 'cleanly sort of tall man . . . about him' and provided food for a host of 'idle bellies'.[3]

Such vast households served a variety of purposes. They might still have a residual military function and be responsible for discharging one of the bishops' obligations as good subjects. Rowland Lee bitterly resented the fact that he was forced to have two hundred men in livery by virtue of his office as president of the Council of the Marches. Their purpose was clearly defensive. Other bishops used members of their households to lead or serve in the companies which they sent

2. *Ibid.* p. 63.
3. Pollard, *Wolsey*, p. 327. PRO, E 179/69/9. *LP*, III, i, 702. N. Harpsfield, *Historia Anglicana Ecclesiastica* (1622), xv, c. 20. Godwin, *A Catalogue of Bishops*, p. 279. PRO, E 163/24/19. Quoted in L. B. Smith, *Tudor Prelates and Politics* (Princeton 1953), p. 58.

upon royal service in time of war. Some may even have done as
Whitgift did at the end of the century and kept trained captains in
their households to ensure some degree of military preparedness.
The flock of men in livery also enhanced the power and prestige of
the bishop: they formed the backcloth to the ceremonial occasions
of his life and were a visible sign of ecclesiastical strength. When a
prelate travelled through the country with his full train he expected
the appropriate deference to be shown him by the populace. Bells
would be rung at his approach to communities within his own
jurisdiction. This had a more than ceremonial significance, as is shown
by a complaint of the bishop of Hereford that the abbot of Reading
had overstepped his rights in allowing his tenants to ring the bells to
celebrate his arrival at a manor within the bishop's jurisdiction.
Larger towns felt an obligation to receive their lord with a ceremonial
which was a modest copy of that offered to the monarch. The treasurer's accounts for Cambridge note a characteristic occasion when
the bishop of Ely was welcomed with speeches and gifts, 'viz. ii couple
of capons, ii pikes, a marchpane and a gallon of iprocras – xxxs iiiid'.[4]

The main purpose of the armies of servants, however, was to provide due entertainment within the household. 'Hospitality' is a
delicate word, subject to a whole variety of nuance and meaning in
the Tudor period. It was enjoined upon the bishops first and foremost
as a godly duty towards the poor, as an important aspect of their
work of charity. The almoner and his assistants were responsible for
distributing part of the products of the kitchen to those in need.
This was an obligation which many of the early Tudor bishops
continued to take seriously, if the reputation which was handed down
into the seventeenth century can be trusted. Nicholas West won
particular praise for his habit of feeding up to two hundred men daily
at his gates with hot meals. Thomas Ruthal always produced meals
for the sixty to eighty beggars at his gates during his visit to his diocese,
though his complaints on the subject suggest that he found charity
a burden rather than a pleasure. Foxe was praised by Nicholas Harpsfield for providing the destitute of the Winchester area with food,
clothing and money. But hospitality meant far more than just this
assistance offered to the poor: it meant providing in the episcopal
household a focus for entertainment and meetings commensurate
with the status of the prelate. All who had any claim upon him must

4. *LP*, xii, i, 973. G. Paule, *Life of Whitgift* (1612), p. 78. *Registrum Bothe*, p. 135. C. H.
   Cooper, *Annals of Cambridge* (Cambridge 1842–1908), ii, p. 175.

be entertained according to their correct degree: a little later in the century the ordinances of Archbishop Cranmer's household offered elaborate guidance to the officers upon how to receive guests and ensure that they were properly bestowed. A bishop expected a constant stream of visitors, though certain times of year or certain occasions were by convention the most open. The Christmas season was the one in which the prelates most commonly played host to all comers, and it was predictably expensive: one year Robert Sherburne spent £77 on food and wine during the twelve-day festival. When parliament and convocation were in session there was little relief from the round of entertainment, and the same was true when a bishop went to his diocese, especially for the first time. The household accounts of Thomas Goodrich show that he incurred particularly heavy expenses when he was first consecrated: in London he had to entertain a succession of courtiers, and then, as he moved in to his diocese, all the local gentry flocked to sample his food. Thomas Ruthal visited his see of Durham for the first time in 1513, four years after his consecration, and then he was appalled by the expectations of his tenants and dependants. 'That I spend here', he wrote to Wolsey, 'would make many towns and refresh my ruinous houses.' He had left London with eight tuns of wine in his train, and all but two had been consumed within two months by thirsty northern throats.[5]

These elaborate establishments offering such a wide-ranging hospitality were not entirely divorced from the spiritual concerns of the prelates. Although the episcopal *familia* was no longer the focus of diocesan administration and pastoral care as it had been in the early Middle Ages, it still offered a bishop the opportunity to meet his spiritual subjects informally when he was within his jurisdiction. Events such as ordinations, which a conscientious prelate might perform in person, sometimes took place on one of the episcopal manors, within the context of the household and the private chapel, rather than in the full public view of the cathedral. Most bishops retained some of their personal chaplains within their own establishments, and inventories often refer to rooms allocated to their use. The 'best' households may have been marked off from those of the lay peerage by a greater sobriety of organisation and behaviour. Edmund Dudley certainly advocated this as a desirable principle, implying that some, but not all, of his contemporaries, ordered their

5. Godwin, *A Catalogue of Bishops*, p. 279. Harpsfield, *Historia Anglicana*, xv, c. 20. LPL, MS. 884. WSRO, Cap. I/14/4a, fo. 46. EDR, D/5/8. *LP*, I, ii, 2394.

servants in a manner befitting their office: 'it is not unfitting that
there were a plain diversity between their servants and the servants
of other temporal men as well in the honesty of their demeanours
as in the sadness of their vesture'.[6] A century earlier Margery Kempe
had been appalled by the laxity of Archbishop Arundel's household
and had rebuked him for it. It is difficult to imagine that all those
gorgeously apparelled gentlemen who so offended George Joye were
any more likely to be models of sobriety and godly conduct. Nevertheless, prelates and their retinues who showed scant regard for the
virtues of moderation and devout behaviour were the subject of
critical comment by the early sixteenth century. James Stanley and
Thomas Savage, whose aristocratic birth had left them with more
interest in the hunting-field than the study or chapel, were attacked
for their misplaced sense of values. The household of a prelate was
at least expected to be regular in its devotions and not blatantly
immoral in its daily activities.[7]

One other function of the episcopal household may also have marked it off from households of the laity and extended its personnel.
Some of the bishops retained an interest in education and learning
which they still fostered through their own establishments. At least
a hundred of Wolsey's dependants had studied at Oxford before
entering his service, and it was through their intimate connection
with him that the careers of a handful of future bishops were made.
Much of this was, of course, but the routine process by which a man
seeking advancement through the church became chaplain to some
great figure as the first step upon his upward road. But the household
could also be a conscious place for the pursuit of learning and culture
and for the stimulation of the young. The best-known evidence for
this sort of activity comes from the establishment of John Morton,
who patronised drama, cultivated good conversation and provided
the young Thomas More with one of the most important intellectual
experiences of his adolescence. Other households were also open to
the learned and generous in their entertainment of scholarship:
William Warham, Richard Foxe and John Fisher were among those
who became foci for the second generation of English humanists.
It is less clear if they were providing any formal education within
their own mansions: Morton's pages obviously benefited from hearing

6. EDR, G/1/7, fos. 80v–88. Dudley, *Tree of Commonwealth*, p. 43.
7. *The Book of Margery Kempe*, ed. W. Butler-Bowdon (1936), p. 64. Godwin, *A Catalogue of Bishops*, pp. 223–4, 484.

the conversations of the great, but were they actually given scholarly training? The one firm piece of evidence is that Thomas Langton, bishop of Winchester until 1500, did have a private school within his household. By good fortune, one of his scholars was Richard Pace, who in later life described the bishop's close interest in the humanities which led him to encourage learning. His concern for his school was so close that 'he was delighted to hear the scholars repeat to him at night the lessons given them by the teacher during the day'.[8] It is impossible to assess how common arrangements of this type were.

While some of the gentry continued to send their sons to be trained in the episcopal household, as they did at Durham, for example, there was probably some expectation that they would receive a grounding in good scholarship. This must have been the main advantage that it had in comparison with a noble establishment, where training in the martial arts would probably be given priority. On the other hand, we might infer from the surviving evidence that the bishops regarded formal education as taking place principally in institutions not directly under their charge. A good deal is known of the foundations which they endowed in the early Tudor period, and there was a concentration both on colleges and grammar schools. Most of the resources that the bishops invested in education must have gone to these establishments rather than to private training of a privileged few within the traditional setting of the *familia*.[9]

The range and diversity of the functions that the household was expected to perform inevitably suggest that it was costly to maintain. Precisely how costly is often difficult to evaluate, both because of lacunae in the records and because of the need to define what constituted household expenditure. The problem of evidence is a serious one, since expenditure accounts had none of the permanent value that was assigned to the records of estate income, and they were often discarded as ephemera. Much that does survive is merely the day-by-day notes of sums expended within the kitchens, which cannot be made to yield any general totals. The situation is also confused by the variety of spending agencies within a large establishment. In some

---

8. Richard Pace, *De fructu qui ex doctrina percipitur* (1517). Langton's attachment to Pace is shown by the will in which he left him £70 as his 'scholar'. *Sede Vacante Wills*, ed. C. E. Woodruff, Kent Archaeological Soc., Records Branch, III (1914), p. 110. Ruthal may also have had some teaching arrangements within his household, since one of his senior servants was 'master of the children'. PRO, E 163/24/19.
9. A Bygod and a Grey were among the gentlemen of Ruthal's household.

sees the receiver-general, treasurer or cofferer handled almost all monies, kept a centralised record and passed only limited sums to the clerk of the kitchen. Elsewhere the steward of the household was still a central figure, taking money and food partly from the receivers, partly from the bailiffs, and having responsibility for such items as travel and the bishop's own charges beyond the confines of the household proper. The bishop himself might be closely involved in spending and act as his own cofferer, keeping his cash within his chamber and dispensing it to his officers as necessary. At Exeter it was Hugh Oldham who usually gave money to the clerk of the kitchen when he needed to make purchases. A further problem is that even the best of the expenditure accounts make no distinction between monies being spent from current income and from accumulated capital. Thus a major building project or land purchase could create the impression that expenditure exceeded income in a particular year, while in fact the prelate was merely drawing upon some of his reserves. Only a series of accounts can correct this impression, and it is only the excellent Exeter series that provides a continuous record of both income and expenditure over a number of years.[10]

Before we can begin to assess whether the great episcopal establishments did consume anything resembling the ideal third of income mentioned by Dudley, it is necessary to return to the notion of disposable revenue. In chapter 3 the main concern was with gross receipts, with the yield of the estates before any deductions other than those of the local officials. To translate this into net disposable income the Tudor accountant deducted a series of allowances and added together actual receipts from the current financial year and any arrears that had been collected. The result appears in tables 3:2 and 3:3 as the livery made to the bishop. Sometimes the allowances include items such as building works and repairs, a part of which might more suitably be placed under the heading of disposable revenue. The other obligations discharged before money came into the hands of the bishop or his cofferer were virtually inescapable: the payments to the feed officers, annuities, decays, pensions and the costs of running the estates. Fees and annuities could certainly be varied, but their holders were sometimes in possession of patents which gave them a life-interest or were at least recognised as long-

---

10. Ely, Exeter and Rochester are examples of sees where the receiver-general or cofferer dispensed monies directly to the clerk of the kitchens; Canterbury, of one where the steward played a central role. Exeter Cathedral, MS. 3690.

established officials. Contemporaries would not have recognised the payments made to them as part of the income over which the bishop had full discretion and control.[11]

The fixed charges obviously varied according to the size and complexity of the estates which a prelate had to administer. In a large bishopric the central officials might be feed at £50 or £60: receivers-general averaged about £10; stewards, between £10 and £20; surveyors and auditors, £6. 13s. 4d. The best-paid officials were Reginald Bray at Winchester and Thomas Cheney at Canterbury, both of whom received £40. Smaller sees could pay less, but even at St Asaph £15 was needed to fee the central officials. Since St Asaph only had £25 worth of temporalities in 1535, it would seem to have been paying a disproportionately high sum to its administrators. The complete list of feed officers included park-keepers, woodwards and guardians of manors, their numbers and cost usually being a function of the scale and complexity of the estates. It cost the bishop of Winchester £123 to pay his officers in 1503, though by the 1530s, when Bray's fee no longer had to be paid, the figure had dropped to £101. Durham had even higher charges because of its palatine administration; in 1512 the sum was £208, though this included some bailiffs' fees which Winchester deducted at the local level. The middle-sized estates of Salisbury cost £56 in fees and retainers in 1533, and this seems a fairly representative figure for those bishoprics which were neither extremely rich nor verging on poverty. The Salisbury totals include the only sort of annuity paid by that see – retainers to various learned counsel that cost £6. Such retainers seem to have been common in the pre-Reformation period: for example, a 1478 account for London describes in detail payments of between £1 and £2 to five lawyers acting in various central courts. It also lists annuities to four laymen of the rank of knights, who may have been protecting the interests of the see by more physical means. On the whole, though, annuities paid to laymen, as opposed to the specific retainers for lawyers, are not often found in the records of allowances. If the bishops did give annual grants as a form of reward or pension, it was not mentioned, with the notable exception of the great sums paid by Wolsey from Winchester to members of the circle of Anne Boleyn. They belong to the Reformation story and are discussed in a subsequent chapter.[12]

11. See above, pp. 56–61.
12. *VE*, I, p. 7; IV, p. 7. HRO, Bpric 155648. *VE*, IV, p. 433. SRO, LM/927/3. DDR, Bpric CC 189833. SRO, LM/1895. PRO, SC 6/1140/27.

D

Other necessary deductions such as audit expenses and pensions rarely added more than £30 to episcopal costs. Only when a prelate was charged with the maintenance of a hospital or other charitable institution through a pension did the sums involved become at all large. The archbishops of Canterbury regularly paid £160 to the hospital of Northgate Canterbury, and the bishops of Winchester produced £26 in alms for the hospital of St Mary Magdalene, but these payments seem exceptional, since most of the foundations endowed by the prelates were intended to be self-financing. These various figures suggest that in most sees fixed costs did not need to exceed £100, though the greatest and richest among them could generate charges of as much as £400. A very crude estimate for all bishoprics might be that 10 per cent of gross income was consumed by fees, pensions and other charges of organising the estates. This does not include any calculation of the cost of repairs deducted by the central officials. Small repair bills were usually met by the local bailiffs from their rents, and it is not easy to disentangle which of the central charges should more properly be considered as construction costs rather than repairs. They are therefore all discussed below under the general heading of building. The mixed group of accounts in tables 3:2 and 3:3 show an average difference of 14 per cent between gross income and livery (after the exclusion of two extremely low, and one extremely high, net payments). Such a small sample cannot necessarily be claimed to be typical of all sees, but the figure is not far from our estimate of 10 per cent for fixed charges and may be taken as a possible indication of the difference between gross revenue and disposable income.[13]

The wealth which remained after the allocation of fixed charges could then be used for the purposes suggested by Dudley, plus the payment of royal taxation and other dues. It was the household that was the main spending agency for the bishops, whether the monies were to be consumed in meat, drink and wages or in activities more loosely connected with domesticity, such as alms, rewards, gifts, travel and so on. When the expenditure accounts are good, it is possible to separate these various categories, from one another but more often all or many of the charges are comprehended under one or two general headings. Food costs are among the easiest to isolate, since they were usually the subject of separate accounts by the clerk

13. *VE*, I, p. 7. SRO, LM/927/3. The net payments excluded are those for Worcester in 1535, Coventry and Lichfield in 1522 and Bath and Wells in 1520.

of the kitchens. Even though most prelates could rely upon their home farms to produce some of the grain and much of the meat that they consumed, they still had to make large purchases of luxury items and of such staples as fish to maintain their establishments and provide the requisite standard of entertainment. Chichester accounts for the 1510s show that fish days were almost always more costly for the bishop than meat days, when much of the food was drawn from stock. The same was true at Ely in the 1530s, even though Bishop Goodrich had extensive fishing rights in the fens, where eels formed a key part of the local diet. Even important items such as grain could not usually be supplied exclusively from the estates: in 1517, for example, the steward of Exeter was allocated £10 to pay for wheat, and such a procedure was common in the Exeter accounts. Particularly valuable evidence about food costs comes from Rochester in 1532/3. There the clerk of the kitchen received from the home farm eleven cows, seventy-seven sheep, forty quarters of wheat and forty-two quarters of barley, plus a little fish, to a total value of £73. In the same year he had to spend on food, drink and household goods purchased on the market £122. Of course the home farm was not without its own expenses: restocking, repairs and wages amounted to £60 in this year, so the saving on market costs was much less than might at first be assumed.[14]

Daily charges for feeding the household obviously varied according to its size and the amount of hospitality that it offered. The two best account series, those of Chichester in the 1510s and Ely in 1533/4 show weekly food bills ranging between £2 and £30, though the latter figure is very unrepresentative, since it refers to the Christmas season. Normal weekly spending by both Sherburne and Goodrich, when they were in the country, was in the range of £3 to £5, while in London Goodrich's costs were always at least £6 and sometimes considerably higher. London was often felt to be expensive by the bishops, partly because it was more difficult to use the resources of their estates when they were at a distance from them. In 1534 Bishop Longland of Lincoln complained that he was being detained in the capital by royal business and was consequently being put to much greater expense than if he had been able to go down to the country. Against this must be set

14. WSRO, Ep/4/1. EDR, D/5/8. Exeter Cathedral, MS. 3690. PRO, SC 6/H. VIII/1699. High costs on the home farm were not unique to Rochester. See for example of the stock experiment at Durham cited above, p. 33; also the demesne at Otford, which yielded the archbishops of Canterbury an average of £76 but cost £67 to maintain. Du Boulay, p. 226.

Ruthal's lamentation about the costliness of a visit to his diocese: it may be that the country was only less expensive for those prelates who were fairly regular residents and who had organised their estates to provide a part of their household needs. A resident bishop could also expect some help towards the costs of entertainment from the gifts of his neighbours: both Ely and Chichester accounts show regular presents of game meat and fowl being added to the bill of fare. The donors were often other clerics, especially the heads of the local monastic houses, which suggests that the episcopal table may have been one of the minor sufferers at the time of the dissolution.[15]

General figures for food expenditure show a predictable diversity. In 1485/6 the bishops of Carlisle paid out only £73 to keep their establishment in food and drink. In the next reign Bishop Fisher of Rochester spent £128 in 1521 and £122 twelve years later, which suggests that he, like the northern prelate, was not lavish with his hospitality. Robert Sherburne spent rather more, as we might expect from the reputation which he had for good entertainment. He paid out £229 in 1512 and £244 the following year, and by 1522 his total household charges had risen to £350. During the first year of Bishop Goodrich's tenure of Ely his steward paid out £288 for food, drink and fuel. The two other sees which produce evidence of expenditure cannot readily be compared with this first group, since they offer figures for total household spending, not merely the immediate items of consumption. Nevertheless, they may be presented here, since they offer a marked contrast with the rather modest sums already cited. The excellent Oldham accounts for Exeter provide the only complete evidence for costs that span several years. They show that household charges during an eleven-year period averaged £844 per annum. In two cases, 1512 and 1519, they exceeded £1000, and it is interesting to note that these had been preceded by two years when income was much higher than average. Net income at Exeter averaged just under £1600, so about 50 per cent was being consumed by the episcopal establishment. Although this figure includes some general items such as wages, it is still not comprehensive. Under one year it is specifically noted that charges for the marshalsea, for alms and bounties and for the bishop's privy purse are excluded. At Canterbury the monies paid to the steward and the clerk of the kitchens were intended to cover these costs as well. In the three years preceding 1531 the clerk of the kitchens spent an average of £1920 and the

15. WSRO, Cap. I/14/4a. EDR, D/5/8. *LP*, VII, 541.

steward an additional £921. Since Canterbury had a net income of around £3000, it would seem that the household, defined in its widest sense, used almost all the resources of the archbishopric. It may be that a different scale of hospitality was expected of the leader of the English church and that this placed a strain upon his budget. William Warham did not leave large sums of money at his death and claimed in his will that he had used his income for the benefit of his see. His household costs go some way towards substantiating his claim.[16]

It is difficult to isolate other domestic costs such as wage payments and the purchase of manufactured goods and fuel. Nevertheless, the few figures that survive suggest that these were never so important as the basic costs for food and drink. At Canterbury, where the scale of provision would argue for a large group of servants, the steward paid £160 in wages in 1523 and allocated a further £61 to pay for the diets of the household officials. This may not be the highest figure for wages in the period: even if we discount Wolsey it is unlikely that Foxe's army of servants could have been rewarded for under £200, and if Ruthal's men were paid an average of only £2 a head he would still have had costs as high as the archbishop's. Others obviously managed to lay out less upon wages: Hugh Oldham paid £24 as a quarter's salary to his servants, and at Rochester Fisher covered his wages and all other general necessities for £82. The only manufactured item which was likely to be of major importance was cloth, since it was needed not only to provide for the immediate household but also for any men feed by the bishop who were entitled to their livery. The Canterbury steward paid £107 for cloth to make the archbishop's livery, and even in the reign of Edward IV the London receiver-general had purchased cloth worth £69. Many of the other requirements of the prelates could be supplied from their estates. The most vital was fuel: the purchase of wood is hardly ever mentioned in the accounts, but one of the extra charges regularly included is the payment for the carriage of wood from one episcopal estate to another. Only when the bishop of Ely was in London did he purchase wood or coal, presumably because transport costs were too high to justify the use of his own fuel. Other products such as salt, wax and

16. CuRO, DRC/2/28–9. BL, Harl. MS. roll AA/27. PRO, SC 6/H. VIII/1699. WSRO, Ep/4/1/fo. 10; Cap. 1/14/4a/fos. 54v and 60. Exeter Cathedral, MS. 3690. *LP*, v, 450. PRO, E 101/518. Earlier Canterbury accounts studied by Professor Du Boulay confirm that most of the budget of the archbishops was used for housekeeping. Du Boulay, pp. 262–3.

lime were sometimes supplied from the bishop's own lands or provided by their tenants as part of lease agreements. The furnishing of
the episcopal manors, which each generation had to undertake
afresh, must have been the most obvious occasion for substantial
expenditure on manufactured goods. No details are available for the
early sixteenth century, but under Elizabeth William Overton of
Coventry and Lichfield laid out £158 to equip his two houses. The
pre-Reformation bishops might have four or five dwellings in regular
use, and therefore have incurred higher costs, though it is worth noting
that both inflation and changes in furnishing fashions probably made
the exercise more costly for Overton per house. Even if one assumes
an expenditure of several hundred pounds by the leading diocesans before the Reformation, it is still likely that the costs of food and drink
remain the most important in their household budgets: the evidence
of sees such as Exeter, Rochester and Chichester suggest that the
ratio was approximately 3:2 for these items against the rest.[17]

Bishop John Young of Rochester, writing towards the end of the
sixteenth century, offered as the conventional wisdom of his age the
statement that 'no man can well uphold his state, if he spend above
a third of his yearly revenue in meat and drink'. Those bishops whose
accounts we can study did not spend more than this proportion,
with the possible exception of the archbishops of Canterbury. Even
in the case of Warham it must be remembered that he had a substantial income from office in addition to the profits of his archbishopric.
The net revenues of the latter may have been heavily committed
to providing for the bellies of the household and its numerous guests,
but Warham could still summon reserves of money to pay his other
costs such as rebuilding and offering the crown financial support.
Yet it is important that the bishops had to spend even as much as a
quarter or a third of their receipts upon food, for it was food prices
that rose most sharply during the century of inflation. The bishops
were committed to a system of large establishments offering lavish
hospitality and had only limited reserves of food from their own lands
to protect them against inflation. Although the demesnes ensured
that the effects of price rises were softened, the prelates nevertheless
experienced some of the same difficulties as those who were completely
dependent upon the market to supply their provisions.[18]

17. PRO, E 101/518. Exeter Cathedral, MS. 3690. BL, Harl. MS. roll AA/27. PRO, SC
    6/1140/27. PRO, E 135/9/6.
18. BL, Lans. MS. 79/42.

It was less easy to determine the proper level of investment in building and reconstruction than in the household. The bishops had, of course, an obligation to keep all their existing properties in good repair, and when they failed to do so, they or their executors were liable to pay dilapidations to the next incumbent of the see.[19] But the evidence cited in an earlier chapter suggests that there was no consensus among the early Tudor bishops on the subject of new building. The great improvers, such as Morton and Sherburne, must have used much of their spare capital upon buildings while others such as the bishops of Hereford, were quietly allowing some of their older houses to fall into total disrepair. Morton's great constructions proved nothing but a source of anxiety to his successors: Warham claimed that he spent £30,000 upon repairs during his time at Canterbury, and he was still concerned lest a dilapidations suit should be brought against his executors. Even after Henry VIII had obligingly taken some of the greatest houses from Cranmer, he found the costs of repair very burdensome, as did the Elizabethan archbishops who followed him. Dudley seems to have had no doubts that the prelates should continue to build their mansions, but already there were voices of dissent among the laity. Wolsey's grand passion for construction helped to crystallise this dissent, and from the earliest stages of the official Reformation the great houses of the bishops became targets for the demands of king and courtiers on the grounds that they were not necessary for men of the church.[20]

One would expect that, had full records of the costs of building and repair survived, they would show a very mixed picture and a level of expenditure far more varied than that of the clerks of the kitchen. The actual evidence is so thin that it can hardly be used even to confirm or challenge this general impression. Only at Durham are there reasonably full data upon construction work in the records of the clerk of works. These show that repair costs were always an item of some importance for the administration: this was especially true of mill repairs, which had not been made the responsibility of the lessee as in some bishoprics. Occasionally the total repair bill might be as low as £30 in the early sixteenth century, but in some years when no new work was undertaken it cost £100 just for routine

19. The sums involved could sometimes be large; see for example the 3000 marks paid to the new bishop of Lincoln in 1473, or the 2200 marks that Walter Likert left his successor as bishop of Norwich. BL, Cott. MS. Cleo E III/105.
20. PROB, 11/24/26. *Parker Correspondence*, pp. 454–5.

maintenance. An absentee like Ruthal was liable to find that the buildings of the see had not been given adequate care: on his first visit to Durham he told Wolsey that his houses were in a state of decay 'the like whereof I trow never Christian man looked on'. When circumstances were as bad as this the division between repairs and new construction was almost non-existent. The works that successive bishops undertook at Durham Castle served to maintain the ancient fabric in reasonable good repair as well as adding to the interior some of the modern conveniences that made it a tolerable home for a sixteenth-century gentleman. As one would expect, the Durham records show peaks of expenditure when new buildings were commissioned. In 1518 the construction that Ruthal had ordered at Auckland cost between £300 and £400, but average spending during his episcopate was £188 per annum. Later in the century Cuthbert Tunstal built a new gallery at Durham: in 1541/2 this cost him £285, but during his long tenure of the see his average expenditure was somewhat lower than that of Ruthal, £174 per annum.[21]

The Durham example is particularly useful because its bishops were neither great improvers nor totally negligent in their care of their manors. Since they were often absentees, their care was spasmodic, but nevertheless they did undertake some major works designed to improve the condition of their main residences. In some other bishoprics very little was spent on repairs or buildings: at Rochester in 1521 costs were only £14, while at Norwich in 1524 they were only £3. The very low figure for Norwich may be explained in part by Nix's efforts to shift the cost of repairs to his farmers, but it is surprising that the episcopal palaces alone did not require more than £3 for routine maintenance. Nix is not known to have been particularly interested in improving his dwellings. In larger sees the regular round of repairs was inevitably more expensive: at Winchester, for example, the crown actually had to expend £237 on repairs *sede vacante* in 1531, although it normally preferred to leave the costly business of reconstruction to the incoming prelate. Much must have depended upon how conscientious a bishop was in keeping all his dwellings in good repair. In the 1520s an estimate of building and repair costs was drawn up at Salisbury, perhaps for the benefit of Wolsey when he undertook the protection of the see on behalf of its absentee bishop. This showed that if all the properties were fully

21. DDR, cc 190054, 190056, 190062, 190066, 190071, 190074. *LP*, i, ii, 2394; iii, i, 440; vi, ii, 4416. Horton, 'Durham Bishopric Estates', p. 164.

restored and improved the total cost would be £793. This sum included £200 for the reedification of Woodford, which was no longer in use and was probably already completely decayed, since its remains were demolished by Bishop Shaxton in the next decade. If William Warham is to be believed, he spent the much larger sum of £1000 per annum in keeping all the buildings of Canterbury from this fate.[22]

The costs of ordinary maintenance provide justification for the efforts made by Robert Sherburne to shift much of the burden of repairs to his tenants. Once freed from the need to reconstruct mills and barns, he could more easily concentrate part of his resources upon the episcopal mansions. In two years which are documented in detail, 1512 and 1513, Sherburne spent £191 and £223 on his building works, that is, something near to the third part of net revenue suggested by Dudley. It is not clear that many others followed his example. The fact that the bishops were only life-tenants must often have discouraged them both from undertaking adequate routine repairs and from new buildings. Some of the most impressive works of the early Tudor bishops are not those on their estates, but the colleges which they endowed and the chantry chapels which they had constructed in the English cathedrals. For those with a passion for building, notably Wolsey and Morton, there was enough energy and money for their own endowments and for the property of their bishoprics. Other prelates seem to have reserved their best offerings for their own foundations, or within their sees only been concerned with the comfort of one or two favoured palaces.[23]

More important than the expense of repairs for many bishops must have been the financial demands of the crown. Even before the Reformation the Tudors expected much of their clerical servants. They were liable for the payment of taxes such as the fifteenth and tenth and subsidy which convocation granted with some regularity, especially during the reign of Henry VII. In approximately three years out of four the bishops were required to pay some tax to the crown, and they had the added burden of being responsible for collecting the payments of the rest of the clergy. Until 1522 they at least had the benefit of paying at the old assessment rates fixed by the lists prepared for the taxation of Pope Nicholas IV in 1291. This did

22. BL, Harl. MS. roll AA/27. PRO, SC 6/H. VIII/1699. NRO, Ep. EST/15, 1/6. SRO, LM/927/3. PRO, E 101/519/33.
23. WSRO, Cap. I/14/4a/fos. 54v, 60. Lander, 'The Diocese of Chichester', p. 113.

not value the episcopal estates as highly as the 1535 survey: the bishop of Hereford, for example, was assessed at £449, and the archbishop of Canterbury at £1985.[24] After 1522 even this advantage was no longer available, for in that year the clergy, together with the laity, were compelled to provide new evidence of the value of their property for the general proscription prepared on the instructions of Wolsey. Some, at least, of the new returns brought the assessments of the bishops nearer to the realities of the sixteenth century: the bishops of Ely, to take one instance, were now to be taxed on an income of £2003, not far short of that calculated for the *Valor Ecclesiasticus*. Others still managed to cling to the older estimates: Bishop Booth of Hereford claimed that his receipts after deductions were worth only £463, although accounts for his period in office show that his revenues were far closer to the £769 estimated in 1535. Even if some men such as Booth were still able to value their possessions at less than their true worth, the government had now given notice of its intention to collect tax upon an assessment of all clerical goods, and the way was opened to the closer examination undertaken in 1535.[25]

The rate at which tax was demanded varied according to the nature of the grant and the period allowed for payment. Some of the grants levied by Henry VII involved a lump sum which was then raised by convocation by a system of local apportionment. More commonly, a certain percentage of clerical income was granted as subsidy and paid in equal proportions over several years. In the period of the second French wars of Henry VIII the clergy were induced to offer the unusually large subsidy of 50 per cent of the value of their goods and property, payable over five years between 1523 and 1527. In the first year of this grant Bishop Sherburne recorded that he had to allocate £47 to the exchequer for tax, and at Rochester £15 was noted as paid, though this seems to be only half the sum owed by Fisher. In one year during the payment of the 1522 subsidy the bishops as a group produced £1896, ranging from £14 produced by St Asaph to £396 from Winchester. Although this figure must have been paid according to the new assessments, it still fell short of 10 per cent of

24. *Taxatio Ecclesiastica Anglicae*, ed. S. Ayscough and J. Coley (1802). Property acquired by the bishops between 1291 and the later fifteenth century was subject to direct taxation with that of the laity, but few manors fell into this category, since the pattern of episcopal landholding was fixed by the late thirteenth century.
25. C. Goring, 'The General Proscription of 1522', *EHR*, LXXXVI (1971), 681–705. EDR, A/6/2. *Registrum Bothe*, p. 149.

the value of the revenues of the bishops, which, as we have seen, were closer to £30,000 than to £20,000. If Wolsey's determined efforts to raise revenue in the mid-1520s failed to make the bishops disgorge a true tithe of their income it is unlikely that they were doing so at any point before the Reformation. Such relatively small sums as the prelates did pay were not liable to disturb the general pattern of their spending.[26]

A far greater irritant was the various loans that the Tudors so regularly required of their more affluent subjects to make good the deficiencies and slowness of the normal system of taxation. In one case, that of the forced loan or benevolence of 1491, the grant was a complete substitute for parliamentary taxation and received retrospective sanction in legislation of the 1495 session. John Morton paid no less than £1500, or approximately half the income of the archbishopric, in 1491 as benevolence for the support of 150 men for the defence of the realm and the recovery of France. Other prelates seem to have contributed a large part of their revenues to the benevolence with no prospect of recouping their losses, since this was an outright grant and not a loan.[27] After 1491 this method of raising money lapsed, and instead the bishops were asked for loans, which were repaid, though often slowly. It was the government's requests for loans, as well as direct taxation, that made the French wars of the 1520s a burden to the prelates. The initial year of the wars was financed by loans, since there was no meeting of parliament or convocation until 1523. Several of the bishops were asked for £1000, and although the payment could in theory be spread over time, most of them produced what was requested within a year. It is possible to observe how Bishop Sherburne set about raising his £1000 for the king. In 1522 he sold £641 worth of plate and then collected together another £307 from unspecified miscellaneous sources. Since Chichester's annual income was only about £700, this must have been a considerable short-term sacrifice. Bishop West of Ely was less willing to produce his loan. His response to Wolsey's request for £500, not a large sum in view of the wealth of the bishopric, was that he had not been 'barer' of money since his second year in the fens and that the utmost he could scrape together without breaking up his household or selling his plate was

---

26. F. C. Dietz, *English Government Finance, 1485–1558* (Urbana 1920), p. 54. D. Wilkins (ed.), *Concilia Magnae Britanniae* (Oxford 1761), III, p. 699. WSRO, Ep/4/1. BL, Harl. MS. roll AA/27. LPL, CM/1/76.
27. *CPR, H. VII,* II, p. 60. S. B. Chrimes, *Henry VII* (1972), pp. 202–5.

£300. Since West ended his days with a great mass of plate and an establishment rumoured to number a hundred persons, a little breaking or selling might not have left him so impoverished as his letter implies. But even Archbishop Warham protested vigorously when a second loan was demanded of the clergy in 1525. The clerics of his diocese, he wrote to Wolsey, showed more 'untowardness than towardness in this behalf'. He was himself willing to bear all the costs that he could for the king, but he had already advanced £1667 in loans 'whereby I was promised to be repaid long before this time and as yet am not paid'.[28] The costs of his housekeeping were so great and his properties in such urgent need of repair that it was difficult to do more. The figures for the archiepiscopal establishment lend colour to Warham's claims that he could not easily produce more loan money. However, Warham's difficulties cannot be taken as typical either of the situation of the rest of the bishops in the 1520s or of their general experience in the early Tudor period. The second French wars were the occasion on which the crown attempted to exploit every fiscal device available: the only other times when loans were asked of the bishops at large were the early years of Henry VII's reign. Even in the 1520s the archbishops had far less elasticity in their income than other bishops whom we have been able to study. It may be that most prelates were able to manage their loans by the same methods as Sherburne without imposing long-term strain upon their finances.

The time when external charges proved most burdensome to the bishops may well have been at their consecration or translation, rather than in periods of high government demands. Both the crown and the papacy had the right to exact large payments from a cleric at his elevation, the former for restitution of the temporalities, the latter for bulls of provisions and the other common services of the curia. The new bishop had to pay to the crown approximately one year's income from his temporalities. The accounts of the treasurer of the chamber under Henry VII show the bishop of Exeter being bound to pay 500 marks yearly for three years, the bishop of Norwich paying 1000 marks and the bishop of Ely £2000 within three years. When Henry Deane was promoted to Canterbury he was asked for the relatively low sum of £1600 but was allowed only two instalments for payment, with a year between them. At the same time Rome demanded almost a year's income for the safe passage of the bulls

28. WSRO, Ep/4/1, fo. 10. PRO, sp 1/29/fo. 1; sp 1/243/fo. 242.

on terms which were likely to be harder than those of the exchequer or chamber. In his early years the charges of a bishop could therefore actually be larger than his income. If he remained in one place for a reasonable period these initial costs could be recovered, but rapid promotion was a guaranteed road to impoverishment. Henry VII, who was attracted by the financial benefits of moving his bishops, ensured that at least some of his clerical servants suffered this fate. During his reign new services and fines had to be paid in each see on average once every nine years, while in the first half of Henry VIII's reign the average was only once every nineteen years. Henry Deane was the most notable victim of the cycle of promotion, since he was moved three times within six years and died less than two years after reaching Canterbury.[29]

Later in the century James Pilkington, bishop of Durham, comparing the situation of the Protestants with that of their Catholic predecessors, argued that the latter can have had no difficulty in financing their promotion, since they had 'divers fat benefices and prebends . . . [and] they were stored of all necessaries of household afore they entered'. Their earlier careers may indeed have done something to ease the transition, but the evidence suggests that many new incumbents had to borrow heavily to finance their initial charges and that this was a source of anxiety to some. When Cuthbert Tunstal was offered the possibility of moving to Ely in 1525 if West, who was then seriously ill, should die, he replied that he was reluctant to leave London, since he had not discharged his debts from his first promotion and did not wish to leave a financial burden to his relatives if he should die. West had himself found it difficult to raise the money for his bulls and restitution, since he was from a poor family and heavily dependent upon the favour of Wolsey. The cardinal may actually have lent him part of the money to pay to Rome, since he was able to transmit his 7500 florins to the curia only three months after making a direct appeal to his patron for assistance. Other bishops turned to their fellow clerics for assistance: William Barons, bishop of London, was one of those who guaranteed the payments to the crown of Henry Deane, and Richard Nix had Stephen Gardiner as one of his more substantial debtors at his death. Some loans were presumably arranged commercially with London merchants and others, though

29. J. J. Scarisbrick, 'Clerical Taxation in England, 1485–1547', *JEH*, XI (1960), 41–54. PRO, E 101/414/16/fo. 209; 415/3/fos. 184v, 200v, 202. *DNB*, Deane.

the evidence for such agreements is now lacking. Whatever the source of support for the bishop, the consequence was a commitment to repayments which could last for some years: Tunstal had been at London three years when he was approached about the see of Ely, and Gardiner had occupied Winchester for almost five years before Nix's death. During this period a prelate could not deploy his resources to their full. For example, Nicholas West was faced, in the year after his promotion, with disastrous floods in the fenlands, which needed 1000 marks to make good the damage to the dikes and drainage system. However, his great charges for promotion left him with less than £100 and therefore prevented him from acting as a good lord to his diocese. Even allowing for the fact that West was liable to cry wolf about his finances, his general complaint must be taken seriously, for a bishop who appeared very wealthy yet could not fulfil his obligations was liable to bring the hierarchy into disrepute.[30]

While the fine for the restitution of temporalities was the largest sum that the Tudor monarchs exacted from their bishops as tenants-in-chief, neither Henry VII nor Henry VIII scorned other feudal exactions. Fines were imposed for the infringement of royal preroga-tives and for neglect of their obligations by the prelates. Twice these fines were imposed in a manner which can be described as systematic: once during Henry VII's last years when all possible sources of finance were being tapped and again on the eve of the Reformation. In the first period the bishop of Salisbury had to pay 500 marks for a mort-main licence, the bishop of Coventry and Lichfield was asked for £300 for a decision in a dispute with Sir William Knyvett, and the bishop of Ely was expected to produce £100 because he had allowed some prisoners to escape from the episcopal gaol at Exeter when he was the incumbent there. On the eve of the Reformation fines were used as a form of threat against the bench: the bishops of Bangor and Dublin were asked to pay £333 and £1467 respectively when they sought pardon for praemunire offences, the bishops of Bath and Wells and of Lincoln were fined £700 and £667 for allowing prisoners to escape from their gaols, and even the relatively trivial error of giving an inaccurate certificate of non-bigamy cost the bishop of Hereford £667. The culmination of the use of the fine as a political weapon came in 1534 when Nix was ordered to pay £10,000 for his infringement

---

30. J. Pilkington, *Works* (Cambridge 1842), p. 594. *LP*, IV, i, 1264; II, i, 299. W. J. Lunt, *Financial Relations between England and the Papacy, 1327–1534* (Cambridge, Mass. 1962), p. 802. PRO, E 101/415/3/fo. 200; SP 1/101/p. 92. *LP*, II, i, 1733.

of the privileges of the town of Thetford. Although some of these fines were not paid in full, they remained a threat both to the revenues and the independence of the episcopate.[31]

The main feature of the various demands made by the government upon the bishops was their unpredictability. Loans, fines and the payments made at translation might be required at very short notice and might consume as much as a year's income from the see. It therefore behoved a prelate to keep a part of his wealth in the form of plate which could readily be cashed to meet an emergency. Yet too large a reserve was already liable to tempt the government to make extra demands: the huge fine imposed upon Nix was prompted in part by the information that he possessed a great heap of wealth. In the incident already noted when Wolsey discovered Ruthal's affluence after the wrong account book had been passed to him, he is supposed to have commented to the king, 'you see where you may at any time command a great mass of money if you need it'. Already before the Reformation there was a symbiotic relationship between the wealth of the crown and that of the bishops; the obligation of the latter as good subjects was to provide a reserve of money on which the former might draw when there was any legitimate excuse to do so. Already the bishops were expected to be more pliant to the will of the government, more willing to offer it support from their revenues, than were the lay aristocracy. The way was well prepared for the legislation of the 1530s which secured for the crown a regular income from all the clergy.[32]

The need to keep a substantial reserve of wealth to answer the wishes of the crown may help to explain why many of the greatest charitable endeavours of the pre-Reformation bishops were reserved for their last years or even made after their death in their wills. When Edmund Dudley wrote that works of charity should absorb a third part of a prelate's income he no doubt thought principally of the traditional support of the poor that was enjoined upon him by the canon law. By the law a cleric was in fact enjoined to allocate to the poor 'a good portion . . . which is the fourth part'. We have seen that at least some of the bishops had a good reputation for feeding and supporting those who flocked to their gates, and they continued to

31. PRO, E 101/415/3/fos. 200, 202v, 206, 275v, 296. *LP*, V, 657; VII, 171. PRO, KB 29/166/ro. 42; KB 29/1091/ro. 13. The fine imposed upon the bishop of Lincoln was pardoned in 1534 or 1535. G. R. Elton, *The Tudor Revolution in Government* (Cambridge 1953), p. 269.
32. Godwin, *A Catalogue of Bishops*, p. 530.

employ almoners to 'keep hospitality and be men of alms'. Since the almoner was primarily responsible for dispensing food and was only secondarily concerned with cash payments, it is impossible to calculate if the bishops whose accounts survive were in fact spending generously on the poor. When there is mention of sums paid to the almoner the amounts are usually small, only a few pounds at a time to be handed out in dole. On the whole it seems unlikely that the poor received a large part of the episcopal budget, except at those times such as Christmas when completely open entertainment was part of the accepted social pattern.[33]

If, on the other hand, the foundations and endowments of the early Tudor prelates are included under the heading of charity, the picture changes very markedly. The leaders of the Henrician church scarcely needed the promptings of Dudley that they should spend yearly some 'part of their portions' on the support of learning. They were themselves the product of a scholastic system of education, and some of them added to a traditional belief in the importance of learning a new, humanist, enthusiasm for its wider dissemination. They therefore continued and expanded a process commenced much earlier of founding and endowing schools and colleges. Among the thirty-four bishops for whom there is some detailed evidence, twelve founded twenty-two schools or colleges. Twenty bishops, in some cases the same men as the original twelve, provided endowments and scholarships at Oxford or Cambridge, some of them of such large value that they virtually represented a second foundation. The great importance of education is suggested by comparing these figures with those for other forms of charity. Ten bishops provided some sort of support for their cathedrals over and above bequests of plate. Eight endowed other churches, and a further four provided money for monastic churches, while only six gave revenue for secular works of any importance. Appendix III offers a detailed list of the endowments which can be attributed to the pre-Reformation bishops, with some estimate of their value where possible.[34]

Most of the great endowments of the bishops were made late in life or funded by their wills and were made possible by the accumulation of revenue over some years. The well-documented example of Hugh Oldham shows that he had almost half his income in hand after the

33. W. Lyndwood, *Provinciale seu constitutiones Anglie* (Oxford 1679), bk 3, tit. iv, c. 4; bk 1, tit. xiii, c. 1.
34. See also W. K. Jordan, *Philanthropy in England, 1480–1660* (New York 1959).

payment of his household costs. Even after the deduction of taxes and his personal expenses he must have been able to retain several hundred pounds a year from the see of Exeter. In 1516 he was able to show his affection for his birthplace and honour the memory of his brother by establishing a free grammar school in the town of Manchester. He paid £218 for its buildings and also provided lands to endow it; but this by no means exhausted his surplus revenues or his desire to aid education. Oldham therefore also became a benefactor of Bishop Smith's new foundation of Brasenose at Oxford and took almost as active a part in the establishment of Corpus Christi College as his good friend Richard Foxe. He is reputed to have given the latter the immense sum of 6000 marks, which, if true, suggests that his total charitable endeavours must have amounted to over £5000. Since Oldham held various government offices in addition to his bishopric and clearly lived far within his means, these figures do not entirely strain one's credulity. Some of the other great supporters of education must have provided just as much from their revenues. There was John Alcock, bishop of Ely, who established Jesus College at Cambridge, founded a free grammar school at Hull, and helped to finance the building or rebuilding of a number of churches. Or Thomas Rotheram, archbishop of York, who gave large sums to several Oxford and Cambridge colleges and established an elaborate college and grammar school at Rotheram. In the next generation came William Smith, with Brasenose College and three schools within his diocese; Richard Foxe, who founded Corpus Christi and established two grammar schools; and John Fisher, who cooperated with Lady Margaret Beaufort to establish St John's College, Cambridge, and re-found Christ's College. The case of Fisher is particularly outstanding: he held a poor see and never had the advantage of government office, yet he provided St John's with gifts to a total value of £1128 and was still able to afford £43 for Christ's and to finance the rebuilding of Rochester bridge. His accounts suggest that he did so with some difficulty: in 1532/3 he withdrew £230 to spend upon alms, gifts and taxes and in consequence spent £75 more than the net income of his see.[35]

Not all the bishops waited until their later years to undertake investment for charitable purposes. William Warham made his major gifts when he had not long been in the archbishopric, donating lands

35. Mumford, *Hugh Oldham*, pp. 105–23. Exeter Cathedral, MS. 3690. *DNB*, Alcock. W. K. Jordan, *The Charities of Rural England* (1961), pp. 304–5. *DNB*, Smith, Foxe, Fisher. PRO, SC 6/H. VIII/1699.

in Hampshire to Winchester College and New College, Oxford. Robert Sherburne, whose chief interest was in the welfare of his cathedral, had spent £3717 on repairing it and providing the chapter with lands before 1529. There were risks in too long a delay for those who wished to direct their charitable endeavours towards a particular establishment. Their executors and successors were unlikely to have the same keen interest in the institution as they themselves, and therefore it was necessary to balance the need to accumulate sufficient financial reserves against the desire to see a college, school or collegiate church well established before death. Several prelates specifically requested their successors to be good to the foundations they had erected: Sherburne in the insecure 1530s even asked Cromwell to be generous to his executors and allow the works of charity which he planned to proceed unimpeded. Another motive for passing on land or money as soon as it was available was that it removed it from the demands of the government. Bishops such as Fisher or Warham, whose normal expenses were not far short of normal income, may have felt the need to do this more urgently than those such as Sherburne or Oldham, who had a handsome reserve available to them.[36]

The creation of new institutions was inevitably in some degree linked to the more private use of wealth, to provide for the health of the soul. The purchase of paradise was as much a concern of the bishops as of those laymen whose wills have been studied for the fourteenth and fifteenth centuries. The founder or benefactor of an Oxford or Cambridge college might be motivated first and foremost by an interest in education, but this did not preclude a desire to ensure that prayers were said for himself and his family. Indeed, the establishment of a large organisation made the arrangements for prayers all the more secure and enduring. When the collegiate structure was a church served by canons as well as, or instead of, an educational institution, the emphasis on perpetual prayer for the founder was liable to be more important. This was the situation at Thomas Rotheram's college in his home town. Another archbishop of York, Thomas Savage, had plans for an elaborate college of the same kind at Macclesfield, though these were never realised. James Stanley of Ely spent much of his spare revenue on the collegiate church of Manchester, within which he eventually established his own chantry chapel. Most of the rather limited bequests that the bishops still passed to the monastic orders and the friars were specifically desig-

36. *DNB*, Warham. Lander, 'The Diocese of Chichester', p. 101. PROB, 11/25/41.

nated for prayers for their souls. Henry Standish of St Asaph, for example, ensured that he would be well remembered by giving small sums to seven different monastic houses or friaries.[37]

Episcopal wills record many small charitable bequests not listed in appendix III which were designed for the soul's health. These included the monies dispensed at the funeral, at the month's mind and on various other occasions to a specified number of the poor and also to any clerics who attended. In the pre-Reformation period the residue of a bishop's goods was more commonly left for generalised works of charity than assigned to a relative, and again the executors were usually admonished to bestow the goods in ways that would be beneficial to the soul of the deceased. All this is, of course, consistent with the attitude towards purgatory that was the shared heritage of the late Middle Ages. A bishop was just as entitled to use his vast resources to limit his own period of purgation as were those laymen who were establishing chantries throughout the country. When these resources served the dual purpose of aiding the prelate and promoting learning or assisting the poor, there was no serious conflict between public and private advantage. Potentially more sensitive was the spending of large sums of money on chantries and chantry chapels that benefited principally the bishop and his family. Some of the richest and most elegant of our cathedral tombs and chapels belong to the early Tudor period and are the work of the prelates. James Stanley left £260 to build two chantry chapels, one at Manchester and one at Ely, and most of his lands and other surplus to finance the two. His successor, Nicholas West, was equally concerned that his soul should not be neglected and created two chantries, at Ely and Putney, leaving the majority of his estate to their support. In his case this meant that almost £2000 went to this end. Among surviving wills for the period 1492 to 1536 ten show most of the remaining wealth of the prelate being used for a chantry and its building. This suggests that roughly the same number of prelates concentrated upon their own spiritual needs as expended large sums on new educational institutions.[38]

37. *DNB*, Savage. PROB, 11/18/7; 11/25/26.
38. PROB, 11/25/13. In West's case his relatives were given some benefit in his property, since after twenty years the lands he had loaned to the priory of Ely to finance his chantry were to be seized to his nephew, Thomas Megges, in return for a payment of £640. The ten wills showing large payments for a chantry are those of West, FitzJames, Stanley, Mayhew, Langton, Booth, King, Redman, Savage and Vaughan, though of this list Vaughan, Langton and King also gave generously for charitable works.

Edmund Dudley, as a conservative critic, dissociated this concern for the soul from the use of episcopal revenues for the advantage of relatives, which he specifically attacked. His only comment on the subject was that the support of education was an important duty of the higher clergy, for 'a better chantry shall you never found'. Only when the general sumptuousness and extravagance of episcopal expenditure came under the criticism of the reformers were the chantries taken as an example of private greed, of the misappropriation of funds intended for the support of learning and the aid of the poor. Many of the early Tudor bishops were able to discharge their obligations to society and care for their souls; again the example of West is pertinent, since he left behind him a great reputation for generosity to the poor. If they were able to avoid being promoted too often and lived for a reasonable number of years in one see, they were more likely to have the pleasurable task of choosing how to spend their surplus than to suffer any serious financial strain. There were, of course, bishops who could not expend large sums because of their limited endowments. The Welsh prelates were always among them: Richard Rawlins, for example, who was bishop of St David's until his death in 1536, had an estate valued at only £487, much of which was committed to pay for his funeral and discharge his debts. At the other extreme Warham struggled with the duties of the archbishopric and apparently had little to save from his current income. In between were those sees which provided their occupants with the opportunities to become outstanding patrons of learning. The efforts of the minority who did so much to change the face of Oxford and Cambridge were remembered throughout the century and the successors of the early Tudor bishops had to face the charge that they were doing far less. Yet the very scale of their charity may have served to foster doubts in the minds of some reformers. If some of these rich clerics could offer so much, why not all? Might not it be better if the crown compelled them to generosity by taking their surplus wealth into its own hands and using it to transform the society? In the 1530s, the decade when all seemed possible, Thomas Cromwell was regularly proffered advice based upon these notions. Affluence of the sort displayed by the early Tudor bishops bred envy and the conviction that others were better equipped to manage these monies than were the clergy themselves.[39]

39. *LP*, x, 431.

5

HENRY VIII AND THE
BEGINNINGS OF APPROPRIATION

The early years of Henry VIII's reign witnessed some increase in that hostility to the established church which is loosely classified under the heading of anticlericalism. In the major incident associated with the case of Richard Hunne resentment of clerical privilege was expressed both by the citizens of London and by the House of Commons. A decade later, as Lutheran influence began to penetrate the country, anticlerical writing became common. The authors ranged from those who had a deep commitment to the new theology, such as Tyndale or Jerome Barlow, to those who expressed principally the negative aspects of criticism of the clergy, such as Simon Fish. Yet whatever their starting-point and approach, most of the writers shared in common at least two assumptions: that general reform within the church was necessary if it were once again to fulfil its true function of ministering to the faithful and that clerical immunities and privileges were one of the main obstacles to such reform and must therefore be abolished. Immunities and privileges included not only the legal advantages enjoyed by the clergy but also the secure possession of wealth. The reformers were already arguing that great wealth was not compatible with devotion to spiritual duty: 'love of worldly things', commented the lawyer Christopher St German, 'strangleth the love of God'. An attack upon the riches of the church was also one of the best ways to rally support for the cause of reform; the cry that the clergy were too affluent, that they held in their hands a disproportionate part of the wealth of the realm, had an immediate appeal that needed no reference to any change in doctrine. The popularity of a work such as Fish's *Supplication for the Beggars* lay in its skill in touching the resentments and anxieties felt by various sections of the community towards the church, resentments which did not necessarily have any profound theological implications.[1]

1. C. St German, *A Treatise concerning the Division between the Spirituality and Temporality* (1532?). S. Fish, *A Supplication for the Beggars* (1871). For a summary and discussion of some of this literature see A. G. Dickens, *The English Reformation* (Fontana edn. 1967), pp. 140–7.

It is important, however, not to exaggerate the significance of this literary outburst in the second decade of Henry's reign. Had the crown not wished, for its own purposes, to exploit the agitation, it is difficult to believe that the reformers would have made much progress. The Lancastrian kings had been able to manage the protests against the powerful church precipitated by the Lollards, and Henry VIII could surely have done likewise. The infant Protestant movement offered as yet no major challenge to the authority of the Establishment. The bishops, once freed from the constraints of Wolsey's period of control, showed confidence and enthusiasm in assailing their critics and in reiterating the claims of their estate to privileges and immunities. Only when Henry found it politically expedient to move against the church did they begin to waver and eventually to succumb. Even then they were not easily cowed, and throughout the 1530s a variety of incidents bear witness to the fact that the higher clergy were still endeavouring to protect the remnants of their former position. After the summoning of the Reformation Parliament the interests of the gentry, and especially of the lawyers, helped to dictate an early assault upon the legal immunities of the English church, but from the very beginning the attack upon the clergy had economic implications as well. Legislation of the 1529 session, which was aimed principally at limiting pluralities, included a clause which denied clergy the right to take farms and leases and another which forbade them to trade in corn and other commodities, except the by-products of their own estates. Here the initiative probably came from the Commons, but the crown was also ready to use financial weapons against the clergy as and when it proved appropriate. The specific writs of praemunire issued against those bishops who had been implicated in Wolsey's use of his legatine power were translated into the general charge of praemunire, from which the church had to buy pardon. There were other pinpricks against the higher clergy: the large fines that were demanded for offences such as allowing convicted clerks to escape from episcopal gaols. These offered another means to assert royal influence and to confuse and demoralise any of those prelates who might show a disposition to oppose the royal will.[2]

In the years of uncertain policy between 1530 and 1532 financial demands upon the clergy had rather limited objectives. Only when the movement away from Rome had begun in earnest did any general threat to ecclesiastical wealth become likely. In January 1533 the

2. 21 Henry VIII c. 13. J. J. Scarisbrick, *Henry VIII* (1968), pp. 273–5. *LP*, v, 657.

imperial ambassador, Eustace Chapuys, reported to his master that Lutheran doctors were coming to England to advise the government upon a variety of topics including the alienation of church property. Chapuys was in this case being needlessly alarmist, but it is not clear that Henry needed the aid of the continental reformers to prepare a scheme for profiting from the wealth of his clerics. In the same month the ambassador also reported that church goods were to be used for financing a regiment of horse, which seemed a likely project in the tense political situation created by the divorce crisis. Henry himself revealed some of his mind to Chapuys in March 1533 when he told him that he wished to free England from papal subjection and to reunite to the crown all the goods which churchmen held of it, as he was bound to by the terms of his coronation oath. Here was proof positive that the king planned to profit from his attack upon Rome, though the device chosen, an assertion of feudal rights and of the claims of the king as descendant of the founders of many monasteries and bishoprics, was fraught with practical difficulties. It is not perhaps surprising that, when the government was once again free to give attention to the alienation of church property, this mode of appropriation was quietly forgotten.[3]

The rapid changes of 1533 thrust the issue of church lands into the background for a time, but expectations of further alterations were high. At the beginning of 1534 Lord Lisle's agent, John Husey, informed his master that it was widely rumoured in London that the temporal revenues of the clergy were to be removed in the coming session of parliament, 'whereof many be glad and few bemoan them'. Chapuys picked up the same information and added that the profits were to be divided between the king and the nobility of the realm. These rumours, in so far as they have a sound basis, probably refer to the projected legislation upon first-fruits and tenths which was introduced into the 1534 session. If other possibilities were contemplated at this time the evidence has not survived. It was only in the summer of 1534 that the plans for profiting from the church assumed a new urgency with the Irish revolt of the Kildares. Irish revolts were always a grave embarrassment, and this one occurred at a moment of particular international tension. The real possibility that the emperor might come to the aid of the Irish, who appealed both to him and to the pope, made it urgent to raise an adequate army to suppress the

3. *LP*, vi, 89, 180, 235. On Cromwell and his plans to assert founders' rights see Youings, *The Dissolution*, p. 41

revolt. An army had to be financed, and the church was now an obvious source for the money. This is the background to an interesting paper filed by Cromwell's clerks, which can be dated to the latter part of 1534. It advocated that the monastic orders and secular clergy should have their surplus wealth pruned away, that they should lose their liberties and franchises and pay first-fruits to the king. The money saved by these changes should be given to the crown and used for the defence of the realm and suppression of the Irish revolt. Both the diplomatic of the document and its idealistic assumptions and framework suggest the work of a private individual. It stands at the beginning of a succession of 'commonwealth' proposals offered to Cromwell in the 1530s for the reform and renewal of the society. On the other hand, it shows some insight into the priorities of the government in arguing for the suppression of small religious houses and the abolition of franchises. It may be that the writer had some contact with Cromwell and was amplifying proposals that he knew had already received some consideration in official circles. Some suggestion that the wealth of the bishops should be limited probably came before the council, for a paper survives in Wriothesley's hand, noting that the king had the right to all the temporalities of the bishops except for sums of £1000 or less reserved to the prelates. Unfortunately, the paper bears no date and could relate to any year up to 1540. The most that can be said is that it fits well in the early years of the breach with Rome, before the assault upon the monasteries had begun, when the government needed revenue to suppress the Irish revolt. In the end the threat of external intervention in that revolt receded, and it was possible to finance an army from the normal sources, including parliamentary grants.[4]

The private paper of 1534 for the alienation of superfluous church wealth is important as the first of a series of reform-minded proposals prepared in the heady atmosphere of the Cromwellian decade. A wide range of topics was embraced by these proposals, but only those which related to the church and its property can concern us here. Most were evidently of private origin: they bear witness to the re-forming urge of the decade and to the conviction that it was worth presenting Cromwell with radical social and religious proposals, but

---

4. *LP*, vi, 14, 24, 114. BL, Cott. ms. Cleo e iv, fos. 174–5; printed in Youings, *The Dissolution*, pp. 145–7. PRO, sp 1/86, fo. 145. On the Kildare revolt see B. Bradshaw, 'Cromwellian Reform and the Origins of the Kildare Rebellion, 1533–34', *TRHS*, 5th ser., xxvii (1977), 69–94.

they cannot be taken as direct evidence of government thinking. In 1535 one projector advocated the use of superfluous church revenues for the improvement of highways and for turning parks to tillage, which acts, since they would help to restore harmony within the realm, would lead to concerted action towards converting the Turks to Christianity! Not all suggestions tried to be quite so comprehensive as this, but it is common to find the authors invoking as many of their favourite ideas upon social organisation as they could within the scope of one document. Thus when John Parkins offered a set of proposals to Cromwell he included in them an attack upon the church, especially the remains of the monastic order, suggestions for alterations to the organisation of Oxford and Cambridge, and a strong emphasis on the need for preaching. His specific idea for the bishops was that they should be made to live entirely upon their spiritualities, supplemented by an annuity from the council if necessary, and that all their temporal possessions should be given to the laity. A third plan, probably the work of Thomas Gibson, dating from 1539, returned to a concern with defence and the need for a standing army. In an elaborate argument that has attracted considerable attention from historians the author proposed the establishment of a Court of Centeners, one of whose duties would be the financing of the army from the surplus revenues of the monasteries and bishoprics. In this proposal the bishops were left some lands, but only to the value of 1000 marks per annum. Finally, there was a bill prepared for the Parliament of 1540, but never introduced, which argued that the episcopate should be left with only enough revenue for 'the reasonable maintenance of a preacher of God's word without superfluity'.[5]

Although superficially similar, these schemes really fall into two groups. Those of Parkins and the 1540 bill are principally concerned with the reform of the church; they allege that the removal of wealth would actually benefit the clergy morally and spiritually. In the case of the 1540 bill the author seems to have assimilated the Lutheran ideal of a called ministry needing only modest resources for its support. Parkins adds a view which was to enjoy some popularity later in the century, that only 'spiritual things', revenues from within the church itself, were truly appropriate for spiritual men. The other projects are perhaps more typical of the schemes propounded in this

5. BL, Cott. MS. Cleo E IV, fo. 172. PRO, SP 1/115, fos. 97–101. L. Stone, 'The Political Programme of Thomas Cromwell', *BIHR*, XXIV (1951), 11–17. PRO, SP 1/152, fos. 11–13; printed in Hembry, pp. 260–1.

decade. They are concerned with the regeneration of secular society, and the interest of their authors in the church and its wealth is confined to the practical need to finance their elaborate plans. What cannot be claimed is that either set of ideas necessarily represent any general public opinion upon the need for reform. The authors are highly committed, sometimes slightly eccentric, individuals. Parkins, for example, was an Oxford common lawyer with a propensity for engaging in disputes and an unbalanced attitude to his opponents which suggests mild persecution mania. However, their ideas do take their place alongside a number of others urging upon Cromwell change and reform in all aspects of the life of the society. They do indicate that some men were viewing church wealth as more than a means to self-enrichment and that the changes already begun by the government gave them the confidence to urge further amendments. The authors seem to have believed that Cromwell at least was on their side and was ready and willing to undertake further drastic reforms in the body politic.[6]

Thomas Cromwell may have had some sympathy with certain of the suggestions presented to him, but he had to consider the political possibilities open to the Henrician government. He certainly appreciated the importance of financing any scheme adequately and had no particular love for wealthy churchmen, whether abbots or bishops. But whereas most of the private projectors urged that money should be taken from both the monasteries and the higher secular clergy, it was the monasteries alone that were selected for direct assault in the 1530s. It is not difficult to guess why they offered an easier prey than the bishoprics. The order of bishops was necessary for the preservation of traditional Catholic discipline and for the enforcement of the changes introduced by the Reformation Parliament. It was the bishops who were required to defend Henry's caesaropapism before the international community as well as to their own parochial clergy. The prelates had to digest many bitter pills in the 1530s as their control over jurisdiction was usurped by the vicegerent in spirituals, and a major crisis over lands and revenues might have lost the grudging support of such key figures as Stephen Gardiner and Cuthbert

6. On the spate of reform proposals put to Cromwell in the 1530s see G. R. Elton, *Reform and Renewal* (Cambridge 1973). There is a more detailed discussion of the proposals affecting church wealth in F. Heal, 'Henry VIII and the Wealth of the English Episcopate', *Archiv für Reformationsgeschichte*, LXVI (1975), 289–92. On the diplomatic and provenance of the documents see G. R. Elton, 'Parliamentary Drafts, 1529–40', *BIHR*, XXV (1952), 117–32.

Tunstal. The monasteries were an easier target, especially when approached by the 'divide and conquer' principle espoused in 1536. Even then the dissolution of the monasteries provoked strong, if intermittent, opposition and absorbed much of the energies of the government in the last four years of Cromwell's period of power. In these circumstances any notion of 'rationalising' episcopal wealth, which the chief minister himself might feel disposed to favour, had to be deferred in favour of resolving the more immediate political and financial problems created by the dissolution of the monasteries.[7]

Yet the absence of grandiose schemes to appropriate episcopal wealth does not mean that Cromwell took no action or was content to maintain the *status quo*. It was of the utmost importance that the royal authority over the church should be asserted at every opportunity, even if it was not exploited to its full practical limits. Thus, even before the first-fruits and tenths legislation, Cromwell had begun the task of examining and supervising the wealth of the bishoprics. As one of the treasurers of the king's revenues in the early 1530s Cromwell made it his business to supervise the collection of income from episcopal sees *sede vacante*. The temporal income of the English and Welsh sees accrued to the crown during a vacancy as part of its regalian right, while the spiritualities passed under the administration of the metropolitan. Direct control of the temporalities by the royal escheator was common, especially during the thirteenth and fourteenth centuries, and still sometimes occurred in the early sixteenth century. The escheator could, on the other hand, vest the crown's rights in the cathedral corporation in return for a fixed annual payment, ostensibly agreed afresh at each vacancy. In some dioceses this arrangement had been given the full sanction of a royal charter: Lincoln, for example, possessed a charter dating from the reign of Edward II. So firm was St Paul's hold upon the London lands *sede vacante* that episcopal leases regularly included a clause specifying that when there was no bishop rents were to be paid to the dean and chapter. In other sees the arrangements never reached this degree of formality, but the normal custom was for the chapter to take control. Even the monies paid to the exchequer tended to be fixed by the early sixteenth century. The chapter at Ely paid the same sum at three vacancies separated by over a century, a sum which

7. On opposition to the dissolution see G. R. Elton, *Policy and Police* (Cambridge 1972), chs. 1–3; Haigh, *The Last Days of the Lancashire Monasteries*.

seems to have been based upon the taxation assessments of Pope Nicholas IV.[8]

Cromwell apparently decided that royal income could be enhanced by a return to the system of direct royal control over the temporalities. When the see of Ely fell vacant in April 1533 one of Cromwell's own servants, William Cavendish, was sent to supervise the temporalities. The prior of Ely vigorously resisted this intrusion, claiming that he had the right of supervision both by tradition and by charter. His legal proof must have been defective or non-existent, for he was formally excluded from care of the temporalities, but emotions ran high, and the prior still apparently tried to extract from the tenants some of the dues to which he felt his house was entitled. In 1534 the bond tenants of the manor of Bishop's Hatfield were exonerated from the payments of recognisances to the incoming bishop because they had been subject to the double exactions of the crown and the prior *sede vacante*. The direct financial benefits of Cromwell's initiative do not seem to have been very great: Cavendish accounted for £2033 collected during his year at Ely, while the priory had traditionally compounded at £2000. However, the crown would also have had access to all the casualties of the see, especially to the woodlands, which were particularly useful as a source of quick profit during a vacancy. It was certainly felt sufficiently worth while for the same policy to be pursued in the subsequent year, when the temporalities of Bangor were supervised for Cromwell by the Bulkeley family and the claims of the chapter ignored. Again in 1536 the chapter of St David's were not allowed to intrude upon the collection of revenues, which was delegated to James Lathe. None of the chapters seem to have had the secure legal claims to control possessed by Lincoln or St Paul's Cathedral, and they offered Cromwell one of numerous opportunities to assert royal authority over the church.[9]

During the watershed year of 1534 these opportunities greatly increased. This was the year in which the government had to decide, amidst its other multitude of preoccupations, how to use the wealth of the church. 'The clergy', as an official apology for the Reformation explained a few years later, 'have submitted to the King, from whom they have immediately jurisdiction and goods, except mere spiritu-

---

8. Howell, *Regalian Right. LP*, III, ii, 1408. StPDC, Dean Sampson's book, *passim*. *LP*, II, i, 472.
9. *LP*, VI, 977 (2), 1244, 1381–2, 1494. Hatfield House Estate Docs., Court Rolls, 11/19. *LP*, XXI, i, 148 (29); VII, 257; X, 556.

alities granted by the gospels and Scripture, and have acknowledged that without his assent and confirmation they could pretend none other.'[10] The first general result of this financial submission was that the crown now chose to replace Rome as the beneficiary of the taxes of the clergy. Taxation needed to be based upon accurate assessments, and therefore the first-fruits legislation initiated the great survey of all clerical possessions which appeared in the following year. The survey was also necessary before there could be any proper appropriation of lands or revenues: the word of the clergy about the extent of their possessions needed to be tested against the relatively objective standard of the reports of the local commissioners. While, therefore, Henry and Cromwell may have toyed with various schemes for the use of church wealth during 1534, such as the payment of troops for Ireland from the surplus revenues of the bishoprics, it was only in the light of full knowledge acquired late in the subsequent year that they were able to proceed. It may have been during this period of waiting that a new policy towards the lands of the episcopate was devised.

If Cromwell's ideas had ever turned towards a general rationalisation of episcopal wealth, that moment had passed by the end of 1535. Even the decision to attack the smaller monasteries seems to have been accompanied by hesitation upon methods. Was it best to proceed by a frontal assault via parliamentary statute, to assert the king's rights as heir to the founders of many houses, or to follow the pattern used in many Lutheran lands of encouraging men and women to leave the cloister voluntarily and allowing the orders to atrophy slowly? If the challenge to the small monasteries provoked these heart-searchings, a direct appropriation of episcopal land must have been almost unthinkable. Yet the king wished for more than taxes from his prelates. There were their desirable hunting lodges, their great town houses, their carefully managed swelling acres, all of which attracted the avarice of the monarch and his leading lay subjects. Some device was therefore needed to translate this avarice into actual possession, without provoking violent opposition from the clergy and while retaining the semblance of equity. The method chosen was the exchange, the offering of one set of estates as substitute for another which had long been a common mode of transaction among the laity and between the crown and its subjects. There was, of course, no legal precedent for the use of such a method between the crown and the church, but once the king was firmly established as head of both

10. *LP*, xiv, i, 402.

church and state there was no fundamental objection to such transactions taking place. It was a far more refined and flexible idea than
that displayed by Henry in his only earlier attempt to take property
from the bishops. This was in 1530, when he simply took York Place,
Whitehall, from Wolsey at the time of his fall. Unlike Hampton
Court, or Cardinal College, Oxford, York Place was the property of
the see of York, and Wolsey entered a dignified protest at its surrender.
'If every bishop', he argued, 'may do the like then might every prelate
give away the patrimony of the church which is none of theirs.'
Some less provocative method had to be found in the circumstances
of the early 1530s, and the notion of using the exchange suited the
government's purposes most admirably.[11]

The idea of using exchanges to benefit from episcopal lands cannot
be directly attributed to any one individual, but it is reasonable to
surmise that Cromwell had a major hand in its development. The
first two sees to be the subject of royal demands both had a particular
interest for the secretary. Canterbury and its new archbishop were a
major concern: from 1534 onwards Cromwell's notes and remembrances contain several references to valuations of the estates of the
archbishopric, and the manors of Mortlake and Wimbledon attracted
him as desirable lands for his own possession. Norwich, the second
see, had been brought to his attention by the disputes with Richard
Nix and by the fine of £10,000 which was imposed upon the bishop in
1534. During the remaining year of his life Nix paid close, almost
obsequious, court to Cromwell, and after his death in early 1536 it was
the latter's agents who supervised the ordering of his goods and the
completion of his estate.[12] Furthermore, these two bishoprics offered
the ideal opportunity to test the acceptability of the new policy:
Norwich was vacant and its temporalities in the king's hands during
1536, and Canterbury was occupied by the leading exponent of Henry's
new order. Cranmer's deference to the royal will and to the political
expertise of Cromwell made him an ideal target. As early as 1533,
soon after his promotion, Chapuys had surmised that he would be
willing to renounce all his temporalities and encourage the other
bishops to follow his example. This was a misassessment of Cranmer's
attitudes, which tended to favour the continuity of episcopal tradition

---

11. Scarisbrick, *Henry VIII*, p. 237. The dissolution of the monasteries stimulated
an increase in the number of exchanges between laymen and between king
and subjects. See for example W. K. Jordan, *Edward VI: The Young King* (1968),
pp. 103ff.
12. *LP*, VII, 923. PRO, KB 29/166/ro. 42; 27/1091/ro. 13. *LP*, X, 236.

in this field, but the archbishop was certainly not opposed to some financial readjustment between church and state and did not stand upon the prerogatives of his office as a Warham or Gardiner would have done. When he was asked to exchange some estates in 1537 he wrote to Cromwell, 'as concerning such lands of mine as the King's highness is minded to have by exchange ... forsomuch as I am a man that hath small experience in such causes, and have no mistrust at all in my prince on that behalf, I wholly commit unto you to do therein for me as by you shall be thought expedient'.[13]

In 1536, therefore, two bills were introduced into parliament. The first was for an exchange between Cranmer and the king of the manors of Mortlake and Wimbledon for lands belonging to the priory of St Radegund's, Kent, the other for an exchange between Henry and William Reppes, the bishop of Norwich, of all the ancient estates of that see for a collection of monastic lands, including those of St Benet's, Holme, whose abbot Reppes had been. The use of monastic lands as recompense to the bishops in both these cases suggests that the policy of exchanges may have been devised as a by-product of the plans to dissolve the smaller monasteries, as a way of ensuring that more desirable estates accrued to the crown. There the similarity between the two exchanges ends: the Canterbury transaction was relatively modest in scale and set a pattern for many of the later arrangements made under Henry VIII. The two manors were close to the capital and therefore particularly attractive to a leading layman: they were passed from the king directly to Thomas Cromwell. The Norwich exchange, on the other hand, is comprehensive and drastic; it substituted a group of very small monastic estates for the larger manors of the see and worked to the financial disadvantage of the bishops. Chapuys heard rumours that the lands were to go to the earl of Wiltshire, but the object seems to have been the augmentation of crown estates in East Anglia, for most of the lands were retained at least until the 1540s. Although this transaction occasioned some ambassadorial comment, there is no evidence of outcry from churchmen of any religious persuasion. Reppes himself was almost embarrassingly eager to cooperate with the government in order to obtain the prized office of bishop and proved equally pliant to the laity once he was installed at Norwich. In these circumstances it is interesting to ask why the plan executed at Norwich was not repeated elsewhere,

---

13. *LP*, ix, 331; x, 912. On Cranmer's losses see F. Du Boulay, 'Archbishop Cranmer and the Canterbury Temporalities', *EHR*, lxvii (1952), 19–36.

why Hereford, St David's, Chichester and Carlisle were not made the subjects of massive exchanges as they came vacant later in the decade. It is possible that some major change was contemplated at Chichester where Cromwell made a considerable effort to persuade the aging Robert Sherburne to resign, but Sampson was installed without any losses to the see except the London mansion. Most of the bishoprics which happened to become vacant in the 1530s were relatively poor and therefore not perhaps worth the attention of the government. It is more likely, however, that the complexity of the management of the monastic lands through the newly established Court of Augmentations discouraged Cromwell from adding further to its burdens. For most of the rest of the decade the only exchanges undertaken were those in which the king or a leading layman had a specific interest in acquiring a particular property from the bishops.[14]

The estates which were taken from the prelates in this way can be divided loosely into two categories. First, there were the London manors, which had been coveted and admired by the laity since well before the Reformation. A large residence in the capital was becoming one major way of displaying political influence and status, and there can have been no sharper indication of the loss in status that the bishops experienced in the 1530s than the loss of many of their great urban 'inns'. In the early sixteenth century the crown already expected the bishops to be hosts to a range of government guests, to make good the deficiencies of royal accommodation in the capital. When Catherine of Aragon came to England in 1501 she was lodged in a series of episcopal houses: the home of the bishop of Bath and Wells at Dogmersfield, Hants., the archbishop of Canterbury's palace at Croydon, the bishop of London's main house at Fulham and finally the bishop of Rochester's residence in Lambeth. Ambassadors, especially those who came to negotiate for a limited time, were often assigned to the homes of the prelates. Bishop Clerk of Bath and Wells was offended to find that he was expected to accommodate Cardinal Campeggio on his crucial visit in 1528 to hear the divorce case, merely because Campeggio had lived in the Bath inn on his previous visit in 1519. The honour had also been offered to the bishop of Norwich, but Nix's agents had persuaded the cardinal that Norwich Place resembled a

---

14. 27 Henry VIII cc. 34, 45. *LP*, x, 295. The only Norwich lands that were granted away quickly were the London house, the Essex estates which passed to Thomas Audley and the manor of Thornage which was given to Sir William Butts. *LP*, xi, 202 (1), 943 (8). *LP*, x, 1146–7. 28 Henry VIII c. 23.

'pigsty'. Clerk suggested that Wolsey should undertake his own hospitality, since he was so interested in the cardinal's visit, and lodge him at Durham House, but to no avail. From this use of the homes of the bishops it was but a small step in practice, if not in theory, to Henry's action at York Place, which after 1530 formed the centre of his burgeoning palace of Whitehall. In the same year the king arranged that the earl of Wiltshire, father to Anne Boleyn, should have permanent tenure of Durham Place, while the new bishop, Cuthbert Tunstal, was given a home in Coldharbour Lane. This arrangement was given no formal sanction until 1536, when the beginning of the exchanges allowed the earl to confirm his position by an act of parliament.[15]

After 1536 the laity began their scramble for London property. Norwich Place, alienated from the bishopric in the great exchange, was given to Charles Brandon, duke of Suffolk. The lawyers of Lincoln's Inn secured the house of the bishops of Chichester by a series of astute manoeuvres. In 1537 the house of the bishops of Coventry and Lichfield in the Strand was surrendered, under pressure from Cromwell, to Lord Beauchamp, and in 1539 Bath and Wells Inn in the same street was given to the earl of Southampton in return for a dwelling in the Minories. Finally, there was a tripartite exchange by which Lord Russell took the bishop of Carlisle's palace outside Temple Bar, Carlisle moved to the home of the bishops of Rochester at Lambeth and Rochester went to the Russell manor at Chiswick about five miles up the Thames. In at least one other case a palace seems to have been taken over without the formal sanction of an exchange: John Gostwick, a friend and servant of Cromwell's, held Hereford House, but he could not prevail upon his master to arrange for his occupation to become possession. Presumably there was a question of status involved in this case: the houses of the other bishops had been taken by their social equals, the peers, and Gostwick was too lowly an intruder in such company. When the bishops lost their London homes they were less likely to receive adequate compensation than in the case of their rural manors. Even when another house was given in exchange, it was often smaller and certainly less well located than the one they had been compelled to vacate. This made little economic difference to the prelates: the great inns were a financial burden rather than an advantage, and the urban rents which

---

15. *Letters and Papers Illustrative of the Reigns of Richard III and Henry VII*, ed. J. Gairdner (1861–3), I, p. 408. *LP*, VI, ii, 4553–4; V, p. 758. 28 Henry VIII c. 33.

E

accompanied them were in several cases detached from the house and remained with the bishops throughout the century. The real loss was in political prestige, for the appearance of laymen in permanent occupation of these great homes was one of the most visible signs to the world that the power of the hierarchy had been gravely weakened by the events of the Reformation.[16]

Henry VIII had no interest in more homes within the city once he had swallowed up York Place, but he had an insatiable appetite for the second type of property lost by the bishops, large rural manors with hunting facilities. Otford and Knole, owned by Canterbury; Bishop's Hatfield, held by Ely; and Esher, held by Winchester, all passed to the crown during the 1530s. Only Gardiner raised any overt protest that has survived. He told Cromwell that he would surrender but that he did so very unwillingly. His resentment was perhaps caused by the fact that he received no compensation for Esher, while others were given good monastic lands in exchange for their sacrifice. No doubt there were many who would have liked to follow the king's lead, but outside London the crown in the 1530s kept a tight check on the lands it was prepared to pass on to laymen. Apart from the grants made to Cromwell, there were only some of the Essex manors formerly belonging to Norwich, which were given to Thomas Audley, and Frekenham, which Edward North, chancellor of Augmentations, extracted from the bishop of Rochester in return for two appropriated churches. By the time of Cromwell's fall there had been fourteen separate transactions involving the episcopal estates. The number of manors lost by the bishops and their approximate annual value are given in table 5:1. It can be seen that only Canterbury and Norwich experienced major financial loss and significant disturbance to their pattern of landholding. In return for the manors they surrendered the bishops received a variety of ex-monastic properties, including a number of appropriated rectories and other spiritual dues. These possessions were often less attractive and compact than the lands they lost, but the financial loss was not usually very great. Only at Norwich, where annual income fell from an estimated £979 in 1535 to £681 in 1543, was the transaction obviously unjust. Cranmer also appears to have lost some revenue, but the Canterbury lands were exchanged and reassembled and exchanged again with such bewildering frequency in this decade that it is difficult to be sure which prop-

16. 27 Henry VIII c. 39. *Acts of the Chichester Chapter*, p. 51. *LP*, xii, i, 807, 820, 1139, 1199. 31 Henry VIII cc. 25, 26. *LP*, xiv, ii, 527, 548.

Table 5:1 *Manors lost by the bishops, 1529–40*

	No. of manors	Estimated annual value
Canterbury	29	£1243
York[a]	1	–
Winchester	1	£21
London	1	£27
Ely	1	£64
Norwich[a]	22	£816
Bath and Wells[a]	2	£26
Chichester[a]	1	–
Rochester[a]	2	£55
Coventry and Lichfield[a]	1	–
Carlisle[a]	1	–
		Total £2252

[a]These sees lost a London property, to which no income value can be assigned

erties formed part of the endowment of the see at which date. A crude calculation suggests that the bishops received new income of about £1900 per annum as compared to the £2250 which they lost.[17]

The methods adopted by the Henrician government in the 1530s seem to have ensured that there was no vocal criticism from the bishops. The most that Cromwell's correspondents were prepared to do was to enter a mild protest against his proceedings. Thus when John Stokesley, bishop of London, wished to resist the alienation of Lodsworth he hid behind the persons of St Ethelbert and King Offa, who had given the manor to the see and had hedged their gifts with 'strange imprecations *contra alienatores*'. Nevertheless, neither he nor Gardiner was prepared to take a principled stand against the monarch whom they had acknowledged as head of the church, and the exchanges proceeded as the government wished. Meanwhile the monasteries continued to occupy Cromwell, and any question of more general expropriation from the bishops was left strictly alone. In 1536 we find the English ambassador to the Scots, Bishop Barlow of St David's urging James V to reform the clergy and to increase his

17. *LP*, xiii, ii, 904; xii, ii, 1004. Hatfield House, Deeds of Purchase and Exchange, A21, E7. *LP*, xii, ii, 1004; x, 1087. NRO, Ep. cc 100094. After the exchanges begin it becomes increasingly difficult to identify manorial units, for much of the property that accrued to the bishops was now merely rents. However, a rough estimate suggests that about fifty-six estates came to the bishops in the 1530s as compensation for their losses.

income by restoring all church emoluments to the crown, to whom they rightfully belonged. This statement, for external rather than domestic consumption, suggests that the idea of asserting founders' rights was still at the back of the minds of Henry and Cromwell even after the beginning of the attack upon the monasteries. What it does not show is that Cromwell intended to apply the notion to the rest of the English church. It was still merely one of a range of possibilities that the government could consider.[18]

The final dissolution of the larger monastic houses revived a plan which had first been mooted by Wolsey a decade earlier for the creation of some new bishoprics. In 1532, after protracted negotiations with the curia, bulls had actually been issued for the erection of six new sees. Events had overtaken this initiative, and it was not until 1539 that there was a serious prospect not only of creating the bishoprics but of financing and accommodating them fairly painlessly from some of the larger of the dissolved houses. Henry himself chose to take a personal interest in the establishment of the sees, and he was enthusiastically seconded by Stephen Gardiner, who was always concerned to extend the influence of the clergy. The original proposal included twenty-one possible sees, most of the bishops being assigned an income of £333. 6s. 8d. This list was reduced finally to only six new foundations, with their attendant cathedral establishments, presumably because the cost of the original idea was too high for Henry or his advisers to stomach. Thomas Cromwell may have argued against this lavish scheme for new bishoprics: in one of his remembrances for the year 1539 he noted the need to 'diminish some of the bishoprics' and in another list suggested that the existing poor see of St Asaph should be united to the proposed foundations of Chester and Wenlock. The latter arrangement would have had the advantage of creating an entity which was well financed but would have established a see that was even more unwieldy than the one that finally emerged as the diocese of Chester in 1541. The six bishoprics which were established between 1539 and 1542 were given endowments of approximately the order originally planned, except for Westminster, which was blessed with rents and property worth almost £600 a year. Peterborough, Gloucester, Bristol, Chester and Oseney/Oxford were left with revenue that would barely have been adequate in a period of economic stability; in the inflationary situation of the mid-Tudor decades their bishops were condemned to a cycle of indebtedness and

18. *LP,* XIII, i, 1500; IX, 730.

fiscal problems. The extent of the changes could not, of course, have been foreseen by the king and his advisers when they fixed the endowments for the new sees, but they allowed little margin in their calculations for any crises. The establishment of the new dioceses may represent Henry's affirmation of his belief in the episcopal order and the traditional forms of ecclesiastical government, but the affirmation is severely circumscribed by the grudging provision made for these extra servants of the Tudor church.[19]

After the foundation of the new dioceses and the fall of Cromwell, political events appeared to move modestly in favour of the traditional church, and for a time proposals to assail the bishoprics were no longer put to the government. Nevertheless, after a brief pause in 1541, demands for episcopal property continued briskly. During the 1540s the laity as well as the crown began to reap the benefits of trafficking in these lands, although it was still the king who dominated the major exchanges. Royal interest was concentrated upon the continuing attrition of the Canterbury estates and upon the diocese of York, where, in two major transactions in 1542/3 and 1545, the territorial basis of the northern see was fundamentally changed. The Canterbury losses in this period included most of the Sussex manors and those in Middlesex centred on the Harrow estate. Although some Kentish lands were taken, the policy of the government, if it can be dignified with the title 'policy', was to remove from the archbishop those manors which were not close to the heart of his jurisdiction. Monastic lands were still an important part of the recompense offered to Cranmer, but as these became more precious to the government their place was taken in part by appropriated rectories. Moreover, recompense of any kind was often given late and was of too low a value: the king was clearly aware of his failure to reimburse Cranmer and in his will he ordered that the three Lancashire rectories of Whalley, Blackburn and Rochdale be given to the archbishop. At York the exchange of 1543 was made between Archbishop Lee and the king: the lordships of Beverley and Southwell were alienated from the see and a mixture of manors and rectories given in return. The success of this inroad into the great estates of the north apparently encouraged Henry to try again when the see was vacant and to arrange a second exchange with the new archbishop,

19. *LP*, VI, ii, 4920. P. Heylyn, *Ecclesia Restaurata* (Cambridge 1849), I, p. 38. PRO, SP 1/243/fo. 59. BL, Cott. MS. Cleo E IV, fos. 303, 304. *LP*, XIV, ii, 424, 427, 259, 260. PRO, SC 11/roll 845.

Robert Holgate. This second transaction of 1545 marks a turning-point in the history of the episcopal estates rather similar to the Norwich exchange of 1536. The baronies of Hexham, Ripon, Sherburn, Scrooby and Churchdown in Gloucestershire were given to the crown, and in return the archbishop received only rectories, the appropriated benefices that became known in York as the 'great collection'. The practical reason for this change to spiritual property was presumably that there was a shortage of monastic land by the mid-1540s and that it was no longer convenient or desirable to offer it to the bishops. This practical consideration could easily develop a theoretical justification: the notion already espoused by Parkins that spiritual things were most appropriate to spiritual men, that the church should generate its own wealth by its spiritual services to the community. In the case of the bishops this idea was absorbed into official ideology in 1559, when it was used to justify the giving of spiritualities to the bishops in return for their ancient temporalities.[20]

Apart from these large exchanges, the crown took a less active part in the demands for episcopal estates in the 1540s. It was the interests of the laity and their ability to force compliance from the bishops that predominated. Laymen gained property in the dioceses of Norwich, Canterbury, Exeter and St David's and in each of these cases the crown's consent was sought only in the form of the purchase of licences to alienate land. The beneficiaries tended to be peers or gentlemen with strong local interests who could presumably exploit the weakness of the Henrician bishops and their need for support and patronage. William Reppes, bishop of Norwich, had already shown himself to be so cooperative with the crown that it is not surprising to find local gentlemen extracting estates from him. He agreed to three exchanges in the 1540s: the first gave the priory of Hickling to William Woodhouse, who founded a local dynasty based upon that estate; the next gave Paston and Haedale to Thomas Paston, not only a member of the important local family but a gentleman of the Privy Chamber; and the third provided John Corbett with the manor of Woodbastwick. In each case the bishop was recompensed with other lands, but not necessarily with ones which were conveniently located or which improved the property

---

20. For a detailed consideration of the York exchanges see C. Cross, 'Economic Problems of the See of York', *Agricultural History Review*, supp., XVIII (1970). *LP*, XIX, i, 226 (66); xx, i, 465 (39). Du Boulay, 'Archbishop Cranmer', p. 27. See below, ch. 9.

arrangements of the see. These arrangements with the laity are scattered throughout the later years of Henry VIII's reign, but the majority occurred during 1545 and 1546. Between 1541 and 1544 there were five exchanges; in the subsequent two years, seventeen. Some of these seventeen still directly concerned the crown: the second exchange at York, the 1545 transaction with Canterbury and the dissolution of the new see of Oseney with the consequent loss to the church of all its lands. Most of the rest profited laymen. Small prizes could be won from the bishops by local pressure of the sort which the Norfolk gentlemen must have exerted, but the greatest benefits had to be achieved through the court and through proximity to the king. William Paget gained most from the bishops by this method: in 1546 he was given six Staffordshire estates belonging to the bishops of Coventry and Lichfield and the one manor, Weston in Derbyshire, which the bishops of Chester had possessed. This haul was sufficient to support his new title of Lord Paget of Beaudesert. Sir Edward North followed his early success at Frekenham by purchasing part of the Kentish estates that Cranmer had been compelled to exchange in 1545. Wriothesley, earl of Southampton, took the so-called 'golden prebends' of Charminster and Bere from the bishop of Salisbury, and Edward Seymour, earl of Hertford, began his exploitation of episcopal land with the grant of Ramsbury and Boydon from the same bishopric.[21]

The crown was not necessarily the loser in this rush to acquire episcopal property. Paget had to pay in excess of £5000 for the lands needed to support his barony, and Edward North had to part with £7337 to the king and 500 marks to Cranmer for his Kentish estates. During the 1540s the sales of monastic lands were accompanied by a small but steady flow of sales of properties which had formerly belonged to one of the bishoprics. Nevertheless, the last years of Henry VIII's reign show the crown under increasing pressure to make grants from the episcopal estates and some evidence that influential laymen were demanding exchanges not favoured by the king. For example, Seymour's and Wriothesley's transaction with the bishop of Salisbury mentioned above, apparently provoked some royal criticism. Paget told Seymour that the king was refusing to write the necessary letter to the bishop demanding the Ramsbury and Boydon estates because

---

21. *LP*, XVII, 283 (26); XVIII, i, 66 (c. 47); XX, ii, 707 (8). On the local standing of these families see A. Hassell-Smith, *County and Court: Government and Politics in Norfolk 1558–1603* (Oxford 1974), pp. 39, 68, 312. *LP*, XXI, ii, 332 (47). 37 Henry VIII c. 26.

he believed that there had been general agreement between the parties that the properties could not be granted away, as they lay too near the centre of the diocese. Paget exerted all his well-known powers of persuasion, and Henry was eventually content to let him draft the appropriate letter. The type of missive that Paget sent may be guessed from a surviving Exeter example, when the bishop was required to part with Crediton Park to Sir Thomas Denny:

> He [Denny] would gladly obtain the same at your hands either by exchange or in fee farm as you shall together agree and think most convenient. You shall understand that being no less desirous that our said counsellor should obtain his suit in this behalf, than firm and constant in opinion that as well you my lord Exeter will most gladly gratify us in granting of the same, as you the dean and chapter of the cathedral of Exeter will do the semblable . . . we have thought meet to write these letters unto you.

If such a request was accompanied by more explicit bullying from the petitioner or his friends, it was a brave bishop who opposed or questioned the royal will. In the Exeter case the bullying came from Lord Russell, whose West Country interests gave him a special influence over the bishop. 'I may say to your lordship', he wrote to Bishop Voysey, 'that the King is very earnest in it and fully determined that the said Sir Thomas Denny shall enjoy the same by other lawful means if need be.'[22]

Henry was certainly aware that his servants were eager to exploit the episcopal lands and to use his name to threaten the bishops if necessary. This emerges from the famous story told by Ralph Morice, Cranmer's secretary, about the conflict between his master and Thomas Seymour. Seymour, apparently wanting some of the archiepiscopal estates, tried to discredit Cranmer by telling the king that his hospitality was poor. Henry arranged for Seymour to visit Lambeth at a time when the archbishop was keeping lavish open house and compelled him to admit that he had maligned the prelate. The king's lecture to his courtier is of particular interest. 'I know your purposes well enough,' Morice reports him as saying; 'you have among you the commodities of the abbeys, which you have consumed . . . and now you would have the bishops' lands and revenues to abuse likewise.' The bishops, if they kept good hospitality and engaged in charitable acts, should be helped rather than hindered. 'And there-

22. *LP*, xxi, ii, 332 (76); xxi, i, 149 (6); xx, ii, 524. DRO, Chanter 15, fos. 111–12.

fore', he concluded, 'set your heart at rest; there shall be no such alteration made whiles I live.' It would be pleasant to be able to accept Morice's story as reliable evidence of Henry's attitude to the wealth of the bishops. However, the secretary had obvious reasons for bias in his account: he wished to present his master in the best possible light, and he was anxious not to provide any ammunition for those who assailed the church and its goods. The image of Henry as the protector of the rights and wealth of his leading clerics is flawed by other evidence. The king was bitterly opposed to clerical marriage on the grounds that it would allow priests to ally themselves with the great of the realm and might lead to benefices and ecclesiastical property becoming hereditary. He consistently sought a view of orders that would not allow the clergy to account themselves independent of royal control: indeed, at times he seems almost to have sought the *potestas ordinis* for himself as head of the church, though the claim was never made overt. His suspicion of wealth and influential priests sometimes appears as sharp as that of his Swedish contemporary, Gustavus Vasa. If Henry did indeed defend the wealth of the bishops to Seymour, it is likely that he was motivated by a wish to maintain control over his church rather than by any altruistic concern for the good works it undertook.[23]

Even the notion that there would be no general change in the financing of the bishops during Henry's life must have seemed doubtful in the circumstances of 1546. The crown was in urgent need of new sources of income, especially to finance the Scottish campaign planned for the subsequent year. There were men of influence at court who favoured a further appropriation of church goods: Morice claimed, for example, that the Seymour group contemplated introducing a bill into parliament for the alienation of episcopal lands. Henry's belief in purgatory and in the efficacy of masses for the dead had not prevented him from presenting the Chantries Bill of 1545 to parliament. In these circumstances rumours which had been dormant since the 1530s were revived. The new imperial ambassador, Van der Delft, saw a connection between the losses to the chantries and those the bishops might experience. He suggested that 'they may feel what they fear at the next Parliament

---

23. *Narratives of the Reformation*, pp. 260–3. The occasion for Henry's hostile remarks upon clerical marriage was in 1541, when reports reached him that there had been agreement between the Catholics and Protestants at the Colloquy of Ratisbon on this issue. *LP*, XVI, 733, 737.

which is fixed for November'. The next session did not actually meet until January 1547 and was abruptly terminated by Henry's death, but rumours that it would consider the wealth of the bishops persisted. Chapuys, who returned to London just in time for this session, reported to Mary of Hungary that the Protestant faction was in the ascendant at court and that their only obstacle was the power of the bishops. He therefore feared that they would lose their property and be given royal pensions instead in order to increase their dependence upon the crown. Here Chapuys must have been picking up some echoes of the conflict between the Protestant faction and Gardiner, who was being steadily excluded from power after the fall of the Norfolks. The details of this tension at the centre of power are obscure, but Gardiner certainly fell into royal disfavour for refusing the king some lands in circumstances which suggest that his opponents may have poisoned Henry against him. As for parliament, the only bill planned for the 1547 session that can be described as relevant to the bishops was entitled 'that Ecclesiastical persons having lands belonging to their offices may be restrained from alienating and wasting them'. This scarcely suggests a general attack on the estates: it is most likely to be designed as an answer to a problem that had been worrying Archbishop Cranmer in the previous year. He found that the dean and chapter of Canterbury were alienating their estates to laymen without waiting for any royal letters commanding them to do so. This meant that property which could be turned to the king's use and to the general advantage of the realm was being lost to private men. While therefore there is nothing in Henry's previous behaviour to indicate that he would have held back from demands upon the bishops if they had proved necessary, there is equally no evidence that such demands were actually planned during the last year of his reign. The king probably favoured the preservation of the *status quo*, provided that his government was not in desperate straits and provided that the bishops cooperated with him when he asked for some small part of their possessions.[24]

The consequences for the bishops of the demands that were actually made in the 1540s can be seen in table 5:2. The total annual value of the property lost, which included a few rectories and miscellaneous

24. L. B. Smith, *Henry VIII: The Mask of Royalty* (1971), p. 236, suggests that episcopal wealth was to be used to finance the Scottish campaign, but there seems to be no positive evidence of this beyond the rumours picked up by the ambassadors. *Narratives of the Reformation*, p. 263. *LP*, xxi, i, 37; ii, 546, 756. *Letters of Gardiner*, pp. 246–9. *LP*, xxi, i, 109. Thomas Cranmer, *Remains* (Oxford 1833), i, p. 319.

Table 5:2 *Manors lost by the bishops, 1541 to the death of Henry VIII*

	No. of manors	Estimated annual value
Canterbury	17	£784
York	73	£1563
London	3	£143
Norwich	9	
Bath and Wells	1	£55
Salisbury	2	£84
Worcester	2	£123
Exeter	2	£231
Coventry and Lichfield	5	£140
St David's	1	£35
Chester	1	£50
Oseney	9	£333[a]
		Total £3541

[a]Includes spiritualities lost as well as the manors and their perquisites.

possessions as well as the manors, was of the order of £3700. The recompense given to the bishops eventually amounted to about £2850, though in some cases there was a delay of several years between the alienation of a property and the provision of compensation. Cranmer had to wait for the execution of Henry's will before he was recompensed for estates he had lost in 1545, and the bishop of London endured a six-year wait between the loss of Lodsworth and the receipt of some property in exchange. Yet the problems created for the bishops by this second phase of demands for their lands was greater than the discrepancy in the income figures implies. If the 1530s had been the years when the symbols of episcopal power had been threatened, the 1540s were years when many sees began to surrender vital rural estates on which the prelates depended for rents, casualties and, in some cases, income in kind. The rectories and spiritual dues which were used to compensate the bishops at Coventry and Lichfield and at Chester as well as at York and Canterbury were less easy to exploit than the manors. Rectories were almost always in lease: this of course prevented the bishops from benefiting from any upward movement in the value of the tithes that formed the appropriation. Since most of the rectories had previously belonged to monasteries and had been the subject of new, long leases in the last days before the dissolution, it was often many decades before the bishops could even take an entry or renewal fine upon their possessions. At Chester, for example,

four of the five rectories that passed to the see in 1546 were cumbered
with leases that did not fall in until late in the sixteenth century.
Worst of all was the precedent which Henry established: that it was
acceptable to make the prelates more dependent upon spiritualities.
There is no evidence that this practice was challenged by the higher
clergy, who seem to have been grateful to obtain what they could at
the hands of the king. But it stored up problems for their successors,
who were open to the charge that they were taking from the parishes
the endowments which would have served to provide them with a
proper teaching ministry.[25]

The practice of compelling the bishops to exchanges of land with
the crown and laity, of taking their London homes and some of their
most attractive rural estates, had demonstrated the control which
Henry could exercise over his higher clergy. It was as convincing a
demonstration of the victory of the laity in the English Reformation
as was the dissolution of the monasteries, though it naturally attracted
less general attention and comment. The church possessed few political weapons against this onslaught, and the spiritual constraints upon
which it had depended for so long to keep its property intact had been
gravely weakened by the events of the 1530s. Yet while Henry lived
the demands were kept within bounds and the bishops were in some
measure compensated for their losses. The attitudes of the king
imposed some limits upon action against the prelates for three reasons.
First, there was the royal determination to be the main beneficiary
from any exploitation of church lands: laymen could only gain
access to this rich source of profit if they were extremely fortunate or
favoured. Secondly, Henry may have been restrained by a desire to
retain the traditional role of the bishop as the doer of good works
and the source of charitable giving, a role which could only be fulfilled with a reasonable economic surplus, and also by a wish that the
prelates should still be men of worship and dignity, worthy to serve
as leaders of his newly purified church.

Thirdly, and of most importance, was the ambivalence that still
surrounded the authority of the bishops. Henry was hostile to any
overt claim by the bishops that they derived their authority from God
rather than from himself as God's chosen representative. He showed

25. Haigh, 'Finance and Administration', in *Continuity and Change*, p. 151. At Coven-
    try and Lichfield the bishops were actually allowed to take into impropriation
    rectories which had previously been free of external encumbrances. *LP*,
    XXI, ii, 770.

on occasion sympathy with Cranmer's view of orders, which allowed that the king could appoint ministers to spiritual office just as he appointed to secular office, should the continuity of ecclesiastical succession be broken. Much of the energy of Cromwell as vicegerent was bent upon demonstrating the practical extent of the royal authority over the jurisdiction and ordinary power of the bishops. But these tendencies were never pushed to their logical conclusion. The bishops retained much of their jurisdiction; their mode of appointment was as it had been before the breach with Rome, though shorn of course, of its papal elements. Conservatives such as Gardiner were therefore still able to believe that the episcopate was of divine institution, and it suited Henry's purposes not to challenge this assumption directly. The insistence that the bishops should be treated with the appearance of equality in exchanges of their estates may be connected with this view of authority. They were still not salaried officials of the state but men set apart for the spiritual labour of securing religious conformity. They retained their connection with the episcopate of the pre-Reformation period, including, in weakened form, the claim to control over their property. This is not to argue that Henry would have continued to find it desirable or right to allow the bishops their illusions of authority over their wealth: the royal mind was liable to move in unexpected ways, especially when the royal purse was empty. Nevertheless, the king never did rationalise the system of authority or financial control which he exercised over them. Some of the logical consequences of the government's actions in the 1530s were not pursued until the subsequent reign.[26]

---

26. On Henry VIII and his view of episcopal authority see Scarisbrick, *Henry VIII*, pp. 413–17; D. M. Loades, *The Oxford Martyrs* (1970), pp. 38–50.

6

CHANGE AND RESTITUTION

The death of Henry VIII, which occurred in the middle of a period when there were intense demands for the lands of the church, could well have been followed by a complete expropriation of episcopal property. The group of men who were now able to assume political power were precisely those who had been busy in the transactions and exchanges of the old king's last years. William Paget, William Herbert, John Russell, Edward North and Anthony Denny were among the sixteen executors of Henry's will and were therefore members of the privy council. They were also supporters of the new leader of the realm, Edward Seymour, soon to be duke of Somerset. Seymour's own attitude to the lands of the church had yet to be clarified; his only excursion so far into exchanges with the episcopate had been the 1545 agreement with Wriothesley and the bishop of Salisbury. Nevertheless, the general behaviour of his friends and the disposition towards Protestantism that he had already demonstrated suggested that he would be even less indulgent towards independent bishops than Henry VIII had been. And indeed it transpired that consideration of the sensibilities of the higher clergy was rare for either of the régimes that held power during the minority of Edward VI. One of the first actions of Somerset's government was to require the bishops to accept new commissions for the exercise of their authority, an authority which they henceforward held only during the prince's good pleasure. This was followed by the decision to abolish the system of *congé d'élire*, by which the church had been able to retain at least the semblance of independent election of its highest officers. Later the revised version of the Ordinal and the deprivation of the conservative prelates underlined the dependence of church upon state. These changes did not only represent an attack by the powerful laity upon the ecclesiastical leadership: they found much support from within the ranks of the reformers. Although the abolition of the office of bishop seems scarcely to have been contemplated, even by such radicals as Hooper and Coverdale, there was enthusiasm for the idea of reducing the lordly prelate to a more modest station within the church. On the one hand there was Cranmer's Erastian belief in the guidance and control of the Supreme Head of the English Church. On the other there was the standard of Scripture to use as a reference, so that Hooper could argue that the prelates must be humbled because they had departed from their original functions, and 'Bishops became princes, and princes were made servants: so that they have set them up with their almose and liberality in so high honour, that they cannot pluck them down again with all the force they have.'[1]

The new commissions which the council decided to issue to the bishops on 6 February 1547 were one of the most important symptoms of the direction church–state relations were to take during the reign. Their form was not new; with minor exceptions they resembled the commission issued to Bonner in the previous reign when he became bishop of London: even the specification that they were only valid during good pleasure had already been included in the earlier document. But, as Gardiner recognised, they could be construed as more than a means to secure the legal authority of the bishops after the change of monarch. He wrote to Paget at the beginning of March, objecting strongly to the inclusion in the commissions of the word 'delegate' with its implication that the bishops could not exercise jurisdiction by virtue of their power as ordinaries but only as royal deputies. Since the original commissions excluded certain of the regular functions of the bishops, especially that of visitation, Gardiner had good reason to complain of the form of the grant. He also saw behind it a deeper intention to assail episcopal power. 'What are you the better', he asked Paget, 'if ye be called of some a pincher of the bishops, and, among them, me?' The conservatives were already especially vulnerable, and the government was here employing a weapon which could both limit their immediate authority within their sees and provide the means to remove them from power if they failed to fulfil the terms of their commission. Paget in his reply tacitly admitted that some general alteration in the situation of the bishops was in the minds of the council: 'and if the estate of bishops

1. On government policy under Edward VI see M. L. Bush, *The Government Policy of Protector Somerset* (1975); D. Hoak, *The King's Council in the Reign of Edward VI* (Cambridge 1976). Hooper's comment is from J. Hooper, *Early Writings*, Parker Soc. (Cambridge 1843), pp. 396–7.

is or shall be thought meet to be reformed, I wish either that you were no bishop or that you could have such a pliable will as could bear well the reformation that shall be thought meet for the quiet of the realm'.[2] For all the bishops, whether reformist or conservative in their religious views, the new commission served to reemphasise their dependence upon the monarchy and the similarity between their power and that of the crown's temporal servants.

The new Protestant rulers of England could have followed this attempt to humble the political and spiritual pride of the prelates by adopting a reformed view of their wealth. In practice both Somerset and Northumberland proceeded far in this direction: the latter in particular appears to have favoured the idea of the prelate as a preaching supervisor, supported by an appropriate 'competent maintenance'. There were those, both laymen and clerics, who urged that the system of episcopal finance should be thoroughly changed in order to ensure that the Reformation was better secured. Philip Hoby, writing from Germany in 1549, quoted with evident approval advice which he had received from some local Protestants. They warned of the dangers of episcopal power and advocated that the council should 'appoint unto the good [English] bishops an honest and competent living, sufficient for their maintenance, taking from them the rest of their worldly possessions and dignities; and thereby avoid the vainglory that letteth them truly and sincerely to do their duty, and preach the Gospel and the word of Christ'. In a similar vein Hooper urged that the wealth of the bishops was nothing but vanity and that its redistribution could be of great benefit to the whole commonweal: 'If the fourth part of the bishopric remained unto the bishop, it were sufficient; the third part to such as should teach the good learning; the second part to the poor of the diocese; and the other to maintain men of war for the safeguard of the commonwealth, it were better bestowed a great deal'.[3] Such ideas were by no means new – we have already encountered very similar proposals from Cromwell's correspondents – but under Edward an influential section of clerical as well as lay opinion found nothing objec-

2. The text of Cranmer's commission is published in Burnet, *History of the Reformation*, II, ii, pp. 131–3. For Bonner's 1539 commission see *ibid*, I, ii, pp. 288–91. *Letters of Gardiner*, pp. 268–72. P. Tytler (ed.), *England under the Reigns of Edward VI and Mary* (1839), I, p. 24. For a discussion of the commissions see Loades, *The Oxford Martyrs*, pp. 52–3.
3. BL, Cott. MS. Galba B XII, 4 (2). Hooper, *Early Writings*, p. 397.

tionable in the notion that the bishops should be parted from much of their ancient wealth.

But though advocates of a complete 'rationalisation' of episcopal finances were not lacking, neither Somerset nor Northumberland undertook the sort of general reform envisaged by Hoby. Somerset in particular, only took lands in a piecemeal fashion from the prelates and has left no evidence that he was interested in initiating a more general change. Some reasons for this reluctance to embark upon grandiose alterations can be inferred from the circumstances of the reign. There were internal constraints imposed by the relative weakness of government during a period of minority. It was a sufficient challenge to initiate major changes in religion, without undermining the bishops, who still served as important guarantors of stability. Then there was the problem that a general expropriation of lands would have stimulated competing claims for patronage, claims which might make it difficult to retain the benefits for the crown and the small circle of the ruling élite. There was even the risk of creating divisions within the council. The delicacy with which even commonplace exchanges of episcopal estates were handled between members of the council is shown by a letter from Warwick to Somerset early in 1548. Warwick was engaged in the apparently unremarkable manoeuvre of exchanging lands with the bishop of Worcester, to the latter's disadvantage. Nevertheless, he felt obliged to justify his behaviour to the protector, and stressed that 'in this bargain I desire no penny disparate [?] to the said bishop, but rather his commodity and advantage . . .' It is true that Warwick concluded by calling his business 'a trifling matter', but his letter suggests an awareness of the importance of political consent and agreement in these land negotiations.[4]

There were also external constraints to be considered. It has been suggested that a principal reason for the caution of Somerset's government was his reluctance to antagonise the emperor. The protector's energies were bent upon achieving victory in Scotland, and this was only feasible if Charles V maintained his distance. The fear that had been felt so strongly in the aftermath of the Henrician Reformation, that the emperor was only waiting to be free of other commitments in order to invade England, revived in the later 1540s. Charles's successes in Germany prompted William Thomas to ask, 'where shall he end his fury but against us?' Paget among others advocated pre-

4. PRO, sp 10/3/1.

senting the changes of religion in England to the emperor as little more than alterations in external ceremony, which might legitimately be adopted at the will of the prince and with the consent of parliament. The imperial ambassadors under Henry VIII had always been closely interested in any hints that the lands of the bishops might be expropriated. Such an expropriation, Chapuys had urged, would have as its primary objective the weakening of the conservatives, whose capacity to influence the religious settlement would be much reduced. It may therefore have seemed injudicious, at least during the first two years of the new reign, to give the emperor further cause for alarm. The chantries presented an easier target for the government at this time, since their loss had fewer repercussions upon the structure of the church than an attack upon the bishops. In observing the significance that the government attached to good imperial relations, however, we should not assume that they were the crucial determinant establishing the pattern of internal religious change. Only in the early part of the reign could this have acted as a serious check upon the government, and even then Somerset could be ruthless in pursuing changes which he felt to be necessary. The imprisonment of Gardiner and the beginnings of action against Bonner are evidence enough of this.[5]

The main reason why no systematic moves were made against the bishops seems to be less the constraints of high policy than the fact that those with political power could take what they wanted by other means. Those close to the protector were beneficiaries from a series of exchanges or outright grants by the bishops which were even more advantageous to them than the pickings of Henry's last years. Somerset himself set the precedent with his spectacular inroads into the property of Bath and Wells and Lincoln. Table 6:1 shows the losses of the bishops between January 1547 and October 1549, and the losses of these two sees, along with those of Exeter, are its most pronounced feature. Since many of the grants made by the bishops during these years were not compensated for by any equitable exchange, the economic circumstances of these three sees were fundamentally altered by the action of Somerset and his circle. The bishops of Lincoln were given some rectories, and the bishops of Bath and Wells for a time gained possession of the deanery of Wells, but not even official government pronouncements pretended that these were a

5. Strype, *Ecclesiastical Memorials*, ii, i, p. 383. *LP*, xxi, ii, 756. J. A. Muller, *Stephen Gardiner and the Tudor Reaction* (1926), pp. 166–9.

Table 6:1 *Losses of temporal property of the bishops, 1547 to October 1549*

	No. of manors	Valuation (from 1535 survey)
Lincoln	30	£1374
Bath and Wells	20	£1448
Exeter	9	£322
Worcester	4	£102
Coventry and Lichfield	3	£91
Norwich	12	£70[a]

[a]This estimate is taken from the 1543 valuation.

fair exchange for the lands taken. Such compensation as was given under Edward was usually in the form of rectories and other spiritualities: the only exchange in which manors of any value were given to the bishop was that effected between the earl of Warwick and the bishop of Worcester in 1548. The rectories were a problem, not only because their value could rarely be increased but also because they were often burdened with high fixed charges: the group that were given to Lincoln in 1547 had fees and other costs of over £160 dependent upon them. The protector and the council never found it necessary to produce any formal justification for their actions against the bishops, though one may surmise that they found some general moral support in the hostility which the leading Protestant thinkers exhibited towards wealthy and powerful clerics.[6]

If the three sees that suffered the greatest losses in the early years of Edward's reign are examined in detail, the influence of the lord protector becomes clear. Lincoln had not been touched under Henry VIII, but it offered a valuable opportunity to Somerset when the death of Longland opened the way to the appointment of the reformer Henry Holbeach. As price for his promotion Holbeach had to make two substantial grants. The second in time, which was formalised in September 1547, gave to the king twenty of the episcopal estates, including concentrations of property in Oxfordshire, Nottinghamshire and Leicestershire. The bishop received in compensation the college of Thornton and a large group of rectories in Lincolnshire and elsewhere, whose fixed costs have already been mentioned. The model for this transaction was probably the York exchange made two years previously, and its object was to supplement the landed

6. PRO, E 305/G/11. *CPR, Ed. VI*, II, pp. 254–5; I, pp. 153–7.

property of the crown, for most of the estates were retained for several years. Somerset may also have intended to disguise the impact of the first transaction, by which he had obtained nine of the most important manors of the see, including Banbury, Dorchester and Buckden in Huntingdonshire. The see received nothing in exchange for this grant, but the dean and chapter recorded that Holbeach himself was a beneficiary. In their confirmation of the indenture they commented that the lands had been given in return for 'certain great sums of money paid over at the sealing of this indenture'. Holbeach had little alternative but to consent if he wished to occupy the bishopric, and the precedent for money payments as a compensation for manors had already been established on a modest scale by Cranmer in the preceding reign. Nevertheless, the Lincoln agreement marks another stage in the failure of the bishops to protect their ancient inheritance, a stage at which even the semblance of care about the future of their property was sacrificed to saving what could be salvaged by the grace of the powerful laity. No evidence of Holbeach's view of the transactions has survived, but the chapter confirmation of the grant to Somerset expresses the distaste and alarm of the cathedral clergy. Somerset benefited both by the general increase in his landed resources and particularly by the acquisition of the Oxfordshire estates of the bishopric, which became the northern flank of his West Country interests. Some of the other properties became useful in the perennial business of consolidating those interests: Stow in Lincolnshire, for example, was sold to Thomas Heneage in return for Cheddar, which was in the area of the country that most interested the duke. Meanwhile, Holbeach was left to struggle with an income derived only from his spiritualities plus five small manors, and a diocese in which he held no estates or residences outside Lincolnshire.[7]

The tale of Bath and Wells is similar, though more complex. Again there was a vacancy at the beginning of the reign and again the new man was a reformer, William Barlow. Somerset had an even closer interest in this area than in that of Lincoln, and the collapse of episcopal finance must be attributed to his desire to increase his landholdings. Again, the protector's own interests were associated with an attempt to increase the endowment of the crown: the largest

---

7. PRO, E 305/F/2. *Chapter Acts of Lincoln*, III, pp. 1–3. *CPR, Ed. VI*, I, p. 184. *Chapter Acts of Lincoln*, II, p. 150. Cranmer was paid £200 in recompense for lands given to the crown and £240 for the 'overplus' of the manor of Charing. *LP*, XXI, i, 643. Hembry, pp. 108–9.

exchange placed ten manors in the hands of the king, and only two of these then passed to Somerset. The Cheddar estate was granted to Heneage and thence given in exchange to Somerset, but the rest remained with the crown until at least 1550. The duke benefited directly in two grants from the bishop: the first gave him six of the most important manors, including Wells, which was the heart of the bishopric; the second added the Wookey estate. Even Somerset's fall in 1549 was of little advantage to the see: during the interval of his imprisonment Barlow managed to recover Wells and two other manors, but in 1550 he was able to retrieve his position for a time. By 1550 Barlow was reduced to living in the deanery of Wells, as even his central palace had been taken from him, though this was restored by the council at the time of Somerset's final fall. The government recognised the dramatic change in the fortunes of Bath and Wells when it permitted the bishop to compound for his first-fruits at a new rate: £480, as compared to the original *Valor* assessment of £1844.[8]

If Lincoln and Bath and Wells demonstrate the aggrandisement of the lord protector, judiciously associated with action to strengthen the endowment of the crown, Exeter stands as an example of the more open competition for advantage in an area where no one lay interest was dominant. The collapse of the fortunes of Exeter must be attributed much more directly to the behaviour of the bishop than can that of the other sees. Holbeach and Barlow acted from a position of weakness: they were new appointees closely dependent upon the goodwill of the protector. Their Protestant convictions may also have made them less confident of the right of the episcopate to the great wealth represented by their estates. Voysey of Exeter, on the other hand, acted from a position of relative strength and was a conservative who might have been expected to defend his property on grounds of conviction as well as self-interest. However, his age and his affection for his home town of Sutton Coldfield prevented him from offering any effective resistance to the laity. The bishop now resided in Warwickshire and directed the affairs of his see at a distance – or rather by this time failed to direct some of them. For example, he kept no check upon his deputy collector of taxes, who for several years failed to perform his duties and accumulated vast arrears. Voysey had already been under pressure to grant long leases in the

8. Hembry, pp. 105–23. *CPR, Ed. VI*, ii, pp. 128; i, p. 275. *Foedera*, ed. T. Rymer and R. Sanderson (20 vols., 1727–35), vi, 166. *CPR, Ed. VI*, ii, p. 128.

last years of Henry's reign, and under Edward he apparently abandoned any attempt to protect his see and surrendered, or perhaps
sold, the best of his manors to the nearest bidders. Thomas Darcy
made sure of the great prize of Crediton, Paget took the London inn,
Thomas Fisher – a noted dealer in episcopal property – the estates in
Surrey, Sussex and Middlesex and Lord Russell took Bishop's Clyst
and Tawton. By the time Andrew Dudley and Sir Thomas Speake
had had their share a little later in the reign, the bishop was left with
only the palace at Exeter and a few poor manors in Cornwall. At this
point, confronted by poverty and a large debt to the crown, Voysey
allowed himself to be eased from office to make way for the reformer Miles Coverdale.[9]

The situation of Norwich is similar to that of Exeter, since Reppes
had proved himself under Henry VIII even more compliant than
Voysey. In 1548 Sir Francis Brian managed to secure an extraordinary
grant of the palace at Norwich and eleven of the best remaining
estates of the see. For some reason the grant never became effective
and had been cancelled by 1550, if not before, but it is difficult to
believe that the bishop himself did much to retrieve it. Possibly the
grant was security on a loan, for Reppes, like Voysey, was badly in
arrears with his taxes during these years; if so, it was of little help in
his general troubles, for he was also compelled to resign in 1550 upon
the promise that his debts would be remitted to him. In all the sees
discussed it was the leading members of the court circle or the central
government who benefited from the episcopal estates. Although
some properties changed hands in the lively land market of Edward's
reign, there is no evidence that the men at the centre of affairs who
secured the first grants intended to act as agents for others who could
not hope for direct patronage. Most episcopal estates were highly
desirable prizes and were therefore retained as part of the landed
property of a peer or politician of influence. Only towards the end of
the reign, when some of the manors which had come to the crown
were sold as part of the general effort to clear royal debts, did some of
the lands pass to lesser men.[10]

The list of bishoprics which had to accept the decimation of their

---

9. This appears to be in contrast with the late Henrician period when Bishop
   Voysey was making some effort to control his officers through detailed
   'remembrances'. DRO, Russell Docs., G2/27. PRO, SP 11/1/2. *CPR, Ed. VI*, II,
   pp. 16, 171, 402; III, pp. 7, 19, 50, 164. J. Vowell, alias Hooker, *A Catalog of the
   Bishops of Exeter* (1584).
10. *CPR, Ed. VI*, II, pp. 67–8.

property under Somerset does not exhaust those which were exposed to the demanding attention of the laity. Salisbury, Hereford, and Llandaff escaped without much outright loss, but their bishops gave leases of such generosity that they can sometimes scarcely be distinguished from outright grants. John Salcot, bishop of Salisbury, made two 200-year leases, one of the key manor of Sherburne to Somerset and one of his London home to Sir Richard Sackville. Anthony Kitchin of Llandaff retained so little control of his estates after the 1540s that one of his successors offered John Harington the terrible joke that all his land was 'aff'. Even those bishops who took seriously their obligation to protect their lands had to make the occasional sacrifice to those in power: Bonner gave Somerset a 200-year lease of part of the Fulham manor at the end of 1547, perhaps as an expression of gratitude for his release from the Fleet, which had occurred two months earlier. Paul Bush, of Bristol, was compelled to yield his estate at Leigh to Sir George Norton, though only after he had been the subject of several requests from the council itself. In the circumstances of the reign there was little point in carrying opposition to a determined government any further.[11]

Two groups of the prelates escaped much of the difficulty of these years, though for very different reasons. First, there were the leading reformers, Cranmer, Goodrich, Holgate and Ridley, who were not subjected to the attentions of the protector or those who enjoyed his patronage. This could be mere accident – their lands did not lie in the path of his ambition or greed – but an element of policy also seems likely. These were the men who were most deeply involved in the construction of the new religious ideology. They were important to Somerset, both because he respected many of their views and because they were the voice of the English Reformation. Their favourable attitude to the 'good duke' was valuable before the court of international Protestant opinion. Cranmer formed the link with such influential figures as Bucer, Peter Martyr and, somewhat later, Henry Bullinger, whose support was a major part of the process by which the English Reformation won respectability. On the whole, Somerset won golden opinions from these men, though his relationship with Bucer was cool after his initial reception in England. No doubt he could have taken most of the wealth of the reforming

---

11. BL, Harl. ms. 604, fo. 244. SaRO, Bpric 460, fo. 156. StPDC, Dean Sampson's Book, fo. 200. Strype, *Ecclesiastical Memorials*, ii, i, p. 525.

bishops and still retained their adherence, provided that he continued on a course towards Protestantism, but it was tactful not to make the issue of the episcopal lands too obtrusive and to assume the mantle of one who was 'a most firm supporter of religion'. Among the reforming bishops and the foreigners who came to England at their behest, only Bucer was eventually willing to point a finger of accusation at the duke who had some responsibility for 'the desolation and betrayal of the churches' and who was one of the many noblemen 'enriched by the possessions of the church, who themselves consider the present desolation of the churches will be more to their interest, than the godly reformation of them'.[12] Such explicit criticism could only damage the image that Somerset strove to establish both at home and abroad. Crude demands for land from Cranmer or Ridley could have been equally counterproductive, and it was possibly for this reason that the reformers were relatively well treated during the earlier part of Edward's reign.

The other group who did not suffer were the leading conservatives, Gardiner, Bonner, Tunstal and Heath. Here the reasons must have been different. From the very beginning of the religious changes Gardiner and Bonner showed signs of resistance, signs which led on to their eventual downfall. It quickly became evident that they would not cooperate with any enthusiasm in the new religious policies of the reign, and the issue of their lands was therefore dependent upon some general solution to the problem of their resistance. Meanwhile, the conservatives were likely to take a more principled stand against laymen who asked for their lands than were the reformers. It is interesting that the only transaction in episcopal estates during the Somerset years in which the bishop was offered a reasonable return was that between Warwick and Nicholas Heath of Worcester. Did Heath make a stronger stand for adequate recompense than Barlow or Holbeach? His dealings at Worcester certainly suggest that he was a shrewd protector both of the interests of his see and of those of his family. His brother, William Heath, was given an extensive lease of one of the important new properties accruing to the see, Richard's Castle, but the bishopric gained a useful group of manors on the borders of Shropshire and Hereford in return for the loss of a set of

---

12. For some views on Somerset from churchmen see *Original Letters Relative to the English Reformation*, ed. H. Robinson, Parker Soc. (Cambridge 1846–7), I, pp. 50–67; II, pp. 481–93. Bucer to Calvin, *Original Letters*, II, p. 547. WRO, CC 900/1, 4768.

estates among which only Old Stratford was particularly desirable. The conservatives certainly had every incentive both in theory and in practice to resist any piecemeal decimation of their estates and to protect their own families and servants rather than offer any further assistance to the ruling élite.[13]

Somerset's own behaviour towards the property of the church appears essentially acquisitive: it is difficult even to dignify it with the title of a policy. Even when he took some pains to secure new estates for the crown, as at Lincoln and Bath and Wells, the choice of dioceses to be assailed seems to have been determined largely by his own personal concerns for the construction of a suitable landed base for his power. Nothing is more characteristic of his casual disregard for the possessions of the church than the demolition of three episcopal palaces in the Strand, those of Worcester, Llandaff and Carlisle, to make way for his splendid new Renaissance town house. White Kennett quotes a letter from Gardiner to Somerset, written from the Tower, in which the bishop warns against this passion for gain: 'Take not all you can, nor all you may, for there is no greater danger in a nobleman than to let slip the reins of his lusts and not be able to reform them with the strong bit of reason.'[14] Such a warning would not seem amiss in one of the court sermons of Hugh Latimer. Although the views of the conservative and reforming leaders had by now polarised so sharply, they could both recognise that the godly ends and aims of the church were threatened by the greed of the laity. The lord protector's use of the resources of the church for his own aggrandisement consorted very poorly with his pretensions to a policy of social justice. There is no evidence of an attempt to use the income he had acquired to further those aims such as preaching, education and care of the poor to which the reformers around him wished to dedicate the wealth of the proud prelates. It cannot even be said from the surviving evidence that Somerset, in making his demands, was guided by any principles concerning the status of the bishops. The idea of a salaried bishop, giving good preaching in return for competent maintenance, began to influence the thought of Northumberland and of Edward himself later in the reign but did not apparently concern Somerset in 1547 and 1548. His lack of thought is illustrated by the Lincoln exchanges, in which the bishop retained the responsibility for his vast diocese but had no houses outside his

13. PRO, E 305/G/11.
14. Jordan, *Edward VI: The Young King*, p. 498. BL, Lans. MS. 980, fos. 154v–155.

own county from which he might visit and supervise the work of his clergy.[15]

Yet despite his casual appropriations, the protector retained the support of most of the reform-minded clerics, and few voices were raised against his activities. We have already suggested that he may himself have taken care not to alienate the most influential of his supporters; there was also care on the side of the clergy, who presumably saw the losses of the church as the necessary sacrifice to secure suitable reforms. The episcopate was divided against itself and no longer shared any common view of its purpose or powers. It became a matter of urgency to men such as Cranmer and Ridley that the conservatives, and notably Gardiner and Bonner, should be removed, since they were an obstacle to the proper dissemination of the religious settlement. Such a removal must have some financial consequences for their sees, but again these were apparently the necessary sacrifices to achieve a godly episcopate. The downfall of the leading conservatives involved not only Somerset but most members of the council. Bonner's deprivation was already in process before the crisis of 1549, and that event had little effect upon the council's willingness to proceed. The bishop of London's removal from his see was confirmed in February 1550, and in the same month Nicholas Heath was imprisoned for his refusal to support the Ordinal. By the summer of 1550 the long-deferred decision to threaten Gardiner with deprivation was taken, though formal proceedings against him were delayed until the autumn of that year. The principal motive in the assault upon the conservatives was no doubt religious: they represented an obstacle to change and were both articulate and influential in defence of traditional spiritual values. Since the king had commissioned them to perform their duties, the king could also remove them from office for their failure to discharge those duties. If, by happy accident, their deprivation brought the lands of some of the kingdom's richest sees into the crown's hands, it was almost inevitable that the government would use the opportunity to part the prelates from some of their property. Since there was a fairly long period of time between the decision to proceed against one of the conservatives and his final deprivation, the question of the estates could be given more careful thought than was possible when a see was vacated by death and needed to be filled quickly.[16]

15. On Somerset's social policy see Bush, *Protector Somerset*, pp. 40–84.
16. Bonner was under surveillance by the council throughout 1549. He was

This was the situation for the London estates when Bonner became the first victim of government policy. The council, with the earl of Warwick as its leading figure, had to decide if any action should be taken before the promotion of Nicholas Ridley to this most crucial of sees. The choice of the government was an interesting and complex one. Ridley, after his consecration, granted away four of the most attractive manors of his bishopric to the crown. However, he was not the principal sufferer from this arrangement. At the beginning of 1550 the ageing Bishop Reppes of Norwich was persuaded to resign in return for a pension and the remission of his substantial debts. This provided an opening for Thomas Thirlby, bishop of Westminster, whose cautious conservatism made him something of an embarrassment to the government. He had not actually resisted the royal will, and although the reformers referred to him as 'Gardiner's student', he showed little disposition for controversy or martyrdom. He was therefore removed to Norwich, where, as Christopher Hales commented, 'he will do less mischief' and where the Reformation was already reasonably well advanced without much assistance from the bishop. As an inducement to move he was given a series of small estates to augment his new bishopric. The see of Westminster was suppressed in March 1550 and its lands divided between the crown and the bishopric of London, so that Ridley lost very little by his surrender of estates. Westminster had in some ways been an anomaly from its inception: unlike the other new sees, it had no natural jurisdictional territory and was in competition with the senior diocese of London. It was ideal for a 'court' bishop: one who could serve the government in secular affairs without being too far removed from his seat. The value of such a position diminished under Edward, since both Somerset and Northumberland subscribed to the general Protestant belief that the prelates should be active in their own jurisdictions rather than in government. Even the church had little to gain from a bishopric such as Westminster, and its suppression appears dangerous only as a precedent, as an incident that could all too easily be repeated in areas much more vital to the interests of the clerical hierarchy.[17]

In the assault upon the conservatives there is little evidence that

placed under house-arrest in August and imprisoned at the beginning of October. Muller, *Stephen Gardiner*, pp. 191–5. Full proceedings against Gardiner are recorded in J. Foxe, *Acts and Monuments* (1837–41), VI, pp. 24–264.

17. PRO, E 305/G/25. *CPR, Ed. VI*, II, p. 385. *Original Letters*, I, p. 185. *CPR, Ed. VI*, III, p. 287. PRO, E 305/G/23. The valuations made by the government for the London exchange suggest that Ridley actually benefited from the transaction.

he events of October 1549 made any difference to government policy, although they gave brief hope to Gardiner, who saw them as a coup against the reformist ideals of Somerset. The most obvious effect for episcopal property of the fall of the protector was that it brought to political prominence a new group of men, who naturally expected land to enhance their position. Thus Andrew Dudley, Warwick's brother, was able to gain three estates from the decayed see of Exeter, and Lord Russell, the victor of the campaign against the western rebels, finally secured Bishop's Clyst and Tawton. Yet the emergence of Warwick and his supporters was not immediately followed by the orgy of exchanges that might have been anticipated. Instead, 1550 was marked by some modest restitutions to those who had suffered so badly under the previous régime. Holbeach regained the important manor of Buckden in Huntingdonshire for the see of Lincoln, a prize that was made more valuable by the remission of first-fruits and tenths on the property. Barlow had the great, but brief, satisfaction of re-capturing Wells manor as well as the estates of Chard and Huish. Thirlby, as has already been mentioned, was given some help in restoring the flagging fortunes of Norwich. He acquired a house in Ipswich and sixteen small manors to augment his living. Apart from this last grant, the restitutions may have been an attempt to concili-ate those reforming bishops who had suffered the extortions of Somerset: Voysey, as a conservative, was given no such relief. The gift of the properties 'as alms', to use the terminology of the Lincoln donation, also suggests an awareness that some of the prelates now needed the direct assistance of the government if they were to per-form their spiritual duties satisfactorily.[18]

By the middle of 1550 it was becoming clear that the deprivation of Bonner was the beginning rather than the end of the eviction of the conservatives. It was at this moment that the council had most incentive to organise a radical approach to the possessions of the bishops. As the imperial ambassador Scheyfve reported at the time of Gardiner's deprivation early in 1551,

> It is believed that all the Catholic bishops will be stripped and deprived of their sees and dignities and, if they persist in the old religion, condemned to perpetual imprisonment; and that, in any case, the temporalities will be applied to the Crown and the

---

He surrendered lands assessed at £480 per annum and received in return property valued at £527.

18. *CPR, Ed. VI*, iii, pp. 164, 167, 178, 180, 287.

King's domain. It seems that hereafter the Government will treat all bishops alike, and assign them pensions of one or two hundred pounds sterling for their maintenance.[19]

Such actions could in some measure have been inferred from the general attack on the Catholics and from rumours which had probably reached the ambassador of the government's plans for the Winchester lands. It would have been a logical progression to move from the view that the bishops were royal officials and exercised their authority only by virtue of the king's commission to the view that their property was vested in the crown and that the monarch was at liberty to determine how much should be used to support the higher clergy. The young king himself seems to have thought that this was the case at Winchester when he noted in his diary under April 1551, 'Ponet, bishop of Rochester, received his oath for the bishopric of Winchester, having 2000 marks of land appointed to him for his maintenance.' An official memorandum made much the same point when Miles Coverdale was given the see of Exeter after Voysey's resignation. It recorded that he received lands worth £500 'of the King's favour', though the estates were the remnants of those left from the debacle of the few years preceding.[20]

In practice the crown could not have exercised this degree of control over the episcopal estates without either legislative action or a direct surrender by the bishops who held the lands. The former course was adopted only at Durham, which was properly dissolved by act of parliament in 1553. Elsewhere the council chose to continue the by now customary method of persuading a new bishop to surrender some part of the patrimony of his see into the crown's hands, the transaction being properly confirmed by the addition of the chapter's seal. Had the council wished to adopt the policy indicated by Scheyfve they would have had to introduce general legislation, and this they still chose not to do. Therefore, in law the ancient estates of the prelates remained theirs until they chose to dispose of them. Continuity with the past was not broken except at Durham. As with consecration, the bishops could still see themselves as heirs of the traditional ecclesiastical system if they so chose. Under Edward VI such ideas became irrelevant and redundant, but their survival into Elizabeth's reign eventually helped to strengthen the revival of a

19. *CStP, Spanish*, x, p. 215.
20. *Literary Remains of King Edward VI*, ed. J. G. Nichols, Roxburghe Club (1857), III, p. 312. PRO, SP 10/19.

iure divino concept of episcopacy which culminated in the ideas of the Laudian period.[21]

For the moment the survival of these traditional forms was of much less significance than the continuing movement towards the 'rationalisation' of episcopal wealth. Gardiner's deprivation and the appointment of Ponet to Winchester were followed by a massive alienation of land that reduced the income of the see to the sum mentioned by Edward, 2000 marks. The removal of Heath from Worcester offered an ideal opportunity to the government to pursue both its spiritual and secular objectives. John Hooper, already bishop of Gloucester, was given greatly increased responsibility by the addition of Worcester to his area of jurisdiction, and he was relieved of too much secular anxiety by the alienation of two-thirds of the Worcester lands to the crown. Finally, the much-criticised imprisonment and deprivation of Cuthbert Tunstal provided the opportunity to dissolve the great bishopric of Durham and erect in its place two new sees at Newcastle and Durham. Yet not every deprivation of a conservative was followed by alienations: when George Day lost the relatively poor bishopric of Chichester its property passed intact to his successor, John Scory. This pattern of appropriation suggests that Northumberland and his colleagues were most anxious to take the rich pickings of the wealthy sees for themselves. The dispersal of the Winchester lands provides a classic example of this process: the earl of Wiltshire was given five manors, the marquis of Northampton one, William Herbert one, Henry Seymour three, Henry Neville three, Andrew Dudley three, John Gate, the vice-chamberlain, four, and William Fitzwilliam and Philip Hoby of the privy chamber two and one respectively. John Dudley himself took none of the Winchester lands: he had his eyes upon Worcester and Durham. He already held some Worcester estates exchanged in 1548, and to these he added four of those properties which passed to the crown in 1551. Even then, his interest was not permanent, for he sold the two most attractive estates, Hartlebury Castle and Wichenford, to Francis Jobson and Walter Blount.[22]

Northumberland's role in the expropriation of episcopal property

---

21. Even at Durham the first intention was to persuade the new bishop to a surrender in the usual form. In November 1552 Northumberland wrote that the king must commit everything to a new bishop, 'otherwise his Majesty can have no surrender'. PRO, SP 10/15/57.
22. *CPR, Ed. VI*, IV, pp. 178–9, 231, 374–5. PRO, SC 12/19/32. *CPR, Ed. VI*, IV, pp. 139, 441, 196–7, 151, 153–4, 166–7. WiDC, Ledger Book IV, fo. 82. *CPR, Ed. VI*, V, pp. 180, 117.

is something of an enigma. The immediate profit that he derived from the process must have been far less than that which accrued to Somerset. Much land formerly held by the prelates passed through his hands during his years of power, but only as an incidental part of his immensely complex exchanges with the crown and others. Even in the north, where he was certainly anxious to increase his power, he was more interested in controlling the palatinate of the bishops of Durham than in retaining their estates. He must have sanctioned the scramble for episcopal manors by members of his circle, since his priority was to retain the loyalty of his colleagues. This concern to secure and stabilise his régime certainly took precedence over any consideration for the church. He even presided over the dispersal of some of the lands which Somerset had won for the crown: at least seven of the Bath and Wells estates were lost between 1550 and 1553. A few of these losses represent sales intended to help towards a reduction of the royal debt, but others are exchanges disadvantageous to the crown, or in two cases, outright gifts. Dudley had to tune his own ambitions and beliefs to those of the council whom he dominated but with whom his relationship was often uneasy. Somerset's fall provided a warning against the arbitrary exercise of authority.[23]

In addition to this willingness to accept the continued attrition of church wealth, Northumberland was far more overtly critical of the bishops than his predecessor had been. His relations with the 'moderate' leadership of the church became notoriously uneasy, both because he appeared to champion drastic change within the church and because of his reluctance to take advice upon ecclesiastical affairs. The suspicion with which Cranmer viewed the duke was coloured by many things, but one of its roots was dislike of Northumberland's attitude to the wealth of the church. When Tunstal was imprisoned the archbishop pleaded for his release, and in 1553, when the duke attacked the agitators who had been preaching against changes in the bishoprics, Cranmer coolly replied that such preaching was intended to correct vices and abuses. The duke proceeded far more publicly against the church hierarchy than Somerset had done: his actions against Gardiner and Tunstal in particular compelled general

23. There is an attempt to make sense of Northumberland's land transactions in B. L. Beer, *Northumberland: The Political Career of John Dudley* (1973), pp. 167–98. The most recent account of the duke's role in the dissolution of Durham is D. M. Loades, 'The Last Years of Cuthbert Tunstall, 1547–1559', *Durham University Journal*, LXVI (1973–4), 13–17. *CPR, Ed. VI*, III, p. 426; IV, pp. 31, 188, 401; V, pp. 59, 175, 304.

attention, and in the latter case at least it was widely assumed that greed for land and power was the main reason for the attack upon Durham. While Bishop Hooper was still in 1553 describing Northumberland as 'a diligent promoter of the glory of God', most of the correspondents of the Zurich divines either ignored him or commented in general terms upon the avarice of the laity. Even firm supporters of the radical reformation, such as John Knox, lectured the duke upon the dangers of secular ambition and lusts. These lectures sometimes provoked a sharp response. When Northumberland's plans for Durham were thwarted by Dean Horne, who refused to take the see with its diminished revenues, he commented angrily that the clergy were 'so sotted of their wives and children that they forget both their poor neighbours and all other things.' The duke may also have been behind the charge of Secretary Cecil in 1552 that the clergy were covetous, a charge which Cranmer solemnly and firmly denied, alleging instead the poverty of most of his order. Such outbursts have led some historians to assume that Northumberland had a deep-seated hostility to the prelates, that, like Gustavus Vasa in Sweden, he would have rid himself of the order had he dared.[24]

This interpretation seems to elevate the impatience of a vulnerable ruler to the level of principle in a manner not warranted by the surviving evidence. The duke certainly had little time for the old concept of prelacy or for those notions of separation and divine right still valued by the conservatives. Like Somerset, he was deeply influenced by the Zwinglian reformers, but they did not argue explicitly for the abolition of episcopacy, at least until 1554, when circumstances had altered once again. From men such as Hooper, Northumberland was more likely to have derived the idea of the bishop as a painful supervisor and preacher, worthy of a reasonable hire. It could be argued that such an idea lies behind his plan for the dissolution of Durham and its reerection as two sees presided over by godly Protestants. Or rather that this lay behind his second plan, by which the new see of Durham was to be given an income of 2000 marks and that of Newcastle 1000 marks and sufficient revenue was to be found for a cathedral establishment at Newcastle. This was the scheme eventually enacted in March 1553. In the preceding autumn the duke

24. Tytler (ed.), *England under the Reigns of Edward VI and Mary I*, II, p. 142. *Original Letters*, I, p. 99. PRO, SP 10/18/3. Cranmer, *Remains*, II, p. 437. W. K. Jordan argues, in *Edward VI: The Threshold of Power* (1970), p. 377, that Northumberland had a deep-seated antipathy to the bishops.

had proposed a plan which fitted better with his conventional characterisation as a man of greed and ambition. By this arrangement the promotion of Dean Horne would have been accompanied by only an extra 1000 marks, and Newcastle would have been financed from the suffragan bishopric of Berwick 'with a little more to the value of 100 marks'. This would have left the king with two important castles, Durham and Bishop Auckland, and a surplus revenue of £2000 from the old see. It may be that the incident with Horne, although it stimulated an angry outburst from the duke, also encouraged him to think again about the endowment proposed. He certainly continued to be deeply interested in the choice of a new candidate for Durham after Horne's refusal. In 1553 he urged Cecil from his sick bed that the northern see needed 'a grave and learned man', and, after some delay, Ridley was persuaded to accept Durham and William Bill, Newcastle. But the council moved slowly, to the duke's evident annoyance, and the crisis of Edward's final illness and death intervened before arrangements could be made to implement the Durham legislation.[25]

There are various reasons to suggest that the Durham affair should modify our view of Northumberland as the enemy of episcopacy. The second set of arrangements, embodied in the 1553 legislation, would have provided two bishoprics in the far north that would have been comfortably endowed, from which the Protestant Reformation could be promoted. If the austere and exacting Ridley, no unqualified admirer of the duke, was prepared to abandon London to take up this new post in the north, he must have believed the rearrangements to be worth while. It could be argued that plan two was not the responsibility of Northumberland, that it reflects his declining influence upon the council in the early months of 1553, while plan one more correctly indicates his attitudes of casual greed towards the church. But the duke retained his interest in the Durham arrangements throughout early 1553, and his correspondence suggests that he was urging forwards the scheme in the face of indifference or hesitation on the part of the rest of the council. A glance at the other changes in the episcopal estates undertaken during his period of influence tends to confirm this image of a man who had some concern that the

25. William Turner attacked the bishops and the idea of episcopal office in *The Hunting of the Romish Wolf*, published at Basel in 1554 or 1555. C. Sturge, *Cuthbert Tunstal* (1938), pp. 281-96. Loades, 'Cuthbert Tunstall', p. 16. PRO, sp 10/15/35; sp 10/18/8.

F

preaching of the gospel should be properly financed. At London, Winchester and Worcester the bishops were permitted to retain a reasonable income for the support of their office. Is it merely coincidence that both Winchester and Durham were 'allocated' 2000 marks and that London under Ridley was worth about £1200, a very similar sum? Hooper was somewhat less fortunate at Gloucester and Worcester but must have had an income of about £800 from his combined livings. Then there were the modest restitutions made in 1550 which began the process of recovery for Lincoln, Bath and Wells, and Norwich. Nowhere under Northumberland's régime was a see reduced from great wealth to very limited means, as Bath and Wells and Exeter had been under his predecessor.[26] At Winchester and Worcester the bishops were allowed to retain some of the manors closest to the heart of their dioceses: there was no repetition of the behaviour of Somerset at Wells. It was, moreover, the council under Northumberland that was responsible for most of the successful appointments of Protestants to bishoprics: Ridley to London, Hooper to Gloucester and Exeter, Coverdale to Exeter, Scory to Chichester. This was partly the accident of timing – there were more vacancies after the deprivation of the conservatives than there had been under Somerset – but Northumberland and his fellows were willing to appoint men of strong views and known capacity rather than clerics who would necessarily accede to their every wish.

It can therefore be argued that Northumberland and the council did give thought to the church as well as to their own private ends in the alienations and changes of the last years of Edward's reign. The drastic reduction in the wealth of some of the bishoprics can be seen as part of the pattern of reform which the government wished to impose upon existing institutions. The régime might in time have achieved a levelling of all episcopal wealth without resort to legislation and so humbled the remaining pride of the higher clergy while leaving them with the means to perform their new duties as Protestant supervisors. But time was not available, and the attention of Northumberland was more closely directed towards his own political survival than towards a rational solution to the organisational problems of the church. Even when he did concern himself with the welfare of the church, the leaders of reform had good reasons for

26. Bath and Wells was worth only *c.* £680 even after Wells and two other manors had been restored to it. Exeter probably yielded less than the £500 to which its first-fruits were reduced upon the promotion of Coverdale.

their mistrust of his motives. The duke was inextricably connected with a group of men who still wished to profit from the casual exploitation of church property, and he still needed to offer them this property to retain their political loyalty. Moreover, even his most serious concern for the future of the church was not matched by an interest in consulting its leaders. It was the arbitrary nature of his proceedings and those of the council that did much to alienate men such as Cranmer. Under Northumberland churchmen were removed not only from the centre of political power but from any immediate influence over the direction of ecclesiastical policy. Cranmer was not permitted to introduce the reform of ecclesiastical law over which he and his fellow bishops had laboured: the black rubric was inserted into the second Prayer Book against his wishes. The direction of spiritual affairs was more obviously in the hands of laymen than at any time since the fall of Cromwell, and the duke did not enjoy the same loyalty that Protestant churchmen had accorded to Henry VIII's chief minister. In these circumstances even moves which might have helped to introduce a form of organisation more closely approximating to that of the continental reformed churches that the Protestant bishops admired were greeted with suspicion. The objectives of the Edwardian council were to retain control over the English ecclesiastical hierarchy and to judge for that hierarchy what was most fitting for the furtherance of the Reformation in England.[27]

Even those bishops who were not compelled to resign and whose property was not decimated under Edward VI were not free of government intervention in their affairs. In most cases this intervention was associated with the problems of taxation and tax-collection. Edward's advisers inherited the assumptions of the previous reign that the clergy could safely be taxed more heavily than the laity, that they could pay subsidy as well as the regular first-fruits and tenths. They also inherited a war policy, which Somerset extended by his determination to subdue Scotland, and therefore a continuing need for income from all possible sources. In 1548 the annual subsidy payments demanded for the clergy fell from 3 shillings in the pound to 2 shillings, but this offered little relief to those bishops who had already fallen into arrears. In Henry's last years, when the French wars were at their height, some prelates were already failing to collect all the dues of their clergy and to produce all their own payments. The

27. On the ecclesiastical politics of these years see Dickens, *The English Reformation*, pp. 317–18, 349–54.

general difficulties that they encountered in these years probably
provided the bishops with less incentive to work for the full collection
of the government's money. By 1549 Bath and Wells owed £1176,
and two years later the poor diocese of Llandaff owed £502. Worst of
all was Exeter, where in 1553 total indebtedness stood at £2353. Other
sees of medium size such as Norwich, Coventry and Lichfield, and
Worcester all owed large sums to the government. Only the large
sees such as Durham and Lincoln seem to have kept entirely free of
debt – perhaps a tribute to the superiority of their administrative
machinery. Taxation debt, as we have already noted, played a part in
the changes in the middle of Edward's reign when Voysey and Reppes
were eased from their sees in return for a promise that they would
have their burdens remitted.[28]

Behind most of the debts seems to lie the incompetence of the
bishops who failed to establish an adequate system for the collection
of these revenues. But a foolproof system was difficult to design,
and the prelates might be forgiven for having little interest in struggling to raise money for régimes which were consistently hostile to
their position. The main problem was to retain proper control over
those deputy collectors who actually raised money from the clergy
and transported it to the exchequer. It was still the bishops, rather
than these underlings, who were accountable at the exchequer and
were therefore liable when they failed through incompetence and
dishonesty. Gradually the government began to offer some assistance
to the prelates in controlling their deputies. From at least the middle
of the Edwardian period the deputy collectors had to account directly
for their own arrears in first-fruits and tenths and, provided that the
bishop had taken a proper bond from his collector to save him harmless from the responsibility for any debts, they were answered against
the estate of the deputy. After some confusion this happened in the
case of the Bath and Wells debt; John Payne, the deputy collector,
was made liable for the repayment of £1800. But not all prelates were
sufficiently aware of the dangers to make a proper bond, and not all
bonds were made in a legally binding form. Hence the difficulties of
Reppes and Voysey, or the problems of a minor debtor such as
Robert Aldrich of Carlisle, whose servants embezzled £163 they were
supposed to deliver to the exchequer. It was not until the last years
of the reign, as part of the organised attempt to improve royal finances

28. On the taxation of the clergy see F. Heal, 'Clerical Tax-Collection', in *Conti-
    nuity and Change*, pp. 107–11. PRO, SP 11/1/2; SP 10/16/91ff; E 347/1/bk 5.

that the government came to the assistance of the bishops. By an act of 1552 (7 Edward VI c. 4) sub-collectors were bound to answer for the sums due within their appointed areas and were compelled to give the bishops bonds to save them harmless from all charges. The act was informed by a concern to secure royal income rather than to aid the prelates; it reflects the knowledge of the council that they had proved inadequate in this crucial task. The council also undertook a much more direct supervision of revenue-collection towards the end of the reign, with checks upon individual bishops and their deputies. Had Edward VI lived, the collection of clerical revenue might gradually have moved under the direct control of the council, another move which would have been compatible with the reformed ideal that the secular commitments of the leaders of the church should be reduced or removed.[29]

Any summary of the policy of the ruling élite towards episcopal wealth and rights under Edward VI is compelled to stress the casual plunder, the quest for immediate profit and for short-term political advantage. It was a Venetian, reporting to his government in 1551, who summed this up in terms which we more readily associate with Spelman and his successors: 'of the church revenues they have made sheer plunder and one enormous act of sacrilege'. In September 1552 a minute in the council notes, possibly by Cecil, recorded that there must be 'some device to stay the great waste that Ecclesiastical persons do make of their livelihoods'. But this was too late; the example had been set all too clearly by the laity, and the ecclesiastical persons had an obvious interest in taking what profit they could while no legislation prevented them. Northumberland has at least some claims to aims other than immediate political and financial advantage. Like Somerset, he believed in minimising the secular role of the episcopate and using it as a force for the conversion of England by Protestant preaching. Unlike Somerset, he and his council seem to have been concerned to provide the prelates with adequate means of support for this task and to have thought carefully about the best ways of expropriating the surplus wealth of the bishoprics. Yet even those most deeply committed to the idea of the bishop as a painful supervisor, shorn of his worldly glory, could scarcely trust Northumberland to have the best interests of reform in mind. When his religious policy conflicted with his political advantage the duke was liable to favour the latter. Moreover, his power was not absolute; he had to

29. PRO, e 347/1/bk 5; c 1/file 1366/5–7. *APC*, 1552–4, pp. 71, 250.

carry with him the rest of the council and to remember the fall of the protector. One means to retain the loyalty of his colleagues was to allow the plunder of the church to continue, to provide patronage without personal cost and without serious loss to the royal possessions. Thus it was that changes in the structure of the church and its finances, however well they might appear to suit the circumstances of a Protestant nation, were still associated with lay greed. Reformers as different as Latimer and Knox recognised that no truly Protestant polity could be constructed until the laity as well as the clergy were willing to support the ideals for which they strove: an educated body of clerics, a well-financed parochial system and social justice. Northumberland did little to promote these ideals, and, indeed, few of the leaders of Edwardian England seem to have paid them more than lip-service. Latimer could remind them of their sins and fulminate against avarice, but power lay elsewhere and many of the pleas for the reformers fell upon deaf ears.[30]

II

It could be argued that it was not until Mary's reign that the laity demonstrated how deaf they were to appeals to support the church, for only then did the crown urge restitution and only then did the ruling classes refuse to follow their monarch upon a religious issue. At the beginning of the reign Mary seems to have been able to command support for most of her moves towards the old religion, even in cases when her actions were as arbitrary as those of the previous régime. Only when the question of church lands was raised in parliament did the laity show concerted opposition to the queen's wish for a steady return to the Roman fold, and that opposition was so prolonged and intense that at one time it threatened the cherished royal plan for an end to the schism. Members of the two houses of parliament were most concerned that there should be no agreement to surrender the lands of the monasteries, which were by then scattered throughout the landowning classes, but the property of the bishops was an important secondary issue and was the one which first forced the government to raise this awkward subject in the political forum.

The problem of the episcopal estates gained prominence because

30. *CStP, Ven.*, v, p. 347. PRO, sp 10/15/10. For Latimer's views on avarice see H. Latimer, *Remains*, Parker Soc. (1844), i, pp. 398–401.

of the anomalous situation of the conservatives. At Edward's death there were five bishops in captivity and a sixth, Voysey, living in retirement. In the eyes of the queen all six had been unlawfully deprived or ousted from their sees, and one of her earliest actions was to free them and begin the process of their restoration. The legal basis for her actions was very unsound: Tunstal and Gardiner had originally been appointed before the schism with Rome, and in the eyes of the papacy their deprivation could therefore be argued to be invalid, but Day, Heath and Bonner, who had reached the bench after the breach with Rome, could not easily be placed in the same category. In practice Mary seems to have assumed that her predecessor had no right of deprivation as part of his office as Supreme Head of the church but then to have abrogated this right to herself when she deprived and ejected seven of the married bishops in 1554 by royal commission. She was determined to have her senior clerics back in positions of power at all costs. Gardiner regained Winchester almost at once with no formal process: Ponet was merely ejected for having intruded himself into the see. The rest apparently petitioned for restoration, and the process by which Bonner regained London was fully recorded in the patent rolls. The most interesting case is that of Tunstal, for he had lost not only his title but the whole see, which had disappeared in the Edwardian reorganisation. In the first few months of the reign, however, Mary contented herself with restoring him to the title of the see of Durham, leaving aside the issues of his jurisdiction and possessions. In August 1553 a commission similar to that established in Bonner's case was appointed to judge if his deprivation had been lawful. It concluded that the actions of Edward's commissioners had been invalid, since no time had been allowed for the preparation of Tunstal's defence and since the judges had all been laymen. These technical justifications for Tunstal's restitution helped to avoid the impression that the queen as Supreme Head of the church was challenging her brother's right to take action in the same capacity, but they left awkward questions unanswered. Could any deprivation procedure established by the Church of England have been valid in Catholic eyes? What about Gardiner's case, in which the crown had been careful to provide both lay and ecclesiastical judges and in which the length of the trial offered the bishop ample opportunity to offer his defence? Since the Edwardian government never formalised the procedure for deprivations but depended in each case upon the appointment of a royal commission to oversee the process, there remained a variety of these grounds for uncertainty.[31]

Permission to reenter their sees did not always guarantee the bishops easy access to their old property. For George Day there was no problem: since no alienations had taken place at Chichester, he merely regained possession of the existing manors of the see. Elsewhere the bishops were in theory allowed to resume the lands they had held at the time of their deprivation. As the order of the commission established to restore Bonner expressed it, he was to be returned to the bishopric 'and to the estate in which he was when summoned for trial'. This meant that he was entitled to reclaim the manors of Braintree and Southminster, given to the crown by Ridley, and lands in Hackney, which his predecessor had granted to Lord Wentworth. Bonner was peculiarly fortunate, for he was also permitted to retain the ex-Westminster lands that had been offered to the see in exchange for Southminster and Braintree, since Mary showed no inclination to revive the short-lived second diocese of the metropolis. Stephen Gardiner at Winchester and Nicholas Heath at Worcester had the same right to reverse the transactions of the last years of Edward's reign and enter once again into the possessions they had held before their deprivations.[32]

Although Mary's government, by its actions, might seek to obliterate the changes undergone in the bishoprics of the men deprived under Edward, it was not so easy in practice for the lands to be retaken. The issue of the ecclesiastical estates was a highly emotive one from the very beginning of the reign, and the laity showed that they were unlikely to surrender their gains without a struggle. In the case of the restored bishops the struggle was muted: Gardiner, with his great political influence, felt himself strong enough merely to reenter his estates and eject the Edwardians. Others had less success: Nicholas Heath regained the rents from his lost lands, but he could not completely remove the new occupants. The most prestigious of his manors, Hartlebury Castle, continued to be tenanted by the Edwardian patentee, Sir Francis Jobson, who would not even provide the bishop with the full rent. Eventually Heath's successor, Richard Pate, took the issue of his title to Hartlebury before parliament in

31. On the arbitrary nature of Mary's actions see Loades, *The Oxford Martyrs*, pp. 112–17. HRO, Ecc. II, 155892. *CPR, Mary*, I, pp. 74–6, 377–8. Loades, 'Cuthbert Tunstall', p. 18.
32. *CPR, Mary*, I, pp. 119–20, 121, 232–3; IV, pp. 146–7.

1555. Judgement was given in favour of the bishop, who was then able to extract the full annual dues, but Jobson did not surrender his hold upon the castle, for he remained keeper of the heath and so well entrenched that in the next reign he was able physically to prevent the representatives of Bishop Sandys from entering the property. There were similar happenings at London, where Bonner found it very difficult to reenter his former estates: the 1557 accounts show that they were not yielding him rents, and in July 1558 he appealed to Pole for assistance in the case of Southminster. He asked that the queen help him to resume full possession of the estates, 'seeing I never did any act whereby in law I have forgone them'. Even at Winchester the bishops felt less than secure in their lands: Gardiner's successor, Bishop White, who seems to have been uneasily aware of the arbitrary nature of the lord chancellor's return to his see, obtained from Mary an order to Nicholas Heath and the master of the rolls instructing them to cancel all grants and deeds made by Bishop Ponet to Edward VI. The grants thus nullified were then formally given to White as part of new letters patent furnishing him in 1558 with all the ancient estates of the bishopric. Unfortunately for the bishop, this careful legal manoeuvre did little to protect his property when Elizabeth came to the throne.[33]

Despite these difficulties, it was at least consistent to argue that, if the deprivation of the conservatives had been unlawful, their lands had been improperly dispersed. Even parliament was willing to support this view in the case of Worcester. The Durham case was somewhat different: Tunstal had been deprived by much the same process as his fellows, but his lands had been lost by act of parliament. Therefore, at the end of November 1553 a bill was introduced into the Commons 'for the confirmation of the bishopric of Durham and Durham Place, to Cuthbert Tunstall, bishop there, and his successors'. Even after the clause upon Durham House, which had been lost at the Reformation, was removed, the bill was rejected upon its third reading. Mary was determined to circumvent this challenge from the Commons and in January 1554 took the extraordinary step of re-erecting the see of Durham by letters patent which did not even

33. House of Lords Record Office, Original Acts, 1 Eliz. I. HRO, Ecc. II, 155892. WRO, cc 900/1, 179/925 (20); cc 900/1, 43697/p. 5. PRO, sc 6/P. and M./193. G. C. Gorham (ed.), *Gleanings of a Few Scattered Ears during the Reformation* (1857), p. 357. CPR, *Mary*, IV, pp. 146–7. N. L. Jones, 'Faith by Statute: The Politics of Religion in the Parliament of 1559', unpub. Ph.D. thesis, Cambridge University (1977), pp. 228–9.

attempt to argue that the Edwardian act of dissolution was technically invalid. This was an exercise of royal power more arbitrary than the acts of the régimes of Somerset and Northumberland and a very rare example of a Tudor attempting to override a valid act of parliament. The queen's determination for the restitution of the true religion overcame any scruples that she might have had about due process of law. But such an arrangement could not outlast another session of parliament, and so in April 1554 Gardiner had the unenviable task of seeking the support of the Commons for the restitution of Durham. A bill was introduced into the Lords to repeal the Edwardian act of dissolution and also a second act which had annexed Gateshead to Newcastle. This latter repeal aroused opposition in the Commons, and there was also an attempt in the lower house to safeguard the interests of Sir Francis Jobson, who had gained Howdenshire after the dissolution of the bishopric. This time, however, Gardiner prevailed, though the strength of feeling against the government is indicated by a comment of Renard's to the emperor: 'The chancellor has proposed the restitution of the Bishop of Durham's usurped property, and succeeded in carrying it by a majority against the will of the heretics, who are raising a clamour . . . so serious as to damage the Queen's popularity . . .'[34] When the House of Commons divided upon the Durham bill the measure was passed by 201 votes to 120, a degree of opposition that indicates that not only heretics wished to oppose the return of wealth to the church.

When property which had only recently been removed from the bishops was returned so reluctantly, more general projects for the restoration of church lands were liable to court political disaster. Yet some restoration was necessary both to clear Mary's conscience and to strengthen the church in its efforts to return England to the Catholic faith. As early as August 1553 one of those who offered the queen advice upon the state of the realm argued that 'impropriations lately made' should be returned to the church and that 'lands of prebends and bishoprics taken away want present recompense since the death of King Henry VIII'. The writer even touched upon the difficult subject of first-fruits, though only to argue that some moderation might be used in their collection. These suggestions were of themselves modest enough, but, like the restitutions to the conservatives they pointed towards a more general surrender of the profits of the

---

34. *Commons Journals*, I, p. 31. *CPR, Mary*, I, p. 378. Sturge, *Tunstal*, p. 298. *Commons Journals*, I, p. 34. *CStP, Spanish*, XIII, p. 221.

Reformation. To this the landowning classes were implacably opposed: Renard argued that they would maintain their opposition to the
death if necessary. The determination of Mary, Pole, Gardiner and the
papacy that there should be restitution eventually had to yield to this
united view of the laity. Julius III first accepted political realities by
issuing his bull of dispensation, allowing those who had taken lands
from the church during the schism by lawful purchase, gift or exchange to retain them after the reconciliation to Rome. It was, as he
argued in a letter of November 1554, 'far better for all reasons human
and divine, to abandon all the church property, rather than risk the
shipwreck of this undertaking'.[35]

Of all those involved in the compromise with the laity, Cardinal
Pole was probably the most reluctant to abandon the idea that true
reconciliation with the papacy should be followed by a surrender of
the church lands. He delayed his acceptance of the parliamentary
position until Renard persuaded him that to wait any longer before
receiving the submission of the English would seriously damage the
Catholic cause. Even after he had ended the schism and the papal
dispensation had been incorporated into the act repealing all anti-
papal legislation, Pole did not cease to feel that true reconciliation
and repentance would have included the willingness to restore lands.
In 1555 he was so angered by the attitude of parliament that he
planned a speech condemning the lay retention of estates as sacrilege
and was only dissuaded from giving it at the last moment. Two years
later he was still willing to point out to the laity how wrong their
stance was: 'and this I say to you now that by licence and dispensation
enjoy, keep and possess such goods and lands of the church as were
found in your hands, that this was done only of the church your
mother's tenderness unto you, considering your imbecility and
weakness, after so sore a schism'.[36] Pole found an untimely supporter
of his views in the new pope, Paul IV, who, on his accession, issued a
bull condemning the alienation of ecclesiastical property. Unfortunately for his conscience, the archbishop was forced to sue for a
special exemption from his bull for the English and a confirmation
of Julius's dispensation. He had by this time had to accept the political
realities of the English situation, but the ideal of restitution was

35. PRO, sp 11/1/8. *CStP, Spanish*, xi, p. 307; xiii, p. 80.
36. W. Schenk, *Reginald Pole, Cardinal of England* (1950), p. 130. P. Hughes, *The Refor-
    mation in England* (1951–4), ii, p. 227. For a general discussion of Pole's attitude
    to the finances of the church see R. Pogson, 'Revival and Reform in Mary
    Tudor's Church: A Question of Money', *JEH*, xxvi (1975), 249–65.

never abandoned, and the need to strengthen the finances of the church remained an urgent priority for Pole.[37]

Even the restoration of ecclesiastical property held by the crown proved far more difficult than the archbishop would have wished. The queen's own attitude towards the possessions her predecessors had acquired was inevitably somewhat ambivalent. On the one hand, she earnestly desired the well-being of the Catholic church and was reluctant to be associated with any of the actions her father or brother had taken against Rome. On the other, the crown needed revenue from the English clergy and from the estates formerly held by the monasteries and bishops. Moreover, there were problems such as the payment of monastic pensions to be considered. It is therefore not surprising that during the first busy years of her reign, Mary and her council proceeded to help the clergy in a piecemeal fashion, alleviating needs as necessary rather than changing the basis of the crown's financial relations with the church. Some help was offered to the bishops, largely as relief for those sees which had suffered from chronic indebtedness in the previous reign. The new bishops of Gloucester, Chester and St David's were exonerated from payment of the debts of their predecessors. In these dioceses the debts had been the personal liability of the bishops; in others, where the deputy collectors could be held to account, the government continued to press them for repayments. Other prelates, either those newly consecrated or those translated from one see to another, were allowed longer periods for the payment of their first-fruits, and some, such as Thirlby who was moved to Ely in 1554, were eventually exonerated from all payments. Another form of assistance to the bishops which began early in the reign was the grant of patronage within the cathedral churches. When the new chapters had been erected in the 1540s Henry VIII had retained most of the major appointments in the hands of the crown. In 1553 Mary began the reversal of this policy by giving the bishop of Worcester the right to appoint to the ten prebends in his cathedral, and the bishop of Peterborough the right to the six in his former abbey. Only the patronage of the deanery remained with the queen. Some of these first grants were personal to the bishops, rather than permanent gifts to the bishopric, but later in the reign they were extended to other sees and made permanent. The prebendal stalls were valuable both as a means to provide the cathedrals with men who

---

37. PRO, sp 11/6/16, 18. E. H. Harbison, *Rival Ambassadors at the Court of Queen Mary* (Princeton, N.J., 1940), p. 272.

would assist the bishops in the care of their dioceses and as a means of support for some of those who depended upon the prelates, most notably their chaplains.[38]

Thus, Mary's initial support of the bishops took two forms: one the rather limited sacrifice of patronage in order to assist in the revival of Catholicism within the cathedral hierarchy, the other the beginnings of a reduction in the tax burden upon the clergy, a move which pointed forwards to the major alterations made in the middle of the reign. Despite these moves to benefit the prelates, Mary and her council showed little interest in restoring the lands taken from them by her predecessors. Although the queen was disposed to aid the church, lands were of great importance to the financial stability of the crown and, unlike taxes, could not be replaced at all easily once lost. So, while Mary deplored the losses to the bishops under her predecessors, she felt obliged to help only those conservatives who had been wrongfully deprived and to give aid to a few others who enjoyed her personal favour. Of the prelates on whom the queen bestowed her favour, Nicholas Heath and Reginald Pole were undoubtedly the most fortunate. Heath was made archbishop of York in 1555 and chancellor on the death of Gardiner. His service was rewarded first by the release of the archbishops from a rent payment of £258 that they had had to pay since the great exchange of 1545 and then by the grant of Suffolk Place, Southwark, in recompense for York Place, which Henry VIII had taken from Wolsey in 1529. Then in 1557 Heath was offered some of the most important of the ancient lands which his see had lost in 1543 and 1545: the lordships of Southwell, Ripon and Scrooby. Pole was even more fortunate, for in 1556 Mary gave him, to support the dignity of his office, all the ancient possessions of the see of Canterbury that remained in her hands. The return of these estates, together with the foreign income that he still received, made Pole the richest of the sixteenth-century archbishops of Canterbury with revenues that only those of Wolsey had exceeded. Yet the grants were for his life only and are therefore difficult to categorise as part of the restitution that Mary made to the church. They were a gift to Pole the nobleman and cousin of the queen as well as a visible sign that the church was powerful again.

38. *CPR, Mary*, I, pp. 112–13, 389. PRO, E 337/2, fo. 252. *CPR, Mary*, I, pp. 60–1, 329. By the end of Mary's reign the bishops of Peterborough, Worcester, Ely, Winchester and Carlisle had been granted the permanent rights of appointment to canonries in their cathedrals.

One may surmise that they would have returned to the archbishops permanently had Mary lived to appoint Pole's successor, but she was under no obligation to continue the grant if circumstances dictated otherwise.[39]

Beyond the charmed circle of the court bishops, the arrival of Pole and his firm attitude to church property extracted some concessions for the other victims of the Edwardian period. Some of the prelates tried in 1555 to petition parliament for the return of estates taken from them, but according to Renard their petitions were rejected as contrary to the terms of the dispensation. Mary was a little more helpful: she returned the rich manor of Crediton to the bishopric of Exeter, though only in exchange for a rent payment of £146 which absorbed most of the profit of the estate. Bishop Bourne of Bath and Wells was able to retrieve Banwell, but again only for a reserved rent of £115. Scott of Chester was rather more fortunate, perhaps because the see was so clearly in financial difficulties: in 1558 the queen licensed him to annex the rectories of Cartmel and Childwall and a reserved rent from the estate of St Bee's. The rectories were supposed to support the archdeaconries within the diocese, but Scott immediately absorbed them into the bishopric properties. The limited nature of royal assistance is most clearly shown in the case of Lincoln: both the Marian bishops, John White and Thomas Watson, were favoured by the queen, and several of the properties of the see were still in crown hands, yet there is no evidence of any attempt to restore the depleted Lincoln estates. There are, of course, reasons and justifications for the reluctance of the Marian régime to surrender lands to the bishops. The manors had come to the crown by perfectly lawful exchange and therefore did not burden the queen's conscience as did the monastic lands that had been forcibly expropriated. Most of the bishops still had considerable property and wealth and were less obviously in need of help than, for example, the poorer parish clergy. The crown had already lost much of the land it had accumulated after the dissolution of the monasteries in the great sales of the early and late 1540s; it could ill afford to part with more. The queen's decision to give most help to those close to the centre of government was in one sense arbitrary, a characteristic result of her loyalty to those who served her well. In another sense, it may represent a sound political judgement, for by giving some bishops the capacity to display

39. *CPR, Mary*, III, pp. 188, 264. Cross, 'Economic Problems of York', pp. 72–4.
    CPR, Mary, III, pp. 69–72.

once again the wealth and dignity of their position the queen may have hoped to strengthen Pole and his colleagues and to make their spiritual task easier. Even the provision of suitable London homes for Heath and Tunstal was in some ways a political choice, for the loss of the great town inns had been one of the most visible signs that the leaders of the church no longer held political power after the Reformation.[40]

The queen's attitude to the taxation of the clergy was less equivocal than her approach to the bishops' lands. First-fruits and tenths payments to the crown were a product of the schism and must eventually be abolished, though the practical steps towards such an end were probably the work of Pole rather than Mary. The decisive change came in 1555 when it was enacted that first-fruits and tenths should no longer be paid directly to the crown but should be paid instead to the bishops. From these payments the bishops were to provide for the monastic pensioners who had previously been paid directly by the crown. As the costs of the pensions decreased by natural wastage, the surplus was to be used to provide for the poorest of the parochial clergy. Had Mary lived longer and the bishops had the opportunity to overcome the initial administrative problems associated with so complex a change, all the clergy would have derived some benefit from the new system, either because their tax burden would have decreased or because they would actually have received supplements to their income. After the death of Mary there was a delay of a century and a half before similar help was given to the poorest clergy through Queen Anne's Bounty. Meanwhile, after the loss of first-fruits revenues, the crown was still in need of financial support of the clergy, and the council therefore turned once again to subsidies, a form of payment untainted by schism. Since the church was in disarray, it was no easier for the bishops to collect all their dues than it had been under Edward VI. By 1557 the council was again undertaking the role of its Henrician and Edwardian predecessors in urging the bishops to perform their duties properly. In that year the bishops of Norwich, Winchester, Coventry, Llandaff and Rochester were all summoned before the council to explain their arrears. The correspondence of Elizabeth's reign shows that substantial parts of the last Marian subsidy could not be collected. The combination of inflation, epidemic disease, a shortage of parish priests and the con-

40. *CStP, Spanish*, XIII, p. 134. *CPR, Mary*, III, pp. 276, 193. Haigh, *Reformation and Resistance*, p. 198.

stant demands for taxation made the church a very poor source of income for the crown.[41]

The problems and ambivalence of the Marian government's approach to the wealth of the church are essentially the product of the previous twenty years during which the realm had moved away from Rome. The Reformation had fostered a dependence upon ecclesiastical sources of income in the crown as well as in the land-owning laity, and it was very difficult to find an acceptable way of restoring those revenues which would not increase the financial embarrassment of the government. It had also fostered in the clergy a dependence upon the monarch as Supreme Head of the church, upon royal assistance for the enforcement of discipline and upon royal initiative in controlling their relationships with the laity. In the first years of Mary's reign, before Pole had established himself as the principal figure of influence upon the queen, her arbitrary approach to the management of the church did little to lessen this clerical dependence, to wean the leaders of Catholicism towards a more Roman view of their functions and powers. After 1555 Pole began the slow process of erasing the marks of the schism, including the tendency to look constantly towards the crown for initiative in spiritual matters. Given time, his cautious march towards reorganisation might have succeeded: in taxation, for example, the changed arrangements upon first-fruits and tenths were beginning to work to the church's advantage by 1558. In that year also Mary finally fulfilled her declared intention of returning crown impropriations to the bishops for the benefit of the parishes. But against success of this type must be set the church's continued need of lay support in the ecclesiastical commission to enforce religious conformity. The bishops were no longer capable of disciplining the realm without the assistance of the crown, and there is no evidence that more time would have altered this situation. Similarly, there is very little to suggest that Mary's own concern to restore property, wealth and power to her clergy was shared by more than a small minority of her subjects. The prevailing attitude, demonstrated in the Commons' implacable opposition to any restitution of monastic or episcopal lands, continued to be that the laity and crown had as much right to ecclesiastical wealth as the churchmen and to undoubted and rightful possession of those lands they had acquired under Henry and Edward. With

41. Pogson, 'Revival and Reform', p. 260. *APC*, 1556–8, p. 143. Heal, 'Clerical Tax-Collection', pp. 111–13, 117.

time these difficulties might well have become less acute, and an effective adjustment between the interests of the crown and laity and the needs of the Catholic church might have emerged, but even then the church could scarcely have returned to its pre-Reformation position. Since time was not available to Pole, and his work of renovation was only half completed, the Marian attempt to strengthen the church and make it more independent inevitably appears to be a failure. Elizabeth found little problem in returning to the policy of her father and brother, that of subordinating the church both spiritually and financially to her own needs and wishes.[42]

42. On Pole's approach to healing the schism and his reluctance to proceed hastily see R. Pogson, 'Reginald Pole and the Priorities of Government in Mary Tudor's Church', *HJ*, xviii (1975), 3–20. *CPR, Mary*, iv, pp. 449–50.

7

THE CONSEQUENCES OF THE BREAK
WITH ROME: THE BISHOPS AND SOCIETY

I

The middle decades of the sixteenth century were therefore years of crisis for the English bishops. Their political influence was in decline, their spiritual authority under attack from above and below, their identity as a separate order questioned and their wealth eroded by inflation as well as the demands of the laity. Underlying all these problems except the last, inflation, was the changing attitude of the laity to the church. Long before there was official acceptance of the Protestant doctrine of the priesthood of all believers, the intermediary role of the church was weakened by the introduction of the English bible, by the criticisms of an articulate minority of reformers and by the emergence of the Supreme Head as the effective controller of doctrine. One of the most familiar arguments employed by the conservative prelates against the reformers was that they failed to understand the nature of authority and discipline. Authority was all of a piece: when men were allowed to read the bible and interpret it according to the light of the spirit, or their own fancy, it was not only certain doctrines that were challenged. Instead, the whole fabric of belief and the whole social order, which rested essentially upon the proper exercise of authority, were liable to be overthrown. 'Follow God and his ministers whom he ordereth to rule', wrote Gardiner in 1547, 'and rather conform knowledge to agree with obedience.'[1] In theory the authority of the Supreme Head of the church could be integrated into the pattern of ecclesiastical domination without weakening it: in practice almost every move that Henry made increased the vulnerability of the hierarchy. The pattern of traditional control was questioned at every point, either by the monarch's probing the full extent of his power or by laymen who saw in the new situation the opportunity to increase their own wealth or influence.

When the established position of the bishops was challenged by the

1. *Letters of Gardiner*, p. 249.

events of the 1530s one possibility open to them was to respond by a corresponding revision of their own idea of the role of the episcopate. The reformers, those who were influenced in greater or less degree by the new views emanating from the Continent, had some positive incentive to undertake such a revision. But they were always in a minority upon the bench, and even this minority was prevented from any radical action by the attitudes of the king and of lay society. The incident narrated by Morice, when Henry protected his archbishop from the allegations of Seymour, shows that he still expected his prelates to maintain all the pomp and outward display that had been associated with their predecessors. The bishops still stood as spiritual peers high in the formal counsels of the realm: they still held their place in the ranks of precedence, though in the 1530s Cromwell as vicegerent in spirituals was able to displace the archbishop, first in convocation and later, by special legislation, in the House of Lords. The Supreme Head required on the one hand dutiful subservience to his will, on the other the full panoply and display of ecclesiastical power. In these circumstances there was only limited opportunity for new ideas to grow and flourish. The only area in which there was the beginning of major change was in the understanding of the authority of the bishops, since this was a subject on which Henry and the reformers could make some common cause. When Cranmer answered the king's questions upon the nature of the sacraments in 1540 he offered the thoroughly Erastian view that the monarch could, in exceptional circumstances, both appoint and consecrate his own ministers. This brought into question the whole idea of a separate *iure divino* episcopate and was to have important consequences in the following reign. Under Henry, however, the change of attitude did little more than confirm the existing trend towards dependence upon the monarchy which perforce influenced the whole of the episcopate.[2]

It is perhaps uncharitable to argue that a movement towards greater dependence upon the monarchy was the only change initiated by the reformers. There were also some genuine attempts to alter the spiritual direction of the church. Cranmer was one of those who looked for a more active, preaching ministry and who made some

---

2. *Narratives of the Reformation*, p. 264. It required an act of parliament to adjust the situation in the House of Lords so that Cromwell, as vicegerent, took precedence over the archbishop (31 Henry VIII c. 10). For the 1540 answers see J. Strype, *Memorials of Thomas Cranmer* (Oxford 1840), I, app. xxvii.

attempts to redirect the resources available to the church to this end. When the king proposed to reerect the cathedral foundation at Canterbury and to establish twelve prebends, the archbishop protested that prebendaries were liable to be as redundant as the monks who had preceded them and that the money would be better employed if it were used to fund lectures in divinity and preachers. Several of the reform-minded bishops shared Cranmer's concern that there should be greater provision for proper preaching, that injunctions and exhortations were not enough. Bishop Barlow of St David's told Cromwell in 1536 that he wished to maintain a household of men learned in divinity and law and he made serious efforts to move his establishment to Carmarthen in the centre of his diocese, so that preachers might from there more easily influence the unregenerate Welsh. Bishop Bird of Chester attempted a similar move in 1546 when he sought the wardenship of Manchester College to provide a centre from which he could evangelise and control his unwieldy see. Neither of these attempts succeeded, since they would have meant the surrender of attractive property by the crown; indeed, all poor Bishop Bird got for his pains was an unequal exchange, in which he lost the manor of Weston which he had proposed as a possible gift to the crown in return for Manchester College. Any real change clearly had to come from the prelates' own efforts, using the resources with which they were still endowed. Much could be done within these limits, as was shown by the preaching ministry of Bishop Hilsey in and near London or by the activities of Nicholas Shaxton, who succeeded Campeggio as bishop of Salisbury in 1535.[3]

None of the Henrician bishops seem to have made so much progress towards putting reformed ideas into action as Hugh Latimer. This may in some measure be an illusion created by the sources, for Latimer was articulate, close to members of the court and always willing to provoke a confrontation in defence of his beliefs. But his work in the south-west was seen as important and controversial by contemporaries, and there is little doubt that he was less inhibited by the constraints of office and power than most of his reforming colleagues. Latimer's attitudes are interesting in two respects: first, because he was frankly hostile to traditional notions of episcopal wealth and power, and secondly, because he saw himself as an evangelist, not merely as a conscientious and learned preacher but as a minister

3. Cranmer, *Remains*, I, pp. 292–3. *LP*, XI, 1428. BL, Harl. MS. 604, fo. 75. *LP*, XXI, i, 967; ii, 183.

whose essential duty was to win souls to God. The wealth that accrued to him as bishop of Worcester he saw primarily as a means of implementing those ideals of social justice about which he preached. He was famed for the free entertainment that he gave to the poor of Worcester, and, as he said of his own hospitality, he was more inclined 'to feed many grossly and necessarily than a few deliciously and voluptuously'.[4] His charitable behaviour fitted well enough with traditional notions of the role of the episcopate, but to neglect at the same time to give rank and power their proper due was a grave challenge to the assumptions of his contemporaries. Latimer's estate policy also reflected his concern for the least advantaged of his tenants. He made a series of leases to his tenants-at-will, giving them the security of ninety-nine-year grants at fixed rents. These were men who held only small parcels of episcopal demesne and who had previously had little or no security in their estates. For once there is little reason to doubt the sincerity of a preamble when the introduction to the Hartlebury lease states: 'Witnesseth the said reverend father for the good zeal and love he beareth to his said tenants wishes for their estates severally to be assured unto them in manner and form as hereafter ensueth . . .'[5] Unfortunately for Latimer's successors, generosity of this sort made no economic sense in a century of inflation. Even he, with good resources still at his disposal, found it difficult to acquire the necessary reserves of revenue to undertake the charitable work he regarded as so important.

Latimer as evangelist was also potentially subversive, not only because of the message that he preached but also because of the methods he adopted. His energies were directed towards promoting reform in the market-place as well as at court, to attacking the old superstitions wherever they might be found. Such activity inevitably crossed social barriers and brought the bishop into contact with his people in a way that had become uncommon in the later Middle Ages. One might, for example, contrast Latimer's behaviour with that of such humanist preachers and bishops as John Alcock or John Fisher. Much of the important teaching that these latter figures offered was given before assemblies of the clergy, at the court or at a funeral of some influential layman. The bishop was likely to remain distanced

---

4. On Latimer's ministry in the south-west see A. G. Chester, *Hugh Latimer: Apostle to the English* (Philadelphia 1954), pp. 134–44; K. Powell, 'The Beginnings of Protestantism in Gloucestershire', *Trans. of the Bristol and Gloucestershire Arch. Soc.*, xc (1972), 141–57; Latimer, *Remains*, II, p. 412.
5. WRO, cc 900/1, 438/37 (iii).

from his flock, except from the parochial clergy if he was interested in maintaining good discipline among them. It was this sense of distance that some of the reforming bishops sought to diminish by their popular preaching at centres like Paul's Cross. Latimer again went further than many of his colleagues: in his campaigns against the old faith in the West Country and in his London preaching he already demonstrated those qualities which were to make him one of the greatest of popular teachers.[6]

Latimer offered an example to his successors both of the possibilities of change within the episcopate and of the difficulty of achieving any fundamental transformation in the office. It was with relief that he surrendered his see at the time of the Six Articles crisis, for its multifarious demands impeded his fundamental wish to evangelise. Under Henry it was almost impossible for the reform-minded bishops to proceed any further than Latimer, and most hesitated to make any major change in the patterns established by their Catholic predecessors. Even under Edward, when the rulers of the realm were so receptive to foreign models of Protestantism, the basic continuity in episcopal authority made it difficult for individuals to wrench the ecclesiastical establishment from a predetermined social course. It required a man of the strength of character and purpose of John Hooper to demonstrate the practical possibilities of change. At Gloucester Hooper endeavoured to live the life of a reformed supervisor, a life no doubt patterned upon his knowledge of the leaders of the Swiss Reformation. His modest household was devoted to works of charity and to the care of the poor, a care in which the instruction of the mind and spirit was linked with the support of the body. Foxe describes the assistance that he gave to all comers, provided that they accepted instruction in the Lord's Prayer and the elements of faith as a part of his care. Miles Coverdale, who succeeded Voysey at Exeter, made a less obvious external impact upon his see but at least provided in his own life an exemplar of the behaviour of a reformed minister and offered in his household a centre of prayer, charity and modest living. John Ponet at Winchester may have been struggling to achieve something similar, though his endeavours were impeded by an embarrassing matrimonial crisis.[7]

6. J. Blench, *Preaching in England in the Late Fifteenth and Sixteenth Centuries* (Oxford 1964), pp. 263–77. H. S. Darby, *Hugh Latimer* (1953), ch. 5. Elton, *Policy and Police*, pp. 112–20.
7. Foxe, *Acts and Monuments*, VI, pp. 644–5. Vowell alias Hooker, ‘A *Catalog of the Bishops of Exeter*. W. S. Hudson, *John Ponet* (Chicago 1942), p. 155.

Coverdale and Hooper still remained exceptions among the Edwardian prelates in adopting a way of life fundamentally different from that of their Catholic predecessors. Elsewhere, a decline in conspicuous consumption and the active display of authority seem to have been dictated by economic constraints rather than by ideological ones. The bishops were perforce compelled to occupy fewer houses as some of their best residences were taken by the crown and laity, and wills indicate some decline in the number of servants. Goodrich at his death, for example, had a household of fifty-three, compared to the hundred servants supposedly employed by the last pre-Reformation bishop, Nicholas West. Nor were most prelates any longer able to leave ostentatious monuments behind them: chantries were precluded after 1548, and giving to educational and other charitable establishments also declined sharply. When resources were available to them it is hardly surprising to find that even convinced Protestants such as Cranmer and Ridley felt it necessary to provide as large a household as possible and to retain the trappings of wealth and power. The enforcement of the Reformation was a complex task, and the prelates needed all the strength they could command to undertake it. In Tudor society strength and authority sprang partly from the display of wealth; since the bishops had had much of their natural spiritual authority undermined by the actions of the crown, they needed to husband their surviving image of power more carefully than ever before.[8]

This at least would seem to be the most appropriate interpretation of the behaviour of the leader of reform, Thomas Cranmer. Cranmer's attitudes were perhaps more instinctively conservative than those of most other leading Protestants, and issues of order and social harmony held sway in his mind in far greater measure than in that of Hooper. His own personal life, if we are to accept Ralph Morice's description of it, was restrained and sober to the point of frugality. Morice suggests that he often avoided eating lavish meals by the simple device of keeping his gloves on at the board, while still being present in order to participate in the discussion. Yet his household was as hierarchical, as well ordered and probably as large as those of his predecessors. The surviving household ordinances reveal an elaborate system ruled by a council of officers, who held regular meetings to discipline the servants and to 'take order for the Lord's better service'. Only the

8. PROB, 11/37/F10. W. K. Jordan, *Philanthropy in England, 1480–1660* (New York 1959), pp. 330–9.

insistence that all members of the household must hear daily service does a little to separate these rules from those which might have governed the establishment of any senior nobleman. The resources of this household were directed towards the maintenance of hospitality, as Thomas Seymour had discovered to his embarrassment, and by the Edwardian period this included much entertainment of foreigners and native Englishmen involved in the labour of reforming the theology and liturgy of the church. Cranmer's generosity to foreigners certainly served the fledgling English church well, and Foxe, who clearly felt somewhat ambivalent about the outward display of the archiepiscopal establishment, defended Cranmer on these grounds. But the formality which surrounded the archbishop must have appeared unusual to men who had also sat at the board of Bucer in Strassburg or Bullinger in Zurich. Cranmer explicitly condemned covetousness in the clergy when he was challenged by Cecil in 1552, and most of the trappings of wealth and power with which he was surrounded were undoubtedly intended to enhance the public authority of the church. Nevertheless, he was not immune from the personal temptations of wealth: he purchased or otherwise acquired three estates at the expense of the see and was as adept as any of the other prelates at finding desirable leases for his relatives.[9]

There is surprisingly little evidence of attempts to formalise the sort of attitudes implicit in Cranmer's behaviour into an effective defence of the wealth of the hierarchy. This is partly because at no time between 1535 and the death of Edward was the episcopal bench itself united on these issues. At the one extreme stood the conservatives, with their argument that authority was all of one piece and that changes in the religious fabric would inevitably tend towards social disintegration and conflict: at the other, men such as Hooper and Turner who were questioning the general validity of ecclesiastical wealth. Moreover, the lay environment was so hostile to all claims of clerical privilege that the bishops must often have found silence their most practical defence. Such quiescence must have appealed particularly to those conservatives or neuters who still clung to their places upon the episcopal bench. These were men to whom, as Bucer sourly remarked, 'the idleness and luxury of antichrist is more agreeable than the cross of Christ'.[10]

9. LPL, MS. 884. PRO, E 154/2/41. For Peter Martyr's description of Bucer's household see Gorham (ed.), *Gleanings*, pp. 21–2. Cranmer, *Remains*, I, p. 352.
10. *Original Letters*, II, p. 548.

Theoretical claims for church wealth by the Protestant hierarchy therefore proceeded little further than the forum of the academic disputation. Two such formal defences survive for the Edwardian period: one dated December 1552, must have had relatively wide circulation, for three different copies are still extant. The author argued that goods and wealth designated to the clergy should not be alienated to the laity and that the bishops could not in good conscience consent to such alienations. He was of Protestant persuasion, for he urged the magistrate to maintain and support the church and to improve the quality of the ministry and its opportunities for propagating the gospel. A high calibre of ministry meant sufficient financial aid: money must be found to offer a competent maintenance to the parochial clergy, to encourage scholarship and study in the universities and to support the poor and needy. Much of this money was already available through the wise provision that previous monarchs had made for the bishops and higher clergy. To alienate this property and impoverish the prelates would be an act of folly. It could also be construed as an act of sacrilege, and here the author adduced some lively biblical examples of the consequences of such royal impiety. The time had not yet come when the laity could be trusted to provide for the needs of the church, although in a true commonweal they would undertake this burden. Towards the end of the treatise the author descended to a particularity that suggests some personal acquaintance with the process of alienation. The remarkable feature of episcopal alienations in England, he commented, was that they were made by the prelates' own letters of grant, as though the transactions were spontaneous. The second defence considered the traditional conundrum, whether it was lawful for a cleric to alienate the goods of the church. It adopted the same general arguments as the first defence, with the interesting addition that the higher clergy would be brought into contempt if their wealth was removed and that the authority of the church would consequently suffer.[11]

II

When even men with strong convictions and strong views about the church dared not to air them more openly, Bucer's conservatives

11. PRO, sp 10/15/77. CCCC, ms. 113, nos. 25–6. Both treaties are bound together in the Corpus ms.

and neuters may be forgiven for clinging quietly to their traditional paths and the remnants of their tattered authority. And many such men remained on the bench throughout the mid-Tudor years. Only ten of those appointed between the breach with Rome and Henry's death can be reckoned as being even in general sympathy with reform and four of these were dead or had resigned before the end of the 1530s. The Edwardian episcopate obviously became more firmly committed to Protestant ideals, but in 1553 there were still nine men in office whose religious views were either conservative or are unknown from the surviving evidence. Those who possessed neither spiritual zeal nor a particularly clear vision of their function in the English church were liable to lapse into apathy, to fail to supervise and control their diocesan officials and to lose much of the humanist momentum towards internal reform that had been such a feature of the 1520s.[12]

At Chichester, for example, Bishop Sampson did little to restore the diocesan administration to working order after it was disrupted by Cromwell's prohibition in the 1530s. Bishop Reppes at Norwich also allowed an organisational system which had worked well under Nix to deteriorate alarmingly. Indeed, Reppes seems the classic example of a man promoted to high office who was totally unable to cope with the circumstances in which he found himself. He allegedly tried to live in the same style as his predecessor on a much diminished annual income with no accumulation of capital, and as a result lurched from one fiscal expedient to another. These difficulties left him no time, or perhaps inclination, to handle the more serious problems of discipline or of enforcing the Reformation within his see. Cromwell, who apparently realised that his appointment had been a grave mistake, endeavoured to remove him, but the bishop stuck fast until his debts finally undid him during Edward VI's reign. One of his servants could not resist a lament upon his poverty and failure:

> Poor Will, Thou Ruggered art and ragged all,
> Thy Abbie cannot bless thee in such fame
> To keepe a Pallace state, and Lordlie hall
> When gone is thence yt shoulde maintaine ye same.
> Best paye they debts, and hence retourne to Cell . . .[13]

12. On the episcopate and their views see L. B. Smith, *Tudor Prelates*.
13. Lander, 'The Diocese of Chichester', pp. 45ff. R. Houlbrooke, 'Church Courts and People in the Diocese of Norwich, 1519–70', unpub. D.Phil. thesis, University of Oxford (1969). *LP*, Add. I, ii, 1328. CUL, Mm/3/12, p. 287. The 'Ruggered' refers to Reppes's alias of Rugge.

The case of Reppes highlights one of the major weaknesses of royal policy towards the bishops. It was not merely that Henry failed to appoint reformers: indeed, given his own reluctance to initiate religious change, it is surprising that so many were placed upon the bench. Rather, there were too many appointments that could not be justified by any standards, either reformist or conservative. The regulars, who were recruited in some numbers after the dissolution, proved particularly ineffective. A few, such as Robert Holgate, John Hilsey and William Barlow, showed some competence, but most of the rest were at best nondescript and at worst resembled Reppes. When the new sees were established in 1540–2 the government was offered a particularly good opportunity to insert men who would provide strong spiritual guidance in their areas of jurisdiction. Instead, the only cleric of any distinction who was promoted was Thomas Thirlby, given Westminster more for his diplomatic abilities than for any spiritual contribution he could make. Otherwise, the new appointments went to men with little evident merit: particularly bad mistakes were made at Peterborough and Gloucester, where the old abbots took over the sees and proved able to adjust to new circumstances only when it came to exploiting their estates.[14]

The principal reason for this series of poor or indifferent promotions by the government must surely be expedience. It was convenient to employ the local abbot who had cooperated in the dissolution of his house: he had the advantage of knowing his cathedral establishment, and some pension costs were saved by the manoeuvre. It was convenient to find a bishop like Reppes, who was as pliant in agreeing to the dismemberment of the episcopal estates as to the dissolution of his own monastery. There were also some advantages in recruiting a few nonentities to the bench at a time of spiritual disharmony. A few clerics like Latimer and Gardiner were sufficient in any body politic, and Henry VIII no doubt appreciated the dutiful conservatism of many of his appointments. It may also be that the pool of potential candidates for the episcopal bench was smaller in the 1540s than in the preceding decades. Between 1533 and 1546 thirty-five consecrations or translations took place, compared to twenty-one in the first twenty-three years of Henry's reign. Many of these changes occurred because of death, deprivation and the establishment of new bishoprics,

14. T. F. Shirley, *Thomas Thirlby: Tudor Bishop* (1964), pp. 27–40. Wakeman at Gloucester seems to have started the see on a disastrous downward path, partly as a result of the long leases he granted.

rather than because the government made a conscious choice to move men from see to see. At just the time when more prelates were needed, religious conflict among the senior clergy served to rule out some of the most able candidates. Thus Robert Barnes and Miles Coverdale, both men of great ability, were unacceptable because of their total commitment to reform. On the conservative side there were few men of the type of Gardiner, few who had been reared in canon and civil law and in government service: Bonner, Thirlby and Nicholas Wotton, who became dean of York, are the last of the clerics who reached high office by this road. It may therefore be necessity as well as convenience that turned Henry and his advisers towards the regulars to staff the higher levels of the church. The ex-abbots in theory had the experience and the skills to control a diocesan organisation and impose discipline: unfortunately, those who had been able to adjust to the great changes of the 1530s were not neces-sarily the men best able to undertake the spiritual and political leader-ship of their sees.[15]

One interesting consequence of the increase in the number of regulars serving on the bench in the later years of the reign of Henry VIII is that we know less of the social origins of the episcopate in this period than in the early part of the sixteenth century. The question of origins is of some importance in understanding the authority which the bishops were able to exercise. However dependent the prelates might be upon the crown for promotion, they could still derive advantage from the support of a wealthy or influential family. The family might provide some economic support, aid in paying first-fruits and assistance in the early years of an episcopal career, which enabled the recipient to avoid local obligations and retain some independence. Bishop Goodrich's family did this at Ely, and Cuthbert Tunstal also seems to have received help in financing his first promo-tion to London. An established family might also offer an effective entry into local politics for a bishop who was fortunate enough to return to his home area, as Tunstal did at Durham, Savage at York and Arthur Bulkeley at Bangor. Above all, respectable, preferably gentle, origins protected the bishop against the charge that he was an upstart, wielding power far greater than he could legitimately claim by right of birth. Such criticisms from the laity are a feature of the post-Reformation era, especially of the late sixteenth and early

15. On the men promoted to the bench in these years see L. B. Smith, *Tudor Prelates*, pp. 9ff.

seventeenth centuries. As the concept of gentility hardened and the religious policies of the hierarchy became less universally acceptable, criticism of the proud bearing of the prelates and aspersions upon their birth became common. Yet, with the possible exception of the regulars, there do not appear to be great contrasts between the origins of the post-Reformation prelates and those of the early sixteenth century.[16]

Table 7:1 gives the basic data for the social origins of the bishops who were on the bench at fifteen-year intervals during the first half

Table 7:1 *Social origins of the English bishops, 1500–45*

			Family background of English-born prelates			
	(1)	(2)	(3)	(4)	(5)	(6)
			Gentry connec- tions/pro- pertied	Mercantile/	Lower social	
Year	Nobility	Gentry	families	burgess	group	Unknown
1500	–	3	5	1	2	7
1515	2	1	3	3	4	5
1531	–	5	3	3	4	3
1545	–	5	7	4	2	8

Note: 1531 has been chosen in preference to 1530 in order to avoid the period when Wolsey controlled several sees.
Sources: J. J. Scarisbrick, 'The Conservative Episcopate', ch. 1. L. B. Smith, *Tudor Prelates and Politics* (Princeton, N.J., 1953), pp. 9–38.

of the sixteenth century. The figures are in some measure conjectural: at one extreme there are the group about whom nothing is known except perhaps their county of origin; at the other those who belonged to readily identifiable gentry families or who left specific biographical information behind them. In between are the majority, whose family connections can be established with varying degrees of certainty from other sources, who were often from a relatively wealthy or landed background, but who cannot be positively connected to the gentry. The numbers in column 3 of the table are an

16. The prelates listed in col. 3 of table 7:1 are as follows: 1500: John Morton, John Morgan, John Arundel, Richard Foxe, John Blythe; 1515: Richard Foxe, Thomas Skevington, William Warham; 1531: Henry Standish, William Warham, Thomas Skevington; 1545: Thomas Sampson, George Day, Anthony Kitchin, Edmund Bonner, William Reppes, Arthur Bulkeley, William Barlow.

attempt to represent this group, which does not fit readily into the social categories established by contemporaries. The first and obvious conclusion to be drawn from the table is that noble prelates were a rarity and were extinct by the end of the period. Only James Stanley and Edmund Audley were scions of noble houses. For much of the later medieval period nobles were a rarity on the bench: strong monarchs preferred to appoint administrator bishops from a less exalted background, and the nobility themselves displayed little enthusiasm for sending their younger sons into the church. The early fifteenth century had seen some growth in the number of bishops from noble houses, but by the reign of Edward IV this trend had again been reversed. By the time of the Tudors it was well established that the greatest prizes in the church would go to those who served the crown best, and few men of noble family seem to have been willing to enter this contest. On the other hand, the next ranks of society, the gentry families and those with gentle connections or landed wealth, appear to have been fully represented in the episcopate both before and after the Reformation. It may be that there was some shift within these broad categories from the greater families to the less – there were, for example, no bishops who came from families of first importance among the gentry in 1545, while there were two such men in 1500. Nevertheless, there does not seem to have been time before the end of Henry's reign for the career choices of gentry sons to have moved decisively against the church and for this to be revealed in the figures for those promoted to the bench.[17]

The final column of table 7:1 shows the number of men for whom no adequate biographical information about origins is available. Throughout the early sixteenth century the two groups most likely to be found in this category are the Welsh bishops, who often led lives of such obscurity that they left very little mark upon the records, and the regulars. Not all the regulars were of unknown antecedents: Standish and Reppes, for example, were both connected with gentry families. But the majority can no longer be tracked back to their roots; their loyalty and commitment were presumably given principally to their own monastic establishment. Since they could not make wills or retain possessions, their kin might have less incentive to maintain their contacts, though the offices and patronage to be

17. Six of those for whom there are no data among the 1545 group were regulars: John Salcot, Paul Bush, Henry Holbeach, Robert Parfew, John Bird and John Wakeman.

dispensed by the head of an establishment still tempted some of them. Such studies as have been undertaken upon the origin of the regular clergy suggest relatively humble beginnings, even for these who later rose to positions of authority within their order. It is therefore probable that most of the regular 'unknowns' who appear in the final column of the table would have sprung from fairly lowly positions within society.[18]

Family support and the natural confidence that derived from secure gentry status could strengthen the social and political position of a bishop, but this paled into insignificance when compared with the power which the crown could exert over them. In addition to the control over promotion and taxation which it had exercised before the Reformation it could now examine and criticise the spiritual attitudes of a prelate, his enforcement of discipline and his general conduct of diocesan business. Occasionally this close dependence upon the crown could lead on to positive achievements: in the obvious case of Cranmer the cooperation between the archbishop and Cromwell as Henry's vicegerent in the 1530s was very fruitful, and the spiritual successes of the decade more than compensated for the price paid, that is, the loss of part of the Canterbury estates. Even the economic and social relationship between king and archbishop was not entirely one-sided, for Cranmer felt able to ask for favour for his clients, to use the royal favour to promote his own modest suits. When, on the other hand, the relationship worked badly, as it did for a conservative such as Edward Lee, archbishop of York, who was suspected of involvement in the Prilgrimage of Grace, it could undermine episcopal authority and create an enduring sense of insecurity. In Lee's case, the great exchange of 1542/3 was part of the extended price he was compelled to pay for the return of royal favour. Above all, the comprehensive and threatening nature of royal command over the church was liable to create a mood of silent acquiescence in any change that we have noted in many of the weaker bishops. It took courage and a strong sense of the spiritual rightness of one's position to question the direction of Henry's religious policy. Even in the following reign, when the reformers appeared to have the sympathy of the ruling élite, their exclusion from power was in practice as absolute as before. Not surprisingly, many of the bishops,

18. On the regulars and the prohibition upon will-making see Lyndwood, *Provinciale*, bk III, tit. xiii, c. 2. In 1535 Standish made a will, but his executors were challenged and a complaint was made to Cromwell. *LP*, IX, 34.

like the parish clergy for whom they supposedly cared, preferred to keep their opinions to themselves except when directly challenged by the crown.[19]

Edward's reign introduced one novel element into this complex of relationships. Clerical marriage meant that the bishops had to consider not only the welfare of their extended families but also the much more immediate security of their wives and children. The effects of this change can already be seen before the demise of the young king, especially in the areas of land purchase and leases. In addition to Cranmer's land purchases there was the case of Robert Holgate, almost certainly the well-endowed bishop mentioned by Cranmer in his letter of 1552. He is known to have purchased three estates during his time at York: one, Sand Hutton in the North Riding, was left to his hospital at Hemsworth; another, the ex-archiepiscopal estate of Scrooby, was left to his wife Barbara in survivorship and after her death reverted to the see; a third, the priory of St Mary, Yedingham, was retained in his family, apparently by his children, though no children are mentioned in his will. Other bishops favoured the cheaper method of providing leases for their children and wives: Bishop Barlow's infant son, for example, was given the parsonage of St John's Glastonbury, in reversion. The support of a nuclear family was a pressing obligation upon the bishops, and the issue of provision for children was to become a contentious one under Elizabeth, exacerbated by the queen's pathological dislike of clerical marriage. It is important, however, not to exaggerate its economic consequences under Edward. Marriage was only allowed to the clergy in the last four years of the reign, which afforded a rather limited time for procreation and the formation of dynasties. Only ten of the prelates married, and of these only seven are known to have produced children while in office. It is interesting that Cranmer should have been one of those who actually purchased estates for his heirs, since he had been married since the 1530s and had grown children. For the rest, the arrival of infants does not seem to have afforded much contrast with the preceding situation, since many of the extended families of the prelates were already profiting enormously from the wealth of their relatives. As for the additional cost of a family, the large households of the bishops could presumably absorb a few more

19. Cranmer, *Remains*, I, pp. 61, 130, 145. *DNB*, Edward Lee. Our best knowledge of the views of the episcopate comes from the two questionnaires addressed to them in 1540 and 1548. Strype, *Cranmer*, I, app. xxvii.

individuals without difficulty, and in theory a woman might do something to bring closer supervision to the organisation of these predominantly male establishments.[20]

The marriage of the prelates probably made more impact in a social than in a purely economic sense. When they chose a partner the bishops were compelled for the first time to submit their status and wealth to the judgement of society. So far, they had been able to consort with the magnates of the realm on equal terms on state occasions, even if their diminishing real wealth made them more comparable with the county gentlemen with whom they sat in the commissions of peace. Their quest for marriage partners tended to reveal that they were not considered by either of these groups as reliable or desirable spouses. Those wives whose origins can be traced were drawn from the ranks of the urban bourgeoisie, were foreign or came from even humbler backgrounds. These lowly connections are not purely a reflection of the landed classes' doubts about the wealth of the bishops or their standing in society. Marriage was such a novelty, and the religious settlement so fluid, that any squire might be forgiven a reluctance to have a lordly prelate as his son-in-law. It is only from the 1570s onwards, when marriage for the clergy was widely accepted and the Elizabethan settlement seemed more secure, that the bishops began to have a greater choice of partner.[21]

The social acceptance of clerical marriage was not facilitated by some of the bishops themselves, who, in their eagerness to take advantage of the new situation, contracted disastrous unions. Both John Ponet and Robert Holgate were charged with marital irregularity: in Holgate's case because his Barbara had been precontracted as a child to another man, and in Ponet's with bigamy. These problems offered invaluable ammunition to those who were opposed to the concept of clerical marriage. Henry Machyn, the London diarist, recorded with delight the news that Ponet had been divorced from the lady of his choice 'with shame enough'. Little detailed evidence

20. *VCH, Yorkshire North Riding*, II, pp. 95, 436. Cross, 'Economic Problems of York', p. 73. Hembry, p. 85. The married bishops were Holbeach, Hooper, Ferrar, Cranmer, Holgate, Coverdale, Ponet, Scory, Barlow and Bush. There is no evidence that Coverdale, Bush or Holbeach had children.

21. Mrs Barlow was a former nun, Mrs Hooper and Mrs Cranmer were foreigners, Mrs Holgate was a lady of 'good family'. Mrs Coverdale was of uncertain origin but was the sister-in-law of the reformer Dr Joannes McAlpine. Ponet married twice, first in a bigamous association with the wife of a butcher and secondly Maria Haymond, of respectable parentage. Nothing is known in detail of the background of the other episcopal wives.

G

of the hostility shown to clerical wives survives, but there are hints
of it in the sour criticism of Northumberland, who attacked Dean
Horne for devotion to his family at the expense of charity. John
Hooker, the Exeter writer, recorded the hostility that Coverdale
encountered in that city both for his religious convictions and for
his marriage, even though his wife was 'a most sober, chaste and
godly matron: his house and household another church in which
was exercised all godliness and virtue'. A part of the problem was
that some of the prelates hastened to marry out of a sense of Protestant conviction, rather than for affection. When the two were combined, as they seem to have been, for example, in the union of John
and Anna Hooper, the bishops no doubt found a source of inner
support that more than countered the effects of this public hostility.[22]

At no time before the mid-sixteenth century had the English bench
contained men with such diametrically opposed religious views or
habits of life. All was novelty and flux, especially during the brief
Protestant triumph under Edward. Few generalisations are therefore
relevant to all the prelates holding office during these disturbed
years. Some of the more radical reformers appear to have been feeling
their way tentatively towards a new view of the episcopate, despite
all the practical impediments which lay in their paths. Others followed the example of Cranmer in moulding the traditional pattern
of episcopal behaviour into a spiritual life that was unequivocally
Protestant. At the other extreme a few leaders of the Catholic prelates, notably Bonner and Gardiner, continued to maintain all the
port of a bishop as part of their general defence of the authority and
independence of the episcopate. Between these fairly clearly defined
paths of behaviour lay, no doubt, the practice of most of the rest of
the bench. Many of their energies were consumed in the attempt to
enforce the royal will and to bring some spiritual order within their
dioceses; their hold upon office can rarely have seemed less secure,
and their hold upon their lands was even less certain. At best, this
insecurity and the difficulty of ensuring conformity bred a type of
political quietism such as that which Cuthbert Tunstal displayed at
Durham. He consistently expressed himself in favour of the conservatives in the great religious disputes of the 1540s, but he enforced
the royal will within his diocese, at least until the Prayer Book crisis

22. A. G. Dickens, *Robert Holgate, Archbishop of York* (York, 1954), pp. 24–5. H. Machyn,
    Diary, Camden Soc., 1st ser., XLII (1848), p. 8. See above, p. 144. Vowell alias
    Hooker, *A Catalog. Original Letters*, I, pp. 64, 92, 106–7, 111–13.

of 1549. Meanwhile, he gave care and attention to the supervision of his see, following here the initiative that he and his fellow bishops had begun in the 1520s, and was sufficiently devoted to his office to continue a major building programme at Durham at a time when many episcopal palaces were suffering neglect. It was maybe only in the north that such a combination of external obedience to the crown and inner adherence to a traditional pattern of behaviour could have survived the reigns of Henry, Edward and Mary almost intact. Elsewhere the bishops found themselves constantly exposed to crown and lay pressures and vulnerable because their place in the commonweal was go longer clearly defined or universally accepted. In the circumstances it is scarcely surprising that greed, pusillanimity and equivocation appear as the dominant social characteristics of the mid-Tudor episcopate.[23]

---

23. Loades, 'Cuthbert Tunstall', pp. 10–19. Sturge, *Tunstal*, pp. 281–97. DDR, cc 190066/9.

8

THE CONSEQUENCES OF THE BREAK
WITH ROME: FINANCIAL PROBLEMS

The preceding chapters have shown that the episcopate underwent a major crisis between the breach with Rome and the death of Mary. It is now time to try to give this crisis a specifically economic dimension, to assess the financial significance of the loss of lands. This is no easy task, since there are no general figures for episcopal revenue to replace those that are available for 1535 and since the further we move forward from the date of the *Valor Ecclesiasticus* the more conjectural must be our global estimates. Individual episcopal accounts are available, and in a few dioceses series of such accounts make it possible to offer effective comparisons with the earlier figures. In other sees, for which only the occasional record of income survives, the receipts are valuable mainly as a guide to the margins of error which may be expected in any final calculations. Table 8:1 gives the income of some of the English sees for various dates between 1540 and 1558. The pattern is by no means consistent: several sees show an increase in money income as compared to the estimates of the *Valor* or even to the episcopal accounts cited in chapter 3; others appear to have remained constant or even to have lost value. This latter situation can be observed at Salisbury and Worcester as well as in the lands of those victims of the Reformation Norwich, Canterbury and Winchester.[1]

For any general estimates of the revenues of the bishops in these difficult years we remain dependent upon the 1535 survey, amended by information upon the losses of land and such data as are available from the accounts. From these sources it would appear that in 1541 the total receipts of the English bishops were larger than they had been six years earlier: approximately £31,500 as compared to £29,550. This was the moment after the creation of the six new bishoprics when the fortunes of the episcopal order were temporarily in the ascendant. By 1547, making allowances for the changes initiated by

1. Series of accounts for this period survive only for Durham and Winchester.

Table 8:1 *Temporal income of the bishoprics, 1540–58*

| See | Year | Episcopal or crown accounts | | *Valor Ecc.* |
		Gross receivers' receipts	Livery	Gross income
Winchester	1546	£4452	£3928	£3888
	1552	£1334	£1103	
	1555	£4255	£3468	
Durham	1540	£2738	£2206	£2431
(co. only)	1548	£2629	£2047	
	1553	£2617	£2111	
	1556	£2611	£1999	
Canterbury (Kentish lands only)	1552	£1671	£1483	£2022
London	1550	£1114	£776	£1181
	1556	£1420	£1072	
Ely	1542	£2306		£2205
	1549	£2400	£2260	
Lincoln	1542	£1611	£1450	£1438
Worcester	1542	£1110	£655	£980
	1556	£1018	£670	
Hereford	1547	–	£653	£718
Salisbury	1549	£1261	£1096	£1284
Norwich	1549	£678	–	£979

Sources: HRO, Ep. 155887; 155890; 155893. DDR, cc 189847; 189851; 189854. PRO, sc 6/Ed. VI/240; sc 6/Ed. VI/307; sc 6/P. and M./193 (London figures are reproduced in Alexander, 'Victim or Spendthrift?' in *Wealth and Power in Tudor England*). EDR, D/5/9. BL, Add. Roll 34274; BL, Harl. ms. 7505, fos. 15ff. WRO, cc 900/1, 718, 719. Bodl., Hereford Roll 35. PRO, sc 6/Ed. VI/491. NRO, har/3. The figure for Norwich is a valuation.

Henry VIII in his will, total revenues had fallen to around £30,000. Edward's reign marked a predictable nadir in the finances of the order, until at the young king's death in 1553 annual income can have been little higher than £22,500. In the calmer atmosphere of Mary's reign, when some modest restitution was the object of the queen, the final estimate for receipts is *c.* £28,300. All these figures are, of course, purely calculations of money income and make no allowance for the inflation of the mid-Tudor decades, which must have had serious effects upon the real revenues of every prelate. Average income fell from over £1400 to £865 in 1553. However, these global figures conceal the degree of continuity in some sees and the

very sharp decline in money income elsewhere. Table 8:2 demonstrates not only the general fall in revenues but also the marked
changes in rank and comparative wealth that had occurred by the
death of Edward VI. Mary's reign saw some reversal of this process,
with the restoration of Winchester and Durham to the ranks of sees
worth over £2000 per annum, yet many of the changes wrought
during the early years of the Reformation became permanent features
of the English church.[2]

The same decades that witnessed a decline in the total revenues of
the bishoprics also produced a steady increase in the percentage of

Table 8:2 *Income of the English and Welsh bishoprics, 1553 and 1535*

	1553	1535	Rank in 1535
Canterbury	£3100	£3224	2
Ely	£2420	£2135	4
Winchester	£1580	£3885	1
Salisbury	£1340	£1368	9
Durham (proposed)	£1333	£2821	3
York	£1330	£2036	5
London	£1110	£1119	10
Lincoln	£960	£1963	6
Worcester/Gloucester	£900	£1050[a]	11
Bath and Wells	£900	£1844	7
Norwich	£870	£979	12
Hereford	£768	£768	13
Chichester	£677	£677	15
Newcastle (proposed)	£667	–	–
Coventry and Lichfield	£660	£703	14
Exeter	£530	£1567	8
Chester	£495	–	–
St David's	£470	£457	17
Carlisle	£470	£541	16
Rochester	£411	£411	18
Peterborough	£380	–	–
Oxford	£340	–	–
Bristol	£311	–	–
St Asaph	£188	£188	19
Llandaff	£155	£155	20
Bangor	£132	£132	21

[a]For the diocese of Worcester only, since Gloucester was not established until
1541.

2. See app. I. The six new bishoprics accounted for about £2430 of the total for
the temporalities in 1541. PRO, E 315/389/fos. 6ff.

those revenues that derived from the spiritualities. Incomplete figures for the 1535 survey suggest that about 12 per cent of the total came from rectories, tithes and spiritual dues. After the Reformation it is even more difficult to find information upon spiritual dues than it had been earlier, and it is probable that there were times, notably the years of Cromwell's vicegerency, when very little was available to the diocesans. From the end of the 1530s they did at least enjoy once more the most profitable of the dues – visitation fees – and these, with the rectories and tithes, continued to form the most important part of the spiritualities. One valuation, for Norwich in 1543, shows the pensions, synodals and casualties as worth £188, or exactly the same as the figure in the *Valor*, a small loss on the casualties being compensated for by a rise in pensions. If we therefore make the very tentative assumption that spiritual dues in the long run held their money value, we can estimate that by 1547 total spiritual revenues represented at least 17 per cent of all income and by 1553 at least 30 per cent. Even under Mary spiritualities retained an important place in the episcopal economy, with 24 per cent of receipts from this source. Not only the poor Welsh sees and Rochester and Carlisle now looked to rectories and tithes to supplement their manors, but Winchester, York and London, which had previously derived very little from the body of the church. Most of this new 'spiritual' wealth was in the form of appropriated rectories, passed to the higher clergy as part of the great exchanges of the 1540s and early 1550s. To refuse this form of recompense for lost manors would have left the bishops in an even more parlous financial condition, and so the form of exploitation initiated by the monasteries was perpetuated within the church. Only a few voices were raised in protest, and even they did not single out the return of impropriations to the clergy. Bucer, in a letter to Calvin in 1550, roundly condemned the general practice of detaining revenues that should be used for the benefit of the parishes but implicitly directed his criticism at the lay inheritors of monastic wealth. In the apparent absence of strong and principled objection to the possession of spiritualities from the higher clergy themselves, the crown and its ministers allowed the movement towards spiritual property to continue unchecked. By the reign of Elizabeth the philosophy that such property was most 'meet for spiritual men' was well entrenched in the thinking of the government.[3]

3. The percentages for spiritual income are all probably slight underestimates. Some receipts from the spiritualities, especially from rectories, were included

The general picture of the bishoprics in the mid-Tudor years is therefore one of almost static rent-rolls in the fortunate sees, of a sharp decline in money income in the few affected by the depredations of the crown and laity, especially in the Edwardian years, and of a shift from the holding of manors to the holding of rectories and other spiritualities. Much of this rather dismal picture must be attributed to the policy of the crown, both because of its direct demands upon the bishops and because of the environment of uncertainty and insecurity which was created by fundamental changes in ecclesiastical strategy. Yet many resources still lay at the disposal of the bishops, and the crisis years of the mid-century, with their high inflation rates and their political unrest, might have stimulated them to profit more effectively from the possessions still remaining to them. Instead, the Henrician and Edwardian prelates not only ossified their own rental incomes but ensured that their successors should not have much opportunity to improve their revenues. These were the years when demesne leases were made with a lavishness and a disregard for economic reality that have not been seen before or since in the long history of the English ecclesiastical establishment. To begin with, there was a marked increase in the number of grants made between 1546 and 1553. In the eight bishoprics for which detailed information is given in appendix IV, 87 leases were issued between 1535 and 1541. In those sees for which an adequate comparison can be offered, this represents approximately double the number for a similar period at the beginning of the reign. The last five years of Henry's rule witnessed a further increase to about 130 leases, a figure that compares with that for the slightly longer period of Edward's reign, when the bishops of these eight sees made 123 grants. This is in marked contrast with the years from 1553 to 1558, when Mary's bishops made only 68, the great majority of which were of properties with very low rental values.[4]

Further, as the number of demesne leases increased, so also did their length. There were marked variations in the years for which property was granted out in different sees – in the exceptional case of

---

in the temporal accounts and cannot be isolated from the manorial totals. NRO, CC 100094. *Original Letters*, II, p. 546.

4. Sources for leases in these years are: Ely – EDR, 2/6/1; Winchester – WiDC, Ledger Books III and IV; London – StPDC, Dean Sampson's Book; York – YDC, Wa and Wb; Salisbury – SaRO, Bpric 460; Worcester – WRO, CC lease transcript vol.; Hereford – HeRO, Butterfield's Survey; Lincoln – *Chapter Acts of Lincoln*, vol. I.

Worcester and the periods were actually shorter than they had been before 1535 – but the graphs show a general upwards movement that was very sharp on some estates. In four of the eight bishoprics studied, the lengths of grant rose sharply under Henry VIII and again under Edward, while in three others a marked increase in the later years of Henry was followed by stabilisation or slight decline under Edward. A weighted average, using the rental values of the manors and other properties demised by the bishops, shows the same pattern even more clearly, for it was often the most valuable estates that were put into longest lease. This is especially true for the reign of Edward VI, when ninety-nine-year grants became commonplace in a number of sees: 40 per cent of the manorial leases in the eight sees were for this period or longer. There is also evidence that the practice of demising manors in reversion more than five years before the expiry of the existing lease was on the increase. Between 1509 and the end of 1534 only five of the group studied were made more than five years in advance of the date on which they would become effective. Between 1535 and 1547 there was a long reversionary clause in twenty-six cases, and under Edward VI the figure rose to thirty-five. A few bishops, such as Goodrich of Ely and Salcot of Salisbury made a regular habit of issuing these types of leases on their more important manors.[5]

Why did the bishops embark upon a leasing policy that was potentially disastrous for their successors in an era of inflation? It was certainly not to gain increased rents, for in all but a handful of cases the traditional rents were maintained. In the worst years in the middle of the century they actually ossified their rent rolls still further by leasing out whole manors with all ancillary rights in many cases. This effectively prevented any subsequent exploitation of the ancillary demesne rights and even modest profit-taking from such casualties as court fines. Many prelates at least retained their rights over woodlands, but at Salisbury, Worcester, and Bath and Wells even the woods were often granted away. The only direct financial incentive can have been the chance of immediate profit through the entry or renewal fine. So little information upon fines survives that it is impossible to say how well the prelates could hope to profit. The only evidence which is at all detailed comes from a London survey of 1539 in which the surveyor made some estimates of the sums which could be taken upon renewal of a lease. Several properties were expected to yield little more than one year's rental upon renewal, but

5. Heal, 'The Bishops of Ely', p. 213. SaRO, Bpric 460.

one of the Fulham farms, undervalued by 20 marks according to the surveyor, could realise a fine of £50 on an annual rental of £13. This may be a stray indication of a greater importance attaching to fines after the Reformation, as may be the offer made by a tenant of the bishop of Salisbury to increase his payment for the reversion of his lease from £4 to £13. 6s. 8d. on a grant of sixty years. When Bishop Longland demised Stowe Park on generous terms with a long reversion in 1534 he realised a fine of £50 on a property with a rental value of £16. 12s. None of these scattered examples relate to the really extra-ordinary grants of the mid-Tudor years, which could in principle, therefore, have realised a substantial immediate profit for the prelates. It seems likely that Bishop Voysey, for example, made part of the money which he later bestowed upon the embellishment of his native town of Sutton Coldfield from such payments for leases, and even outright grants, of the Exeter estates.[6]

Although the need for immediate sums of money may be one explanation for the behaviour of the bishops, it is itself scarcely a full and sufficient answer. Other explanations must be sought in the general difficulties of these years, especially in the vulnerability of the prelates in the face of lay demands and pressures. Archbishop Cranmer offers an example of one of those whose leasing policy was apparently determined by these pressures, rather than by his own judgement about the arrangements best for his see. His secretary, Ralph Morice, indicates that he intended at his first entry only to lease his lands for short periods such as twenty-one years. However, he quickly found that unless he conceded longer grants and 'if he had not well-behaved himself towards his prince and the world, his successors should not have been cumbered with any piece of temporal revenue, either in lands, woods or other revenue'.[7] He therefore resorted to the policy of demising many of his estates for eighty or ninety years as a means of restraining lay greed! Plenty of individual examples can be found, especially from the reign of Edward VI, of leading laymen exploiting their power to gain long leases as well as outright exchanges. The most extreme cases are the four two-hundred-

---

6. PRO, sp 1/153. *Chapter Acts of Lincoln*, iii, pp. 120–1. *DNB*, Voysey. Some leases realised rather low fines; e.g. Chardstock meadows, Sarum, were leased in the 1540s for a £25 fine at a rent of £10. PRO, sp 46/2/fo. 193. Hopsthorpe Rectory in Lincolnshire raised a fine of £30 on a rental of £28 and Alvingham and Cockerington rectories in the same county, £10 at a rent of £15. *Chapter Acts of Lincoln*, iii, p. 128.

7. *Narratives of the Reformation*, p. 264.

year grants that were given to Protector Somerset and his brother and to close members of his circle. The most dramatic collapse in the face of these pressures, apart from Voysey at Exeter, was that of John Salcot at Salisbury. Already before Henry's death Salcot had regularly granted out parts of his estates for sixty to seventy years, but from the middle of Edward's first regnal year he began remorselessly to surrender his manors for periods of at least ninety-nine years. Since most of the Salisbury estates were in the south-west, it should come as no surprise to find the Seymour brothers leading the quest for pickings. Thomas Seymour was given Bishop Cannings for ninety-nine years, and Edward gained the prize of Sherburne for two hundred. Other beneficiaries included Herbert, Sackville and Paulet as well as a few of the substantial local gentry. In the end Salcot became so willing to dispose of his lands that men of little evident influence or connection were given extraordinary grants. By the end of Edward's reign fifteen manors out of the total of twenty-three had been committed on a fixed rental for the next century.[8]

It may be a mistake to conceive these surrenders to the laity merely as an example of episcopal weakness. They certainly reflected the insecurity of the new circumstances in which the bishops found themselves, but they are also an exaggerated extension of a tradition which had already existed before the Reformation. Leases were still the most important form of patronage available to the higher clergy and as such continued to be regarded as valuable for reasons that were not solely pecuniary. Was Salcot, for example, using his property in some measure to buy peace from those in power, so that his quiet conservatism would not be challenged by the new Protestant élite? Did some of the bishops actually offer Somerset long leases voluntarily in order to secure the favour of his régime? Whatever the motives in cases which involved leading laymen, there is little doubt that issues of immediate profit did not dominate one area of patronage: the care of family and servants. This had always been an established part of the leasing policy of a number of bishops; indeed, some of the longest and most attractive grants had passed to members of episcopal families well before the Reformation. The only change thereafter is perhaps in the scale of these leases: as the insecurity of the bishops increased and other demands for their lands intensified, there must have been a natural inclination to protect the family even further. This depended, of course, upon the number and closeness of one's

8. SaRO, Bpric 460. BL, Harl. MS. 604, fo. 244.

relatives: Gardiner at Winchester, Salcot at Salisbury and Voysey at
Exeter gave little or nothing to their families, presumably because
they had few relatives for whom they had a duty to provide. On the
other hand, Bonner, Cranmer and Goodrich of Ely provided generously for their families. Bonner was still giving his Mongey relatives
grants of sixty to seventy years from the London estates under Mary,
at a time when many of the bishops were trying to limit their leases
in order to undo the damage of the Reformation period. Cranmer
may have tried to placate the king and the laity by his leases, but he
also ensured that some very lucrative grants were provided for his
brother and son. Most blatant of all was Goodrich, who gave five of
his ninety-nine-year leases to members of his family, another to the
brother of the dean of Ely and two more to trusted servants. By the
time of his death his family dominated the key manors of the Isle of
Ely and retained their influence for much of the remainder of the
century.[9]

Obligations to the family were deeply felt and socially sanctioned
emotions, even if a few of the mid-Tudor bishops interpreted their
duties too broadly. When Edmund Bonner provided a house on the
Fulham demesne for his mother, sister and niece he defended his
behaviour thus: 'I . . . am straightly bound by God's law to take care
of all those that be mine and specially of those that be of the same
house whereof I am, lest I beseem to deny my faith and be worse than
the heathen and infidel.'[10] Beyond the family, those that were 'of the
same house' could include servants and retainers, and once again
many of the prelates in greater or less degree used some of their
leases to provide for their faithful servants. When a crisis threatened,
as it did for many of the prelates during these years, the care of relatives and servants assumed an even greater importance. In 1548 the
imperial ambassador commented that Gardiner, already foreseeing
the possibility of deprivation, 'had provided for his servitors', and we
can establish from the Winchester records that much of this provision
took the form of leases and annuities granted out during that year.
Nearly all the groups of leases examined show an upsurge of grants
at the beginning of each new reign, especially at the beginning and
end of Mary's reign, when the Protestant and Catholic bishops
respectively felt their position to be threatened. Bishop White of

9. EDR, 2/6/1. WiDC, Ledger Book IV, fos. 69v, 70v, 72v, 73. StPDC, Dean Samp-
    son's Book, fos. 186, 191, 205. PRO, SP 12/277.
10. StPDC, Dean Sampson's Book, fo. 165.

Winchester is a prime example of a prelate who, in the early months of Elizabeth's reign, gave away any lease which had any chance of renewal and donated a handsome group of them to his brother, an alderman of the city of London.[11]

A final reason for the long grants may have been that, at least until the middle of Edward's reign, the bishops and their administrators failed to appreciate fully the long-term effects of inflation. This is not to suggest that episcopal estate officials were any more naive than their fellows controlling lay property. There is evidence that they were aware of the undervaluing of land, as in the London survey of 1539, which commented that several estates were undervalued at the old rent and that entry fines should be increased in compensation. But the thinking of such men must still in some measure have been conditioned by the long period of relative price stability and steady land prices that preceded the 1530s. As late as the early 1540s lease lengths were still increasing on some lay estates: a reflection of a world in which the tenant still had to be courted to ensure regular rent payments and in which long leases were a method of encouraging them to improve their lands. In the north, for example in the see of Durham, land prices rose only fitfully until the second half of the century, and there was even less incentive to pursue a novel leasing policy than in the south. When the insecurity of the bishops, and presumably of their tenants, is added to these circumstances, it becomes even less surprising that they allowed long leases and did little to increase the yield from them. Cranmer expressed these feelings of doubt about the future when, in 1534, he rebuked the parson of Chevening for asking £4 more than the accustomed rent for a lease of his rectory: 'Sir, I much marvel that you will desire thus far to exceed, in this uncertain world, from the accustomed rent thereof; I had thought you would rather have minished the old exaction than now to increase the same.'[12] A pride in being good landlords, and not extortionate, which can be found in the comments of a number of the higher clergy, is a concomitant of this attitude. It must often have been easier to accept that one's successors would have a fixed income from rents than to appear to rack or exploit the faithful current tenants of the see.

11. *CStP, Spanish*, IX, p. 278. WiDC, Ledger Book, IV fos. 126v–27v, 132. Hembry, pp. 91–2.
12. PRO, SP 1/153. For rents on lay estates and lease lengths see *Agrarian History of England and Wales*, IV, p. 687. Cranmer, *Remains*, I, p. 58.

Thus, through lay pressures, the need for patronage and support of the family, and a failure to appreciate the long-term damage wrought by fixed leases, the bishops granted away much of the most valuable of their property before the death of Edward. No general attempt was made to inhibit their right to dispose of their property in this manner until the beginning of Elizabeth's reign. But already under Mary there are signs that neither the government nor all the bishops themselves were happy with the freedom which the episcopal order possessed. A council minute of the previous reign, dating from 1552, had already commented that some means must be found to prevent churchmen making spoil of their livings. Among the legislative proposals for Edward's last parliament is the following: 'no spiritual person shall make lease for a longer time than xxi years, nor yet of none of his demesnes of his principal house longer than for his own time'.[13] The idea was not revived officially under Mary, but there are signs that Pole approved of its general sentiments and that certain prelates were implementing a similar policy. Pole, in his legatine decrees, did not direct his attention specifically to episcopal lands but ordered that the parish clergy should make no lease for longer than their tenure of office, except with the consent of the ordinary. Among the rest of the prelates there is evidence of some feeling that the estate policies pursued by their predecessors, both Catholic and Protestant, must now be renounced, even though the damage done in the preceding decades could not be reversed. Bishop Thirlby, who occupied the see of Norwich until 1555 and then moved to Ely, certainly read Pole's decrees as relevant to the bishops as well as to the parochial clergy. He made no lease at Ely for longer than twenty-one years, in marked contrast to his predecessor Goodrich. At Lincoln, rectorial leases, which had commonly been made for sixty years or more under Edward, were limited to an average of thirty years under the second Marian bishop, Thomas Watson. Pole's own Canterbury grants, or at least the few examples that survive, were also made for thirty years or less. Most striking of all is the case of York, where Archbishop Holgate had already pursued a more prudent leasing policy than many of his contemporaries. Nicholas Heath, who at Worcester had shown a tendency to be very generous towards his family, confined all his York grants to twenty-one years with no long reversionary clauses attached. These gestures may seem rather limited, yet they gain further significance from the fact

13. PRO, sp 10/15/10; 10/18/13.

that these prelates had very little left to grant and that their sacrifice of the profits that might have accrued from a few long leases was correspondingly large.[14]

While a few of the Marian prelates appear to have experienced a change of heart and demonstrated a genuine concern to preserve some of the property of the church, there were others who continued much as before. Neither Bonner nor Gardiner deviated from his earlier pattern of behaviour; both continued to dispense leases for sixty or seventy years, often to relatives or members of their household. Their principal concern was probably to reassert their authority over all their estates, to oust lessees inserted by their Edwardian successors and to demonstrate that they once more held full control over matters of patronage. When these concerns are added to the continuing uncertainties of the religious settlement, especially in the year preceding Mary's death, it is understandable that many bishops found it difficult to reverse the policies of their predecessors. It was with some justice that James Pilkington complained at the beginning of Elizabeth's reign that 'Divers of these holy prelates ... had so leased out their houses and lands and parks, that some of the new bishops had scarce a corner of a house to lie in . . .'[15] He should, however, have recognised that much of the damage had already been done before Mary even ascended the throne and that at least some of the Marian bishops had taken advantage of the respite of her reign to halt the depredations of the 'godly Protestants'.

The flood of long episcopal leases that marked the middle decades of the sixteenth century had consequences beyond that of restricting the potential income of the estates. As we have seen in an earlier chapter, land and lordship were still closely linked together, and even estates which had been wholly or partly leased provided men for the episcopal levies and the opportunity for the exercise of judicial authority. It was, moreover, necessary for the bishop to retain sufficient power and influence over his tenants to ensure that rents were properly collected, surveys undertaken and the land used in accordance with custom and equity. It was difficult for any large landowner whose manors were in lease to ensure that his residual authority was upheld, especially in cases where one important tenant had

14. Wilkins (ed.), *Concilia*, IV, p. 123. Burnet, *History of the Reformation*, III, ii, p. 326. EDR, 2/6/1, fos. 61v–62, 64. *Chapter Acts of Lincoln*, III, pp. 92–159. CDC, VI, pp. 40, 56. YDC, Wb, fos. 76–107v.
15. Pilkington, *Works*, p. 595.

rights over others such as the copyholders. Much of the energy of the estate administrators was bent upon ensuring not only that the lord's dues were properly paid, but that tenants abided by the terms of their grants and did not exploit their position. This required considerable vigilance even in stable times, as some of the early-sixteenth-century litigation indicates. In times of disturbance, when the authority of the lord was weak, it was all too easy for the more powerful of his tenants to aggrandise upon their situation. Thus the prelates would probably have found it difficult to control their tenants in the mid-Tudor decades without the additional complication of long leases; with that complication they sometimes found it impossible. One manifestation of this difficulty was an increase in current arrears which some sees experienced, especially during the Edwardian years. At Durham, which has good records throughout this period, current arrears in the early 1540s were normally under £100 per annum. In 1546/7 they rose to £207, and in the crisis year of 1551/2 they stood at £441. Durham is, of course, scarcely typical, because of the upheaval caused by Tunstal's arrest and deprivation: it is known that this caused unrest among the Durham tenants, and in May 1552 Sir George Conyers was ordered to compel them to pay the rents which they had withheld in the bishop's absence. But arrears figures from Winchester and Salisbury tell a similar tale: in both sees a few of the larger tenant farmers were failing to pay their rents or were at least delaying payment for several years, with no evidence of sanctions being applied to them by the episcopal administration.[16]

A decline in episcopal authority could lead to other abuses. In a particularly interesting letter sent to the dean of Rochester and others in 1551, Bishop Ridley complained bitterly that one of his tenants had broken covenants made at the sealing of the lease and had raised the rents of his sub-tenants at Bromley from £14 to £44 per annum. The affair rankled especially because the offender was Robert Deane, formerly receiver to the bishop, and because it appeared almost impossible to intervene on behalf of the exploited tenantry. It was such activities, Ridley remarked sadly, that redounded to 'the great slander of all Bishops (as I take it) that should consent and suffer their poor tenants so to be pilled and polled, and their lands so excessively to be improved by such Leasemongers, which are the utter undoing

16. Horton, 'Durham Bishopric Estates', p. 103. DDR, cc 189851. *APC*, 1552–4, pp. 32–3. PRO, sc 6/Ed. VI/491.

and very destruction of the commonwealth'.[17] How often this form of profiteering occurred must be a matter for speculation, since the episcopal accounts never give details of the monies paid to anyone but the lord himself. It is likely, however, that any substantial tenant who did not wish to farm the land himself would expect a realistic return upon his investment when he sub-leased, that is, a higher annual rental than the bishop extracted from him. Another facet of the same problem was the limited control which the prelates were able to exercise over the sale of their leases. Many grants specifically required a tenant to seek the lord's permission before alienating his lease, but the main purpose of this clause was that the lord would be able to exact his fine for a licence to alienate. As with the crown, which as tenant-in-chief extracted fines on all lands under its direct control when they were bought and sold, so the bishops endeavoured to fine their tenants as lands passed from hand to hand. It is difficult to establish how often in practice their permission was sought: fines for such transactions, like the main entry fines, were accounted a part of the private income of the bishops and did not appear in the records of income. What is certain is that there was a regular market in episcopal leases and that substantial sums of money changed hands in the sale and purchase of long beneficiary grants. In 1556, for example, the countess of Bedford complained that she had paid £300 to obtain a lease of Eybury, belonging to Peterborough, with a rent of £67 a year, but that the bishop was endeavouring to buy in the lease at £200, with the support of Cardinal Pole. In certain parts of the country, such as Wiltshire and Somerset, transactions in these long leases must have had a significant influence upon the pattern of landholding and merit more detailed study in their own right.[18]

Loss of control by the bishops might also be reflected in actual incursions by tenants into lands under the direct administration of the estate officials. Where the surveys of manors were inadequate or outdated, such incursions were always possible. There is some evidence of a failure to keep adequate records in certain dioceses in the mid-Tudor years, but this is a subject which will be examined in more detail for the Elizabethan period. The clearest evidence of problems

17. Kent Record Office, Rochester DC, Egz. 2.
18. *HMC, Salisbury MSS.*, I, p. 137. Many leases, especially at Ely and Winchester, included this specification upon alienation and a licence, but it was not an automatic part of the conditions, as was, for example, the reentry clause. Licences to alienate are rarely recorded among the surviving episcopal documents.

comes from litigation associated with actual exchanges of manors rather than with long leases. When a property passed from one owner to another there were often opportunities for enterprising tenants to deny their obligations to the lord. Sometimes it was merely that the period of transition created an awkward hiatus which genuinely confused the tenantry. Thus, in 1545 the tenants of Clacton Wick in Essex found themselves caught between the bishop of London and the crown, paying rents to both parties who were engaged in exchanging the manor. More common was the situation that Cranmer's officers encountered on two of the Kentish manors granted to the archbishop in the exchanges of the 1530s. In both cases one tenant farmer denied that he owed rent for certain parcels of land listed in the deed of exchange, and arrears accumulated while the disputes were taken to chancery. A powerful tenant might even deny episcopal officers any access to view their new property, or at least detain the deeds so that it was difficult to prove ownership. Robert Holgate was compelled to sue William Cavendish for an action of this sort when he withheld from him two of the rectories given as part of the 'great collection' in the exchange of 1545. In such a case recovery of monies and rights due to the see could take a very long time: Bonner, in the middle of Mary's reign, was still suing for entry to two rectories granted at the time of the dissolution of the bishopric of Westminster. These problems were exacerbated when the serving bishop lacked administrative expertise and an understanding of how to manage his officials and tenants. The rapid religious changes of the mid-Tudor decades brought many such men into prominent positions. The consequence must often have been a failure to uphold the rights of the bishopric. As Latimer commented in 1538, 'I trow no man, having the name of so many things, hath the use of so few as I, handled indeed like a ward.'[19]

The fixity of income from rents and the loss of authority over their estates would have been a serious problem for the English episcopate at any period. But in the Reformation decades the order had to face other particularly intractable financial difficulties which increased their existing woes. There was the general threat posed by rising prices, especially those food prices which were inevitably a large part of the episcopal budget. In 1552, when the consequences of the upheavals of the previous decade had become clear, Cranmer complained

19. *LP*, xx, ii, app. 14. PRO, lr 8/158; lr 8/165; sc 6/Ed. VI/240; c 1/file 1303/nos. 47–50; c 1/file 1332/20; c 1/file 1334/nos. 97–9. *LP*, xiii, ii, 1733.

to Cecil, 'I pay double for everything that I buy', and this despite some decline in the money income of his see. Canterbury was perhaps particularly exposed to the problem of rising prices: we have noted in an earlier chapter that its household expenditure represented a higher proportion of total income than that of the other bishoprics for which evidence survives. The Kentish manors provided some income in kind to help to support the archiepiscopal establishment, but food purchases consumed much of the revenues of the see, and many of those purchases had to be made in London at a high cost. Since Cranmer felt compelled for reasons of public policy to continue to maintain the same lavish establishment as his predecessors, he must have suffered the full effects of inflation. By the Marian period Pole was having to pay 750 Italian scudi, or about £240, per month in order to keep his household in food and drink, heat and light. Almost all the bishops must in some measure have experienced the same increase in costs as Canterbury: even sees such as York, Worcester and Ely, which could provide much food from the demesne for the support of the household, were obliged to purchase a part of their stocks, and to maintain the standards of their tables they would have needed luxuries not available from the home farms. It may not be particularly relevant to apply the Phelps-Brown price index, with its weighting towards food costs, to these bishoprics, but if we take that index and the income figures given in appendix I as an indication of the worst that the English sees can have experienced n this period, we could argue that real income had declined by 61 per cent between 1535 and 1553. Even if this percentage is halved to make allowance for provisions from the estates and additional sources of income, it is still clear that the prelates faced a major financial crisis which had its origins in inflation as well as in the depredations of the crown and laity.[20]

As if these combined difficulties were not enough to distress the leaders of the church, there was the additional burden of increased taxation to assimilate. The first-fruits which the post-Reformation bishops paid certainly had their origins in papal taxation, but they were now assessed by the more rigorous standards of the *Valor*, and the annual tenth was added to the crown's demands. These new payments created problems about which the bishops complained

---

20. Cranmer, *Remains*, I, p. 253. See above, p. 168. CCCC, MS. 105, no. 43. E. H. Phelps-Brown and S. Hopkins, 'Seven Centuries of the Prices of Consumables', *Economica*, XCII (n.s. XXIII) (1956).

more loudly than any others. Some of them found it difficult to raise
the capital necessary to finance their entry into their sees: this was
especially true of the new generation of prelates appointed in the
1530s. Thomas Cranmer had to be loaned money by the king to
pay his annates to Rome, and Latimer and Shaxton both had to have
loans, from, amongst others, Anne Boleyn. First-fruits and tenths
and the other costs of entering office meant that most bishops remained in debt for the early years of their episcopate. Shaxton,
for example, was still in debt three years after his entry into the see of
Salisbury and had to borrow to pay for his Christmas liveries. In 1538
Latimer wrote to Cromwell explaining that he could not afford a
generous New Year's gift because of his heavy charges. Since his
arrival at Worcester, £1700 of the £4000 he had received had been
consumed by taxes and repairs. After the payment of his basic household costs and the king's tenth he had little left for any other activities. Even a bishop who was not beholden to the leaders of government
for loans and could depend upon family support, as Bishop Goodrich
was able to do at Ely, might find that the expenses of taxation had
unfortunate consequences. Goodrich raised his money from his
brother but offered as security a 'great lease' on the undemised
property of the see – a lease that was never employed, but never
properly cancelled, so that it remained an embarrassment to his
successors.[21]

During the following decade the bishops' own problems in tax
payments gradually merged into the more general difficulties that
they encountered in acting as collectors of revenues to the government. These seem to have assumed major proportions during and
after the French wars of the 1540s when the clergy were regularly
asked for a subsidy in addition to first-fruits and tenths and when the
level of subsidy on one occasion reached 3s. in the pound. Not only
were the prelates required to pay these sums, they were also asked for
loans to help to finance the war. Most of the richer prelates were
asked for £500 each, and a total of at least £6600 was collected from
them. The unfortunate William Knight of Bath and Wells was rumoured to have considerable liquid capital and was asked for the
quite extraordinary loan of £3000. After some months during which
he struggled to raise the money, the government graciously reduced
its borrowing requirement to £1333, and this was duly paid. The

21. *LP*, ix, 203, 342; x, 1257 (9); vi, 131. Cranmer, *Remains*, i, p. 74. *LP*, xi, 1427; xii,
    ii, 1277. On the Ely loan see Heal, 'The Bishops of Ely', pp. 274–7.

impact of loans and taxation upon the revenues of the bishops during these war years must have been considerable: even those who owed no first-fruits could have found themselves donating between a quarter and a third of their net income to the government for several years in succession.[22]

With such a range of demands upon their revenues, the bishops might have been expected to look outside their sees for means of supplementing their income. The most profitable form of supplement, office-holding, was, however, virtually closed to them after the Reformation. Only Gardiner (under Henry and again under Mary), Goodrich and Heath gained high national office, although both Tunstal and Holgate held the presidency of the Council of the North. For the rest, unless they had independent wealth from their families, the only extra assistance came from the grant of benefices in commendation if their own revenues were obviously inadequate. The arrangement by which certain bishops were allowed to hold livings in commendation predated the Reformation: it had been relatively common early in the century for the papacy to permit the poorer Welsh prelates to retain an abbey or deanery after their elevation to the bench in order to support their households. After the dissolution it was no longer possible for the crown to reproduce this arrangement, but commendations were transferred from the abbeys to parish churches. In time it became a routine decision that all the Welsh sees except St David's should be supported in this manner. The bishop of Bangor was licensed in 1541 to hold three rectories and two prebends in addition to his see, and the Welsh church was embarked upon a course which led to a failure of parochial care and was the subject of bitter criticism from some of the Elizabethan reformers. The system also began to be used outside Wales: Bishop Hilsey of Rochester, who in 1535 complained to Cromwell that he had 'only . . . £200 a year to discharge me every way', pleaded for commendations. He was finally licensed to hold two livings, and a precedent was again set that was followed by all subsequent bishops of Rochester. Edward's counsellors showed signs of unease at this abuse of parochial resources. In 1550, when John Ponet was awarded a *commendam* upon his appointment to Rochester, the council decreed that 'henceforth . . . no Bishop shall keep other benefice than his bishopric only'. It

---

22. Scarisbrick, 'Clerical Taxation in England', pp. 41–54. F. Heal, 'Clerical Tax-Collection', in *Continuity and Change*, p. 106. *LP*, XIX, i, 272 (2), 1032 (5). Hembry, pp. 75–6. PRO, SP 1/190.

is not clear, however, that they adhered to their resolution: Ponet himself had some commended benefices when he moved to Winchester, and the Welsh sees and Carlisle certainly retained theirs even if they were not increased in number. The bishops of Chester also retained an ingenious arrangement which was not dissimilar; they secured for themselves a better revenue by diverting into their own purse £100 which had been designated for the payment of archdeacons in the new diocese.[23]

Commendams remained a last financial resort for the poor of the episcopal bench. Otherwise, most bishops struggled to manage from their own resources, and many obviously found it difficult to do so. Cranmer in 1552 argued that none of his colleagues, with one possible exception, had much wealth and that a number were scarcely able to manage. Bishop Bonner complained in 1558, 'I do spend a great deal more than is my livelihood', and he was better placed than many prelates, for few of the London lands had been alienated to the crown. It is impossible to judge from the surviving sources how many of the bishops were falling into debt: even the obvious cases of indebtedness to the crown under Edward are not easy to evaluate, since they include sums owing from the bishops as tax-collectors. But evidence of financial strain can be located easily enough. In addition to the specific complaints made to the crown and its ministers, there are the long leases already discussed, one of whose objects was probably the raising of income from fines. Then there are the one or two bishops, notably Voysey at Exeter and Anthony Kitchin at Llandaff, who virtually gave away their estates for some financial reward. Another way of raising money, the sale of wood, is not well documented for the mid-Tudor years, but the complaints of Elizabethan bishops in sees such as Canterbury, Worcester and Ely suggest that their predecessors had in some cases been exploiting the woodlands in an unjustified manner. Occasionally there is a hint that economic pressures were forcing some of the bishops back towards farming and a more rigorous exploitation of their tenants. Dean Goodman of Bath and Wells bitterly attacked Bishop Barlow for running flocks of sheep on the Mendips and for evicting poor tenants from their copies. The dean had no reason to love the bishop, but the substance of his

23. Hoak, *The King's Council*, pp. 84–5. W. Wilkie, *The Cardinal Protectors of England* (Cambridge 1974), p. 58. *LP*, XVI, 1391 (6); IX, 693. *CPR, Ed. VI*, III, p. 335. Strype, *Ecclesiastical Memorials*, I, i, p. 343. *CPR, Ed. VI*, III, p. 293. Haigh, *Reformation and Resistance*, p. 8.

charges sounds plausible enough in the circumstances of Edward's reign.[24]

Although actual evidence of economic difficulties can be adduced for only a few sees in these poorly documented years, it must be a reasonable assumption that most of the rest also suffered, at least in comparison to their situation before the Reformation. The weaker prelates responded by abandoning a positive and conservationist attitude towards their possessions: even the stronger and more devoted members of the order seem to have done little more than endeavour to continue traditional policies in difficult times. Only occasionally is there a hint that the bishops and their officials were beginning to devise ways of managing their new situation without resort to gross exploitation. The best evidence for this statement comes from London diocese, where three determined prelates each in his own way struggled to protect his inheritance. Stokesley made one of the firmest attempts to resist the encroachment of the crown when he tried to deny the manor of Lodsworth to Henry VIII, arguing that it had been given to the see by King Offa with the strict enjoinder that it was never to be alienated. The shade of Offa failed to frighten his royal descendant and Lodsworth was lost, but Stokesley had done his best for his estates. There are other hints that he or his officers had a positive attitude towards estate administration. The most interesting is that one of his leases, to a Stepney tenant, included a licence to hunt out concealed demesne lands within the manor and to eject the tenants. This predates by some years the national fever for concealment-hunting and indicates that the bishop intended to control his urban estates. Either Stokesley or his successor, Bonner, also received the interesting survey of the London demesnes, on whose concern for profit and the true value of the estates I have already commented. Bonner in his turn showed a close concern for his lands, even if family protection was one of his main objects. He initiated a number of chancery cases to secure the rights of the see and made energetic attempts under Mary to regain the manor of Southminster which Ridley had alienated. Both he and Ridley were careful to protect a valuable source of income which passed to them in the exchanges of 1550: the grain rents paid by the manors of Greenford

24. Cranmer, *Remains*, I, p. 352. Inner Temple, Petyt MS. 538/47, fo. 3. L. Thomas, *The Reformation in the Old Diocese of Llandaff* (1930), pp. 75–82. Wood sales at Ely in 1549 realised £147, as compared to the estimated figure in the *Valor* of £34; BL, Add. Roll 34274. PRO, SP 10/10/20.

and Stevenage and by the rectory of Ashwell. It has been estimated that in dearth years these rents may have been worth as much as £300 to the bishops, or almost a third of their net cash receipts. The London bishops even attempted to increase their rents in kind when some of the Fulham demesnes were re-leased for grain payments in the 1550s.[25]

It is probable that if the evidence for the mid-Tudor decades were more complete we would be able to cite more examples of attempts to counteract the effects of inflation and lay depredations. Cranmer and Pole at Canterbury both endeavoured to protect their estates, and again there was some movement back towards grain rents on the archiepiscopal estates, though it is difficult to trace their origins. Even clearer is the example of York, where, as we have already noted, both Holgate and Heath adopted a relatively cautious leasing policy. Holgate was also engaged in farming on a scale that must surely have been unique among his contemporaries. His inventory shows that he had a flock of about 2500 sheep, and since he had between eighty and a hundred horses and considerable quantities of grain in store, he must have had a very large and diversified set of farming arrangements. Holgate was certainly wealthy: he had lands of his own which yielded an annual income of £500 and must have been the prelate whom Cranmer had in mind when in 1552 he commented that only one of his colleagues had large revenues. It is important to note that, in the troubled years of Edward's reign, Holgate felt it was worth while to deploy this wealth for the benefit of his see when he purchased the manor of Scrooby to be granted to his successors after the death of himself and his wife.[26]

While the mid-Tudor decades are not therefore wholly devoid of examples of prelates who managed their financial affairs well and provided some care for their estates and some thought for the future of their sees, the circumstances of the age militated against such behaviour. Since the role of the bishops as spiritual leaders of the new church was not itself always clear and the initiative in religious policy lay partly in the hands of the crown and its advisers, their social and economic circumstances were inevitably insecure. Had

25. *LP*, xv, 942 (21). StPDC, Dean Sampson's Book, fo. 39. PRO, c 1/file 1332/no. 20; c 1/file 1334/nos. 97–9; c 1/file 1409/nos. 19–20. Alexander, 'Victim or Spendthrift?', in *Wealth and Power in Tudor England*, pp. 137–9. Mrs Alexander comes to similar conclusions in her article but emphasises Bonner's attachment to family interests even more strongly.
26. CDC, vi, pp. 40, 56. CCCC, ms. 105, no. 34. *CPR, Ed. VI*, v, pp. 298–9.

Mary lived longer, the effects of Pole's attempts to revitalise the ecclesiastical hierarchy might have done much to overcome this insecurity. It is less likely that even a strong Catholic hierarchy would have been able to return to the economic *status quo ante*, to make the English bishoprics once again as wealthy in real terms as they had been before the Reformation. The forces of inflation and the increasing power of the laity placed such an outcome beyond the reach of even the most tenacious church leadership.

9

THE ELIZABETHAN SETTLEMENT
AND ITS AFTERMATH

The accession of Elizabeth almost inevitably meant the end of the attempt to restore England to the arms of the papacy. The precise intentions of the queen, the degree of her commitment to Protestantism and the nature of the religious settlement she wished to impose have been endlessly debated by historians. On two topics, however, there seems little room for controversy: the queen intended to be head of the church once again, and that church would be dominated by the crown in all important matters of policy and finance. This second point was confirmed as soon as the 1559 Parliament assembled: the first government bill presented to it was for the return of first-fruits and tenths to the crown. The purpose was very practical, to help to solve the pressing financial problems of the new régime, but the move was also symbolic, for nothing better represented the subjugation of the clergy to the crown than the regular taxation first introduced in the 1530s. It was no wonder that the Marian bishops felt obliged to oppose the measure, which marked a reversal of the cautious progress towards financial autonomy that had occurred during the previous reign. The severance of all links with Rome by the Supremacy Act also had some political and economic consequences, for it returned to the crown an uncontested control over patronage within the church. As the settlement matured and lost the temporary character that it possessed in 1559, the principles of royal control over the fortunes of the clergy became an accepted part of the pattern of the church.[1]

For the leaders of that new church, royal intervention was the price that had to be paid for the English Deborah, for a queen who provided a bulwark against the forces of antichrist and against the threat of further exile. The reformers might differ among themselves, but all agreed that the protection of the faith was the first priority and that this rested in the hands of the monarch. Elizabeth had evidently

1. 1 Eliz. c. 4. On the reaction of the Marians see Jones, 'Faith by Statute', ch. 6.

been chosen as 'God's silly vassal' for this purpose, and no failure on her part, while she remained Protestant, could allow her clergy to withdraw their support from her. Thus the queen had immense advantages in her relations with her churchmen; she used their support but was rarely dependent upon it; without her favour their cause was lost. As the reign progressed she became increasingly aware of the advantages of a close relationship with her prelates, provided that this did not imply any sort of equality and provided that it did not interfere with her freedom to order the clergy as she wished. Elizabeth remained incontestable ruler of the church, supreme head in practice, even though she had hesitated to assume the title in 1559.

The 1559 Settlement therefore reestablished all the 'Henrician' controls over the English clergy and added to them a specifically Protestant dimension, which ensured the loyalty and cooperation of the new generation of bishops. But in ecclesiastical government it was not quite the Protestantism of Edward VI that was restored. The Prayer Book certainly derived from the reign of the queen's brother, but some of the innovations of that period were quietly forgotten. There was, for example, no attempt to return to the system by which the crown selected bishops and then appointed them without the use of the *congé d'élire* and the formality of appointment by the chapter. The commissions issued to the new bishops no longer included the phrase that they were to hold office during pleasure, a circumstance that was to create difficulties for Elizabeth when she later wished to rid herself of Archbishop Grindal at the time of the prophesyings crisis. The practice of the Elizabethan government might be arbitrary, but the ordering of the church was more traditional than might have been indicated from the changes of Edward's reign. As in the addition of the vestments rubric to the Prayer Book, the queen indicated by her choice of methods of appointing her higher clergy that she did not propose to indulge in rash experiment or to surrender to the example of the continental reformed churches. Decorum must be preserved and the traditional ecclesiastical structure maintained. Even at this juncture the signs were available to be read by bishops and laity alike: royal power might be used to exploit the church, but it would not be used to destroy the pattern that the queen had inherited from her father. The days when change had been enacted at a fast and furious pace and when the development of a wholly reformed church within England had seemed possible had vanished with Northumberland. It took many of

Elizabeth's loyal subjects twenty years to assimilate these basic truths.[2]

Meanwhile, one of the minor pieces of legislation in the first parliament of the reign indicated that the queen and her advisers were not wholly traditional in their approach to the property of the church. By 1 Elizabeth c. 19 the crown was empowered, during the vacancy of an episcopal see, to exchange impropriated rectories, tithes and tenths which it had accumulated since the Reformation for some of the temporal property of the bishops. A subsidiary clause limited the length of the leases which an incumbent prelate might make to twenty-one years, or three lives, *except* when the beneficiary was the crown. The preamble of the act naturally stressed the benefits to the bishops of these arrangements:

> The Lords and Commons perceiving how necessary it is for the Imperial Crown of this realm to be repaired with restitution of Revenue meet for the same ... be ... desirous to devise some good means whereby the revenue of Tenths and Impropriate benefices might be in the governance and disposition of the Clergy of this realm, being most apt for the same, in such sort as yet thereby the said Imperial Crown should not be in any wise diminished in the said restored revenue.[3]

Yet there is no doubt that the immediate purpose was to take quick advantage of the deprivation of the Marian bishops. In this act the Elizabethan government for once went beyond the behaviour of its Edwardian predecessors by providing a general framework for appropriations from the bishops rather than relying upon assailing individual sees. The reason is probably that it was easier to have legislative support for the alienation of land than to depend upon the cooperation of the bishops and deans and chapters that was otherwise necessary. Even with the act, there remained some doubts about estates that were taken without the traditional forms of consent. In the 1562 parliamentary session a bill was introduced 'for the assurance of certain lands assumed by the Queen during the vacancy of the bishoprics'. After two readings nothing more was heard of this bill, but as late as the reign of James I there was controversy about the ownership of some of the Canterbury lands that had supposedly been alienated to the crown in 1559. The preamble to the act should

2. On the nature of royal authority in the Elizabethan church see C. Cross, *The Royal Supremacy in the Elizabethan Church* (1969).
3. For some discussion of the act and its context see Heal, 'The Bishops and the Act of Exchange of 1559', pp. 227–46; J. E. Neale, *Elizabeth I and her Parliaments* (1953), I, pp. 73–5.

not be completely discounted as a piece of self-justification by the government: a part of the thinking behind the legislation may have been that it would strengthen the bishops as patrons and therefore help them to reintroduce Protestantism effectively within their jurisdictions.[4]

Contemporaries were acutely aware that the act was an unusual measure, a novel means of pursuing the old end of profiting from the church. Il Schifanoya, writing to Venice in 1559, commented, 'a statute has been enacted . . . limiting the revenues of the Bishops to (I believe) £500 annually'. A fortnight later his information was more accurate, though he still exaggerated the actual influence of the act. He believed that the bishops had already lost their temporalities and been promised benefices in return, 'which according to my belief they will never obtain, and they will thus remain very poor'. The ambassadors of the Catholic powers were, as we have already seen, prone to be alarmist about the collapse of the English episcopate, but at least some of Il Schifanoya's assumptions were shared by a well-informed Protestant, John Jewel. 'The lands of the bishops are to be made over to the Exchequer', he wrote to Peter Martyr at the end of April 1559, 'and the rectories which heretofore belonged to the monasteries will be given them in exchange.' Another of the former exiles, John Parkhurst, agreed that the results would be serious, though he did not understand the details of the legislation very clearly. He explained to Bullinger that 'the bishops are in future to have no palaces, estates or country seats. The present owners are to enjoy for life those they are now in possession of.'[5]

The purposes of the government can scarcely have been as threatening as the Venetian ambassador suggested. To start with, the act was so framed that it allowed the queen to take temporalities only to the equivalent value of spiritualities that could be offered within a prelate's own jurisdiction. Secondly, it assured to the bishops their own dwelling-houses and any demesne that was in regular use for the benefit of the household. The leasing proviso also assumed that there would still be lands for them to lease, and the caveat in favour of the crown would not have been made if nothing of worth was to remain in episcopal hands. Nevertheless, suspicion of the government's motives was widespread. Even in the House of Commons, whose

4. *Lords Journals*, I, pp. 583, 587. Bodl., Tanner MS. 127, fo. 55.
5. *CStP Ven.*, 1559–80, pp. 66, 73. *The Zurich Letters*, ed. H. Robinson (Cambridge 1842–5), I, pp. 20, 74.

members usually shared with the crown a deep interest in the profits of the church, the act did not pass without a division, and ninety members voted against it. Most of these opponents were probably hostile to the general direction of crown policy, that is, they were conservatives in religion, with some sympathy for the Catholic bishops who still at this stage possessed the estates. They could have included a scattering of men who were tenants of the bishops and preferred the relatively light hand of episcopal authority to the uncertainty of crown or lay ownership. There may also have been a minority of Catholics or Protestants who believed that the resources of the bishops would be best employed by their present owners in godly works. Jewel complained that there had been silence upon the encouragement of learning and the founding of schools. The reformers' doubts about the government's intentions would have been increased by a letter of William Cecil's in which he set out, for the benefit of the Scottish Lords of the Congregation, the priorities in which he believed: 'I like no spoil, but I allow to have good things put to good uses, as to the enriching of the Crown, to the help of the youth of the nobility, to the maintenance of the ministry of the church, of learning in schools, and to relieve the poor members of Christ, being in body and limbs impotent.'[6] The first two causes all too often meant that the rest were left unserved, and opponents of royal policy in the Commons may have been expressing their concern about this danger implicit in the act of exchange.

Did Cecil intend to disperse the wealth of the bishops in order to serve the causes listed in his letter? It seems unlikely that he intended drastic change, especially when the queen's cautious conservatism is considered. However, the government not only furnished itself with the means to threaten most of the temporalities of the bishops, it actually prepared commissions which, if executed in full, would have alienated about 60 per cent of the value of the estates. For reasons discussed below, this initial plan was gradually modified until the act finally had a serious impact on only a few bishoprics. It may be that Cecil, or Paulet, would have liked to seize the opportunity offered by the Settlement to reduce the bishops to dependence upon their spiritualities. Paulet, despite, or perhaps because of, his conservative views on religion, had little sympathy with the idea of powerful bishops. When the new leaders of the church came to him asking for more equitable exchanges, he dismissed them almost contemptuously

6. *Commons Journals*, I, p. 60. *Zurich Letters*, I, p. 20. *CStP For.*, 1558–9, no. 1086.

with the comment 'spiritual things be meet for spiritual men'. Cecil commended to the Lords of the Congregation the Danish pattern of reformation, in which the bishops were reduced to the status of superintendent and were given only modest incomes. This fitted well with the prejudices of their social class and time: there was a general reluctance to allow much power to the clergy, who had shown under Mary how they could escape from the clutches of the laity into high clericalism once more. Some observers recommended curtailing the wealth of the bishops as the best way to avoid a recurrence of this phenomenon. In 1559 Armigail Waad returned to the old 'commonwealth' ideals when, in *The Distresses of the Commonwealth*, he argued that the bishops should cease to be temporal lords and that they should live upon spiritualities – £1000 worth for each of the archbishops and 1000 marks for each of the rest. But such a neat solution to the problems of episcopal wealth and power, if it ever was in the minds of the framers of the 1559 act, had quickly to yield to the realities of Elizabethan politics, not least to the fixed view which the queen herself already held of the new hierarchy.[7]

The portion of 1 Elizabeth c. 19 which controlled leasing policy suggests a somewhat different interest, but one that was thoroughly compatible with the concerns of the crown and laity. The length of episcopal leases under Henry and Edward was a justifiable cause for anxiety for both crown and clergy, since one of the most valuable remaining assets of the church was being rendered almost worthless in some cases. The issue of curtailing lease lengths had already been raised by Edward VI, and the prelates could scarcely resist this attempt to protect their remaining property. Indeed, some of the clergy argued for even closer restraints than those imposed in 1559. Bishop Sandys, whose own record as a lessor leaves much to be desired, presented a paper to the 1562 convocation which urged prelates not to lease any land that had not previously been demised for more than their own lifetimes or tenures of their sees. A set of articles in similar vein, surely originating from a clerical hand, proposed that prelates should agree not to lease any estate in its totality or any demesnes for more than twenty-one years or three lives. Land held for the use of the household should never be demised, great timber should not be sold and no annuity should be granted for longer than the period of a bishop's occupancy of his see. These terms represent ideals which neither prelates nor crown were really eager to fulfil in the circum-

7. *CPR, Eliz. I*, II, pp. 30–1. *CStP For.*, 1559–60, p. 137. PRO, SP 12/1/66.

stances of the reign. Nevertheless, royal officers such as Cecil had a genuine interest in limiting indiscriminate leases and waste. In a set of notes written in the early 1570s, Cecil argued that there must be control so that 'the whole clergy would be restrained from alienation of their lands and from unreasonable leases, waste of woods, and grants of reversions and advowsons'. Thus in 1559, and again in 1571, when cathedral chapters were also restricted to twenty-one-year leases, Cecil began to resolve the problem which had worried him as early as the reign of Edward, how to prevent churchmen from wasting resources which could be regarded as part of the wealth of the crown.[8]

Unfortunately for the bishops, Elizabeth and her ministers did not perceive episcopal estates as a good to be conserved wholly for the benefit of the church. The exemption of the crown from the limitation on episcopal leases was a clear assertion of the royal right to control the flow of patronage from church to laity. It may be seen as one aspect of the consistent attempt to revive royal authority which had suffered such reverses since the last years of Henry VIII. There is some evidence that it was intended to use the exemption only sparingly, although by the 1580s it had become the most important and exploited feature of the 1559 act. But the intended use of the clause is less important than the fact that it was another clear demonstration of how Elizabeth and her ministers perceived ecclesiastical property. It reinforced the old assumption of the Reformation that the queen's unique position as head of the church gave her unique rights to its possessions and that it was she and her ministers who could determine the economic destinies of her clerical subjects. While the bishops and higher clergy might possess considerable formal and legal rights in their property, their political dependence upon the will of the sovereign meant that these rights offered little protection against her wishes.

The wide discretion which the 1559 act offered to the queen made her own attitudes of particular importance in the preservation or

---

8. *The Sermons of Archbishop Sandys*, ed. J. Ayre (Cambridge 1842), p. 434. PRO, SP 12/8/38. The proposal in State Papers is listed under 1559, but there is no conclusive internal evidence about its date. It resembles closely a document in the Cottonian collection which refers to an agreement between the queen and the bishop of Winchester, which is again undated. One possibility is that Pilkington, who was interested in protecting episcopal property and was offered the diocese of Winchester, was behind both projects. BL, Cott. MS. Cleo F II, fos. 44v–49v. BL, Lans. MS. 104/12. 13 Eliz. c. 10.

dispersal of the episcopal estates. There is no reason to suppose that Elizabeth favoured any fundamental change in the position of her higher clergy: it is difficult to imagine that she would have commended the Danish Reformation as enthusiastically as Cecil did to the Scottish Lords of the Congregation. Her reluctance to dispense with the traditional forms of religious organisation and worship is well known, and one of her main complaints against the first generation of her bishops was that they were indifferent to that hierarchical structure which suited her view of the reformed religion. Their successors met with more consistent royal favour, partly because of their modified zeal for the purification of the church, but partly because their leaders were careful to maintain the port and countenance which the queen considered appropriate in her spiritual deputies. Archbishop Whitgift, with his sixty well-clad retainers and formal courtliness, was always particularly careful to appeal to his sovereign's social prejudices. In the propitious circumstances of the later years of the reign, Elizabeth was sometimes moved to defend the privileges of her clergy, especially when the assailants were suspected of puritan ideals. In a general sense, the queen no doubt always believed herself to be the defender of the church, and her correspondence with the bishops is scattered with assurances of her tender concern. However, this gracious interest was given real political significance only during the 1580s. An interesting illustration of the new attitude comes from an audience between the queen, her councillors and some of the leading bishops in 1585, on the occasion of the presentation of the clerical subsidy. Elizabeth was irritated by the puritan agitation of the Commons and therefore disposed to be particularly gracious to the clergy, who gave their mites 'of themselves, not moved'. She expressed her concern at the attacks upon the bishops which had occurred in the House and assured them that the perpetrators would be called 'to an accompt', even those members of the council who were implicated. Although the interview did not entirely favour the prelates, since the queen accused them of failing to restrain dangerous preaching on the one hand and to provide good ministers in the parishes on the other, she clearly demonstrated her support for the prelates before an audience of councillors who were far from sympathetic. Often in the latter years of the reign the queen left her advisers in no doubt of her support for Whitgift's campaign for conformity in the church; positive tokens of her favour, such as his appointment to the council, were invaluable in furthering his

H

aims. This contrasts with the way in which she kept the first generation of prelates apart from the business of state and was notoriously
fickle in the help which she gave to the devoted Matthew Parker.[9]

Some part of this change must be attributed to the queen's recognition that the puritans posed a threat to her authority as well as to
her view of the religious settlement. Neither papists nor puritans, she
told her bishops in 1585, could be given any trust, 'for neither of them
would have me to be Queen of England'. The articulation of the
notion 'no bishops, no king' had to wait for Elizabeth's impolitic
successor, but there is no reason to suppose that the queen had not
understood the importance of the connection. Indeed, after 1583 she
seemed to some of her councillors to be exploiting and enhancing
the power of her prelates in a way that threatened the cause of
moderate reform. What Elizabeth never fully accepted was that a
strong episcopate capable of enforcing the royal will had to be an
episcopate that could command respect both spiritually and socially.
If the bishops were constantly at the mercy of lay patrons and of the
financial wishes of the crown, it was unlikely that they could exercise
authority with anything resembling the ease they had known before
the Reformation. The secular aspect of the queen's thought would
anyway have revolted against an episcopal bench such as that created
by Archbishop Laud under Charles I. She saw, or professed to see, no
difficulty in keeping her prelates under the close control of crown
and powerful laity in economic and social affairs, while insisting that
they played a strong and apparently independent role in enforcing
her religious settlement. Her skills as ruler, and the deep loyalty and
dependence of her churchmen, permitted her to continue to have the
best of both worlds, though there was no shortage of clerics who
suggested that the hierarchy could not long endure under their dual
role. Hooker best expressed the needs of the leaders of the church
when he wrote, 'Where wealth is held in so great admiration, as
generally in this golden age it is, that without it angelical perfections
are not able to deliver from extreme contempt, surely to make
bishops poorer than they are were to make them of less account
and estimation than they should be.'[10]

The queen might well have found Hooker's general argument
unexceptional, but as the ruler of a complex society she could ill
afford to take its central message to heart. Her prime interest was in

9. *CStP For.*, 1558–9, no. 1086. Paule, *Life of Whitgift*, pp. 78–9. PRO, SP 12/176/68.
10. R. Hooker, *Of the Laws of Ecclesiastical Polity* (1888), III, pp. 395–6.

the maintenance of effective political control and of her own prerogative power. In the circumstances of Elizabethan England this
necessitated the sacrifice of the weak to the mighty, or more specifically in this case the grant of episcopal lands to those who had a
claim upon the patronage of the crown. Royal resources were never
sufficient to meet lay demands, and the queen had no hesitation in
turning to the bishops for their assistance in maintaining the health
of the body politic. Any resistance on their part was, she chose to
believe, motivated by self-interest and was an affront to her majesty.
When crossed she could be, as one courtier commented, 'right King
Henry her father' and cause the bishops to tremble and wilt before
her righteous anger. A fine example of the biting sarcasm of the
angry queen can be found in the letter which her secretary was ordered to write to Richard Cox of Ely after he had refused a lease of
his manor of Somersham to Lord North. Smith wrote as follows:

> The Queen's majesty ... wills me to signify unto you by letter
> that her Majesty liketh your letter very well for the eloquence
> and the great persuasions which you make to persuade her
> Majesty to be the protector and defender of the church and of
> the possessions thereof... the which thing her Majesty hath always
> done, and no prince more desirous than her Highness to keep
> her Church and clergy in their right lands and goods ... But
> now seeing both you and almost all other bishops, deans and
> Prebendaries do of themselves so dispense to others by leases and
> fee farms the possessions of their Churches ... her Highness
> cannot but think much unkindness that to do the same to other,
> their wives, children or friends they make no conscience, when
> her Majesty requireth any thing for her servants ... there is such
> conscience and scrupulosity made and scripture ready to be
> alleged ... Her Highness willed me to write unto you to consider
> how great cause she hath to note your unkindness and unnatur-
> alness towards your prince, who hath given you the whole, and
> now requireth but part in lease.[11]

The demands for patronage were unceasing, and the behaviour of
the bishops provided ample excuse for the exploitation of their
property as a means of offering the laity satisfaction. The ingratitude
of the prelates towards their gracious sovereign, their greed on behalf
of their children and kin and their coldness in the service of the

---

11. *HMC, Salisbury MSS*, II, no. 339. Gonville and Caius Coll., Cambridge, MS.
   53/30, fo. 32v.

church became common themes in the repertoire of royal anger. Those close to the queen knew well how to stir her enmity towards the bishops and often only had to threaten the latter with her displeasure to gain their ends. The few such as Cox, Sandys and Matthew Hutton who stood firm against these pressures had to face searing royal criticism, though it may be significant that Elizabeth never forced the suspension or deprivation of a cleric in a dispute upon land. Few men, however, had the courage or the desire to put the queen to the test. Indeed, they may have regarded some degree of complaisance as the necessary price for royal support of their ecclesiastical policy. The leaders of second- and third-generation Elizabethan Protestantism – Whitgift, Bancroft and Matthew – certainly avoided direct conflict with the crown in economic affairs: they sought to achieve their ends by politic means rather than by the adoption of rigid and principled stands upon the position of the church.

The queen's behaviour towards the church must be seen in part as a product of the attitudes of her leading advisers and supporters. The delicate political balance wrought and maintained by a judicious patronage policy was a concern to all leading laymen. Exclusion from royal favour meant the incapacity to further one's own suits and those of friends and dependants and might lead on to the dangerous political suicide espoused by the duke of Norfolk. Noblemen and government officers inevitably thought it essential to be able to succeed in their petitions, both for their own financial advancement and for the maintenance of their influence. And the church was once again under Elizabeth an obvious area in which to seek power and profit. The bishops and higher clergy were now normally dependent upon the recommendation of a lay patron for their advancement, and the importance of the patron increased as the reign progressed and the pool of potential clerical candidates grew. The fortunate men thus advanced were naturally expected to show some gratitude to their patrons; they should not cavil at the leases and exchanges which were required of them through the crown. Cecil and Leicester, to take the two prime examples, each stood at the centre of a whole network of such dependent relationships, and regarded the rewards which the system brought to them as their natural right. There were few Elizabethan bishops who did not owe something to William Cecil, either because of his share in their advancement or because of support he offered when they were faced by other opponents. Even men, such as William Chaderton, who looked to Leicester as their principal patron often had to turn to Cecil for the furtherance of their career. In Chaderton's case two offices, the headship of Queen's College, Cambridge, and the deanery of Winchester owed much to Cecil's influence. The correspondence of the prelates abounds with references to the secretary as 'the only stay and patron of the church', and, indeed, one of his personae was that of the defender of ecclesiastical interests against the inroads of the puritans who looked to Leicester for support. But Cecil, who as a public officer was concerned for the preservation of episcopal property, saw no incongruity in exacting a price for his support in the form of leases and exchanges under the 1559 act. Though his demands never had the brash quality of those of Leicester or Hatton, this was more a function of the secretary's politic character than of any reluctance to profit from the church. The course of events, particularly in the second and third decades of the reign, favoured Cecil's cautious approach. He was able to increase his ascendancy in matters of patronage and as intermediary between queen and prelates, until in the years after Leicester's death he was unchallenged.[12]

The *status quo* on episcopal lands, as defined in the Elizabethan Settlement, suited the 'radical' Leicester as well as the politic Cecil. He too had special claims upon a group of the bishops and was less cautious in exploiting his position. It was Leicester who procured one of the most inequitable of the long leases granted by a bishop via the queen. His servant Thomas Sutton was given the coal-mines of Whickham and Gateshead in the bishopric of Durham and became in consequence one of the wealthiest men in England. Harington hinted darkly that he was involved in other schemes to take money and land from prelates such as Archbishop Young and Bishop Godwin. Samuel Harsnet charged that Leicester led a faction dedicated to taking episcopal property on long leases, and this fits with the known behaviour of the favourite as well as with the comments of that hostile source *Leicester's Commonwealth*. He was certainly the author of an interesting scheme of 1587 by which exchanges were to be arranged in the vacant sees of Durham, Ely, Oxford and Bristol. The exchanges

---

12. On the patronage networks of Leicester and Burghley see W. MacCaffrey, 'Place and Patronage', in *Essays Presented to J. E. Neale*, ed. S. Bindoff (1961), pp. 108–10; J. A. Berlatsky, 'The Social Structure of the Elizabethan Episcopate', unpub. Ph.D. thesis, Northwestern University (1973), pp. 61–9. F. Peck (ed.), *Desiderata Curiosa* (1732–5), II, nos. 4 and 5. On Burghley and Peterborough see W. Sheils, 'Some Problems of Government in a New Diocese: Peterborough', in *Continuity and Change*, pp. 169–70.

would have brought the queen £1200 in return for spiritualities of equivalent value, and Leicester generously proposed that she should retain £200 worth, while he took the other £1000. This was evidently a little too blatant for the royal stomach, for nothing more was heard of the plan, but it indicates very well the casual and calculating spirit in which a man like Leicester considered gaining at the expense of the church. His support for the puritan cause can be seen as offering a legitimisation for these attitudes, though in practice Leicester would have been as unhappy with a thoroughly reformed presbyterian church as with a powerful episcopate. The interests of the laity were best served by dependent clergy of whatever religious persuasion; the existing structure of the ecclesiastical establishment offered ample opportunity both to promote moderate reform through patronage and to gain substantial profits through the dependence which patronage created. Although the sincerity of Leicester's puritanism is no longer questioned by most historians, he was too committed economically and politically to the existing system to accept wholeheartedly the challenge posed by presbyterianism. Leicester's scheme that failed to find royal favour also suggests a reason why the leasing clause of the 1559 act achieved such prominence. Long leases allowed the laity to take substantial profit from the church without any loss to the crown and with only a very temporary need for royal involvement.[13]

The behaviour of the two great advisers to the queen was both a mirror of, and example to, that of the rest of the political nation. Differences of religious politics usually counted for little when there were opportunities for financial gain. Sir Christopher Hatton, a much more energetic champion of episcopal government than Cecil, forced Cox to surrender much of his London home to him and held 105 tithe leases. The earl of Essex was given much of the property alienated by the bishop of Oxford to the crown in 1589. Those who could not hope to command the ear of the crown directly sought to do so through one of the great officers of state or waited until services rendered entitled them to royal favour. Lord North, for example, had to wait until after he had completed an embassy to France before his suit for the Ely lands was considered. Those who had no means of exploiting the 1559 act either directly or indirectly might try other

13. Horton, 'Durham Bishopric Estates', p. 285. J. Harington, *Nugae Antiquae* (1804), II, pp. 231–3. *Letters of Thomas Wood, Puritan, 1566–1577*, ed. P. Collinson (1960), pp. xxxiii–xxxiv. BL, Lans. MS. 31/39.

tactics to gain their share of ecclesiastical property. Commissions issued to discover concealed lands, that is, lands which should have passed to the crown, usually as a result of the monastic dissolution, were a particularly popular form of profiteering in the later years of the reign. The bishops of Worcester, York, St David's, Winchester, and Norwich were troubled by the zealous questers for concealments, as were several of the cathedral chapters. At every level the spirit of plunder, the conviction that there was still an easy profit to be made from the church, remained alive and well under Elizabeth. Although the justification for the activities of the laity was now often couched in 'puritan' terms, it related more closely to a general anticlericalism that had become almost an automatic reflex for the landowning classes. The assumption, which rarely found full or explicit formulation, was that the clergy misused and abused their wealth and power, which therefore ought naturally to be handed to those best equipped to use it for the general good – the nobility and gentry. Armigail Waad argued specifically in *The Distresses* that the lands and titles taken from the bishops should pass to the nobility, since one of the reasons for the weakness of the commonwealth was the poverty of the leading magnates. Such arguments were sufficient spur and justification to the natural desire for profit. The concentration of patronage in the court, part of a conscious policy to increase the power of the crown, may actually have stimulated demand for the property of the secular church. The willingness of the government to take lands from the bishops and to exempt the crown from controls upon episcopal patronage was a signal that ecclesiastical property was still an acceptable target for lay ambitions: these could often more readily be pursued via the central agency of the court than through contacts with the individual bishops.[14]

If the laity at large sought no further for justification for demands upon the church than the sanction of the crown and a general mistrust of powerful clerics, there were those who saw in puritanism a more specific reason for attacking the wealth and ambition of the clerics. Puritanism was different things to different men, but one might place at its heart a strongly bibliocentric faith that sought to submit all actions and institutions to an exacting test of scriptural

14. Gon. and Caius, MS. 53/30, fos. 54–5. H. Lansdell, *The Sacred Tenth* (1906), p. 308. BL, Lans. MS. 27/73; 79/41. G. Williams, 'Richard Davies, Bishop of St. David's, 1561–81', *Trans. of the Hon. Soc. of Cymmrodorion*, 1948, p. 163. *CStP Dom. Eliz.*, 1591–4, p. 576. BL, Harl. MS. 589, fo. 92. PRO, SP 12/1/66.

purity. It was inevitable that many aspects of the Elizabethan church should fail to satisfy those who applied this standard, since political compromise had little to do with the advancement of pure religion. On the subject of the bishops and their wealth and power, the puritans spoke with a variety of voices, all of them in some measure hostile to the existing arrangements. One of the most common voices was that which continued the earlier tradition of Reformed Protestantism exemplified by Latimer, Hooper and William Turner. This view did not normally involve a total rejection of the episcopal office, but instead perceived the prelate as a preaching 'supervisor', set apart from his fellows principally by the excellence of his learning. The appeal of this notion was very broad: a number of those returning Marian exiles who were persuaded to take office in the church clearly saw themselves in these terms. John Aylmer, in his famous attack on the Marian bishops while still in exile, had urged the prelates to be content with a limited income 'as they be in other reformed churches where be as great learned men as you are'. Jewel hoped that the act of 1559 might be the beginning of such a ministry for the bishops.

> We require our bishops [he wrote to Simler in 1559] to be pastors, labourers and watchmen. And that this may the more readily be brought to pass, the wealth of the bishops is now diminished and reduced to a reasonable amount, to the end that, being relieved from that royal pomp and courtly bustle, they may with greater ease and diligence employ their leisure in attending to the flock of Christ.[15]

This version of the painful supervisor, although never abandoned by the prelates, became in its more limited form the property of their opponents. The puritans argued the impossibility of a bishop ministering by personal example to a whole diocese, and suggested various limitations on the geographical area served by each leading cleric. One of the most interesting proposals, which survives among Robert Beale's papers, argued for a diocese in which no cleric was more than three or four hours away from his superior and where the group of ministers could meet at least once a week for 'a lesson of divinity'. The new prelates would be paid a fixed salary of 200 marks besides house and some spiritualities from the revenue of the existing sees. The rest of the money would be spent on schools and exhibitions

---

15. J. Aylmer, *An Harborowe for Faithfull and Trewe Subjects* (Strassburg 1559), O 4, printed in Cross, *The Royal Supremacy in the Elizabethan Church*, p. 121. *Zurich Letters*, I, p. 51.

at the universities, and by towns for the better maintenance of the peace. Rather similar, though less elaborate, was a petition to the Parliament of 1587 that the title of bishop should be abolished, and there should be instead superintendents paid a salary of £200 with a limited group of ministers under their care.[16]

Plans to turn the bishops into preaching ministers without secular or judicial functions probably commanded wide sympathy among reform-minded clerics and laymen alike. So also did the attack upon the prelates for failing to live up to the standards of sober and godly leaders of the church. The criticism of the leaders of the puritan movement often has a touch of resentment, of the feelings of those who had failed to capture the church for their own religious standpoint. That earnest puritan gentleman Thomas Wood quoted a friend who claimed, 'Let the godliest man, and best learned within this realm be chosen, and put once a rochet on his back, and it bringeth with it such an infection as that will mar him forever.' No doings of the bishops, thought Wood, could find favour in God's sight as long as they continued in their great pomp and wealth.[17] It became a familiar theme of the puritan ministry that the failures of the Elizabethan church were to be blamed in large measure upon the greed for great possessions that had overwhelmed its leaders. It was greed that encouraged Overton of Coventry and Lichfield to make all sorts of mechanics and unworthy men priests, greed that made episcopal visitations so regular and yet so perfunctory, greed that led clerics to spend their time in the court rather than fulfilling their painful duty as preachers. In the Marprelate tracts the greed and incompetence of the bishops became the subject for some of the most daring and popular jesting of the century. Those ever-hated figures, the bishops' wives and children, were a particularly useful butt for this humour. 'To what end else is John of Cant unmarried', asked Martin Marprelate, 'but to provide for the bishops' children who shall be poorly left?' All this was undeniably entertaining and a valuable stalking-horse for those laymen who needed justification for their own profiteering from ecclesiastical lands. Moreover, all those with reformist leanings were prepared to argue in unison that learned ministers must be provided for the church and the abominations of

16. BL, Add. MS. 48066, fos. 2–15. *The Second Parte of a Register*, ed. A. Peel (Cambridge 1915), II, pp. 209–10.
17. *Letters of Thomas Wood*, p. 19. Professor Collinson suggests that the comment may have been made by Knollys.

pluralities and absenteeism removed. Since a full resolution of these problems would certainly have threatened the property rights of the laity in impropriations, it was natural that it was easier to criticise the bishops' failure to aid learning and the parishes than to attempt root-and-branch solutions to the financial ills of the clergy.[18]

These ideas were acceptable to a range of courtiers, gentry and committed clerical puritans. But the aims of many of the clerical leaders differed from, and went beyond, the concerns of the majority of the laity. A complete presbyterian system, as first advocated by Cartwright in the 1570s, would have allowed none of that modified episcopacy, that tidying of the existing order, that the schemes cited above were advocating. More important, dedicated presbyterians, whether clerical or lay, could scarcely have accepted the dispersal of ecclesiastical wealth into the hands of the laity nor the degree of lay control and patronage that the creaking mechanism of the Anglican church permitted. Prelates such as Richard Cox and John Whitgift were happy enough to see in puritan attacks only greed and ambition for their property. The radicals, claimed Cox, 'bawl out to those harpies who are greedily hankering after plunder and spoil . . . that the estates and houses of the bishops should be appropriated to pious uses'.[19] But most of the leaders of presbyterianism would have denied that they were offering any such encouragement to the laity. *The Book of Discipline* took particular pains to refute the charge:

> Our speeches against Bishops etc. pleaseth well those who do already gape for this prey and hope for this great inheritance. They thinking that we seek only that the Bishops might be put down wait for the like prey as they had sometimes at the overthrow of the Abbeys. For as for religion they care not what become of it . . . and would not stick to crucify Christ again so they might cast lots for his coat and divide his garments among them.

Their true intention, they alleged, was to convert the bishops' livings, and those of the cathedrals, to the uses of presbyteries, for the payment of learned ministers, the fostering of education and works of charity. There can be little doubt that these were the fixed intentions of those godly who wished to change the English church to a fully fledged presbyterian system. The help of the laity, and therefore some compromise with them, might be a necessary part of furthering this

18. *The Marprelate Tracts*, ed. W. Pierce (1911), p. 283. For a more detailed consideration of these puritan attitudes see Hill, ch. 3.
19. *Zurich Letters*, I, pp. 298–9.

scheme, but there were few of the ministers who were so naive or so desperate as to appeal directly to their greed. An exception was John Penry, whose passionate desire for the abolition of episcopacy led him to seek the help of the earl of Essex with the words 'I offer your lordship of her [the church's] spoil.'[20]

For the rest, it was probably fair enough of Christopher Hatton to oppose the presbyterian Bill and Book in the Parliament of 1586 partly on the grounds that it would threaten the property and vested interests of the laity. A convinced presbyterian, with his bibliocentric creed, his denial that forms of organisation and discipline were things indifferent and his stress on a learned ministry, ultimately offered less economic and social role within the church to the layman and could certainly be expected to take a stronger stand against expropriation than some of the existing bishops. Some of the leaders of Elizabeth's church in the last decades of the reign recognised in this 'stiff discipline' of the presbyters a way of recalling lay interests to their own cause. Richard Bancroft, who may as Hatton's chaplain have been responsible for the 1586 speech, was especially energetic in his pursuit of the extremist implications of puritanism. He urged that the best interests of the laity were to be served by cooperation with prelates and crown against the sort of radicalism that threatened to subvert property rights within church and state. Unfortunately for Bancroft's argument, there were still many resting-places for the laity between these two extremes. The claim that puritanism was subversive had little impact upon those gentlemen and others who saw in it a useful means to godly reformation and a sanction for their hostility towards affluent and powerful clerics.[21]

The practical consequences of these various attitudes were constant pressures upon the bishops and higher clergy. They could rarely depend upon the support of crown or influential laity for help in retaining their property and were constantly cast into a defensive posture, preoccupied by the need to maintain their estates and to justify their economic position in the eyes of the Elizabethan world. This need was recognised as soon as the act for the exchange of bishops' lands became a reality in 1559. The first five bishops to be appointed – Parker for Canterbury, Cox for Ely, Grindal for London, Scory for Hereford and Barlow for Chichester – showed none of the

---

20. LPL, MS. 178/62. *The Notebook of John Penry*, ed. A. Peel, Camden Soc., 3rd ser., LXVII (1944), p. 93.
21. PRO, SP 12/245/90. Bodl., Tanner MS. 79/fos. 133ff.

naivety of Jewel or Parkhurst. They recognised the legislation as a way of taking income from them without providing any corresponding relief from the multifarious obligations of an administrator-bishop. Much of their correspondence with the government proceeded upon the assumption that exchanges were inevitable and sought to mitigate their worst effects. But Richard Cox prepared a paper, perhaps as spokesman for the whole group, which set out principled objections to the crown's intervention. These resemble in some respects the arguments of the treatise of 1552 against the alienation of church goods. Kings and queens were designated in the scriptures to be patrons and nurses of the church, and earlier English monarchs had fulfilled this role in their grants to the clergy. The lands which they and others had given in their wills should not be alienated, for St Paul argues in Galatians that a godly testament should never be broken. Moreover, Cox argued, with a shrewd eye to the government's European preoccupations, any alienation of church land would be criticised throughout the Continent. The bishops had always played an important part in the provision of education and the support of learning, and they would no longer be able to do this if their property was taken from them. Their wealth had also always provided a means to relieve the crown when it needed monies quickly in a crisis; this source of supply would no longer be available if the prelates were impoverished. Finally, 'concerning the exchange of lands for impropriations it will be a grievous burden to take benefices impropered, because we are persuaded in conscience that the parishes ought to enjoy them, in such sort and for such end as they were godly appointed at the beginning'.[22]

Here was a collection of arguments that the clergy might use against the ranged forces of secularism and puritan idealism. The issue of impropriations was quickly overlooked and rarely raised again by the prelates, who had to stifle their consciences and take spiritualities from the crown or have nothing for their pains. For the rest, it was the argument about education and the encouragement of learning that proved most attractive to the leaders of the church under Elizabeth, both because of their commitment to the spread of the Protestant message and because this was the one reason for the godly laity to look favourably upon episcopal wealth. When Matthew Parker sought to justify the income of the archbishops of Canterbury he gave pride of place to the works of charity and the support of

22. *Parker Correspondence*, pp. 97–101. Inner Temple, Petyt MS. 538/54, fos. 49–54.

education that his income permitted. They represented only a small part of his expenditure compared to his household costs and fixed charges of about £2250 per annum, but they were disproportionately important to him as a leader of the church. The efforts of Sandys, Jewel, Grindal and even Parkhurst, on his limited income from Norwich, to help foreign scholars and further the work of the English universities suggest that the first generation at least took seriously the notion that their wealth was in trust to aid the reforming cause. The problem was that, given the other demands upon the prelates and the fixity of their incomes, their efforts must often have appeared pitifully small, especially when compared to the great foundations of the pre-Reformation bishops.[23]

The other obligation which Cox failed to mention specifically in 1559, but which was often employed in argument later by the bishops, was the duty of hospitality. It was in recognition of the importance of their role as hosts that the government excluded episcopal demesnes in regular use from those lands that might be exchanged under the Settlement legislation. It is common to find in episcopal letters claims that they would not be able to 'discharge their duties to their poor neighbours' if any more was taken from them in land or taxation. Such pleas might have had more influence on godly opinion if the bishops had not still been caught in the old dilemma that hospitality was enjoined towards the poor but was more often given to the rich and influential. Thus the author of the reform proposal which would have reduced the dioceses to a few parishes each bitterly criticised the higher clergy for 'maintaining a great rout of people about them like princes, apparelling them in chains of gold, silks and other costly apparel, feasting, banqueting and entertaining with great rewards and fees'. Yet the critics of the higher clergy were able to have it both ways, for those prelates who entertained their neighbours more sparingly under Elizabeth than had been customary were often accused of parsimony and avarice. This was a particularly useful charge with which to rouse the queen, for, like her father, she firmly believed that it was the duty of the higher clergy to be generous hosts.[24]

Those arguments most calculated to appeal to the godly, that episcopal wealth should be conserved for pious uses, therefore failed

23. *Parker Correspondence*, pp. 454–5. *Zurich Letters*, I, p. 264.
24. *HMC, Salisbury MSS.*, VI, pp. 64–5. BL, Lans. MS. 79/38; MS. 84/76; Add. MS. 48066, fo. 8.

(largely) to convince, because so little income was used directly for these ends. For many of the bishops themselves these objectives ceased to be the main justification for their retention of wealth. Men such as Cox and Sandys, from the first generation, pointed the way to another argument used by such later leaders as Whitgift and Bancroft. The church had to be wealthy to be powerful and had to be powerful in order to secure unity and order. Whitgift's well-known comment that 'the Temporalty seek to make the clergy beggars that we may depend upon them' demonstrates the fear lurking behind the careful arguments of Hooker. If the clergy were to command obedience they must have the means to enforce respect. This was the lesson which Laud was to assimilate, unfortunately to the exclusion of almost all others. As the concerns of the hierarchy changed, appeals to 'commonwealth' and Protestant sentiments were heard less often, and legal and scriptural defences of episcopal property gained prominence. Thus Cox opposed Lord North, and Sandys resisted demands for a lease of Bishopsthorpe, both on the grounds that the public credit of the episcopate would be diminished by a lay victory and that they could not surrender what had been given to them in trust. Towards the end of the reign Bancroft argued that the crown must, in its own interest, uphold the authority of the bishops against the laity and return to its traditional role as the nurse of the established religion. Such views could make little practical headway under Elizabeth, but they provided one of the foundations for the revived clericalism of the early seventeenth century.[25]

II

The use to which the 1559 act was put gives us a good view of the consequences of lay attitudes and of the difficulties the prelates encountered in opposing them. The immediate intention of the act was apparently to benefit from any and all episcopal vacancies that might occur as a result of the resistance of the Catholics to Elizabeth's religious settlement. This meant in practice that all sees except Llandaff could have been subjected to exchanges under its provisions. When the first exchequer commissions were issued during the summer of 1559 it appeared that this broad intention was embodied in their provisions. Commissioners were ordered to prepare to survey

25. White Kennett, *The Case of Impropriations Truly Stated* (1704), app. IX, p. 21. Gon. and Caius, MS. 53/30, fos. 31–2. Strype, *Annals*, II, ii, pp. 44–6.

lands within 'every such archbishopric or bishopric being vacant'. The surveys do not survive, but in some dioceses at least they must have been completed by September 1559, for on the sixth of that month William Ward was paid nine marks for his survey and valuation of Carlisle, and on the thirteenth exchequer commissioners were appointed to consider those certificates which had been returned. In this second commission appears the first hint that not all sees were to be subjected to royal demands: the general phrase about every bishopric was eliminated and replaced by the vague statement that the men appointed should do everything as they thought best. Meanwhile, the sees of the first five bishops chosen by the queen were the immediate concern of the exchequer; in commissions issued on 4 October, 105 of their manors and attendant liberties were selected for detailed survey prior to alienation. The choice of this number of manors suggests that in these dioceses the crown did intend to exploit the act to its formal limits, for Chichester, Hereford and Canterbury would have been left with little more than the estates regularly used by the bishops, and at Ely there was a constraint upon taking any more property, since the crown owned relatively few spiritualities within its jurisdiction. Yet even in these cases the exchanges which finally took place were more modest: after a long period of negotiation, Canterbury, Ely, London, Hereford and Chichester lost seventy-three manors, with an estimated annual value of £2899, rather than the £4180 of the original survey.[26]

The signs of retreat from an extensive use of the 1559 act can be seen clearly after the end of 1559. While Parker, Cox and their colleagues struggled to reduce the number of their manors committed to exchange, the smaller and poorer sees were completely eliminated from the projected transactions. Finally only Durham, Winchester, Bath and Wells, Coventry and Lichfield, Norwich and Worcester were added to the first five. Bath and Wells, Coventry and Norwich lost one or two manors apiece, though in view of their sufferings earlier in the Reformation this represented a serious loss. Worcester was finally compelled to grant away five manors, once again after an initial plan to take far more. Durham and Winchester were subjected to the greatest demands, since they remained among the wealthiest and best endowed of sees. James Pilkington actually refused the prize of Winchester, since he believed too much was to be taken from it,

26. PRO, sp 12/6/42; sp 46/13/16; lr 6/114/1; lr 6/115/1; lr 6/105/6. *CPR, Eliz.*, ii, pp. 33–4, 191–8, 224, 285–9, 306.

only to find that his second choice of Durham was to be similarly afflicted. In the end, although these two great bishoprics lost a considerable part of their revenue in 1559, in neither case was the transaction covered by the terms of the 1559 act. The crown withheld from each a large block of manors, but then promised to regrant them in return for a fixed annual payment, an arrangement which allowed it to 'forget' the obligation to compensate the bishops with spiritualities.[27]

Since the crown evidently gained substantial patronage and income in the first few years of the operation of the 1559 act, it is curious that it chose to limit its demands when it was formally and legally empowered to take so much more. There is no conclusive evidence of a change of heart, but it is possible to suggest some reasons why the legislation was used in a less extended manner than might have been anticipated. One was the strong clerical reaction that the attempted exchanges provoked. Cox was not alone in his objections to the principles of the act. Pilkington, despite his strongly reformist bias, quickly became one of the champions of a strong and affluent episcopate. In March 1560 Henry Machyn the diarist noted that the bishop-elect of Durham had had the temerity to preach at court on the theme 'the bishops and clergy to have better living'. Another staunch Protestant, the Frenchman Veron, had offered the queen the same message in the previous October. He had preached that 'the bishops elected should have lands as the old bishops had, or else [they] were not able to maintain and keep good house'. These general complaints were seconded by the struggle of the early appointees to mitigate the effect of the actual exchanges. Parker and his fellows produced a long list of complaints about the inequity of the transactions and suggested ways in which the situation of the bishops might be improved. In October 1559 the imperial ambassador reported that they were grumbling to the queen about their revenues and even beginning to preach against her, though this latter point was probably more the product of Catholic wishful thinking than a serious problem.[28] The more aggressive and tenacious of the bishops, such as Scory and Cox, challenged the commissioners at every point: the exchange at Hereford was not finally settled until 1562, after an investigation had revealed prejudice against the bishop by some of the surveyors. The

27. *CPR, Eliz.*, ii, pp. 323–5; i, pp. 355, 444. BL, Cott. ms. Vesp. f xii, fo. 129v. I owe this last reference to Professor Collinson.
28. Machyn, *Diary*, pp. 214, 227. *CStP Spanish*, 1558–67, p. 90.

government was anxious to appear scrupulously fair in its dealings with the prelates, and each dispute had to be investigated, causing extensive delays and increasing the transaction costs. Not only was all of this activity tedious and expensive, but it was embarrassing for the government to be so visibly at odds with those whom it had just selected to be leaders of the new church. Moreover, slowness in coming to agreement with the bishops-elect meant delays in sending them out with full authority to enforce the religious settlement. Cecil's correspondence in the latter part of 1559 shows that he was anxious about the failure to send bishops out into the diocese, a failure caused by a combination of the queen's reluctance to make decisions on appointments and the difficulties of implementing the act of exchange. By 1560 the task of enforcing religious conformity may have been considered more important than that of extracting a few more manors from the prelates.[29]

An even more compelling reason for the abandonment of wholesale exchange may have been the state of the episcopal lands. The government was aware in general terms of the long leases granted by the bishops under Henry and Edward, which decreased the opportunities for quick exploitation of the estates. However, close investigation by the commissioners could well have revealed a worse situation than had been anticipated: the smaller and poorer sees had so few temporalities that there was little to be taken from them, and elsewhere there was a preponderance of leases not due to expire before the end of the century. Most of these properties, while ultimately good and fineable, could not be expected to give the crown more than the fixed rents for years to come. That these considerations may have discouraged the exchequer is suggested by two specific cases. One of the bishoprics with a reasonable income, and therefore an obvious choice for exchanges, was Salisbury, and indeed the second list of bishoprics to be surveyed still included it. But Salisbury, as we have seen, had virtually been leased away by its Edwardian bishop: no large manor had been granted out for less than ninety-nine years, and the Elizabethan bishops were able to make scarcely any grants on their own account. Salisbury was excluded from the final list of bishoprics to suffer exchanges, and it seems likely that this reflects the crown's detailed knowledge about its circumstances. At Worcester the first list of manors to be exchanged included three that were let out for long periods of time, one of which, Richard's Castle, had come

29. PRO, sp 12/17/32; sp 15/11/38. *CStP For.*, 1558–9, no. 962. PRO, sp 12/6/13.

to the bishop burdened with a two-hundred-year lease. These three were excluded from the final Worcester exchange.[30] Even when the crown took lands which were not encumbered with quite such long grants, it was often difficult to realise more than a modest profit. As table 9:1 shows, the lands which were acquired in 1559 in the counties of Norfolk and Suffolk were by the 1590s yielding only a slightly increased profit to the queen. Since few leases even on these lands could have fallen in before the 1590s, the crown had to make its additional profit from casualties such as woods, which had rarely been leased on the well-managed Ely estates. These were no doubt sufficient to justify the effort of exchange, but elsewhere the incentive to struggle with the bishops was probably lacking.

Table 9:1 *Crown income from ex-episcopal property in Norfolk and Suffolk*

County	Under bishops	In 1560s	In 1590s
Norfolk	£544	£522[a]	£525
Suffolk	£238	£235	£277[b]

[a]By this time the crown had only a reserved rent at Shipdham, which yielded £21 as compared to £58 earlier.
[b]Excludes Wetheringsett, valued at about £25.

Sources: PRO, LR 8/158; LR 8/165; LR 8/243. The episcopal income figures come from BL, Add. Roll 34274 and *CPR, Eliz.*, I, p. 444.

The full enforcement of the act became even less attractive when compared with the possibilities both of the expedient tried at Winchester and Durham and of the leasing provision. The pension which was taken from Winchester and Durham demanded no expenditure or effort by the crown, allowed it to retain the spiritualities that still yielded some income, and offered the bishops the inducement that they would finally be able to make more from their lands than they were forced to pay to the queen. It may even have been the bishops who unwittingly suggested the notion to Cecil or Paulet: in their attempt to avert the exchanges, the first five bishops had offered money payments to the crown during their tenure of office, a total of £633 per annum. Their offer was rejected, but it could well have been the model for the next round of negotiations with the richer

30. SaRO, Bpric 460. *CPR, Eliz.*, I, pp. 354–5; II, pp. 323–5. The other Worcester manors in long lease were Fladbury, granted from 1558 for sixty years, and Withington, earlier granted out with a long reversion.

sees. The arrangements at Durham and Winchester proved doubly attractive, since the lands to be restored for rent payment were retained by the crown until 1566 in the case of Durham and until 1573 in the case of Winchester. Meanwhile, Horne at Winchester was certainly burdened with his rent payment of £400, and it seems that Pilkington was having to pay at least part of his much larger sum of £1020. Only ceaseless struggle and agitation by Pilkington ensured the restoration of his estates in the mid-1560s, and his tenacity made him unpopular with both the queen and Cecil.[31]

Not only did the pattern of exchange established in 1559 prove unsatisfactory to the government in the early years of the reign, it was only once again specifically invoked in the course of the time that Elizabeth was on the throne. There were a few exchanges of episcopal estates, but most conformed to the pattern of the earlier Reformation. In 1564 Richard Sackville gained from Salisbury the London home which he already occupied and gave in exchange Marston Maisie and lands in Ford. Ten years later the next bishop of Salisbury, Edmund Guest, alienated Sonning and Eye in return for property in Dorset and Hampshire. In the same year Burghley profited in an even more dubious way when Edmund Scambler of Peterborough alienated to the crown, for his benefit, the manors of Thirlby and Southorpe and the hundred of Nassaburgh. All these transactions proceeded without any evidence that the 1559 act was invoked. Even in the two major exchanges which occurred late in the reign, only one conformed to the provisions of the act. This was the arrangement of 1589 by which almost all the manors pertaining to the see of Oxford were taken by the crown on the eve of the appointment of John Underhill as bishop. In this instance the crown was scarcely doing more than confirm its own possession, since it had held the see for most of the reign and was to do so again after the death of Underhill in 1592. The final exchange was the great alienation of the Ely lands when that bishopric was again filled in 1599 after a vacancy of nineteen years. This arrangement had some claim to being covered by the provisions of the act but in fact violated a number of its clauses. Two of the usual residences of the bishops were taken from them, the rectories offered as compensation were not all within the jurisdiction of the see of Ely, and three manors were added to the spiritualities offered by the crown. The government was well aware that the agreement with

---

31. *Parker Correspondence*, p. 101. SRO, LM/927/4. BL, Lans. MS. 8/81. PRO, SP 46/27/fo. 84; SP 12/39/81.

the bishop-designate, Martin Heaton, did not conform with the details of the statute and could therefore be challenged in the future. Robert Cecil discussed the possibility of a separate piece of legislation to ensure the crown's possession, but in the end nothing was done. Instead he resorted to the older method of obtaining the manors with the consent of Heaton once the latter was in office. All the estates were restored to him, and he then conveyed the majority to the crown, the arrangement being sanctioned by the seal of a reluctant chapter.[32]

It can therefore be argued that the principal clauses of the 1559 act fell into disuse after the 1560s, remaining in the background as a threat to the prelates and a means of ensuring their continued cooperation in the crown's other schemes. There were occasional alarms that land was about to be taken: in 1588, for example, there was a full survey of the bishopric of Durham, and the dean, Tobie Matthew, could be forgiven for assuming that this was the preliminary to a major exchange. The reason that this and other incidents did not often result in the full-scale alienation of lands was that the crown had discovered in the leasing provision of the act a far more satisfactory way to exploit the possessions of the bishops. When the 1559 legislation exempted the crown from the restriction that all episcopal leases should be made for twenty-one years or three lives only, it gave a clear signal that the greatest fruits of the ecclesiastical estates could only be obtained by royal favour. It is less clear whether anyone in government had considered how extensively this privilege should be used. Since the first efforts of Cecil and Paulet were bent upon taking lands for the queen and for the augmentation of the royal estates, they may not have given much sustained thought to the matter. It certainly seems from the evidence of the early years of the reign that they did not intend that the leasing exception should become a licence for general profiteering by the laity. Between 1559 and 1573 only four long leases were extracted from the bishops and passed to laymen: two to Cecil and two to members of the privy chamber. Thereafter the pace begins to quicken: during the rest of the 1570s at least eleven grants were made by the bishops to the crown, and in the last two and a half decades of the reign forty-six grants have been discovered. The list is unlikely to be complete in the

32. *CPR, Eliz.*, III, no. 438. *Peterborough Local Administration*, ed. W. T. Mellows, Northants. Record Soc. XIII (1941), pp. lxii–lxiii. Willis, *Survey*, II, pp. 416–17. PRO, C 66/1525. For details of the Ely exchange see Heal, 'The Bishops of Ely', pp. 289–94. BL, Harl. MS. 7043. *HMC, Salisbury MSS.*, XIV, pp. 114–15.

absence of the printed calendars of the patent rolls after 1575. These sixty-one leases were almost without exception given to the queen and immediately reassigned to the true beneficiary. Most related to a single manor or other property, but there were a few multiple grants, of which the most notorious were Bishop Scambler's offering of sixty Norwich manors to Sir Thomas Heneage and Bilson's of 2000 marks' worth of Winchester temporalities to Sir Francis Carew. The giving of leases reached a peak in the decade between 1579 and 1589 when three sees, Durham, Winchester and Norwich, demised eighty-five manors and other possessions for periods which were rarely less than sixty years. Only the Welsh sees, Hereford, Bristol and Oxford apparently remained untouched, but they had little that was likely to interest a courtier or ambitious local gentleman.[33]

The beneficiaries in this great scramble for episcopal leases included the greatest men in the land. Cecil, Hatton, Raleigh and Thomas Smith all received their share, as did courtiers such as Heneage and Carew. Occasionally, these men were able to exploit their position by converting tenancy into outright ownership: Lord Howard did this at Esher in 1578, and Raleigh engaged in a peculiarly unsavoury form of bullying to liberate Sherborne from episcopal control in 1599. The greatest prizes were intended for their own use, but the centralisation of patronage in the court enabled the influential to act as agents for others. Thus the lease of Bishop Lavington, Salisbury diocese, was given to Burghley in 1573, but he immediately reassigned it to a Mr Dauntsey, a prominent local man. In other cases, such as Maisemore taken from Gloucester, the secretary was acting on behalf of another member of his family. When the queen made a direct grant to men of little national standing, as for example when a John Stockman, esquire, was given some Winchester lands, one suspects that either a courtier or possibly even the bishop himself acted as agent. It would be interesting, but a task beyond the scope of this study, to trace the permanent recipients of the leases: information upon the immediate beneficiaries is given in appendix v.[34]

The suggestion of episcopal intervention is by no means as unlikely as might at first appear: once the use of the 1559 act to extract valuable leases from them had become a *fait accompli*, some prelates at least

---

33. BL, Cott. MS. Titus B II/fo. 362. See appendix III below for a full list of these grants and the beneficiaries. Bodl., Tanner MS. 135/fos. 125–8. HMC, *Salisbury MSS.*, VII, pp. 220–1.

34. Loseley MSS., 8/21; 9/26. HMC, *Salisbury MSS.*, IV, pp. 507–8; IX, pp. 333–4. VCH, *Wiltshire*, VII, p. 200. CUL, Dd/12/43. PRO, c 66/1112.

seem to have accepted the inevitable and tried to turn the system to their own advantage. At a fairly early stage Matthew Parker, who was perhaps better informed than some of his colleagues upon the inner workings of patronage, conveyed to the queen his manor of Boughton and Blackburn rectory. In 1573 they were both assigned to Richard Wendesley of Derbyshire, who retained Blackburn. The assignment of Boughton in Kent, however, seems to have been a ploy to disguise its real destination, for almost immediately Wendesley passed the property on to John Parker, the archbishop's son, who used it to support his growing influence among the gentry of Kent. A few years later Wolsingham Park in Durham ended in the hands of the brother of Bishop Barnes, having been assigned to the queen's physician Roger Gifford. In this case Barnes does seem to have purchased the lease, but the bishop's land dealings are so dubious that it would come as no surprise to find that he was manipulating the system in favour of his family. Bishop Dove of Peterborough certainly managed to do so when, in 1601, he arranged that the lease of Eye for seventy years be assigned to his son via William Hake. And, beyond the strict limits of our period, Tobie Matthew arranged the most spectacular manipulation of all when he got Tunstall demesnes and various desirable tracts of arable assigned to his son Tobie in 1604. There is one other example in which the bishops concerned benefited in a manner which seemed more appropriate for the general welfare of the see. Bishop Aylmer yielded the queen a lease of Bishop's Wickham and Paddington for seventy-eight years, and, unusually, the crown chose to retain the property. Aylmer, who certainly did not lack enterprise in financial matters, then applied to have access to Wickham in order to use the house as a centre for reimposing conformity upon a difficult corner of Essex. It is not clear if he was successful, but his successor, Richard Fletcher, certainly prevailed upon Elizabeth to assign both manors to him once more. Even this arrangement, which brought the estates once more under episcopal control, had its dangers, for the grant was to the bishop in person and not to his see. It therefore encouraged him to use these manors to his private benefit and that of his family.[35]

These examples apart, the 1559 act became a major means by which the laity could continue to enjoy the advantages of cheap leases at

---

35. CDC, v 3, p. 80. LPL, MS. 737/17v. Horton, 'Durham Bishopric Estates', pp. 277–8. *Peterborough Administration*, pp. lxii–lxiii. Guildhall, MS. 12730. PRO, C 66/37 Eliz./pt 5.

the expense of the church. In the early years of the reign the queen and her advisers may have intended to exercise caution in dispensing patronage. There are several examples of royal letters in which deans and chapters were assured that there was no intention of making a particular grant a precedent for others of similar length. Thus, Elizabeth wrote to the chapter of Ely in 1579 that their confirmation of the lease of Littlebury, Balsham and Hadstock, for seventy-nine years ought 'not to make a precedent thereof for so many years'. Some of the first generation of bishops and the chapters also showed determination in resisting the royal will. The chapter of Wells took a particularly successful stand against an attempt by Lord Henry Seymour to gain a lease of Banwell: despite the spinelessness of Bishop Berkeley, it resisted several threatening letters from the council, and eventually Seymour had to be content with an annuity of £40. Cox and Pilkington opposed attempts to take some of their property with equal vigour: indeed, Cox's case became a *cause célèbre* in the 1570s and will detain us further below. From about the mid-1570s, however, the tide must have been turning against those who wished to conserve their possessions: the crown could ill afford to use its own limited resources to appease all the demands of the land-hungry laity and was more and more inclined to turn to the episcopal lands to supply the deficiency. Very few of the second generation of bishops were actually prepared to resist a demand for a lease that was strongly supported by the queen. Matthew Hutton took a principled stand against such grants, but was eventually persuaded to part with some of the archiepiscopal manors after his consecration, when the transaction did not smack of simony. Most others accepted the situation and surrendered with various degrees of grumbling: a few, such as Scambler, Barnes, and Watson of Winchester, actually seem to have thrust estates upon the laity, no doubt mindful of the sort of dictum later enunciated by Tobie Matthew: 'God loveth, and so do princes, a cheerful giver.'[36]

The crown impinged upon the lands and finances of the Elizabethan church in ways that ranged beyond the 1559 statute. The two most important were through the issue of commissions to seek out concealed lands, and through close control of tax-collection. The two can scarcely be compared in their effect upon the bishops:

---

36. EDR, 2/6/1, fo. 146v. *APC*, 1571–5, pp. 328, 354, 370. Hemtbry, pp. 146–7. *The Correspondence of Dr. Matthew Hutton*, ed. J. Raine, Surtees Soc. XVII (1843), pp. 93–5.

tax-collection was a continuous burden that engaged much of their time and energy, especially in the case of those who failed to pay all their dues. Concealments were a specific annoyance that caused deep anxiety to only a few of the bishops, though rather more general problems to the cathedral chapters. Nevertheless, concealments are worth mention, since they demonstrate once again the assumption of the government that it could make profit from the lands of the church without grave damage to the relations of church and state. The pastime of concealment-hunting had very modest beginnings in the 1560s, when the crown was shown that it could add small sums to its rent-rolls by licensing private individuals to search out lands on which it had a claim by virtue of the dissolutions or by virtue of the attainder of laymen. From the 1570s, what had begun as a quest for small parcels of chantry land or forgotten corners of monastic property had become a substantial business, with courtiers moving in to seek out larger prizes. It was at this point that bishops, deans and chapters became vulnerable, since the changes in their landholdings during the Reformation period meant that their tenure could often be queried on technical grounds. Whitgift was one of the first bishops to be annoyed. Some of those whom he classed as his enemies gained a concealment commission for lands formerly held by the duke of Northumberland and also attempted to prove that Hartlebury Castle was no longer a possession of the see of Worcester. Although they did not succeed in wresting it from him in the short term, the issue was still alive in the 1590s when Whitgift as archbishop addressed a sharp memorandum on the subject to Burghley. St David's, Winchester, Durham and York were similarly annoyed: in the last-mentioned, the concealers threatened the archbishop's possession of the lordship of Ripon, which had reverted to the see under Mary. Meanwhile, several of the new cathedral chapters had actually come near to losing their estates, and in 1593 the lower house of convocation addressed a petition to Burghley complaining that the concealers were ruining their fortunes. Convocation requested that parliament should provide the remedy by securing all grants that had been made in the Henrician period as a result of the act establishing the new bishoprics and cathedrals. Legislation duly followed with an 'Act for the explanations of the statute 34 Henry VIII', though it is a significant comment upon hostility between bishops and laymen that an anonymous diarist in the Commons could write of the bill when it was before the House, 'It was doubted by some that this bill went in affirmation of bishops, therefore suspected by some what purpose it had.'[37]

Even the 1593 legislation did not end the activities of the concealers. A few years later they returned with renewed energy to the bishoprics, especially the bishopric of Norwich. A technical fault was found in the letters patent by which the main episcopal estates had been granted in 1536, and only the intervention of Sir Edward Coke prevented the lands from being taken as concealments. Once again there had to be an act of parliament, this time in the 1597–8 session, when the possessions of the see were protected against 'a certain pretended concealed title made thereunto'. The problems of concealment-hunting continued into the reign of James I; indeed, the king's impecuniousness and the quest for profit by the courtiers stimulated the business for a time. But the bishoprics were not affected as seriously as it seemed they might be in the 1590s. This may be explained by James's strong support for his bishops but may also owe something to the fact that they held relatively little old monastic or chantry property, the obvious targets for the hunters. It may also be because the church was able to defend itself successfully against the major attempts to take its property that similar enterprises were discouraged. In this the higher clergy were certainly helped by some sections of the laity, for their tenants had a strong vested interest in maintaining the *status quo*. When the Norwich lands were threatened, the farmers of the bishopric addressed their own petition to Sir William Periam, chief baron of the exchequer, supporting the bishop's bill. These facts, taken in conjunction with the generally suspicious attitudes which the courts adopted towards concealment-hunters, help to explain their relatively low level of success. Yet the sanction which they were given by the crown to seek for all concealed property including that held by the secular church, and their consequent capacity to cause serious annoyance and concern to the clergy, is one more example of the government's reluctance to subordinate financial profit to the security and well-being of the church.[38]

The issue of tax-collection is altogether more important. As in the earlier years of the Reformation, the bishops remained responsible

37. On the development of concealment-hunting see C. J. Kitching, 'The Quest for Concealed Lands in the Reign of Elizabeth I', *TRHS*, 5th ser., xxiv (1974), 63–78. BL, Lans. MS. 27/72, 27/73. Inner Temple, Petyt MS. 538/38/fos. 95–8, BL, Lans. MS. 79/41. Kitching, 'Concealed Lands', pp. 74–5. 35 Eliz. I c. 3. BL., Cott. MS. Titus F II, fos. 95–5v. I owe this last reference to Mr Leslie Jenkins.
38. E. Coke, *Institutes of the Laws of England* (1797), IV, pp. 76, 256. 39 Eliz. I c. 22. House of Lords Record Office, Main Paper Collection 1596–1607, fo. 59.

for the return to the exchequer of the tenths of the clergy and of subsidies. The only exceptions were the archbishop of Canterbury and the bishop of Ely, both of whom had been granted the tenths of their own clergy as part of the 1559 exchanges. This duty continued to prove burdensome and thankless, largely because it forced the bishops to depend upon deputies whose honesty and efficiency were always in doubt. Many of them also had to struggle to produce their own first-fruits and tenths, and the general consequence was that many ended in debt to the crown. Some specific examples will be considered in detail in a subsequent chapter; here it is just worth making the general observation that the difficulties of the bishops were often increased by the attitude of the government. Under Edward and Mary, despite occasional major efforts to call in debts, financial administration had dealt fairly leniently with the prelates. Undercollectors might occasionally end in prison, as did John Payne of Bath and Wells, but there is no evidence that the bishops ever had their goods distrained for the payment of debts. In the revived exchequer of Elizabeth's reign, however, there was a determination to make them pay their full dues or suffer the consequences. Few of those who fell into debt were allowed to escape without distraint of goods, either in life or after death. The surviving correspondence to and from the exchequer is full of the appeals by the bishops against the decisions of the lord treasurer and his subordinates. The common pattern was that any bishop unable to produce at least half his subsidy or tenth within a term of the due date had writ and process made out against him for seizure of lands and goods to pay the debt. When Overton of Coventry and Lichfield accused Thomas Fanshawe, the remembrancer of the exchequer, of being unjust in making out process against him in 1594, the latter responded that he was only obeying the orders of the lord treasurer and following the practice 'as in former times had been used'. By then the pattern of making distraint upon episcopal goods for unpaid debts was commonplace: Fanshawe commented that writs had also been issued 'against sundry others no less reverend than himself'. Many of the bishops continued to believe that their undercollectors were responsible for debts which in fact redounded upon them or upon their executors after death. the only sure way for a prelate to escape this responsibility was to have a legally watertight bond to save him harmless from the collector, and such a document proved difficult to secure.[39]

39. The correspondence upon episcopal debts is to be found largely in the special

It may have become a commonplace routine of the exchequer to issue writs against defaulting prelates, but for the clerics concerned the activity never lost its terror. Bishop Godwin of Bath and Wells demonstrated why when he pleaded not to have process sent against him for another term: 'Process is so terrible to me, *and so disgraceful to my place*, the credit whereof I would fain maintain for the bettering of my service' (my italics). The treatment of a bishop as a common debtor, even if the crown did not actually throw him into prison, was incompatible with his attempts to maintain dignity and authority within his see. The full consequences of such behaviour can be seen in the famous case of Bishop Parkhurst, discussed in detail below. Parkhurst found himself responsible for very large arrears, in taxation accumulated by his undercollector, and was forced to agree to repay the exchequer, an agreement which left him with scarcely any income during the last years of his life. He retired to live quietly and cheaply upon his rural manor of Ludham, and his capacity to intervene effectively in the affairs of his see was much diminished. If few cases ended quite so dramatically as Parkhurst's, there were plenty of bishops who lived in a state of unease and anxiety because of their own inability to pay the crown, the dubious behaviour of their deputies or threatening noises from the exchequer. One of the letters of Robert Horne of Winchester shows the sort of problems that could arise. In 1574 he wrote to the exchequer claiming that he was entitled to an acquittance for his tenths. However, this had been denied him because he was engaged in a dispute about payments from the Wimbledon area of the diocese, which was an archiepiscopal peculiar, and because a Mr Earith, who had a commission for the collection of arrears, alleged that the bishop himself was in debt to the crown. The rights and wrongs of Horne's case are less relevant than the confusion that it reveals. The bishop seemed genuinely muddled about the sums he owed and was harassed by various functionaries who had a vested interest in passing the blame on to him. In the short term Horne was given the benefit of the doubt by the exchequer, but he failed to clarify his responsibilities and died heavily in debt to the crown, a debt that then became a burden on his estate.[40]

In the 1570s Burghley, at the head of the revived exchequer, was

---

Exchequer section of the State Papers: PRO, SP 46. PRO, SP 46/39/fo. 33.
40. PRO, SP 46/34/fo. 257. On Godwin's debts see Hembry, p. 176. *The Letter Book of John Parkhurst*, ed. R. Houlbrooke, Norfolk Rec. Soc. XLIII (1974/5), pp. 25–30. BL, Lans. MS. 18/25.

often willing to help individual bishops by deferring the payment of their debts or by pursuing their undercollectors instead. But he was, above all, determined that the crown should not lose revenue to which it was entitled through the negligence or corruption of any collectors, whether lay or clerical. He was faced by a group of bishops, many of whom had little administrative experience before they entered their dioceses and some of whom undoubtedly thought their secular duties a hindrance to the labour of enforcing the Reformation. In the field of taxation they did not even have the consolation of those lay collectors the sheriffs, who only held office temporarily. It is sometimes difficult to sympathise with the moans of some of the persistent offenders, such as Overton of Coventry and Lichfield or Cheyney and Bullingham of Gloucester, whose problems with taxation appear in the exchequer correspondence for decade upon decade. Such men could make the normally urbane lord treasurer lose his cool and courteous manner and complain that he was constantly troubled by the bishops. Nevertheless, in these cases a weak bishop only compounded an underlying problem: that the crown was expecting its senior clerics to discharge their secular duties as effectively as they had done before the Reformation, but that it failed to offer them the support which would have given them the authority and enthusiasm to fulfil those duties. When it is remembered that much the same was true in ecclesiastical administration, it is small wonder that a man such as Parker could lament his lot, complain of the attitude of the queen and wish to be a private man again, 'were it not for conscience and duty'.[41]

---

41. *Parker Correspondence.* p. 158.

10

THE SOCIAL RESPONSIBILITIES OF THE ELIZABETHAN BISHOPS

The foregoing analysis of the behaviour of the laity and the relative subservience of the episcopate naturally leads on to two further questions. Why did the bishops not manage to cope more effectively with the pressures upon them, and how far was their role as spiritual leaders of the realm damaged by the attitudes and behaviour of the laity? The second question cannot be answered in any depth here, but it is worth making a few comments before returning to the role of the bishops in society. The church had at its disposal a concept which offered some help in separating the political and economic conflicts of the reign from the essential spiritual task of enforcing the Reformation. This was the notion of *adiaphora*, things indifferent, which had its origins in the very earliest stages of the breach with Rome, but which developed under Elizabeth into an idea which protected the clerical establishment from the demands of the queen and the criticisms of the puritans. Provided that no crucial issue of faith was at stake, the church should accept the guidance, or indeed the domination of the Supreme Governor, who had the right to determine external forms of religious observance, the general structure of the church and so on. Royal control was appropriate on questions of vestments, uniformity of worship and the financial welfare of the clergy, though it was desirable that the advice of the clergy should be sought.

Yet acceptance of this control and of its unpleasant consequences did not imply a change of values on those matters that were not indifferent – the central tenets of the Protestant faith. The ideal of a reformed polity inspired not only the first generation of bishops, many of whom had returned from exile and seen the churches of the Continent, but also those of the second and third generations who are sometimes loosely classified as reactionary because of their opposition to puritanism. Whitgift and Bancroft, just as much as Grindal and Parkhurst, emphasised the importance of the pastoral duties of the prelate, his obligation to be a careful preacher and educator and his responsibility to provide a reformed and well-trained body of clerics. Nor was it only the outstanding names who took their spiritual duties seriously and struggled to make the Reformation a reality throughout the realm. Despite the charges of the puritans and the alarming weakness of a few bishops, as a group the Elizabethans seem to have had more success in providing a pastoral ministry than any of their sixteenth-century predecessors. Most were perforce resident in their sees but made a virtue of necessity by regular preaching, some personal supervision of visitation and the careful examination of ordinands. This direct commitment to the work of conversion is perhaps more characteristic of the first prelates than of their successors: Cox, Horne and Grindal, for example, were enthusiastic visitors, and Jewel and Horne presided in person over their consistory courts. Nevertheless, if later bishops did not always appear in person on such occasions, they were usually careful to choose deputies who would perform their tasks to the same standards. Even weak men such as Scambler, Overton and John Bullingham aspired to these standards and were earnest in their enthusiasm for reform, though hampered by their own ineptitude and by the web of vested interests that they encountered in their sees. The real renegade among the Elizabethans, Marmaduke Middleton, was eventually removed from his diocese of St David's partly because his brash zeal for reform took no account of the sensibilities of the souls under his care.[1]

The social position of the episcopate proved at best a nuisance and at worst a total impediment to the performance of these spiritual tasks. The laity often demanded of the leaders of the church contradictory behaviour. On the one hand, the growing influence of puritanism pointed towards a belief that the bishops should have only a bare sufficiency for their maintenance, that they should derive their authority only from their own qualities as preachers and supervisors. On the other, the bishops were still regarded as a fount of hospitality and charity and as the essential centre of systems of local patronage. It is significant that many of the conflicts between the gentry and the bishops arose from the failure of the latter to oil the wheels of local patronage, to buy the support of the former with leases and grants of office. Since most of the prelates now had fewer

---

1. On the importance of the concept of *adiaphora* see W. Haugaard, *Elizabeth and the English Reformation* (Cambridge 1968). The pastoral activity of the bishops is discussed in R. Houlbrooke, 'The Protestant Episcopate, 1547–1603', in *Church and Society in England: Henry VIII to James I*, ed. F. Heal and M. R. O'Day (1977), pp. 86–97; F. O. White, *Lives of the Elizabethan Bishops* (1898).

resources available and their use of their own possessions was circum-scribed by legislation, they found it more difficult to satisfy the demands made upon them. Moreover, the issues of patronage and hospitality achieved greater prominence now that the bishops were resident upon their sees and therefore subject to the close observation of their neighbours. The very enthusiasm for reform demonstrated by many of the bishops could provoke a crisis: Bishop Curteys of Chichester, for example, raised a storm among the local gentry of Sussex by his tactless aggression towards Catholics and crypto-Catholic families. Here religious and social problems intermingled: the bishop was attacked for his untimely zeal but also for his social presumption in assailing the natural rulers of the country. Examples could be multiplied from various parts of the country of the tendency of the gentry to cling together, whatever their views on religion, in the face of too aggressive a policy by the bishops. Bishop Cox en-countered this problem with both recusants and puritans: the Catho-lic Parys family found support and protection from the bishop's great enemy, Lord North, and the radical gentlemen of Ely were loud in their assaults upon his ecclesiastical leadership. In the circumstances of Elizabethan England, where religious opinion was sharply polarised, the bishops were destined to offend some group. And when they caused offence it was easy to charge them with some failure: failure to live the life of a reformed pastor and painful supervisor or failure to provide the hospitality and care which the laity fondly imagined had been characteristic of the leaders of the 'old' church. No wonder that tact and discretion came to be valued as essential qualities of the successful bishop or that so many were found wanting in this respect.[2]

When contemporaries sought one reason for the failures and difficulties of the prelates they instinctively turned to clerical marriage. The institution which had been a source of embarrassment under Edward VI became a major problem as episcopal families matured, widows had to be cared for and the status of the new arrivals estab-lished. Some of the conservative dislike of clerical marriage that we have noted under Edward VI persisted into Elizabeth's reign. Sir John Bourne, Mary's former secretary of state, who had a series of conflicts with Edwin Sandys at Worcester, was proud to acknowledge that he was a 'misliker of priests' marriage'. Bourne was, of course,

2. R. Manning, *Religion and Society in Elizabethan Sussex* (Leicester 1969), pp. 91–112. Heal, 'The Bishops of Ely', pp. 137–8.

a misliker of reform in general, but his distrust of the wives of clergy was shared by some of those more sympathetic to the new religious order. A private legislative draft of 1575, which is full of admirable Protestant sentiment, advocated that the wives of bishops should be confined to works of charity and the management of their maid-servants 'And not to intrude . . . themselves into the worldly affairs of any such seat of government as now far otherwise at this present is reported to be by the said matrons'. The same note of hostility towards the married clergy appears in the attacks upon such re-doubtable matrons as Mrs Cox, Mrs Freke and Mrs Cooper. The behaviour of these ladies may well have deserved some criticism, but in speaking against them their accusers indulged in a licence and freedom that would not have been permitted against other women of high station.[3]

Thus, Elizabeth's own views on married prelates only gave extreme expression to an undercurrent of hostility towards this new institution which was of benefit to few but the clergy themselves. There can certainly be no doubt of Elizabeth's own consistent antipathy. Her acceptance of Parker and of the leading exiles as her first bishops resolved the settlement in favour of clerical marriage, but she hedged this concession with restrictions and then attempted to impose further constraints with her injuction banning families from colleges and cathedral precincts. In 1561, when this injunction was issued, Cecil believed that she came close to prohibiting the institution: 'Her Majesty', he wrote to Parker, 'continueth very evil affected to the state of matrimony in the clergy. And if [I] were not therein very stiff, her Majesty would utterly and openly condemn and forbid it.' The queen could scarcely have gone so far without questioning the validity of the whole Settlement, and after the first few years of the reign she spoke less often against the principle of clerical marriage. But she continued to mislike the practice, especially among her bishops, and those who were rash enough to remarry while in office incurred her particular displeasure. The courtly Fletcher, who had been one of the few to enjoy her real favour and to gain rapid promo-tion as a consequence, suffered one of the most dramatic falls from grace when he took as second wife the widow of a London merchant. He was actually suspended from his duties as bishop of London for a time and was excluded from court, a fate which can only be compared

---

3. PRO, sp 12/28/38; sp 15/24/8. BL, Lans. ms 20/72. *HMC, Salisbury MSS.*, xiii, p. 208. PRO, sp 15/25/fos. 258, 275, 279.

with that of Archbishop Grindal after the prophesyings controversy.[4]

The queen had a rooted objection of principle to clerical marriage, but for many of the laity marriage merely made the higher clergy more vulnerable to their criticisms. This was especially true as the Elizabethan Settlement endured and the marriage of the clergy became more generally accepted as a social fact. Any sign of resistance to the demands of the laity could now be attributed to the self-interest of the clergy, to the desire to protect and enrich their families. Very few of the leading married prelates avoided some accusation of abusing their position for the benefit of their families. Edwin Sandys was pursued throughout his career by controversy about his generosity to his children; so were Aylmer at London, Cox at Ely, Scory at Hereford, Overton at Lichfield and William Morgan at St Asaph. Pilkington at Durham and Horne at Winchester allegedly invested 'large sums of money' in the marriage of their daughters, and even the cautious Parker was suspected of undue favouritism to his sons, and of destroying woods for the benefit of his family. Many of these accusations came from hostile witnesses, whose own plans for profit had been checked by the bishops, but the chorus of condemnation also included the judicious Burghley and other government officers. In 1572 Burghley was so concerned about the spoil of the estates of the clergy for the benefit of their families that he proposed the following reform in a private memorandum:

> The whole clergy would be restrained from alienation of their lands and from unreasonable leases, waste of wood and grants of reversion and advowsons to any persons, and namely to their wives and children or to others for their use. An Inquisition would be made in the register books, what number of grants have been made within these v or vi years to the disherison of the church, and a resumption would be made thereof by parliament.[5]

As a public officer he took no action along the lines proposed here, though the idea may have been remembered a few years later when the spoil which the bishops had made of their woods was the subject of just such an enquiry.

There can be little doubt that much of the mud thrown at the bishops for their behaviour as husbands and fathers stuck quite correctly. The activity of Sandys, who at York alone managed to give

4. *Parker Correspondence*, pp. 146, 148. White, *Elizabethan Bishops*, p. 312.
5. P. Heylyn, *Examen Historicum* (1659), p. 103. *Letters of Thomas Wood*, pp. 19–20. *Parker Correspondence*, pp. 371–3. BL, Lans. MS. 104/12.

I

his family leases and offices with an estimated annual value of £1700, was not calculated to inspire confidence in clerical marriage. Cox and Aylmer both pursued estate policies and accumulated wealth largely to help their families to important places within society. Cox knew that twenty-one-year leases were more advantageous to his successors than three-life ones, whose term was uncertain, but he gave three-life leases in abundance to his family, while reserving those for term of years to outsiders. The dean and chapter of Lichfield actually refused to confirm some of the grants that William Overton had made to his son Plasted, 'because we fear all will to wrack'. The Godwin family at Bath and Wells proved themselves very adept at exploiting the physical weakness of their father to gain a spectacular array of advantageous leases and offices. Bishop Pilkington paid one of his daughters a dowry of £800, a substantial sum, though rumour so exaggerated his generosity that Thomas Fuller alleged he gave £10,000, and even the bishop's Laudian defender, Peter Heylyn, suggested that the two daughters shared £8000. A few episcopal children also seem to have consumed a large portion of their fathers' income during life. Sylvanus Scory was one such classic wastrel, as was the younger Tobie Matthew, who extracted large sums from his father, even if the £14,000 traditionally claimed is an exaggeration. Henry Cotton's son John was another 'who hath always run an evil course to his own overthrow'. These specific and well-known abuses may be placed alongside the findings of Professor Berlatsky that twenty-four of the seventy-eight episcopal sons for whom accurate information is available established themselves among the local gentry and that of the twenty-eight who entered the church, only one remained at the level of the ordinary parochial clergy.[6]

Some of this behaviour undoubtedly suggests a misuse of the public resources of the church. Nevertheless, it is important to recognise the nature of the dilemma facing the bishops and not to judge them solely by reference to Aylmer and Sandys. It must be noted that the bishops were strongly disposed towards matrimony: among the seventy-six serving during the reign, only eighteen are definitely known to have been single, with three others whose marital status is

6. Borthwick Inst., R/Bsp, 28/18. EDR, 2/6/1. BL, Lans. MS. 36/55. Hembry, pp. 154ff. Borthwick Inst., Chancery 1581. T. Fuller, *Church History of Britain* (1845), IV, p. 399. Heylyn, *Examen Historicum*, p. 103. PRO, SP 12/180/1. Anthony à Wood, *Athenae Oxonienses*, ed. P. Bliss, 4 vols. (1813–20), III, p. 876. PROB, 11/125/49. J. A. Berlatsky, 'Marriage and Family in a Tudor Elite', *Journal of Family History*, III (1978), 12.

doubtful. Eleven of them were prepared for the hazard of a second marriage, despite the queen's known disapproval. Few of the prelates gained a higher social status as a result of marriage: the scattering of the children of minor gentlemen or wealthy merchants among the episcopal wives does not disguise the fact that most were of uncertain, and probably humble, origin. Some bishops certainly derived financial advantages from matrimony: Still of Bath and Wells owed at least part of his fortune to two good alliances with a clothier's daughter and the offspring of a knight, and the wives of John Coldwell and Henry Cotton both brought substantial dowries to their husbands. But in general the bishops must have married for reasons of affection and comfort, and the few harridans and Mrs Proudies among their wives do not necessarily gainsay the advantages for most of them. It may even be that, as William Harrison suggests of the lower clergy, the organisation of episcopal households benefited from the appearance of wives: 'their meat and drink is more orderly and frugally dressed, their furniture of household more convenient and better looked unto . . . than heretofore they have been'. The gentleman who drafted the legislative proposal of 1575 and who was probably a member of an episcopal household, clearly resented the power which a wife could exercise within a traditionally male organisation. He proposed that no wife should be allowed control within the household except over young children and maidservants. So the bishops married: out of affection, and perhaps also for some financial advantage and to have assistance in the control of their large establishments. The inevitable consequence was children and in many cases large families of surviving children: 205 can be traced who lived beyond early childhood. Discounting the bachelors and those whose status is dubious, this means an average of almost four children per bishop, and families of eight or nine were by no means uncommon.[7]

The dilemma for the father of such a family is evident. As the dean and chapter of Lichfield explained in their criticism of Overton, 'The lawful marriage of bishops and ministers is by abuse of the weak sort misliked because they nourish and maintain their children, not according to their calling, which is properly their own, but according

---

7. Hembry, p. 185. PROB, 11/125/49. The other marriages which could well have brought financial advantage to the bishops were those of James Pilkington to the daughter of the chief justice of Common Pleas and of Matthew Hutton to the daughter of Sir Thomas Fincham. W. Harrison, *A Description of England* (New York 1968), p. 37. PRO, sp 15/24/8. Berlatsky, 'Marriage and Family', pp. 11–12.

to their estate of maintenance which should be for the church and the poor.'[8] What they failed to say was that the episcopal calling brought with it no agreed 'private' resources and profits of office to be used for the benefit of the family as opposed to the 'public' income designated for the general good of the church. All the revenues of his see were at the disposal of the prelate, and the use which he should make of them indicated only in the most general terms. Even before the Reformation, as we have seen, the bishops were prepared to divert part of the revenues of the church to two essentially private uses – the support of relatives and the foundation of chantries. Society was not yet accustomed to drawing a sharp distinction between types of income, and the legitimate profits to be derived from office were not specified with any precision. The Protestant emphasis upon ecclesiastical wealth as in trust for the benefit of the whole church should have helped to clarify this division, according to the prelate and his family their competent maintenance. But what was a competent maintenance? Did it include money to educate sons and pay dowries of daughters so that they could marry well? Did it entitle episcopal sons to assume the formal status of their fathers and struggle to enter the ranks of the local gentry or even peerage? What did the 'calling' of a prelate represent in terms of the social hierarchy?

The questions of status raised by the existence of episcopal families have already been touched on for the earlier part of the century. The prelates still had high office, and within the community of the realm were entitled to claim the rank and honour that accompanied it. The name of bishop was still very desirable, even if the office was fraught with problems. When Thomas Cecil recommended that a new bishop of Peterborough should be appointed in 1595 he commented, 'The place is of a small revenue, and *but for the title of a bishop*, I think few sould affect it' (my italics). By the Elizabethan era the prelates, with the possible exception of the archbishops, had ceased to compete for social status with the nobility and leading courtiers but were more closely comparable with the country gentry among whom they worked as diocesans. The honour of the church and their own power to influence the laity were partially dependent upon their maintenance of this status. It would have been difficult indeed to separate their activities in such a way that their public actions in ruling the church, dispensing hospitality and so on accorded with

8. BL, Lans. MS. 36/55.

their position as leaders of the society, while their private actions as husbands and fathers fitted some more modest series of goals.[9]

Even if they did seek an alternative model for the government of their private lives, it is not clear that one was easily available. The bishops would scarcely be content to relate their families to their own early environments. Their origins seem to have been somewhat humbler than those of the Henrician generations: thirteen men came from a good gentry background, a somewhat larger group from reasonably affluent families, especially from a mercantile environment, but the majority from backgrounds with no pretensions to influence or were of unknown parentage. Their entry into the church and the various vicissitudes of their careers tended to detach them from their roots, especially, of course, in the case of those who had suffered exile under Mary. Family affection might remain, but brothers and nephews were more likely to assume the status of their episcopal relatives than vice versa. The only alternative model was that of the Protestant cleric, living modestly in the midst of magnificence, as had Hooper or Coverdale in the previous generation. Traces of this behaviour can be found in men such as Jewel and Parkhurst, but neither of these men had the temptation or pleasure of children, so neither had to decide what might legitimately be done to support the next generation. One solution was to perpetuate the clerical tradition by turning sons towards the church and giving daughters in marriage to clerics of similar status. But even this process could be expensive within a large family, and there were few fathers who could resist the temptation of elevating at least one or two children into the ranks of the local gentry.[10]

It was beyond the capacity of some prelates even to leave widow and children with the bare means of support. Dioceses such as Llandaff and Carlisle simply did not have the resources to maintain a large family, and several of their bishops died in debt leaving nothing to the widows. Mrs Best was allowed to retain Rose Castle at Carlisle between the death of her husband and the appointment of his successor as the only way of safeguarding herself against destitution,

9. *HMC, Salisbury MSS.*, v, p. 333.
10. Thirteen of the bishops were of gentle birth, but most were from the families of minor or impoverished gentlemen. Another thirteen came from wealthy or reasonably influential families, most of them with an urban background. Parental status may have made some difference in the choice of marriage partners: Pilkington, William Cotton and John Still, all of whom came from gentry families, made marriages in the upper ranks of society.

and Mrs Jones, wife of the second Elizabethan bishop of Llandaff, was given the manor of Matherne on the same basis. Those prelates who died in debt to the crown for first-fruits or tenths also found it difficult to provide for their offspring. Bishop Fletcher's rapid promotions and disgrace at court left his family in debt, and Nicholas Bullingham's widow was similarly destitute. Martin Marprelate might gibe that it was the duty of the wealthy bachelor Whitgift to provide for such families, but few contemporaries would have approved of the failure of these bishops. If this represented one extreme, the money that Sandys and Aylmer lavished upon their children represented the other. But Sandys had six grown sons and two daughters to care for by the end of his ministry, and all were in need of security, the security provided by land and dowries as well as leases. Heylyn, in defending the large dowries which he believed Pilkington had given to his two daughters, claimed that he would have been an 'ill husband' if he could not have saved £500 per annum out of the large revenues of Durham for the benefit of his family. He might also have commented that they were fortunate girls to be part of a small family: Bishop Cox, whose resources were equally large, was able to reserve a dowry of only £100 for his youngest daughter, who was unmarried at his death.[11]

Even though Pilkington was evidently willing to spend much of his income upon his daughters, there is no sense that he struggled to acquire wealth for them as did those prelates with several sons. Bishop Cooper is another example of a prelate who did not have to labour on behalf of his family, since he only had two daughters, one of whom was already married before he reached the bench. His skill in managing his revenue even in difficult circumstances must owe much to this relative absence of family responsibilities. For the demands of a large family were never-ending, and once a prelate had decided to offer them all that his position afforded he assumed a life-commitment to the purchase of land and the accumulation of money for dowries. Moreover, a bishop was particularly vulnerable if, in his declining years, he was surrounded by grown and ambitious children. The life-interest of the family in the see and the close access that they had to their head, both informally and often through the possession of administrative office, made them eager for the task of exploitation. Thus a family such as the Godwins at Bath and Wells

11. PRO, sp 46/28/fo. 209; sp 12/99/11. BL, Add. ms. 4123/pp. 133–4. PRO, sp 12/108/46. Heylyn, *Examen Historicum*, p. 103. PROB, 11/63/29.

could strip the bishop of his immediate wealth and monopolise his patronage for their own advantage. The phenomenon of ambitious relatives was not, of course, new in the Elizabethan age, but the close obligations and affection that a bishop felt towards his immediate family increased the possibility of their behaviour impinging upon the welfare of the English sees. No wonder that Whitgift, when asked how he kept such an orderly retinue of men, replied, 'by reason he kept so few women'.[12]

One very obvious consequence of the arrival of the episcopal family was a decline in the charitable activities of the bishops. Professor Berlatsky has calculated that in their wills the prelates designated only £6255 for learning, the poor and other pious works while leaving approximately £22,000 for their own kin. The money left in wills does not, of course, represent all of their payments; apart from the regular almsgiving, support of scholars and so on, it is known that several prelates founded or endowed schools during their lives. But by the same token more money was certainly given to relatives than is shown in the wills: land purchased during a prelate's lifetime and passed on to his children does not appear, nor do most of the dowries. Any figure that was able to comprehend these lifetime payments would almost certainly show an even greater disparity in favour of the family. The most generous charitable bequests did not necessarily come from bachelors, but did come either from this group or from those who had small families. Whitgift founded an elaborate school and almshouse at Croydon, Matthew Parker (with only two sons) provided large endowments for Corpus Christi at Cambridge, Grindal gave to a variety of educational establishments, and Scory (with one estranged son and a daughter) gave large sums to the poor in Herefordshire. Those with more offspring normally only managed to donate small sums to the poor of their own locality or perhaps finance one or two scholars at the university.[13]

There was thus much justice in contemporary allegations and complaints that it was episcopal wives and families who created the economic difficulties of the hierarchy and led them to neglect their duties of charity and care for the good of the church. Yet this easy source of blame was scarcely the complete explanation for the embar-

12. J. V. Redhead, 'Thomas Cooper and the Elizabethan Church', unpub. M.Litt. thesis, University of Newcastle (1975), p. 108. Hembry, pp. 154ff. Harington, *Nugae Antiquae*, II, p. 22.
13. Berlatsky, 'Marriage and Family', p. 19. PROB, 11/103/45; 11/68/39; 11/57/39. E. Grindal, *Remains*, Parker Soc. (1843), pp. 458–64.

rassment of the clerics. The problem of providing for a family was only one aspect of the continuing tension between their inadequate resources and the large demands made upon them. As obtrusive as the family was the crown's need for taxation. William Harrison quite correctly complained that for the clergy taxes were 'certain, continual and seldom abated'. In addition to the first-fruits and tenths received in 1559, subsidy was required eight times during the reign, only five years being completely free of payments. Then there were the additional levies upon the richer clergy for the support of the wars in Ireland and Holland and for the defence of the realm. These took the form either of money to finance a troop of horse – so-called 'lance money' – or of the actual provision of men and equipment. In the worst years of international crisis in the 1580s and 1590s, bishops who happened also to be in the process of paying first-fruits could find themselves in a very difficult financial position. Bishop Cooper showed Burghley in 1587 that out of an income of over £3000 he had only £398 to finance his household and for all other charges. Among his fixed costs he paid £837 for the third part of his first-fruits and also £279 for tenths, even though a bishop paying fruits was normally exempt. Then there were £250 for subsidy and £133 for a benevolence lately granted towards the preparations against Spain. This was merely an extreme example of the demands experienced by many bishops and by other clergy as well. Before 1588 the payments for the support of troops abroad seem to have been particularly resented. In 1581 Cox reported to the council that the payment of lance money was 'much grudged' by the clergy of his diocese, and in 1586 Overton claimed that his clergy would not pay the rest of their lance money for the provision of men for Ireland. When the crisis of 1588 came the bishops and other clergy were more zealous in their support. The council was fulsome in its thanks to the troubled Cooper, who arranged for the clergy of his diocese to raise a whole troop of horse and foot-soldiers at their own expense. Freke and the clergy of Worcester provided a band of 150 foot-soldiers for the defence of the realm. This patriotism was probably as short-lived as the invasion crisis, for again in the 1590s some of the bishops were complaining of the costs of raising troops. Only Whitgift, who knew the value of such gestures and could afford them, maintained a hundred foot-soldiers and fifty horse in constant readiness and kept their captains in his household to train them at his own expense.[14]

14. Harrison, *Description*, p. 30. BL, Lans. MS. 52/61. CCCC, MS. 168. PRO, SP

One of the greatest advantages that the crown could offer to a bishop on his promotion was remission of his first-fruits, for it was often the heavy taxes of their early years that started the bishops on the road to chronic indebtedness. Because it was such a privilege and because it represented a considerable loss to the crown, it was used very sparingly. Only eight prelates appointed under Elizabeth are not recorded as compounding for their fruits in the composition books. In the cases of John Jegon of Norwich and William Wickham at Winchester there are technical reasons for the omissions, and fruits were certainly paid. One of the two bishops of Exeter omitted, William Alley, also probably paid, or at least he was given a commended living to help with the payments. One of his successors, Wolton, may have been excused on grounds of poverty. Two other bishops were royal almoners, and there seems to have been a tradition from the earlier years of the Reformation that almoners could be exempted from first-fruits payments. This was not an automatic privilege, however, for in the 1590s Anthony Watson did his best to escape payments on the grounds that he was almoner but was forced to compound and was merely given slightly longer than usual to produce the money. Coldwell of Salisbury is omitted from the books quite inexplicably. Only one omission reflects poorly on the prelate concerned: Scambler paid no fruits when he was translated from Peterborough to Norwich, almost certainly because the price of his removal was the grand lease of sixty-one estates of the see which the queen conveyed to Sir Thomas Heneage. There may be a few more examples of men who escaped after they had made their agreements. Martin Heaton is known to have been promised exemption from first-fruits as the reward for his surrender of most of the Ely estates, and although he appears in the composition books, it is unlikely that the government went back on its word. Downham of Chester had one payment remitted when he was the queen's chaplain. Some others may have obtained partial remission because of poverty, but the crown was very reluctant to make concessions. When William Chaderton requested that he should pay no fruits on his translation to Chester, Burghley was sympathetic, but warned that 'her majesty be very loath, at this time especially, to hearken to any suit of this kind'. In the end he did not escape; he was merely

---

12/149/37. *APC*, 1587–8, p. 143. *CStP Dom.*, 1581–90, nos. 213/6. Paule, *Life of Whitgift*, pp. 73–4.

allowed the privilege of spreading his payments over several years.[15]

This was the most that the prelates could usually expect: those who had no particular claim to favour had to pay in two and a half years; the rest might be permitted anything up to six years, with the promise that their executors would not be burdened in the event of their death. In the last ten years of the reign, for example, Watson was given six years for his fruits (after much lobbying); Henry Cotton and Richard Vaughan, five at Salisbury, Bangor and Chester; Tobie Matthew, Bilson, William Morgan, Bancroft, Gervase Babington, Henry Robinson and Goldsborough, four years; and Redman, three. This was a valuable and relatively inexpensive privilege that the crown could grant, and one which probably enabled the richer bishops to pay their taxes without borrowing. In earlier years, when payments were more tightly regulated, some of the bishops had had to resort to the old methods of borrowing to finance their first years. John Jewel was indebted to a friend, 'For he hath laid out for me £207, for the first payment of my first fruits', and Cox claimed a few years after his arrival at Ely, 'I am faced presently to remain in debt for that which I borrowed at my first entry.' Even easier arrangements for the collection of first-fruits could not disguise the fact that a new prelate faced an appalling burden as he arrived in his bishopric.[16]

As usual, the story of taxation is only half told when the personal liability of the bishop has been considered. There was still his other role as collector of tenths and subsidies for the diocese, and he was as likely to become a crown debtor for failure in this field as for default of his own payments. This was especially serious when, as we have seen, the Elizabethan exchequer adopted a more rigorous policy towards the collection of debts. The old problem of ensuring the honesty of the undercollectors was still not fully resolved. The collectors now supposedly sealed two bonds on their appointment, one to the exchequer to produce their monies and render proper account, the other to the bishop to save him harmless from any debts. With care and thought a good agreement could be made between bishop and collector. For example, when Matthew Parker

15. PRO, E 334/5–12. *CStP Dom.*, 1595–7, p. 92, indicates that Alley, Bradbridge and Wolton may all have been forgiven their fruits in the end. *HMC, Salisbury MSS.*, VII, p. 145. PRO, E 334/12/pp. 62, 87. Watson claimed that all Elizabethan almoners had had their fruits pardoned. *HMC, Salisbury MSS.*, VII, p. 135. CUL, Mm/3/12. *HMC, Salisbury MSS.*, X, pp. 119–20. *CStP Dom.*, 1595–7, p. 404. Peck, *Desiderata Curiosa*, II, no. 24.
16. PRO, E 334/5–12. BL, Egerton MS. 2533, fo. 5; Lans. MS. 6/53/fo. 133.

appointed Henry Seath and William Woodward collectors of subsidy in Canterbury diocese in 1561, he worded the document very carefully. The subsidy was to be paid to the queen's use, the archbishop to be discharged 'and no penalty to light on him'. Most important of all, the collectors were to obtain the vital exchequer acquittance before the end of the Easter term of the following year, 1562. The whole document suggests close attention to detail by the archbishop or one of his officers and care to circumscribe the activities of the collectors by only allowing them a patent for one subsidy.[17]

Unfortunately, not all Parker's colleagues were able or willing to exercise such care. In some cases the collectorship was quickly granted out for life and was therefore beyond the bishop's power to control. The best-known example of the problems this caused is that of John Parkhurst of Norwich, who was deceived and defrauded by his collector, George Thimbelthorpe. Thimbelthorpe was an established officer of the see, a collector of tenths for Bishops Reppes and Hopton, as well as receiver-general. The inexperienced Parkhurst had little control over his activities, although he did duly extract a bond to save himself harmless from royal debts. This bond was apparently rendered inoperative by the simple expedient of removing one of the sureties' seals. So when Thimbelthorpe accumulated debts to the crown of £1126 it was Parkhurst who was liable and who had to compound for their repayment at the rate of £400 per annum. Diocesan vested interests and dishonesty also caused a crisis for William Bradbridge of Exeter, though in this case the full story was not uncovered until after his death. His undercollector, Henry Borough, actually forged an exchequer acquittance in order to gain the signed discharge of his master. When Bradbridge's estate was valued and his debts counted he was found to owe the exchequer £1235, and there was not enough money even to bury him decently. It can have been of little consolation to the bishops that both Thimbelthorpe and Borough ended in debtors' prison for their part in these affairs. Godwin of Bath and Wells, Cheyney of Gloucester, Aylmer of London and Freke of Worcester all fell into debt partly because they had dishonest or inept collectors who were inadequately supervised. The very fear of being held responsible for the collection of debts often kept the bishops at a distance from their deputies once they had taken what they regarded as adequate bonds. Thus Aylmer's son tried to place responsibility for arrears on the sub-collector for London

17. LPL, CM I/72.

diocese and explained 'neither the late Bishop of London (though he were collector by law) neither myself his son ... ever intermedled with the collection of tenths and subsidies'. Efforts to tighten the legislation governing the behaviour of collectors, which sprang from the notorious Parkhurst case, did something to ensure that the bishops' deputies could have their lands and goods sold if they were found to be indebted to the crown. But none of this really solved the problem that the bishop was ultimately accountable to the exchequer and that, if no one else could pay the taxes, he must.[18]

The amounts which the prelates owed to the government were very variable, and it is not always easy in the surviving evidence to distinguish short-term arrears caused by the late collection of taxes from sums which the bishops were really incapable of paying. Nevertheless, there are a number of well-attested cases of indebtedness, the most important of which are listed in table 10:1. Debts of this magnitude obviously justified energetic pursuit by the exchequer, but lesser sums were also the subject of close inquisition. Richard Curteys of Chichester, for example, owed £150 at his death, and a full exchequer enquiry into his estate was launched in order to recover the money. Two of the major debtors listed below were victims of rapid promotions and early death: Wickham and Fletcher both owed a great deal for first-fruits on the last sees which they had received from the queen. Other bishops escaped this difficulty in the 1590s by inserting agreements into their compositions for first-fruits that they would not be liable for all the payments in the event of translation, nor their executors in the event of death.[19]

The debtors whose difficulties can be blamed most directly on shortage of income to meet royal demands are those who failed to make their own first-fruit payments or who actually embezzled royal taxes to help them over a fiscal crisis. It must have been tempting to adopt the latter course: one of Bradbridge's servants reported with pride that his master would never touch the queen's money, even when he had no reserves of his own. Instead, he would send to Plymouth and other towns to borrow money against the security of future rents. Others, he implied, were not so honest. The very vigour

18. *Letter Book of Parkhurst*, pp. 28–30. Gorham, *Gleanings*, pp. 453–9. PRO, E 178/2074. Hembry, pp. 175–81. BL, Lans. MS. 23/6. PRO, SP 46/40/fos. 81, 164. The legislation was 14 Eliz. I c. 7 'Act against the deceits of undercollectors of tenths'. There was a proposal in 1580/1 to hand the task of collection over to the crown, but nothing came of it. PRO, SP 12/147/85.

19. PRO, E 347/14/pt 2.

Table 10:1 *Debts owed by the Elizabethan bishops to the crown*

Bishop	Date of debt	Diocese	£	Comments
John Parkhurst	1572	Norwich	1126	
Nicholas Bullingham	1576	Worcester	285	Plus £939 in private debts
Richard Cheyney	1576	Gloucester	500	
William Bradbridge	1578	Exeter	1236	
Thomas Bentham	1578	Coventry and Lichfield	1100	Plus £250 to bishopric
Robert Horne	1579	Winchester	1100	
William Overton	1583	Coventry and Lichfield	2270	
John Bullingham	1586	Gloucester	1400	
Thomas Godwin	1587	Bath and Wells	3000	Crown and private debts
Edmund Freke	1591	Worcester	–	
Marmaduke Middleton	1591	St David's	–	
John Aylmer	1594	London	1500	
William Wickham	1595	Winchester	1933	
Richard Fletcher	1597	London	600	Plus £850 in private debts

Sources: PRO, E 347/14/pt 3; SP 12/108/46. BL, Lans. MS. 23/6. PRO, E 347/14/pt 1; SP 46/38/fo. 43; SP 12/131/23; E 135/9/6; SP 46/35/fo. 184. Hembry, p. 176. *CStP Dom.*, 1595–7, p. 454. PRO, SP 46/40/fo. 81. *HMC, Salisbury MSS.*, vi, pp. 64–5.

with which Aylmer, Cheyney, John Bullingham and Fletcher defended themselves against charges of embezzling suggests that the government had some grounds for its suspicions. Marmaduke Middleton was certainly found guilty of appropriating government funds among the other misdemeanours that led to his deprivation in 1592. But it is perhaps William Overton who stands as the prime example of a bishop who managed to compound the problems of a poor bishopric with incompetence in managing his deputies and sheer dishonesty. We are particularly well informed about his troubles because he was not willing to accept quietly the criticism of the government or the dealings of his deputies, but constantly and aggressively brought his difficulties to the attention of Burghley and other members of the government. There is no doubt that Overton inherited a difficult see, which already had a pattern of indebtedness and which had almost been the despair of his predecessor, Bentham. By 1583 he had compounded a bad situation and had managed to fall £2000 into arrears on his payments to the crown – all this after only three years in his bishopric. In a detailed statement Overton attributed his problems to the high costs of gaining and equipping his see – £1328 inclusive of first-fruits – to the expense of litigation and especially a settlement with his hated chancellor Thomas Becon – £1240 – and to the large regular outgoings with which he was faced. Much of the £2000 must have been clerical taxes destined for the crown, for at this time the most Overton himself could have owed was about £900. The bishop was forced to compound for the repayment of his debts, but only after his goods had been seized and he had been subjected to general humiliation. However, this was not the end of his troubles. Dr Becon had succeeded in retaining the patent for collecting the taxes of the diocese, and between him and the bishop there could be no peace. By 1585 disputes erupted again when Overton tried to insert one Mr Fitzherbert into the office of collector. Burghley, who was thoroughly tired of the whole affair, agreed to this arrangement 'so her Majesty might have security for her money . . . [and] I be not further troubled with him'. Yet further troubled the lord treasurer was. Fitzherbert proved a bad choice for the bishop and even more inept in the work of collecting taxes than Becon had been. For a time it seemed that Overton would be made liable for further debts, but the crisis was postponed. By 1594 trouble flared up again, and the bishop eventually dismissed his collector and made himself responsible for all royal payments. It cannot have surprised Burghley that one consequence was that none of the 1594 subsidy was paid into the exchequer until after process for the distraint of goods had been issued against Overton.[20]

The saga of the bishop and his debts shows how easily a difficult financial situation could be rendered totally impossible by failure to manage the diocesan officials and by ambitious schemes and litigation beyond the means of the see. He succeeded in alienating one of his two patrons, the earl of Leicester, and his aggressive attitude probably explains why he was never promoted to a more profitable bishopric. His method of escaping from the trap of poverty – litigation to recover the rights of the see which he believed had been lost – offered some long-term advantage, but at great immediate cost. Yet even Overton was not entirely in the wrong in believing himself oppressed. In the year of his consecration, always a very costly time, he had had to

20. PRO, E 347/14/pt 1. PRO, SP 12/228/15; Sta. Cha. 5/80/25; E 135/9/6; SP 46/33/fo. 291; SP 46/33/fo. 236; SP 46/39/fo. 33; E 347/17/pt 1. On Overton and his troubles see M. R. O'Day, 'Cumulative Debt: The Bishops of Coventry and Lichfield and their Economic Problems', *Midland History*, III (1975), 85–6.

contribute towards the provision of soldiers for Ireland. When he fell into arrears the exchequer would not listen to his ingenious, or perhaps ingenuous, scheme for paying the money without distraint and instead seized his land and goods. In 1586 he was kept in London for many weeks while the exchequer endeavoured to agree repayments with his receivers. He was handled in a way which must inevitably have brought him into disrepute in his own diocese. Indeed, as has been suggested, the regular use by the government of distraint upon lands and goods as a way of settling episcopal debts must have contributed materially to the contempt with which the leading laity often regarded the prelates.[21]

The awkward Overton may have spent too much on litigation, but there is no doubt that his other charges were necessary and were too high for the revenue of his see. A part of those costs related to expenses at court, to the struggle to gain promotion and be properly appointed. Overton was forced to attend the queen on progress for twenty weeks before he was given the appropriate *congé d'élire*, and his charges before he was able to set foot in the bishopric were at least £100. This figure is modest compared to what some bishops had to expend. That notorious self-seeker Richard Fletcher claimed that on his entrance to London diocese he had made at the queen's command 'gratifications' of £2000 to members of the court. This represented almost a year's income from the see. Such *douceurs*, whether in the form of direct payments or of annuities, were a common feature of the Elizabethan church. The diocese of Winchester, by the time of Cooper's consecration, was burdened with annuities of £318, including £100 to that noted critic of the bishops Robert, earl of Leicester. It need hardly be said that evidence about direct payments to the mighty is less easy to obtain, for it was dangerously close to simony, but the obligations of a cleric to his patron were deeply felt and often bordered upon the sycophantic. When Barnes was promoted to the valuable bishopric of Durham he wrote in the following terms to Burghley: 'My singular good lord and patron I most humbly beseech your honour to accompt and accept of me and mine as your own, and so use and command the same.' An obligation once incurred was difficult to evade. Archbishop Young of York refused a loan of £1000 to his erstwhile patron, Leicester, on the grounds that he was too poor, only to be trapped by an astute agent of the earl, who discovered the shipload of lead from the roof of York palace that the

21. BL, Lans. MS. 50/37.

bishop had sent for sale on the London market. To these large sums offered as loans, gifts or annuities should no doubt be added the variety of small payments needed to ease promotion, from the official charges of the scribes and notaries to the entertainment of those who had power and influence.[22]

The lay élite had not finished with the bishops when the struggle for promotion was ended and the obligations of patronage had been met. Matthew Parker was estimated by his son to have spent £2270 on disbursements directly connected with the court. The vast majority of this sum was for the lavish entertainment of the queen when on progress: £2000 had been used for this purpose. Nicholas Bullingham claimed that one of the main reasons for his indebtedness at Worcester was the royal entertainment he had been privileged to give. It is unlikely that any of the Elizabethan bishops rivalled the £3000 that Lancelot Andrewes is alleged to have spent in one week of entertaining James I at Winchester, but the costs of receiving a royal visit were always large, and it was an embarrassment that most of the prelates must have been grateful to avoid. Only the archbishops of Canterbury and the bishops of Winchester suffered regular visitations, though the bishops of London not only sometimes accommodated the queen at Fulham but also had to act as hosts to a miscellany of government visitors and foreign ambassadors. The queen's favourable disposition to the church, or at least to its leaders, could often depend upon her reception on progress. Once again it was Whitgift who demonstrated the best understanding of Elizabeth's character: he entertained her at least once a year, and sometimes two or three times, and had his household perfectly trained in the most respectful style of service. The queen was so pleased by one such visit that she described his servants as her own and spoke affectionately of the archbishop as her 'little black husband'. From his prudent management of the large Canterbury estates Whitgift could still afford such behaviour, but for other prelates, even the Winchester bishops, the entertainment of the court must have seemed a most serious threat to their financial stability. It is interesting to speculate if some of those prelates whom the queen charged with parsimony, such as Cox and Sandys, had in fact attempted to evade their share of royal entertainment.[23]

22. *CStP Dom.*, 1595-7, pp. 247-8. BL, Lans. MS. 52/fo. 179; MS. 24/17. Harington, *Nugae Antiquae*, II, pp. 231ff. Young also remitted a year's rent on the manor of Southwell as a concession to Leicester.
23. LPL, MS. 959/46. PRO, SP 12/108/46. Paule, *Life of Whitgift*, p. 78.

The reception of the court on progress is an extreme example of the general burden of hospitality. Hospitality, in the sense of maintaining 'port and countenance' by entertaining the influential, was still perceived as an integral part of the episcopal role. 'The world expecteth', commented Bishop Berkeley, 'and our vocation is to be hospitales.' Bishops such as John Jewel, who took no pleasure in personal display, might nevertheless keep an elaborate table and elegant establishment because it was expected by their guests and enabled them to relate more successfully to the rulers of local society. In the 1590s Bishop Young of Rochester was proud that he kept 'as good a table as any in England, excepting that which is prodigal', though he did so only by spending too great a proportion of his income on food and drink. At every turn one encounters high lay expectations about the hospitality of the clergy. Elizabeth made it her especial concern that her prelates should uphold the honour of their office by suitable social behaviour and was very wont to associate any lack of generosity with their concern for wives and children. Burghley, in a moment of thorough disillusion in 1585, wrote that the bishops 'have no credit either for learning or good living and hospitality', implying that the one was as important as the other. Even John Harington, who endeavoured to judge them far more sympathetically than most of his contemporaries, was quick in his criticism of those who did not entertain sufficiently. Conversely, a totally ineffectual and weak prelate such as Martin Heaton of Ely won golden opinions from him merely because he was hospitable.[24]

The preservation of an open and hospitable house was undoubtedly very costly and increasingly so as inflation affected food prices. Both the bishops themselves and the government in the 1559 legislation recognised the importance of conserving the demesne as an aid to provisioning the household, but food and drink still dominated the expenditure accounts. At Winchester in 1568 food and its carriage cost Horne £713 out of a total budget of £1489 that passed through the hands of the steward of the household. Parker's son estimated that his father spent £1300 to £1490 a year on household provisions, and although this would have included fuel and manufactured items, the basic cost would undoubtedly have been food. Sandys assessed his hospitality costs at London at £800 a year, while Grindal claimed that when he was bishop of London his ordinary expenses

24. PRO, SP 12/16/27. *Zurich Letters*, II, p. 86. BL, Lans. MS. 79/42. Harington, *Nugae Antiquae*, II, p. 108.

came to £12,524, or £1200 a year, here including under the heading of hospitality all the regular expenditure of the see. Perhaps there was some justice in so doing, for many of the charges upon the bishops, other than food and drink, led back to their obligations as hosts. Large households were needed to provide for the guests, and even the plate that was in one sense an investment was in another needed for appropriate domestic display. When the young Swiss Herman Folkerzheimer visited Jewel he was particularly impressed by his display of plate: 'also when dinner or supper time arrived, how can I describe to you the abundance or magnificence of the silver plate? Yet, great as they are, they do not seem to afford much pleasure to their possessor, and appear to have been provided rather for his guests' sake than his own.' When, on the other hand, a prelate was forced to live in relatively retired circumstances by the poverty of his see, as were the Elizabethan bishops of Norwich, his charges could be very modest. Bishop Scambler's accounts for 1588 show that only £144 was spent on food and provisions, and the steward's total outgoings were only £210. This must have meant a fairly small household and in turn little general hospitality.[25]

Jewel's household, which so bedazzled the young Swiss, was probably small by pre-Reformation standards. His detailed will lists approximately forty servants, though evidently these were sufficient to provide entertainment suitable to his status, for Jewel was widely known as a good housekeeper. Downham of Chester claimed that he must maintain an establishment of forty despite his poverty, the implication being that any less would make it impossible to discharge his local obligations. One of the charges against Thimbelthorpe was that he forced Parkhurst to retire to the rural obscurity of Ludham and reduce his household to thirty persons in order to pay his debts. The subsequent bishops evidently also had to submit themselves to these reduced circumstances, for Jegon had only twenty-three servants active in his household. There were also a few gentlemen retainers, alongside whose names Jegon's secretary, Anthony Harison, commented sourly, 'most of these came gallant to the Bishop like butterflies in the Spring, but when they found little hope of benefit they stayed not'. Although a number of other prelates no doubt had to accept households of this size, the wealthier amongst them still aspired to a retinue little smaller than that of a Foxe or West. Parker

25. SRO, LM/927/4. PRO, SP 12/137/54; SP 12/149/17ff. *Zurich Letters*, II, p. 86. NRO, MSC/1.

described his household in 1563 as 'having not many under a hundred persons uprising and down-lying therein'. Aylmer had an establishment of sixty at London, and Sandys was criticised by the council in 1581 for not providing horsemen for Ireland, 'having so great a household, and travelling in the country and coming up to London with such a number of men'. Here Sandys was neatly trapped by a Catch-22 comment: the servants who were necessary for the hospitality required by the government could also be used as a test of episcopal wealth. It was to avoid this sort of trap that Whitgift trod so carefully: his household of a hundred liveried servants was used ostentatiously for the benefit of the realm, either in a military sense or in providing an effective archiepiscopal presence in the localities. His biographer, George Paule, described in detail his costly journeys into Kent, on which he would be accompanied by his entire household and attended by the local gentry: 'And surely the entertainment which he gave them, and they him, was so great, that, as I am verily persuaded no shire in England did, or could, give greater, or with more cheerful minds, each unto other.'[26]

Here the notion of entertainment in its narrow sense has merged with the broader idea of cooperation. Cooperation for the enforcement of local conformity and for the maintenance of good discipline within the shires was obviously facilitated by good social relationships between bishops and gentry, and these relationships were cemented by hospitality. It was useful for the bishop to be a regular resident and to be visible at two or three houses within his jurisdiction, especially where the diocese was a large or difficult one. For financial reasons many of the bishops continued the process of withdrawing from their outlying manors and allowing them to fall into decay. But the dangers of such a policy were recognised. When Pilkington of Durham was eager to regain the estates that the crown had withheld from him after 1559 he promised to restore the manor of Allerton in Yorkshire, which was on the London highway and 'so decayed these fifty years, that the slates be fallen off, [and] the timber stands bare and . . . rotten'. In such a state it was a source of wonder and scandal to travellers, but restored it could once again become the centre of an effective episcopal administration. Unfortunately, Pilkington did not live up to these professions of concern and was even guilty of allowing

26. PROB, 11/53/43. Strype, *Annals*, I, ii, p. 265. *Letter Book of Parkhurst*, p. 111. Anthony Harison, *Registrum Vagum* Norfolk Rec. Soc. (1963), II, p. 238. *Parker Correspondence*, p. 195. *APC*, 1580–1, p. 224. Paule, *Life of Whitgift*, p. 78.

the other manors of his see to decay during his episcopate. In the 1590s Whitgift campaigned vigorously for the keepership of the old archiepiscopal palace at Otford, claiming that he had 'never a house in Kent fit for him', though both the palace at Canterbury and the manor of Bekesbourne offered suitable accommodation on a more modest scale. The connection between a strong episcopal presence and good religious order was made most clear by Aylmer. In 1586 he was having trouble with the puritans of Maldon in Essex and petitioned the queen for the assignment of the lease of the nearby manor of Wickham, which was in the crown's hands. If it were granted and he lived there, he said, there was no doubt 'but within short space I should bring all the whole country into so good order as any other part of my diocese . . . My being at my other house at Hadham some small time in the year hath made all the country of Hertford . . . now to be most quiet and orderly.' Aylmer no doubt exaggerated the beneficial effects of his presence, and his request for a lease is not known to have met with any response. Nevertheless, a bishop could influence his neighbours for good, the best-attested example being Parkhurst's work in the town of Acle near Ludham, which was described after his death as 'a little commonwealth'.[27]

Parkhurst was evidently able to make a deep impact within a small locality, but only at the cost of loss of power elsewhere. Most of the slightly wealthier prelates struggled to maintain two or three establishments in order to spread their influence as widely as possible. The problem, as ever, was one of cost. Large houses needed regular repairs and had to be furnished in appropriate style. Since few of the Elizabethan bishops had private resources before they reached the bench and since their predecessors were tempted to take away all moveable goods and stock, the charges for building a suitable presence became very large. Nicholas Bullingham, who complained bitterly of the cost of furnishing his houses, was perhaps unlucky to succeed the acquisitive Sandys, who had stripped his three Worcester homes to the bare boards. However, the experience of Overton in paying out £158 to furnish 'my houses in the country' must have been common enough. His predecessor, Bentham, had found that in his castle of Eccleshall 'all the stuff, implements and standards of household' had been taken away, so no doubt his widow felt justified in turn in removing the items of furniture which he had purchased.

---

27. PRO, sp 46/27/84. *HMC, De L'Isle*, ii, p. 447. BL, Lans. ms. 50/40. Hassell-Smith, *County and Court*, p. 104.

These charges for furnishings were but one more aspect of the intolerable fiscal pressures to which the bishops were subjected on their first entry to a see. A prelate such as Bentham, who came from poverty in exile, and to whom the £700-a-year income of the see of Coventry and Lichfield must have appeared as princely riches, quickly found that he was encompassed by a variety of demands and obligations which could not be met from his apparently large sum. Like many others, he bemoaned this situation chiefly because it diminished his standing as a public officer and leader of the church in the eyes of the locality, since poverty would 'redown much to the slander of the gospel, whereby [I] shall be unable either to serve god or your highness, as [my] duty and will is'.[28]

The obligation of hospitality also had its other aspect – charitable behaviour towards poor neighbours. It was the decline of this type of care that the puritan critics of episcopacy had in mind when they alleged that hospitality was offered in 'base and contemptible manner, to the dishonour and reproach of the calling'. It is difficult to produce figures that would support or deny this assertion, as accounts for spending within the household do not usually provide a separate heading for alms and food dispensed to the poor. When Parker wished to stress that he had discharged his obligation of charity he pointed to the £160 per annum which he gave to one of the Canterbury hospitals. Other evidence comes from wills and does not suggest great munificence to the poor. In the wills of three of the Elizabethan bishops of Salisbury, for example, the poor were left 100 marks by Jewel, £20 by Guest and £5 by Cotton. When inflation between 1572 and 1615 is taken into account, the poor of Salisbury may be said to have been suffering serious neglect from their later bishops. The only spectacular exceptions to this general lack of charitable bequests were the £600 left to the poor by Scory and the Croydon almshouses founded by Whitgift. As for immediate rewards within the household, Horne's accounts list £45 as paid out for scholars and the poor, as compared to the £168 for gifts to the bishop's kin and for the queen's New Year gift. Harington commented on only two men as especially generous in their charity: Parkhurst, who was 'ready to do good to all men, but especially to the household of faith', and Overton, who, surprisingly, 'keepeth good hospitality for the poor'. To these we might perhaps

28. PRO, sp 12/107/34; e 135/9/6. J. A. Berlatsky, 'Thomas Bentham and the Plight of the Early Elizabethan Bishops', *Historical Magazine of the Protestant Episcopal Church*, XLIII (1974), 337.

add John May, who was almost compelled by famine conditions in his northern diocese of Carlisle to open his doors to the starving.[29]

It might therefore seem that some of the strictures of contemporaries were deserved, but it is interesting to set against them William Harrison's view of clerical hospitality. He argued that critics were comparing the behaviour of the present clergy with a standard which had never been fully observed. Even bishops and other church leaders used to keep open house 'at Christmas only, or otherwise kept great houses for the entertainment of the rich'. The ordinary clergy were now better able to feed their poor neighbours because of the prudent housekeeping of their wives. As for the bishops, their style might be reduced because of the excessive cost of entertaining and the loss of some of their lands, but 'if you look unto these our times you shall see no fewer deeds of charity done, nor better grounded upon the right stub of piety, than before'. Paule's account of Whitgift's behaviour stands as a perfect example of Harrison's generalisations. Much of his hospitality was directed to those with wealth and influence, but 'at Christmas especially, his gates were always open, and his Hall set twice or thrice over with strangers'. This was the old style of munificence; the archbishop's main efforts for the poor were more specific, more redolent perhaps of the Protestant ethic and of a stratified society. He maintained his almshouses and school and gave money generously to help the poor continue in their proper occupations. He was opposed to raising the expectations of those he aided or making them 'forsake their trade or condition'. It may be that open hospitality was less common among the bishops, not only because of greed and poverty but also because contemporary attitudes were moving against the indiscriminate support of the needy that had been part of the Catholic notion of charity. A few prelates such as Whitgift had something positive to substitute for the munificence of their predecessors; the rest, while accepting the advantage of the new ethos, show little sign of that discriminating charity that had become a feature of lay behaviour by the end of the century.[30]

The Elizabethan bishops were placed at the centre of a nexus of obligation even more complex than that of their predecessors. The most significant new claim upon them was undoubtedly their imme-

29. *The Second Parte of a Register*, ii, p. 210. PROB, 11/53/43; 11/59/12; 11/125/49; 11/68/39; 11/103/45. SRO, lm/927/4. Harington, *Nugae Antiquae*, ii, p. 117. *Illustrations of British History*, ed. E. Lodge (1838), ii, pp. 137–8.
30. Harrison, *Description*, p. 37. Paule, *Life of Whitgift*, pp. 77, 84–5.

diate families, whose demands for lawful maintenance were inexorable. The appearance of the family made it more necessary than before to distinguish between the 'public' and 'private' resources of a prelate, but no such distinction had begun to be made in the later sixteenth century. At the same time, the reformed insistence that wealth could be justified only, if at all, by using it for the advancement of learning and for the poor increased the awkwardness of a prelate's position. Taxation, high fixed charges and the need to satisfy patrons, provide hospitality and maintain a suitably dignified appearance within the localities all contributed to the problems of the episcopate. The crown complicated the situation of struggling members of the bench by its firm attitude to indebtedness. There is frequent and often pathetic testimony from state correspondence of the struggles of the poorer prelates to cope with the range of their problems. Many, like Bentham of Coventry and Lichfield, felt that they were 'in the briars' and had no way of escaping from their encumbrances. Some wrung their hands and wished their episcopal office away, though none except Richard Cox and Edmund Grindal actually made any sustained attempt to resign.[31]

Most serious for the well-being of the church was the amount of time that some bishops had to devote to secular problems and the management of their estates. Bentham's letter-book, which covers two years of his time at Coventry and Lichfield, demonstrates this. Of the 247 entries, 46 per cent are related in some way to the finances of the see, and in other letters the issues of land and litigation are at least mentioned. In John Parkhurst's letter-book, financial affairs do not bulk so large, but the Thimbelthorpe affair proved an overwhelming preoccupation in the early 1570s. It involved the bishop in journeys to London and considerable work with parliamentary legislation as well as all in the upheavals within the diocese itself. Cox's resignation attempt is really a reflection of the exhaustion he felt after his long and mainly successful battle to keep the lands of Ely out of the hands of Lord North. Examples can be multiplied, and although not every Elizabethan bishop had the same titanic struggles as Cox and Parkhurst, everyone had to spend considerable time on fiscal affairs, litigation to defend property rights and so on. As we shall see in the next chapter, much of this activity was intended to assist the bishopric as an economic unit as well as to benefit the bishop and his family. It is less clear that it brought any broader advantage to the

31. National Library of Wales, MS. 4919D, p. 40.

church or to the Protestant faith. The stern moral stance of the puritan divines in this matter was undoubtedly facilitated by their situation as perpetual 'outs', excluded from the best fruits of office. Nevertheless, the words of Sampson to Parker in 1574 are apposite, for they indicate the great difficulty of escaping from that nexus of obligation that made a bishop a lord and yet a reformed minister, a public officer and yet a family man, and a leader of souls but yet a dependant of a lay monarch: 'You say you are not lordly, that you do not set any store by that lordly state . . . if you whom policy hath made a great lord be not lordly but do keep the humble and straight course of a loving brother and minister of Christ's gospel I shall say that you are a phoenix.'[32]

32. *Ibid.* MS. 4919D; the percentage figures are from Berlatsky, 'Thomas Bentham', p. 328. *Letters Book of Parkhurst.* BL, Lans. MS. 25/33; MS. 29/42. Inner Temple, Petyt MS. 538/47/fo. 336.

11

THE RESOURCES OF THE
ELIZABETHAN BISHOPS

I

The howls of anguish that resound through the correspondence of the Elizabethan bishops would suggest that they failed collectively to respond to the diverse demands made of them. They could neither pay their taxes efficiently nor support their families in reasonable style nor serve their cures with appropriate hospitality. But he who cries loudest is not necessarily the most representative, and we need to turn to the resources and income of the prelates to discover if the tangles of Overton or Cheyney are characteristic of the whole order. The seventy-nine men who served as bishops under Elizabeth were very diverse in personality and experience, and the sees which they occupied all presented different problems. It is therefore only to be expected that it is not easy to demonstrate that the prelates failed to manage their finances in an appropriate manner, or that they succeeded in overcoming their difficulties. The most that can be done here is to suggest some of the possibilities open to the Elizabethans, some of the ways in which they could support the demands considered in the last chapter, and to show how a few of the leaders of the church were responding in a positive way to those opportunities.

This involves turning once again to the income of the English and Welsh sees, which we last left at the end of a period of modest financial recovery under Mary. The beginning of Elizabeth's reign provides us with the only general estimate of episcopal income prepared since the *Valor Ecclesiasticus*. Early in 1559, when the rooted opposition of Mary's bishops to her successor's policy became clear, Cecil drew up some estimates of the value of the English sees to help in the choice of new prelates. He turned principally to the information available in the *King's Book*, but his own experience under Edward VI must have led him to believe that some of this material was outdated, for his figures sometimes vary considerably from these estimates. The sees of Lincoln Chester, Exeter, Bristol and Oxford were not included in Cecil's first list: the combined annual value of the remainder was given as

£19,764. This would compare with a figure of approximately £25,500 for the same dioceses in the calculations we have made for the end of Mary's reign. In a subsequent list, written in April 1560 and therefore able to use some of the data provided by the diocesan surveys of late 1559, Cecil amended his figures. York was reckoned to be worth £1100 instead of £1000, Carlisle £500 instead of £268 (which was the value of its temporalities alone) and Durham £3000 instead of £2700. In these second estimates he was certainly including the spiritualities, which he may in some cases have omitted in 1559. Unfortunately, the 1560 list includes only eight sees and cannot therefore be used as a basis for a general calculation of income. But a very crude estimate, using these eight plus the 1559 figures and a rounded sum for the two dioceses which do not appear on either list, would be that the income of the bishoprics according to Cecil was £23,000 as compared to the £28,000 earlier suggested for gross revenues at the time of Mary's death.[1]

Even allowing for the lack of precision in either of these figures, there is a major discrepancy here that requires explanation. The most likely one would seem to be that Cecil was not considering gross income but was assessing the net value of each bishopric and even then was concerned with the temporalities rather than the spiritualities. Thus, £3000 is a reasonable calculation of the amount normally delivered to the bishops of Durham after the payment of fees, as is the £1000 for London, but in both cases the gross receipts would normally have been at least £200 higher. Elsewhere, the estimates are even lower than the net income that could be anticipated: at York, for example, Cecil does not seem to have taken account of the Marian restorations and to have worked instead from the reduced sum levied for taxation after the Henrician exchanges. It is therefore important not to give too much weight to Cecil's efforts, which were no doubt undertaken in haste as an *aide mémoire*. The most that can be said is that they represent a minimum, a figure below which the net revenues of the prelates were unlikely to fall at the beginning of the new reign. By the same token, £28,000 is a maximum for rental and other formally recorded receipts, a sum which is certainly higher than that which the new bishops could hope to receive via their officials from the twice-yearly payments of their tenants.[2]

1. PRO, SP 12/4/39; SP 12/12/2; SP 12/19/62.
2. Cross, 'Economic Problems of York', pp. 82–3. Horton, 'Durham Bishopric Estates', pp. 139, 151. See appendix I below.

No sooner had these calculations been made than they were super-seded by the changes initiated under the 1559 act. The main effect of the first round of exchanges was to place far more spiritual income, and far less temporal, under the control of the bishops. The effect on basic revenues, however, appears to have been rather slight, as table 11:1 shows. Most of the sees lost a little money income, especially if the rather successful Marian years form the basis for comparison, but there is no evidence in the figures of a major financial crisis.

Table 11:1 *Gross income of bishoprics which lost lands under the 1559 act*

	1535	1558	1561	1566
Canterbury	£3223	£3164	£2588	£2815
	1550	*1557*	*1565*	*1569*
London	£1113	£1420	£1127	£1212
	1535	*1541*	*1565*	
Ely	£2135	£2306	£1963	
	1535	*1555*	*1561*	*1579*
Worcester	£1050	£1018	£939	£981
	1535	*1572*		
Chichester	£590	£659		

Sources: PRO, sp 10/13/67. LPL, Estates Docs., nos. 1401, 1406. PRO, sc 6/Ed. VI/307; sc 6/P. and M./194; sc 6/Eliz./1468. Guildhall, ms. 10, 123/4. EDR, d/5/9; a/8/1. WRO, cc 900/1/179; cc 900/1, no. 43694. WSRO, Ep. vi/4/1.

Even Canterbury and Ely, which appear to have lost the most, were in some measure compensated by the remission of their own tenths, worth £323 and £207 per annum. The government commissioners were certainly not encouraged to be generous in assigning values to the property to be exchanged. In an extreme case, Pulham in Norfolk, which belonged to the bishopric of Ely, the bishop was allowed only £88 as compared with the £100 that it normally yielded. But this was an unusual example of a process which often underassessed values by only a pound or two, if at all. On the whole, the royal order that 'the exchange may be such as they the bishops may have in spiritu-alities an equal just value to the temporalities which shall be received from them' was adhered to formally. The only really obvious losses experienced by the bishops were those which arose from burdens upon disposable income: the new spiritualities often required the payment of pensions or fees, and no allowance was made for these in the exchanges. Hereford suffered particularly badly from this problem: the pensions it was required to pay after 1559 amounted to

£55, which was a major imposition upon a relatively poor bishopric. There were other disadvantages: Cox, for example, was critical of the arrangements, which provided no adequate compensation for the woods and parklands that were taken from his see at the same time as the episcopal manors. These had been especially useful, as they had often represented the only demesne kept in hand on the outlying manors, but for that very reson the crown had an excuse not to assign them a high value when the commissioners were at work. The cumulative effect of the exchanges could therefore be inequitable and pose difficulties for a see which was already struggling to survive financially. But it is important not to exaggerate its effect on gross rentals, for the crown undoubtedly fulfilled its part of the legislative bargain: it gave the bishops spiritual property and dues equal to the rental income of their lands, and it used their own accounts to determine that income, not merely the rates already available in the *Valor Ecclesiasticus*.[3]

The exchanges did not, therefore, lead to a major decline in the money income of the prelates. Most of the losses that did occur were confined to the two rich sees of Durham and Winchester and had only a tangential relation to the legislation. Their first losses were a direct consequence of the Marian resumptions. Winchester, Worcester and Durham had been permitted to resume estates alienated under Edward, even though the legal basis for so doing was weak or non-existent. The accession of Elizabeth therefore offered the so-called patentees, who had occupied these lands under Edward, the opportunity to reassert their rights. It seems likely that in practice most had retained their hold upon the estates, even though paying rent to the bishops. Elizabeth's first parliament provided the ideal forum for the trial of their claims, for the anti-episcopal stance of many of the members of the lower house lent them moral fervour. Particularly revealing of the attitude of the Commons is the censure of a member, Mr Story, who 'had not well used himself, being a Member of this House, to go before the Lords, and be of Counsel with the Bishop of Winchester against the patentees, which by the House was taken to be a fault'. Such sentiments may have helped the patentees in their appearance before the Lords, but it needed little support from the Commons to demonstrate that some of their legal claims were very strong.[4]

3. BL, Add. Roll 34274. *CPR, Eliz.*, II, pp. 224, 289. PRO, SP 12/20/17; SP 15/11/38.
4. *Commons Journals*, I, p. 58.

This was especially true of the group of men who had been granted Winchester lands after 1551. When Bishop White appeared before the Commons to defend his title to his lands, the only justifications which he was able to adduce for the resumption under Mary were the general plea that the estates had belonged to the see for 1300 years and the specific claim that Gardiner's deprivation was invalid, since he had appealed against the proceedings of the commission. The first claim was apparently ignored, but the second was potentially dangerous, for it could have called in question the legality of other actions of this sort undertaken during Edward's minority. The queen's attorney therefore appeared in person before the House to argue that the deprivation had been valid and that it was safeguarded by a clause which declared it to be *cum omni appellatione remota*. White's case was rendered even less convincing by evidence that he himself felt unsure of his legal possession under Mary. When Gardiner had resumed all the property of the see he had done so merely by royal fiat, a situation which his successor found understandably awkward. He therefore made an attempt to have his estates confirmed by the Parliament of 1557, but the session was closed before his bill had completed its passage through the Commons. Thereupon the bishop tried the device of arranging for the cancellation of all previous grants and the proper issue of letters patent to himself and his successors. It was this manoeuvre that aroused particular indignation in the Elizabethan Commons, for they saw it not only as a device to protect particular estates but also as a potential threat to property rights, which should not be subjected to arbitrary attack by such methods as the cancellation of chancery enrolments. The result was that the claims of the Winchester patentees were accepted rapidly in both Houses, and the estates which had been lost to the laity under Edward were dispersed once more. This did not represent quite such an economic crisis as 1551 had done, for the lands held by the crown under Mary had been returned to Winchester quite legally and remained with the see. However, income fell from £4255 in 1555 to £1869 in 1570, though it crept upwards to over £3000 again after the resumption of Taunton bailiwick in 1575.[5]

Other patentees did not have such a smooth passage in their attempts to resume the estates lost at Mary's accession. The three occupants of the London manors of Southminster, Braintree, Cogge-

5. *Ibid.* I, p. 56. Jones, 'Faith by Statute', pp. 228–30. HRO, Ecc. II/155907; Ecc. II/155915.

shall and Hackney did manage to get legislation in their favour, for again their legal claim upon the properties was strong, and Bonner had never really succeeded in regaining them in the preceding reign. Jobson and Blount, who wished to gain access to Worcester and Durham estates, were less fortunate: the issue of the lost lands of both sees had been contested in the Marian parliaments and the claims of the Catholic bishops upheld. Perhaps because of this, or because the occupants of the sees were able to adduce stronger arguments in favour of the work of the Marian commissioners, the patentees lost their bills. Also lost were a range of more general devices to restore the deprived Edwardian bishops and declare all their parents and leases valid at the expense of the Marians. Bonner was particularly harried by an attempt to declare all Ridley's grants at London valid, which would in turn have led to the cancellation of some of his own leases. This he opposed with characteristic vigour and, while the Commons was eager enough to pass the bill against him, he had the pleasure of seeing it die in the Lords. The patentees apparently needed a strong legal case and some government support to gain their ends through parliament. It may be that the latter was not always forthcoming because the activities of these private individuals threatened to consume far too much of the time of this first parliamentary session, time which was more urgently needed for the settlement of religion.[6]

After the end of the 1559 session and the partial resolution of the problem of the patentees, Durham and Winchester were further depleted by the variant on the act of exchange by which lands taken from the bishops were regranted to them in return for a fixed annual pension paid to the crown. This cost Winchester £400 as a payment for the bailiwick of Taunton and Durham £1020 for a variety of manors within the county and in Allertonshire. Even after the bishops were allowed to resume their estates in return for these payments, their net income was reduced to between £2800 and £3000 in the case of Winchester and between £2300 and £2500 in that of Durham, in each a decline of at least £1000 on the Marian figures. These are the only outstanding cases of income loss during the Elizabethan era, though to complete the picture one should mention two other dioceses. Ely, which had already lost some revenue in 1559, suffered a further decline of about £100 in the great exchange at the end of

6. *Commons Journal*, I, pp. 56–8. *CStP Dom. Eliz.*, Add. 1547–65, pp. 574–5. Strype, *Annals*, I, i, pp. 94–5.

the century. And at Peterborough Bishop Scambler himself reduced the income of the see when he agreed to alienate to Burghley the manors of Thirlby and Southorpe, which constituted about a third of its temporal endowment. But this was an isolated example of reversion to the worst practices of the reign of Edward VI: on the whole, neither crown nor bishops wished to risk the disgrace to the church that came from such transactions. In most sees the erosion of money income, which had been so common in the mid-Tudor period, was halted under Elizabeth, and the bishops enjoyed a long period of comparative stability in the management of their property.[7]

II

Although one should not expect to find evidence of declining income in many of the Elizabethan accounts, one would still suppose them to show the general fixity of rental income and a failure to compensate for continuing inflation. The long Henrician and Edwardian leases already inhibited improvement on many estates, and the added burden of long grants under Elizabeth took many more properties out of the effective control of the prelates. The 1559 exchanges had brought them some revenues that were totally unimprovable, such as the tenths of the dean and chapters and of the clergy of a few dioceses, and other sources of income, such as tithes and rectories, which were also likely to be difficult to develop. Then there were those other constraints which had prevented substantial increases in revenue even before the Reformation crisis. The estate organisation of the bishops continued to be adapted to the stately collection of customary revenues rather than to the introduction of innovatory techniques of management. The need for patronage and local influence remained at least as important as the exploitation of property for profit. Above all, the bishop was a life-tenant and had very little incentive to improve the basic income of his see, especially when there might be other opportunities to make a handsome profit for the benefit of his family. In these circumstances it is somewhat surprising to find that the sees with good series of accounts, recorded in table 11:2, often do show a modest improvement in income over

7. These payments were still considered important in the 1590s when Burghley was at pains to remind his son that they must be agreed before the installation of a new bishop. Peck, *Desiderata Curiosa*, II, no. 5. BL, Lans. MS. 154/2. W. Sheils, 'Peterborough', in *Continuity and Change*, p. 169.

Table 11:2 *Income of the Elizabethan bishops, 1558–1604*

See	Year	Receivers' receipts (£)	Livery (£)	King's Book (£)
Canterbury	1561–97	2700–900	–	2683
Durham	1558–1603	3300–600	3100–300	1821[a]
Winchester	1570	2868	2408	2491
	1591	3105	2545	–
	1595	3168	–	–
York	1561	1610[b]	–	1610
	1597	1890	–	–
London	1561	898	770	1119
	1565	1127	1032	–
	1569	1212	1073	–
	1574	1147	1086	–
	1581	1280	1390	–
	1586	1334	1222	–
	1591	1369	1328	–
	1604	1404	1334	–
Lincoln	1568	964	–	895
Worcester	1561	939	592	1050
	1576	928	694	–
	1578	1154	833	–
	1579	981	966	–
	1580	995	948	–
	Tempore Whitgift	1034[b]	930	–
Salisbury	1592	1604	942	1368
Norwich	1575	773	425	899
	1576	934	815	–
	1594	1298[b]	1071	–
	1596	977	–	–
	1603	995	–	–
Bath and Wells	1566	770	545	533
	1567	818	593	–
	1571	754	522	–
	1573	989	764	–
	1575	810	685	–
	1595	1435	–	–
	1597	1337	–	–
Chichester	1572	678	50	677
	1573	693	1082	–
	1575	723	638	–
	1582	516[b]	456	–
Gloucester	1561	383[b]	337	315
	1580	393	275	–
	1581	388	240	–

Table 11:2 *Income of the Elizabethan bishops, 1558–1604* (cont.)

See	Year	Receivers' receipts (£)	Livery (£)	King's Book (£)
Oxford	1573	405	312	355
	1594	405	328	–
Bristol	1559	331	313	383
	1595	333	308	–

*This is the reduced sum that Durham paid in taxation after 1561. The gross income and livery include the £1020 that had to be paid in rent to the crown. These figures are valuations.

Sources: Du Boulay, 'Archbishop Cranmer', p. 36. Horton, 'Durham Bishopric Estates', pp. 139–40. HRO, Ecc. II/155907. SRO, LM 927/5. PRO, SC 6/Eliz./806; SP 12/46/83. Cross, 'Economic Problems of York', p. 83. PRO, SC 6/Eliz./1458, 1463, 1468. Guildhall, MS. 10, 123/4–18. Lincoln Record Office, Bp/Rentals 3. WRO, CC 900/1/180, nos. 43693–7. PRO, SC 6/Eliz./2442. BL, Harl. MS. 604/fos. 237ff. PRO, SC 6/Eliz./1566. NRO, CC 100021. CUL, Mm/3/12. Harison, *Registrum Vagum*, I, pp. 105–6. Hembry, pp. 143, 187ff. WSRO, Ep. VI/4/1. PRO, SC 6/Eliz./2219; SP 12/19/62; SC 6/Eliz./762, 763; SC 6/Eliz./1836, 1862; SC 6/Eliz./752, 758.

the reign, or at least show an increase on the taxation estimates of the crown recorded in the *King's Book*. Only at Bath and Wells was the increase very marked, but most other sees above the poorest show some flexibility in their receipts and usually some advance either in gross income or in the actual liveries available to the bishops. At the bottom, Gloucester, Bristol and Oxford may perhaps be taken as typical of the ten English and Welsh sees that had revenues under £500 a year. These had few temporalities, with the exception of St David's and Peterborough, and little chance of altering their rental incomes, which the figures suggest remained completely fixed during the reign. They could just manage by keeping costs to a minimum, as the crown obviously did in the case of Bristol, but not all were successful even in this modest aim. The bishops of Gloucester managed to burden their see with fees and wages higher than those of London, which was about four times as wealthy. In these dioceses, therefore, the full effect of inflation had to be absorbed without any improvement in basic revenue.[8]

At the other extreme stands Bath and Wells, which in the 1590s experienced an increase in revenue that almost compensated for the

8. In 1581 fees and wages at Gloucester amounted to £53. PRO, SC 6/Eliz./763.

great land losses under Edward VI. Bishop Still was entirely responsible for this improvement: it resulted from an energetic exploitation of casualties and from a serious and sustained attempt to raise rents, the only clear example under Elizabeth. The improvement may have been even greater than the figures suggest, since the income from the lead-mines of Mendip was not listed in the ordinary accounts, and their production was increasing in the last decades of the century. Bath and Wells is a dramatic example of a process that one can detect more modestly at work in several other dioceses. It is particularly clear in the good series of London accounts. Here the slow but sustained growth in revenues came from a combination of slight increases in rents and much higher levels of fines on the customary lands, which were included in the accounts under the heading of court perquisites. For example, in a ten-year period during Aylmer's occupation of the see, the court revenues at Feering in Essex moved from £4 to £20 and at Stevenage from £3 to £37. The process was repeated on most of the London lands, and the improvement was sustained through the episcopate of Fletcher and Bancroft into that of Vaughan. Substantial fines also explain the buoyancy of Chichester income under Curteys, although here the levels of income fell for the crown during the vacancy. Unfortunately, few sees have income records to rival those of London, and sustained growth is difficult to trace. Nevertheless, the available evidence does raise an interesting question: should these modest improvements be attributed to the efforts of the bishops, or do they reflect a general change in the land market that led to competition for holdings and hence to increased fines and rents? The London figures would suggest that the land market played a significant part in these developments in the later years of the century. The London estates were scattered around the edge of the metropolis and in Hertfordshire and Essex, all areas where land was increasing sharply in value, making it easier for the episcopal officers to exact higher fines. Even in Durham, where prices advanced more slowly and fitfully than those of the south, the modest increase in the basic income of the bishops can be attributed to rising land values. Nevertheless, episcopal initiative was also of importance: given the traditional nature of diocesan organisation, it required a conscious effort to respond to demands for land by raising fines rather than to continue in the customary way. It was this sort of initiative that seems to have been at work at London under Aylmer, at Chichester under Curteys and at Bath and Wells first under Berkeley and later under Still. More detailed evidence for other sees such as York and Hereford might well yield similar results, though some bishops, for example those of Salisbury, were given no opportunity to raise customary fines, since their rents of assize had been leased out with the rest of their estates.[9]

Other bishoprics in table 11:2 show little change in gross income but a fairly consistent increase in liveries. At Worcester, Whitgift, who was able to effect little improvement in rentals, steadily raised his actual receipts by a careful control of costs and by a determined effort not to allow high arrears to accumulate. Once again there was less excuse for arrears than there had been earlier in the century, because of the general increase in land values, yet not all bishops managed to hold them down. In the first year of Whitgift's episcopate he was not particularly successful: arrears stood at £292, and two of the large farmers, John Abington and the farmer of Richard's Castle, had been allowed to build up large debts. Thereafter, however, he allowed no further increase in arrears, and, indeed, his officers managed to reduce the accumulated debts during the course of his episcopate. At Durham and London arrear levels were also kept in check better than in the mid-Tudor period, though again this probably owes as much to the changing economic situation as to sustained episcopal initiative. Control of fixed costs was more evidently the responsibility of the bishop, and again there is evidence from Durham, London and Worcester of efforts in this direction. At Durham, Pilkington deliberately held twelve minor offices vacant, Barnes sixteen and Tobie Matthew twenty-five, and the consequence of this and of lower arrears was an increase in net income. London charges for fees and wages averaged £40 in the last decade of the sixteenth century as compared to £77 in 1527, and the audit expenses had also been halved. Worcester fees had never been high, so there was not so much scope for savings, but a few pounds were pared from the fees bill, and audit costs and necessary expenses were also reduced. As in the case of gross income, it is risky to generalise from the experience of a few well-managed dioceses to all the rest. In some bishoprics costs were certainly not curtailed; annuities continued to be used as a form of reward, and even the practice of giving offices as sinecures flourished. Gloucester still paid out fees to a plethora of park-keepers, even though in at least two cases the park concerned was not under epis-

9. Hembry, pp. 187ff. Guildhall, MS. 10123/10–18. WSRO, Ep. VI/4/1; Ep. I/44/1. Horton, 'Durham Bishopric Estates', pp. 213ff.

copal control. Winchester had begun to pare away some redundant offices by the 1590s but was still burdened by high fixed costs, because annuities of £199 had to be paid from its lands.[10]

The valuations in the table range more widely than the episcopal accounts, and this requires a word of explanation. None of the informal estimates of income produced by the bishops for the benefit of the government have been included. The incentive to distort the figures was obviously great, as in Cooper's statement in the 1590s which put the gross income of Winchester at £2793. Even when the totals seem more accurate than this, it is difficult to be sure exactly what is included within the estimates. The valuations listed are therefore those prepared for the crown by its own officers or by the episcopal officers for the benefit of their masters. The crown estimates tend to be low in relation to the income raised by some of the bishops but to reflect the actual benefits that it derived from a see *sede vacante*. When the queen was in direct possession of a bishopric her officers tended to minimise costs but also to pursue a cautious policy, not increasing rents or fines and therefore deriving a fixed sum from the see. The static income of Bristol and Oxford partly reflects the fact that the crown held those sees vacant for much of the reign. The two valuations prepared for bishops, on the other hand, those for Worcester and Norwich, offer figures somewhat in excess of the income recorded in accounts for the same period. In the case of Worcester the difference is not great and is explained by the inclusion in the valuation of a few ancillary payments. The Norwich estimate is much more interesting, since it includes a calculation about the value of demesne in hand or let out from year to year only. Ludham demesne and manor were assigned a value of £188 as compared to the usual figures of between £40 and £50, and rent corn and other grains were estimated to be worth £52. Thus the Norwich valuation serves as an important indication of the usefulness of revenues not normally added to the accounts, revenues which the bishops did their best to forget when they complained of their poverty to Burghley or Leicester or Hatton.[11]

One final question to emerge from the revenue lists concerns taxation – the sums paid for first-fruits and tenths based upon the esti-

---

10. WRO, cc 900/1/43694. 43697. Horton, 'Durham Bishopric Estates', p. 360. Guildhall, ms. 10123/3, 15–18. SRO, lm/927/3.

11. *CStP Dom.*, 1595–7, p. 215. This was a safe figure to offer to the government, since it was the sum at which taxation was fixed after the 1570s. CUL, Mm/3/12.

mates of the *King's Book*. Several of the original assessments of the *Valor Ecclesiasticus* had been lowered before the Elizabethan era to take account of the drastic alienations under Edward VI. After 1559 Durham, Winchester and Canterbury also had their taxation burden reduced, but, despite these changes, Whitgift was later to oppose any new assessment on the grounds that 'there is not one bishopric in England but it is valued to the full and the most part as I am verily persuaded overvalued by much'. The figures in table 11:2 do not entirely support the archbishop's claim, although his previous see of Worcester was somewhat overtaxed. Those bishoprics which had their payments revised downwards – Bath and Wells, Coventry and Lichfield, Norwich, Lincoln, Exeter and York as well as the three already mentioned – all seem to have been given the benefit of the doubt and to have been paying tax on less than their full value by the end of the Elizabethan era. On the other hand, those which had experienced some loss of land but had not had their first-fruits revised suffered accordingly: Worcester and Ely were paying at a rate as high as or higher than their rental income until the end of the century. In the poor sees taxation valuations and receipts continued to follow one another closely. Thus the victims of the Reformation had one hidden advantage over their more stable brethren; they paid tax at a rate less than their gross receipts and in some cases at less even than their net income, a situation to grieve the heart of any revenue-collector. Yet this modest good fortune must be set in context by comparing the situation of the prelates with that of some rectors. A group of fifty Lincolnshire rectories, for example, had increased in value by an average of 231 per cent between the 1535 survey, on which their taxation was still based, and 1604. There is no reason to suppose that this was atypical: by 1650 rectories in ten dioceses had increased an average of 549 per cent upon their 1535 figures. These changes make the successes of the bishops seem very moderate; given the regular nature of taxation, it must be said that their burden remained heavy throughout the century and that Whitgift's protective instincts were well justified.[12]

The formal accounts of the Elizabethan bishops tell only part of the tale of their attempts to remain solvent or improve their economic position. The other possibilities available to them may be divided crudely into the internal and external, that is, into resources which

12. Bodl., Tanner MS. 79/fo. 21. Hill, p. 111. These figures are for rectories only; the increases for vicarages were much less marked.

could be acquired from outside the bishoprics and the opportunities from within that did not appear in their rental records. External sources can be dismissed fairly briefly. The profits of political office had by now almost disappeared: only Whitgift was a member of the privy council, and even he held no office under the crown. Bishops were no longer required upon foreign embassies, and even the major regional positions, such as that of the presidency of the Council of the North, had passed to laymen. The only appointment that remained a prerogative of the bishops was that of queen's almoner. which was held by Guest, Freke, Watson, Piers, Fletcher and Underhill (not a particularly prepossessing list). Although the office brought little profit in its own right, it offered certain advantages, such as proximity to the court and the possibility of exoneration from the payment of first-fruits. Of course the bishops were still needed as crown servants in their own dioceses and served on the commissions of the peace: these offered them opportunities for patronage, if not financial benefit. As extraordinary local officials, their influence could at times be decisive: in 1564, for example, they had the opportunity to comment on the religious position of their fellow justices and thereby to influence the composition of the bench in the direction of Protestantism. In Norfolk both Bishops Freke and Scambler were able to 'pack' the bench with men who would support their policies, though their triumph was short-lived. But this local role brought expense and difficulty as well as some power: local political struggles absorbed the energies of the Norwich bishops and of Curteys at Chichester as effectively as economic difficulties absorbed the bishops of Coventry and Gloucester.[13]

Direct financial advantage came from the crown's issue of *commendams* rather than from office, thereby emphasising once again the church's dependence upon the benevolent support of the monarch. By the Elizabethan period commended benefices were an essential part of the support of the poorest Welsh sees and of Rochester, Chester and Carlisle. The Elizabethan government extended their use as a means of supplementing income and often as the simplest way of silencing clerical complaints. Little or no sacrifice was involved, and the policy fitted well with the concept adumbrated in 1559 – that spiritual means of support were best for the clergy. The bishops' own

13. *A Collection of Original Letters from the Bishops to the Privy Council*, ed. M. Bateson, Camden Soc., Misc., IX (1893). Hassell-Smith, *County and Court*, p. 63. Manning, *Religion and Society*, pp. 91ff.

attitudes to these livings must have suffered from the same contra-
dictions as their attitude to impropriations given them in the exchanges. When Cecil asked Parker to comment on the bishop of St
Asaph's request for some commended livings in 1563, the archbishop
set out the position with admirable clarity. The livings were necessary,
he said, if the bishop was to maintain any hospitality, since it had
already been customary to give his predecessors support when livings
were better and food cheaper: 'Though these *commendams* seem to be a
kind of appropriation, yet the inconvenience may be thought less than
that the order of godly ministers in that function should be brought
to contempt, for lack of reasonable necessaries, which though before
God it make no great matter . . . yet the world looketh for port
agreeable . . .' The dangers attendant upon *commendams* were, if anything
greater than upon ordinary impropriations, since the bishop concerned often held them for only a few years and therefore had little
incentive to maintain the churches in good order or support a learned
deputy. Moreover, the livings might be a long way from the diocese,
and therefore the bishop might have little knowledge of their circumstances. In 1575 Grindal wrote to Burghley seeking to prevent the
bishop of Carlisle from renewing his right to the benefice of Stokesley
in Yorkshire. 'It is a market town', he wrote, 'and hath been very
evil served ever sith he had it. I would place a preacher to be resident
upon it.'[14]

Despite such problems, the Elizabethan bishops could not afford
the luxury of renouncing the gifts of the government, and the council
never tried to repeat its prohibition of the Edwardian period. Some
of the larger English sees were now given *commendams* for the first time:
Exeter, Norwich, Salisbury and even Winchester benefited, although
the grants were often short term and designed for some specific
purpose, such as assistance with the payment of first-fruits. The poor
sees held livings more consistently, though even in these the value
could vary considerably from one episcopate to another. Rochester
usually derived between £100 and £140 from its rectories and for a
time even held the archdeaconry of Canterbury in commendation;
St David's gained around £70 and Bangor about £100. Carlisle always
held two valuable benefices, as did the bishops of Chester. An extreme

---

14. *Parker Correspondence*, p. 208. Grindal, *Remains*, p. 354. Grindal as archbishop of
    Canterbury advocated either the total abolition of *commendams* or at least their
    restriction to the very poorest sees only. He also sought to sever the com-
    mended link between the bishopric of Rochester and the archdeaconry of
    Canterbury which had led to administrative difficulties in his own diocese.

example of the profit to be made from *commendams* comes from St Asaph: in 1587 William Morgan was accused of deriving a profit of £400 from the archdeaconry and £520 from other cures, sixteen of them in all. The accuser had clear reasons for malice towards the bishop, and the figures must therefore be discounted, but Morgan did hold an unusually large number of benefices, and it would be no surprise to find that they were worth much more to him than his impoverished bishopric. In a poor area such as North Wales the existence of this extensive network of commended livings and of benefices held in plurality by the other higher clergy had a serious effect upon the provision of preaching and presumably on the conversion of the population to Protestantism. The hospitality provided by the bishop of St Asaph would have had to be good indeed to justify such a severe distortion of the primary duties of the church.[15]

Other external sources of income were probably insignificant. The crown occasionally gave outright gifts to the bishops on their translation or promotion. Sandys and Aylmer received such gifts on their promotion to York and London respectively: Sandys claimed that Aylmer was given £397. More common than direct gifts was the restitution of temporalities from some period before the date of a bishop's translation or promotion: the first bishops appointed in 1559 were given half a year's revenue to pacify them when they objected to the exchanges. In the poorest sees this became a common pattern, but even so it was not an unmixed blessing, for when the temporalities were restored the bishop became responsible for the payment of diocesan taxes, and it sometimes meant that they immediately became crown debtors because they had no control in their dioceses during this interim period. Another possible form of royal reward was the grant of leases or keeperships: we noted in the last chapter the attempts of Whitgift to gain the keepership of Otford. Bishop Fletcher was assigned a lease of Wickham and of Paddington, which the crown held on long lease from the bishopric of London. But such grants seem to have been rare and an exceptional mark of royal favour; substantial rewards for the bishops had to wait for the appearance of Charles I.[16]

The last possible source of external wealth was the bishops' own

15. Strype, *Annals*, I, i, p. 306. *CStP Dom.*, 1598–1601, p. 119. Bodl., Tanner MS. 141/fo. 92. Haigh, 'Finance and Administration', in *Continuity and Change*, p. 157. BL, Lans. MS. 76/89. *CPR, Eliz.*, V, p. 34. Strype, *Annals*, II, ii, pp. 524–8.
16. PRO, SP 12/112/45; SP 46/13/230; SP 12/77/40; C 66/37 Eliz./pt 5.

families and the profits of any previous office they had held. These are much less easy to estimate than the commended benefices. What we know of the social status of the bishops' fathers would not suggest that many had wealth as a birthright; only a few such as Whitgift and Henry Cotton are likely to have derived some advantages from their parents' wealth. Their wives may have been of more help, especially in the later years of Elizabeth's reign, when the position of bishop's wife acquired a higher status. Henry Cotton's wife Elizabeth brought with her a dowry of £700, and Bishop Still's second wife, Jane Horner, brought the even larger sum of £1050 to her husband. But these ladies were the exception rather than the rule: many of the first generation of bishops married wives of obscure rank who can scarcely have aided their husbands by more than £100 or so. Much the same is true of the benefits to be derived from the earlier careers of the bishops: the first generation had been exiles or at least had lived in obscurity for Mary's reign and therefore had had few opportunities to accumulate revenue. Later most men reached their sees by way of respectable office in the universities or via deaneries and archdeacon-ries, which would have afforded an adequate revenue but not the opportunities for capital accumulation offered to their predecessors before the Reformation. On the whole, then, only a minority of the prelates who were of good family or fortunate enough to marry well could expect to have income from sources other than their sees or the crown.[17]

When external means of supplement failed the bishops, and their rentals proved inadequate, the more enterprising among them sought for additional income from their estates and spiritualities. The possi-bilities varied markedly from see to see, as did the energy with which individual prelates attempted improvement. In general, the richer the bishopric the greater were the opportunities for extra profit, though other factors, such as the proportion of temporal to spiritual property or the amount of land retained out of lease, could make a great difference to this simple rule. The most obvious and acceptable means of increasing income remained the entry and renewal fines. We have already noted evidence of the attempt in several bishoprics to increase fines upon customary lands, which were listed in the

17. PROB, 11/125/49. Hembry, p. 185. Berlatsky, 'The Elizabethan Episcopate', pp. 73, 77, 80, 82. Matthew Hutton was exceptional in that he accumulated sufficient funds as dean of York to begin to purchase a landed estate at Hag-thorpe. *VCH, Yorkshire East Riding*, III, p. 54.

annual accounts. In London diocese the yield from these fines increased three to four times over in the Elizabethan period: some of the Bath and Wells copies showed a fivefold increase between the 1550s and the 1560s. If the bishops adopted so determined an attitude to their copyhold tenants, it is tempting to assume that the unrecorded demesne fines moved in the same way. The undervaluation of most episcopal estates certainly provided a major incentive to increase fines. A variety of sources for the late years of the century point to this undervaluation. When a hostile commentator assessed the true value of the lands and leases that Sandys had given to his children, he claimed that they were really worth between four and five times the old rental. This might be thought mere malice but for even higher estimates from other sees. An important London survey, prepared about the turn of the century, gives an estimate of the true value of the estates as eight and a half times the annual rental. Here the urban and suburban manors showed the widest discrepancies: Ealing rented for £13. 6s. 8d. but should have yielded £300 per annum; Wormwood Scrubs gave the bishops £6. 13s. 4d. but could have given £100. When three of the Ely manors exchanged in 1599 were valued in preparation for sale, the ratio of improved value to rent was 9:1. Moreover, these figures can be matched with some from contemporary lay estates: on Petre's Essex manors, for example, the range of rents per acre was as wide as 10:1 in 1566 and 24:1 in the 1590s, the main determinant being the age of the beneficial lease. Since so many of the episcopal leases had been made in the early years of the century, the ratio of 10:1 or even more would not be surprising by the close of the Elizabethan era.[18]

The implications of figures such as these, even when they had not been spelled out in detail, must have been obvious to the prelates. But their desire to improve their rentals was hindered by existing leases and by the strongly established convention that all renewals should be beneficial grants made at the old rents. Even when they had the opportunity to make renewals and when existing tenants with personal claims upon the manors died or disappeared, the life-tenure of the bishops encouraged them to accept a fine rather than take the difficult course of raising rents. The fine, of course, could only partially compensate for the loss in value which the old rent now represented. An example will make this clear. If the bishops of

18. Guildhall, MS. 10123/10–18. Hembry, pp. 141–2. BL, Lans. MS. 50/34. Guildhall, MS. 11927. PRO, SC 12/30/33. *Agrarian History*, IV, p. 689.

London had wished to realise the full market value of the manor of Ealing, mentioned above, they would have had to take a fine of £2746 on a twenty-one-year lease (this includes a discount rate of 10 per cent, which was the figure commonly used in the calculation of rents). No figure among the patchy surviving evidence of fine payments even approaches this level. The highest is a sum of £400 paid to Martin Heaton in 1599 for the rectory of Comberton, which had a rental of £19. This seems to be very exceptional, since no other fine has been found for more than twelve times the old rental.[19]

The evidence for demesne fines is still so imperfect under Elizabeth that it is difficult to base any firm argument upon it. Only twenty-seven items of information have been found which are sufficiently clear for the level of fine to be calculated. In these twenty-seven leases payments range all the way from one of less than a year's rental, Richard Cox's grant of Bramsford manor, to the Heaton example cited above. The average fine is the equivalent of four years' rental; the median, of three and a half years'; but in view of the range of diversity of the grants these are not particularly useful figures. The level of fine cannot readily be associated with any one circumstance, such as the length of the grant or the date of renewal or with a particular type of property – rectories, which might be thought less attractive than manors, yielded very high sums in a few cases. The only example of a fine on one of the long leases given via the crown is that of Bishop Middleham Park, Durham, which afforded Barnes a fine of £100 on a rental of £10. Cox claimed that for a similar lease of Somersham (rent £43) he could have had 1000 marks, and it seems likely that the behaviour of Barnes at Durham and Watson at Winchester brought them considerable short-term benefit. Beyond this, the level of fine was probably determined by negotiation and by a medley of individual circumstances such as friendship with the tenant, family considerations, the nature of the property and its state of repair and so on. The scattered information does not even allow us to say if there was a general increase in fine levels during the reign: the two highest figures come from the end of the century, but the next two derive from the 1560s and early 1570s, and nowhere is there a succession of two grants of the same property. But it seems reasonable to assume that the movement from an average of one or two years' rental as fine, which we have noted for the mid-century, to the

19. The first important series of tables to assist in these calculations was T. Clay, *Brief and Necessary Tables*, not published until 1622. EDR, 2/6/1, fo. 165.

approximately four years' that the Elizabethan figures give happened gradually. The same transition can be observed in the movement of fines on crown estates formerly held by the bishops. In the 1560s two years' rental was not uncommon as a payment on these lands, but by the 1570s the average had become four years', and by the end of that decade few fines were lower than the latter figure.[20]

In good circumstances individual bishops could obviously derive handsome profits from demesne fines. But circumstances were good only infrequently. Even the best-endowed sees were hampered and encumbered by long grants, and the bishops had to respond to a variety of other pressures as well as to the need to increase their income. The first generation suffered particularly badly from the constraints imposed by their predecessors and could make few demises, though the bishop of Lincoln and the archbishop of York had a number of rectories available on short leases. By the end of the century the situation in some sees was improved by the falling-in of long grants: the process is very clear at Canterbury where Parker had been able to make only about 12 leases between 1561 and 1575, while Whitgift issued 105 between 1584 and 1600. One would therefore expect that most of the first generation could not gain much from their fines, and, indeed, Parker complained that all his casualties, including fines and wardships, produced only £300 a year. To assess the impact of fines on annual income we might take three sees for which the evidence of leases is good and calculate their fine receipts upon the hypothetical figure of four times the annual rent of property demised. The multiple of four may err on the side of generosity but is probably the best average for the latter part of the century. On this basis Bishop Cox, during his time at Ely, could have expected between zero and £360 a year from his fines, with an average figure of £124. Since Ely was rich and Cox made a fairly large number of grants, especially in his later years, he would have gained more than most of his contemporaries. In the later part of the century the bishops of Durham might have had £481 from fines in 1595, £215 in 1596 and £414 in 1618. These suggest an average income higher than the Ely figures, but they do not compare with our third example, that of Archbishop Whitgift. In 1584 he could have received £1002 in fines and in 1585, £1187. The average for his archiepiscopate between

20. EDR, 2/6/1, fo. 80. I am grateful to Dr Haigh for information upon Chester leases and fines. PRO, SP 12/157/91. Gonville and Caius Coll., Cambridge, MS. 53/30, fo. 33. PRO, LR 8/158, 164, 243. LPL, MS. 807 (i).

1584 and 1599 would have been much lower, £388, but this excludes any estimate for fines on renewal, and Whitgift began a systematic policy of renewing all his grants at least once every seven years. It is unlikely, therefore, that his fine income was less than £500 a year, and this was obviously a major supplement to his rental receipts. Moreover, it was achieved without any resort to those long grants which Barnes had dispensed at Durham or Watson at Winchester.[21]

The importance of using beneficial leases in this way as a major source of regular income was recognised both by the bishops themselves and by their opponents. When Bishop Fletcher was asked in 1594 for a long lease of some of the London estates, he responded not only with the usual objections but with the claim that his estate was 'impossible . . . to be supported without such poor help as come by fines in the see of London'. While the help that Fletcher derived from his fines may have been poor, some members of the laity apparently already suspected that Whitgift's approach could restore much of the wealth of the prelates. In the Parliament of 1601 a bill was introduced 'for the explanation of such statutes as touch leases to be made by archbishops and bishops'. It was rejected on the second reading and does not survive, but the diarist Townshend summarised its purpose as follows: 'that no Bishop or Archbishop might make any Lease in Remaynder till within three years of expiry of the former lease'. The bill was opposed by none other than Mr John Boys, steward to Archbishop Whitgift and member for Canterbury. He claimed that the bill, which was identical in form to one introduced into the preceding session, would be harmful to the prelates and their regular tenants and would bring benefit only to courtiers. In other words, the prelates would have been denied the opportunity of taking fines at regular intervals, and the security of tenure which most farmers in practice enjoyed, would have been threatened by the intrusion of outsiders. The choice of these last parliamentary sessions of the reign to revive the question of episcopal rights over leases suggests both continuing courtier interest in the exploitation of these grants and suspicion of the sort of policy that the archbishop had begun to undertake.[22]

21. *Chapter Acts of Lincoln*, III, pp. 167ff. I owe the York reference to Dr W. Sheils. CDC, v 1–3. PRO, SP 12/277. *Parker Correspondence*, p. xii. EDR, 2/6/1. Horton, 'Durham Bishopric Estates', p. 143. PRO, SP 12/277. The few fines listed in Whitgift's account book range from two years' to six years' rental. LPL, MS. 807 (i).
22. *HMC, Salisbury MSS.*, XIII, p. 32. S. D'Ewes, *Journals of all the Parliaments* (1682),

Other methods of financial improvement needed close episcopal supervision, especially the direct exploitation of the estates. Direct farming still raised all sorts of problems for the prelates, and in only a few cases can it be said that there was a sharp increase in the level of agrarian activity. Much more tempting were the woodlands and parks, which often remained in the prelates' own hands. The profits from wood were in theory listed in the episcopal accounts, but one's impression is that felling of timber on the demesne was often not recorded, especially the felling of great trees. Nor were the 'sales' of woodland for exploitation by an individual for a fixed term of years always included: these usually appear among the leases, though they do not conform to the ordinary pattern of grants. As we have already seen, the question of the use of woodland had always been a sensitive one. A bishop had an obligation to conserve and maintain his tree-stock but had a right to use his woods for repairs and fuel and to sell any genuine excess on the open market. Both the life-interest of the prelate and the need of the crown for timber *sede vacante* had militated against the preservation of woods, and by the Elizabethan period some sees such as Canterbury, Rochester, and Bath and Wells had had much of their best wood removed. The problem then assumed a new urgency as the government became aware of the depletion of an important national resource, and the bishops recognised their remaining timber as one of their most valuable casual assets. The best solution was to allow the cutting of damaged wood and underwood but to conserve the stock of timber trees. In practice this was very difficult to achieve, since one prelate's timber tree was another's old, redundant log. Moreover, it was tempting to sell timber which was otherwise being conserved only for the benefit of the crown, but at some cost to the bishop, since he had to employ woodwards and sacrifice parkland which might have been turned to other uses.[23]

There had been intermittent warnings from the government to the bishops ever since the Reformation that woods must not be despoiled; then in the later 1570s the privy council decided that more systematic action was necessary. The international situation made the conservation of timber for shipbuilding more important, and there

---

pp. 623, 625. Heyward Townshend, *Historical Collections* (1680), pp. 186–7. I owe this latter reference to Mr L. Jenkins.

23. Part of the Ely woods, for example, were let out under Cox, but this did not prevent him from exploiting the rest. EDR, 2/6/1, fos. 122–2v, 144v, 157. PRO, SP 12/136/33, 71.

had been specific complaints that Aylmer of London was depleting his woods at an alarming rate. An order was therefore sent out in 1579 that no more great trees were to be felled, and the bishops were required to furnish the council with evidence about the number and value of the trees they had already taken. Responses survive for ten bishoprics and can be tabulated as in table 11:3. As an indication of the true profit the bishops derived from their woods, the figures in the table are only marginally more useful than the episcopal accounts.

Table 11:3 *Value of timber trees sold by the Elizabethan bishops, 1559–80*

See	Bishop	Year of entry to office	Estimate of value sold
Canterbury	Grindal	1576	Nil
London	Aylmer	1576	£600–£1000
Rochester	Young	1578	Nil
Salisbury	Piers	1577	£244
Durham	Barnes	1577	Nil
Carlisle	Barnes[a]	1570	Nil
Worcester	Whitgift	1575	£28
Lincoln	Cooper	1571	Nil
Bath and Wells	Berkeley	1560	£4
Hereford	Scory	1559	£230 + 200 trees unvalued

[a]Translated to Durham in 1577.
Sources: PRO, SP 12/136/33, 45, 65, 71, 75, 77, 79; SP 12/137/33, 72.

Even if we accept the estimates for sales at their face value, there is no allowance for one of the major benefits of the woodlands, their use as fuel and repair-timber. Whitgift's careful certificate offers some guidance on this matter. In less than five years at Worcester he had felled sixty-four oaks and three elms just to ensure that necessary repairs could be undertaken. Some sees, notably Rochester and Lincoln, claimed that there was no danger of their selling trees since they did not even have enough for the basic needs of the household and the tenants. However, these seem to have been the exception, and for most of the respondents the woods supplied their needs and left some stock in reserve.[24]

Of course, the estimates of the bishops, placed on the defensive by the council, cannot be taken at face value. The behaviour of Aylmer,

24. PRO, SP 12/136/65.

which triggered the enquiry, was certainly suspect. He was accused of cutting almost all the oaks in Hornsea Park for a profit of £1042, and then there were the famous elms at Fulham, which he is supposed to have felled to earn Harington's pun on his name 'Elm-mar'. The substance of the accusations seems likely to be true enough, given Aylmer's ruthless intentions of building a fortune for his family, though in the case of the Fulham elms there is a delightful (apocryphal?) story that the queen, on being told of the bishop's activities, expressed surprise, since she had recently stayed at Fulham, 'where she misliked nothing but that her lodgings were kept from all good prospect by the thickness of the trees'. Aylmer did his best to blame the depletion of the London woods on Sandys, who was supposed to have destroyed four hundred acres of woodland. Again, given the general behaviour of Sandys, he probably did cut more than could reasonably be tolerated, but relations between the two men were very bad at this time, and the figures given are malicious guesswork. The sums reported by Piers, Barnes and Scory are also likely to be under-assessments: Barnes is known to have been cutting wood at Durham, and Piers was accused of depleting the resources of his bishopric after he had left for York. Other bishops whose replies to the government do not survive were also busy felling their timber. Richard Cox was accused in 1575 of having taken £4000 worth of wood from his estates. He insisted that the figure should be £1000, but even this must represent a considerable part of the value of the woodlands of the see, since some of the best woods had been lost in 1559. Sandys was charged as early as 1563 with selling large parts of the Worcester woods and offering a thousand oaks for sale on the manor of Richard's Castle. Matthew Parker had to defend himself against the allegation that he was selling his woodlands for the benefit of his family. The problem with this welter of accusation and counter-accusation is that there were no independent criteria of what wood could or should have been taken by each prelate without damage to the interests of his successors or irreparable loss to the national stock of trees. The extent of woodland in some of the larger sees is indicated by the list of Canterbury woods in John Parker's notebook. Thirteen are listed, and the ten which have measurements attached totalled 2965 acres. Yet even with woods such as these, the archbishops apparently had to be prudent – Grindal commented in 1580 that he used trees only for repairs and fuel, and Whitgift was equally careful later. The same was true at Winchester, where the very large woods had been exploited and sold steadily throughout the sixteenth century and where, by the 1580s, the bishop claimed to have few timber trees left to sell.[25]

If the exploitation of timber brought royal disapproval upon the bishops, farming for the market seems to have brought the criticism of the laity. This hostility had first been shown in the Reformation Parliament when, by 21 Henry VIII c. 13 the bishops had been prohibited from marketing the provisions of their estates, except those that were a by-product of the servicing of their households. Although the act was not invoked under Elizabeth, its sentiments lingered in the form of criticisms of those bishops who were 'great farmers and husbandmen'. This may have inhibited the prelates' agrarian enterprise, though a more important consideration was that farming for more than the episcopal household involved operations so complex and risky that they often held little attraction. It was necessary to have demesne in hand, to employ labour, to engage in efficient marketing and to have an estate administration directed towards the care of agriculture as well as the collection of rents. It would be an exaggeration to suggest that any of the bishops made the changes necessary to increase their income radically through sales of agrarian products. Such sales as were conducted were still principally of the by-products of farming for the household – skins, wool, a few muttons or beefs, the occasional specialist product such as salt. But within this pattern some evidence can be found of increased interest in marketing estate products. Richard Cox was charged in 1575 with being a great farmer and maintaining flocks and herds for the benefit of his family. His response was that only a few of the excess beasts not needed by his household found their way to the Ely butchers. However, evidence from the Isle of Ely shows that Cox was keeping large flocks of sheep on the summer pastures in the fen, and it seems likely that this overproduction was intentional. Sandys was also accused of selling to the market, as was Bishop Scory, and again these accusations would seem to be consistent with the energetic and exploitative policy of both men.[26]

25. PRO, sp 12/137/10–11. Harington, *Nugae Antiquae*, ii, p. 39. E. Venables, *Episcopal Palaces* (1895), p. 64. PRO, sc 6/Eliz./661; c 66/36 Eliz./pt 11. BL, Lans. ms. 20/72. PRO, sp 12/38/36. *Parker Correspondence*, pp. 371–3. LPL, ms. 737/53v. PRO, sp 12/136/71; e 178/3100.
26. BL, Lans. ms. 20/72. PRO, sp 12/28/36. The flocks kept by such Welsh bishops as Richard Davies and William Blethin also suggest specialisation for the market. PROB, 11/63/45; 11/77/42.

For most of the rest of the bishops the limited demesne still held in hand was probably used for the supply of the household or to increase rents by leasing on a year-to-year basis. The potential value of even a small area held in this way has already been noted for the Norwich estates. A comparable assessment comes from the diocese of Carlisle in the early seventeenth century. A survey conducted in 1627 put the value of the demesne of Rose Castle, the only area retained by the bishop, at £110, or about 18 per cent of the value of the see. When Sandys and Aylmer were busy abusing one another in their dispute upon dilapidations in the 1570s, the latter claimed that the York demesnes were worth £500 a year and that the Hadham demesnes of London had been let out by Grindal for £300. Sandys did not deny the substance of either of these assessments, though he complained that he had had no access to the York demesnes during the first winter of his promotion.[27]

The terms in which Aylmer and Sandys discussed the demesnes suggest that they were seen first as a means to supply the household and secondarily as a source of profitable short leases. Some surviving episcopal inventories for the Elizabethan period help to indicate how far the bishops were engaged in farming rather than leasing. With the exception of two York inventories for Young and Matthew, the ones that give details of farming operations are all for men who died as crown debtors – Kitchin, Parkhurst, Bentham, Bradbridge, Curteys and Howland. As they came from poor sees, one would expect their stock to be correspondingly modest. However, in some cases they owned equipment which would not have disgraced a gentleman farmer or large tenant. Kitchin had the least, perhaps because he had granted away so much of his demesne: he held at death forty-five sheep, eight cattle, and grain and hay worth £7. 13s. 4d. Curteys had eighteen oxen, twenty-seven cattle and no fewer than twenty-one horses, as well as some sown and stored wheat. Bradbridge had fewer horses and ox teams but had a flock of a hundred sheep and lambs, while Howland had eighteen horses, three yoke of oxen and almost three hundred sheep; he also had sown wheat and barley worth £100. This was exceeded only by Young, who had corn in store worth £113 and livestock worth £324, including a flock of over eight hundred sheep. It is interesting that there seems to have been a contraction in the farming operations at York between the death of Young in 1568 and that of Matthew in 1628: the latter had only a flock of a hundred

27. CuRO, DRC/2/46. PRO, SP 12/112/45.

sheep and two-thirds the number of oxen owned by the former. The only man among the crown debtors who was poorly equipped was Marmaduke Middleton: he died owning two old cows and two poor horses 'ready to die'. But Middleton had been deprived of his bishopric some time before his death and probably had little incentive to maintain any stock. In all cases except that of Middleton, stock and agrarian products represented a substantial part of the inventoried wealth of the bishops: 28 per cent for Kitchin, 32 per cent for Bradbridge and approximately the same for Parkhurst and Howland, though the figures are more difficult to disentangle. It is also worth emphasising how important these products must have been for the poorer bishops: Howland's grain, for example, was worth about a quarter of the total value of his rents. Of course, the grain could not be pure profit: seed had to be set aside and labour employed to tend and harvest it. Even so, it must have yielded large benefits to a see such as Peterborough, especially when it is remembered that Howland died at the end of the 1590s, that decade of bad harvests and high prices.[28]

The inventories offer no information upon how much land was retained by the bishops or upon the proportion of arable to pasture. However, some clues are available in the nature of the stock held by each prelate. It is predictable that Curteys, farming the Sussex coastal plain, and Howland, on the edge of the Midlands, should have concentrated upon arable farming, though Howland was also probably able to take advantage of his position on the fen edge to run his flock of sheep. Equally predictably, the inventories of Bradbridge and Kitchin suggest that in the West Country sheep-rearing was the main preoccupation, and sheep were also very important to both archbishops of York. This did not prevent the archbishops from farming the demesne at Cawood near York with forty-six oxen in Young's case and thirty-four in that of Tobie Matthew. It is slightly surprising to find arable farming on this scale, even when the agrarian circumstances favoured crop-growing, for this implies a complex organisation and the payment of wages to a large group of men. On *a priori* grounds it might be assumed that the bishops would look to stock-rearing as the most profitable and simplest form of agrarian activity. The parklands which they still retained in hand offered very useful grazing, and their ancillary rights of lordship also gave them access to common ground for feeding. The wages for stock-farming were lower than for arable, although the cost of replacing beasts could be high, as the bishops of Durham had discovered earlier in the century. Even if a prelate did not wish to organise an elaborate farming operation, he still needed grazing land for horses and so tended to retain this demesne in hand. Both Durham and Canterbury show this pattern of concentration upon stock at the expense of arable. Bishop Barnes of Durham kept in hand the parks of Stockton and Auckland, part of Durham meadows, and gates for 'eight beasts' in the Moor Close. Only two stretches of arable, one at Auckland and one at Stockton, were retained, and even these he leased before his death. Whitgift at Canterbury was certainly not so imprudent as to lease out further demesne, but the land he retained was essentially meadow: fifty-seven acres at Lambeth, thirty-nine at Croydon, parks at Croydon and Ford and some general demesne at Bekesbourne that was often used for geldings. Whitgift was solving the problem of grain partly by taking rents in kind from his tenants, so he avoided the need to organise arable farming on his demesne.[29]

The prelates were united in recognising the importance of a well-stocked demesne. Cooper, Day, Henry Cotton, Aylmer and Redman all complained bitterly that they found their demesnes unstocked and were gravely disadvantaged by the greed of their predecessors. The first generation of Elizabethan bishops seem to have encountered the worst of the problem, for they often arrived in their sees two or three years after the disappearance of the Marian bishops and, not unnaturally, found their land neglected. Berkeley, when he arrived at Bath and Wells, said that he was destitute of all provisions but was expected to offer hospitality in the old style, and Bentham grumbled about the behaviour of his popish predecessor. To blame the previous bishop was no doubt not always fair; executors and servants must often have been responsible for the disappearance of stock and goods, as they were in the notorious case of Bishop Godwin of Bath and Wells. But whatever the agent, the result was the same, and the consequences were clearly explained by Bishop Cooper in a letter to Burghley. He arrived at Winchester after the death of the weak Watson and found no stock or provision on the demesnes. For his first year, always, as has been shown, a time of financial difficulty, he was therefore constrained to buy all his basic foodstuffs 'by the penny', to his grave disadvantage. Other stray indications of the value of demesnes come from some of the battles waged by the prelates to

29. DDR, HC/M64.

retain their property. Cox's determination to keep Somersham and Whitgift's attempt to regain possession of Hartlebury Castle cannot be explained solely by the rental value of the two manors, £45 and £30 respectively. They were, of course, estates to which much prestige attached because of their attractive residences, but the bishops also valued them for their land, which was not leased. Whitgift calculated that Hartlebury had parkland to service twenty horses, six oxen and forty sheep as well as deer, a large heath for coneys, fish-ponds, pasture providing fifty loads of hay and good timber woods. Sandys's reluctance to lease Bishopthorpe may also have been influenced by the availability of its demesne. Finally, that really energetic prelate Bishop Still demonstrated how valuable demesne in hand could be, even if it was not needed for direct exploitation. His predecessors at Bath and Wells had leased all but a home farm or two: as some of these grants fell in he retained the estates in hand, so that by his death four of the eight central manors of the see were no longer in lease. Much of this property was in fact re-leased at higher rents, and thus the fiscal benefits of demesne were made immediately and abundantly clear. In the early Jacobean period some other prelates, such as John Jegon of Norwich, began to take the same road back towards the use of demesne for short leases.[30]

Income in kind could also be derived from the tenants, with the advantage that the bishops incurred none of the hazards or costs of farming. Thomas Wilson suggested that this was the main reason why the clergy were not impoverished, since they had reserved for themselves 'corn, mutton, beef, poultry or such like' in addition to the bare rents. There had always been some grain and other payments in the larger sees, even though they played an insignificant role in total revenue. Revival of food rents was an obvious way of countering inflation, but there were difficulties, since farmers were understandably reluctant to commute from a money payment back to the provision of grain or stock. Most bishops, therefore, seem to have contented themselves with keeping a more accurate check upon the traditional food rents that involved no controversy. There are careful lists of rent corn and hens etc. preserved for the later sixteenth century: at Norwich, Anthony Harison was particularly assiduous in pursuing the bishops' rights to these foods. The Norwich prelates could claim 166 coombs of barley from their tenants. The only really

30. PRO, sp 12/16/27. Berlatsky, 'Thomas Bentham', p. 328. Hembry, pp. 175ff. BL, Egerton ms. 1693/fo. 115. WRO, cc 900/1, no. 43697. CUL, Dd/12/43.

striking use of food rents, beyond this careful enforcement, comes from the see of Canterbury during Whitgift's archiepiscopate. Canterbury had a consistent history of taking food and stock from its tenants, though poor records make it difficult to establish the extent of the practice under Cranmer or Pole. What does seem clear is that Parker began to extend these demands. On the manor of Boughton, for example, he asked for twenty wethers over and above the customary cash rent. Few leases survive for Grindal's period in office, but even if he continued Parker's policy it can scarcely have borne such rich fruit as the behaviour of his successor, Whitgift. During his time at Worcester, Whitgift had been interested in conserving food rents. He devoted much energy to the retrieval of the grain rents of Hallow, leased out by Nicholas Bullingham for only £15 but worth in his estimation at least £59. In the first few years of his tenure of Canterbury he kept careful personal accounts of all the ordinary and extraordinary income of the see and took especial note of the value of grain and food rents. The number of leases he was able to issue offered an ideal opportunity to develop this income in kind. Whitgift's lease book shows that he was able to extract 204 fat wethers, 194 quarters of wheat and 20 loads of hay annually from his tenants. A majority of these rents appear to have been consumed within the household: in 1584, for example, the archbishop received 190 quarters of wheat, of which 132 were consumed within the household, 40 were sold and the rest remained as reserve at the year's end. The full value of these provisions can be appreciated by comparing the Canterbury lists with the expenditure of Horne's Winchester establishment in 1568. Horne's steward had to pay £102 for 170 fat wethers and £55 for wheat, probably about 90 quarters at the prices current in the 1560s By the 1590s, when bad harvests drove prices upwards so sharply, the Canterbury household must have saved several hundreds of pounds on the basic foodstuffs provided by its tenants.[31]

The extensive use of food rents at Canterbury showed a very important way of improving the situation of the bishops without damage to the long-term interests of the see. Unfortunately, few others seem to have had the capacity or the will to follow the example of Whitgift. Indeed, most forms of positive improvement appear to

31. CUL, Dd/12/43, p. 212. CDC, v 2/fo. 88. WRO, cc 900/1, no. 43697. PRO, sp 12/277. LPL, ms. 807 (i). SRO, lm/927/4. J. E. Thorold Rogers, *A History of Agriculture and Prices in England* (Oxford, 1866–1902), iv, pp. 267, 292. Thorold Rogers gives the average price of a quarter of wheat in 1561–70 as 12s. 10¼d.

have been too difficult for a majority of the prelates. There are hints that a few, such as Sandys, Aylmer, Scory, Young, Horne and Cooper, were endeavouring to increase the yield of their lands, yet even if we add this group to those already discussed, only a handful of the Elizabethan bench have been mentioned. The poor prelates, with little demesne and few resources beyond their bare rents, obviously had little opportunity for improvement. But even some of the best endowed were unable to take advantage of their immediate circumstances. Perhaps the most obvious example of this is the failure of the bishops of Durham to benefit from the vast reserves of coal that still lay beneath their estates. The bishops should have been ideally placed to take advantage of the rise in fuel prices. In fact, the corporation of Newcastle was able to monopolise the coal trade and, by the grand lease of the Whickham mines, to take most of the profit of the actual mining operations as well. Although it would have been difficult for any Elizabethan bishop to challenge this monopoly, the Durham prelates seem to have surrendered their rights without any real struggle. Bishop Pilkington was the only one who made any attempt to benefit from the mineral resources of the see. It is interesting that the bishops of Bath and Wells, who also had mines on their property – the lead-mines of the Mendips – were more successful in retaining their rights to royalties, which became a major source of profit under Bishop Still. The difference seems to lie in the scale of the mineral resources and in the timing of their development. The Durham mines had long been recognised as of major importance, and the demand for coal rose sharply during the first half of the Elizabethan period. This meant that the merchants of Newcastle were able to assert their monopoly powers at a time when the episcopate was weak, especially after the appointment of the pliant Barnes. The lead-mines of Mendip, on the other hand, were developed only in the last years of the century and were never of the scale or significance of the Durham mines. They therefore attracted less lay interest, and by good fortune the see of Bath and Wells had a strong and able bishop at the time when they began to yield substantial rewards. But in neither case did the bishops of Durham or Bath and Wells participate directly in the process of mining: that had been abandoned as too hazardous at Durham in the early years of the century and was never even attempted elsewhere. The prelates chose to depend upon the entrepreneurial skill of others.[32]

32. Bodl. Tanner, MS. 79/fo. 84v. BL, Lans. MS. 66/84–7. J. Nef, *The Rise of the British Coal Industry* (1932), I, pp. 37–9, 148–55. Hembry, pp. 187–92.

The benefits and hazards of direct management of the estates can best be illustrated by the well-documented example of Richard Cox of Ely. Cox's conflict with Lord North brought to light a mass of information upon the organisation of the see which would normally have left little trace upon the records. The bishop was accused by North and his supporters of a range of misdemeanours, most of which he vehemently and aggressively denied. From this farrago of charges and counter-charges emerges a picture of a man who sought to make his property pay better than it had customarily done; who did so with little tact and small use of the weapons of persuasion. Cox undoubtedly held sincerely to reformed principles, but when he was appointed bishop saw nothing incongruous about assuming the full authoritarian mantle of his predecessors. Thus, when some of his Doddington tenants presumed to question his judgements in a fenland dispute, he admonished them in pontifical tones, 'ye are so stout disordered and so lawless a people that neither the order of me and [sic] my council can stay you'. His second wife, the widow of the puritan dean of Wells William Turner, helped to reinforce these attitudes: one tenant who was evicted from his land after a dispute with her compared her to Jezebel, and he seems to have spoken for many of his fellows. One could describe the thrust of Cox's policy as follows: first, he sought to undo as much as possible of the damage done by the long leases of his predecessors, and secondly, he tried to use the unleased property of the see more efficiently. He moved towards the achievement of his first objective, though only at the cost of bad relations with many of his tenants. The reentry clauses formerly included in all leases were actually used against those who failed to produce their rents. Thus Alexander East was ejected from the rectories of Dry Drayton and Swavesey, and the important manor of Downham was taken from Austin Steward. In both cases legal battles ensued, but the bishop's claims were apparently vindicated. Where there was no chance of taking back a lease Cox sometimes pursued the more common practice of buying in the grant when it became available on the market. He failed to purchase the lease of Stretham when he offered the existing tenant only £280 but was more successful with the Doddington estate, which he was able to describe in 1580 as 'lately redeemed at great cost . . . for the perpetual quiet of the said see of Ely'.[33]

---

33. For a detailed discussion of Cox's disputes see Heal, 'The Bishops of Ely', ch. 7; *HMC, 9th Report*, Records of King's Lynn, I, p. 296; BL, Lans. MS. 20/73;

His second objective was even less easily achieved, since it had long been customary for the tenants to think of the bishops of Ely purely as rentier landlords. Cox's customary tenants were made to feel that their property was no longer secure: in several cases the bishop was accused of illegal evictions and of rack-renting, though the evidence does not suggest that there was any consistent attempt to raise rents. Cox certainly tried to increase the ancillary duties and obligations of the customary tenants. He claimed extensive rights to carriage duties within the Isle, citing as his authority the 'Old Coucher', the great survey of tenurial obligations prepared for the see in 1251. He also claimed that they should sell him turves and fowl at fixed prices, again rights which the bishops had undoubtedly once possessed but which had been allowed to lapse over a long period of time. Then there were his activities in grazing and farming for the market, which have already been mentioned, and his exploitation of the wood and parklands of the see. There can be little doubt that the principal beneficiaries from Cox's improvements were his family and that Mrs Cox cooperated so zealously with her husband for the advantage of her family and stepchildren rather than that of the see. But the bishop claimed to see in his actions nothing that operated to the disadvantage of the diocese and much that would be beneficial to his successors. There may be some justice in his claim when the individual measures are considered: he did increase the basic revenues by about £100 and rid his living of some of the worst problems of long leases and lay influence. Nevertheless, like too many of his fellow bishops, he left a legacy of bad relations with the laity of his see which was damaging to the interests of the church. His critics complained of his litigiousness: 'Since King Edward the Third's time no Bishop of his predecessors have had so many suits as this bishop within these xvii years.' Cox blamed the times, not his own disposition, and no doubt had ample provocation, but it remains true that he exposed himself to lay criticism by his methods of proceeding. Like Aylmer and Sandys, his approach brought disrepute upon the church which he intended to serve well.[34]

The aspect of Cox's policy found most commonly among other bishops was the plan to resume or repurchase leases. Since fines were still the best form of additional income and since episcopal families

---

PRO, c 3/bundle 58/no. 5; EDR, 2/6/1, fos. 145, 157v–158.
34. BL, Lans. ms. 20/73.

and friends were always hungry for patronage, this proved more attractive than the struggle to improve the limited home demesne. John Jewel, that model of a charitable prelate, was willing to reenter the valuable manor of Sonning when the rents were unpaid and suffered the inevitable chancery suit against him as a result. Thomas Bentham pinned much of his hope for recovery at Coventry and Lichfield upon the lease of Hanberry rectory, which he claimed had been granted out in an invalid manner by his Marian predecessor, Bishop Baynes. Much of his time and energy during his first two years in the see was devoted to its recovery, an exercise which proved a considerable short-term drain on the resources he intended to improve. His successor, William Overton, struggled to regain rents from Lord Paget and the city of Lichfield that had originally been part of lease agreements. At Carlisle in 1583 John Best endeavoured to prove that the lease of Melbourne rectory made by an earlier bishop was invalidated by its reversionary clause. This is a particularly interesting example, since Best's correspondence with the earl of Shrewsbury reveals the whole motivation behind the litigation. The bishop had already been given money in lieu of a fine by Shrewsbury before the case came to court and had granted him a lease. Unfortunately, he failed to prove the existing grant invalid and was left in the embarrassing position of having to repay the fine but not having the money to hand. His solution is equally interesting: since there were still eight years to run on the existing grant, he was at liberty to renew it, and since the existing farmer was eager to retain the property, he could probably be persuaded to part with a lump sum which would help to repay Shrewsbury. This complex transaction neatly reveals both the difficulties of, and the advantages still held by, the landowning bishops. Their lands still afforded them a range of possibilities, but only if they were prepared to be shrewd and aggressive and ever alert to the encroachment of the laity. A glance at the records of Chancery and Requests shows that many bishops were prepared to defend their rights with energy and determination. Yet despite the volume of litigation to which these courts attest, no prelate seems to have achieved a success in the struggle to regain leases comparable to that of the dean and chapter of Durham. The chapter was able to find technical errors in the long grants of the 'corpes' lands or central demesnes, which had been given out on long lease under Edward. The recovery of these lands allowed them to resume both direct farming and short leasing at increased rents and ensured that they were more than able to combat the effects of inflation. The most that the prelates could hope for was the exploitation of lands accidentally excluded from some of the long leases. For example, the diligent Anthony Harison was able to find a variety of small parcels of Norwich lands which had not been included in Scambler's long grant to the queen and to ensure that the bishops realised a profit from leasing these for short periods of time.[35]

When estate-orientated means of improving income failed, the bishops could always turn to a variety of other expedients, most of them even less compatible with the good reputation of the order. The favourite was undoubtedly dilapidations – a means of transferring wealth within the bench rather than looking to outward improvements. Dilapidations assumed a new importance in the Elizabethan age, partly because the neglect of property after the mid-Tudor years was genuine in many sees and partly because of the need for extra income to assist episcopal families. If a new prelate felt that he urgently needed extra revenue on his entry to a see and wished to cause trouble, he could usually find some decayed property and claim money from his predecessor or his executors. A classic example of this process is the use to which the bishops of Norwich put the ruined abbey of St Benet's, Holme, which had been their property since 1536. It had fallen rapidly into decay after the dissolution and was little used by the bishops. In 1579 Freke described the house as 'down' and the site as 'so unwholesome, as neither I am able to rectify the same, nor yet build any other convenient house there'. Yet as late as 1603, when John Jegon succeeded to the bishopric, he endeavoured to claim £3161 in dilapidations for the decayed abbey, as almost all his predecessors had done. Other sees offered similar buildings long since uninhabited but still technically liable to be kept in good repair. This was especially true of the larger dioceses, where superfluous houses still abounded: Durham and Winchester were particularly unfortunate in this respect. The legal position was that houses uninhabited for a hundred years could not be claimed for dilapidations and that a prelate was not responsible for the decays of his predecessors. This last formulation, while admirable in intention, did not prevent endless argument about who was guilty of allowing decays.

35. PRO, c 3/bundle 157/76. Berlatsky, 'Thomas Bentham', pp. 332–4. O'Day, 'Cumulative Debt', pp. 82–3. LPL, ms. 698/29. D. Marcombe, 'The Dean and Chapter of Durham, 1558–1603', unpub. Ph.D. thesis, University of Durham (1973), pp. 117–35. CUL, Mm/3/12, pp. 159, 177, 185.

The incoming bishop, before being allowed to make his own claim, had to prove that his predecessor had not spent all that was reasonable on repairs from his annual rental and from the dilapidations he had received at his entrance. The anxiety created by the question of dilapidations can be seen even earlier in the century in the occasional wills that mention them. Cardinal Pole made a specific request to his successor that his executors should not be troubled by claims, since he had spent more than £1000 on reedifying his buildings. One of the earlier archbishops, William Warham, had made a similar request, having paid £30,000 to keep his property in good repair.[36]

The fragmentary evidence for the earlier sixteenth century suggests that most dilapidation agreements were made between the two parties without resort to litigation and were recorded either in the episcopal register or on the dorse of the Close Roll. The loss of the records of Arches and Delegates, the two courts where disputes between the bishops were heard, makes it impossible to be sure of the scale of litigation even under Elizabeth, but contemporaries were in no doubt that it was on the increase. One commentator, perhaps writing at the time of the dispute between Aylmer and Sandys, noted that in times past the problem of decays had been settled amicably between the parties and that 'it can not be found by search of the records of all these ecclesiastical courts that ten bishops have all gotten any sentence judicial or did sue against their predecessors' executors and vii of those very lately since the Queen's Majesty's reign that now is'. Settlements out of court still occurred: Cooper, for example, accepted £530 from the executors of Bishop Watson, though Sandys was probably right in assuming that he could have exacted more when the manors of Winchester were in a state of decay. No doubt in many of the smaller sees there was still agreement between the parties, since the number and values of the properties involved would scarcely have been great enough to justify the costs of litigation. But elsewhere it became the norm rather than the exception to resolve the issue of dilapidations at law, and a few *causes célèbres* helped to foster an image of the prelates as involved in greedy internecine strife for the loot of the church. The conflict between Herbert Westfaling and the executors of Scory at Hereford was one such case, though it derived more of its drama from the behaviour of Scory's wastrel son, Sylvanus, than from the bishop, who was a man of considerable integrity.

36. BL, Lans. MS. 29/39. CUL, Dd/12/43, p. 277. Strype, *Ecclesiastical Memorials*, III, ii, p. 143. PROB, 11/24/18.

Even Westfaling was not above promoting a claim of £600 for the ruined manor of Bosbury, for which the Scory family almost certainly held no personal responsibility, the incentive being that the rest of the dilapidations amounted to only £250 or so.[37]

The case which brought most critical comment, however, was the great dispute between Aylmer and Sandys about the repairs of London. The affair is of such complexity that it merits a study of its own, but the outline will be considered here to illustrate the depths to which two distinguished leaders of the church could sink when in need of income. Sandys was instrumental in ensuring the promotion of Aylmer to London, and since they were friends at this time, there seems to have been an informal agreement between them that Sandys should pay only nominal dilapidations for damage done at London. The friendship was soon strained by argument about whether Aylmer should receive the rents for Michaelmas 1576, and relations went from bad to worse as the two irascible men assumed entrenched positions. Aylmer no doubt discovered that his predecessor had done little to repair the property of the bishopric, and, faced with the need to support and educate a large family, decided to seek some recompense. Thus, three years after his promotion, he brought a suit against his old friend, claiming £1603 for decays in four manor houses, four appropriated churches and the cathedral of St Paul's. Sandys was infuriated both by the timing and the content of the demands. He claimed to have spent more on the London properties than either of his immediate predecessors and to have done so without any benefit of dilapidations from Grindal at London or York. He was particularly alarmed by the large sum asked for St Paul's, since the decays had been caused by the fire of 1561 and could not be attributed to his negligence or even that of Grindal. Indeed, in claiming money for St Paul's as part of the dilapidations, Aylmer seems to have overstepped the bounds established by canon law, and they were omitted from the final judgement in the case. Apart from the specific accusations of repairs left undone, Aylmer grounded his case upon the claim that canon law demanded that a quarter of annual income should be used for maintenance, an extraordinarily high figure to which even the most conscientious bishop could not have aspired. Grindal, who was drawn into the dispute by Aylmer's claim that £300 was owing from his time at London, showed that he had spent upwards of £1900 on the manors of the see during his ten years' incumbency and that

37. BL, Cott. MS. Cleo F II/fo. 50. PRO, SP 12/149/25. *HMC, Salisbury MSS.*, III, p. 355.

this had maintained them in reasonable condition apart from the disaster at St Paul's. Sandys was on less firm ground, despite his bluster and protestations. After a period of wrangling Aylmer succeeded in having the whole matter examined by a royal commission, which adjudged that Sandys must pay substantial dilapidations, although less than Aylmer wished. The archbishop succeeded in deferring the execution of this judgement, with some assistance from Walsingham, but apparently had to pay up some time during 1585.[38]

The details of the dispute provide a rich mine of information upon estate organisation and income, and not surprisingly both prelates show to great disadvantage as grasping landowners, anxious only to further their own interests and those of their families. Only the discreet Grindal emerges with any credit, and even he sometimes sounds overconcerned with preserving the niceties of his position. In 1579, at the beginning of the dispute, Sandys protested that he wished for 'a quiet end, fit for men of our calling'. Instead, a great deal of episcopal dirty linen was aired, not merely for the benefit of the ecclesiastical courts but for the council and for other influential laymen. The result was undoubtedly that the two prelates lost much sympathy for themselves and for their order and provided further justification for lay attacks upon their property. Ironically, their pugnacity, though damaging to the general interests of the church, was of some advantage in the preservation of their own estates. Both men were as willing to resist the encroachment of the laity as to take up cudgels against one another: Sandys, despite the blackmail scandal that struck him in the 1580s, refused to surrender long leases to the crown, and the most that Aylmer would concede was a modest grant of Dunmow rectory for forty years and a lease of Paddington and Wickham, which was retained by the crown. Aylmer incurred the additional opprobrium of being a vigorous opponent of puritanism within his see, and it is not surprising to find as an epitaph comment upon him the note of Philip Gawdy to his brother: 'Many a dry eye for the Bishop of London, who is dead and buried, and I fear me not ascended into heaven (saving my charity): he hath left £1500 a year to his children.' It would be a mistake to regard the vitriolic dispute between Aylmer and Sandys as typical of the behaviour of the bishops over dilapidations, but its bitterness can be echoed in minor key in several other disputes. At a time when the bench was

---

38. PRO, SP 12/111/41; SP 12/112/45. BL, Harl. MS. 604/fo. 236. PRO, SP 12/131/22; SP 12/137/54; SP 12/149/17ff. BL, Lans. MS. 42/46.

united in its religious ideology for the first time for almost half a century, it was unfortunate that economic divisions should have emerged so sharply.[39]

Dilapidations, even when a large sum could be exacted, were a snare and a delusion, for much of the money had to be spent on repairs if the bishop or his executors were not to suffer later. The most common and legitimate way of extracting money from the episcopal office was to undertake a visitation; indeed, the cynical complained that the only reason for visitations was that they allowed the levying of procurations. In 1582 the dean and chapter of Lichfield complained that Overton had begun his visitation as soon as he possibly could, even though the clergy had just had to pay for an archiepiscopal one. The charge is by no means new: the moralising literature of the fifteenth century criticises the bishops on exactly the same grounds. Anthony Harison copied into one of his commonplace books a mock-Skeltonic verse on this theme, headed

> Skeltonicall observations of Bishops visitations
> Pretending Reformations. Intending Procurations

The financial value of the visitations was not in doubt: at his primary tour of his see in 1604, for example, John Jegon raised £137 in procurations and a further £188 from the issue and renewal of licences, from institutions and so on. Although some prelates claimed that their visitation charges exceeded their receipts, they seem generally to have assumed that they could make a profit from their disciplinary activities. Scambler pointed out to one of his Norwich rural deans that he had omitted his primary visitation which his predecessors had made 'as gainful to them and more chargeable to you' but immediately marred the effect of his words by asking for a benevolence. The archbishops could derive a particularly useful income from the exercise of their metropolitical powers. Grindal argued that Parker had become wealthy partly because he was able to conduct *sede vacante* visitations throughout his province at the beginning of the reign. But the fact that it brought some fiscal advantage should not be allowed to obscure the evidence that visitation was taken very seriously by most Elizabethan prelates. The first generation in particular made great efforts to appear in person throughout their sees and to participate in the preaching that was one of the most important aspects of the local assemblies. Scambler's neglect of primary visitation

39. PRO, sp 12/112/45. BL, Lans. ms. 36/24. Guildhall, ms. 12730. *HMC, 7th Report*, app., p. 524.

reflects far more poorly upon his care for his diocese than does the behaviour of those numerous prelates whose tours of their sees boosted their revenue by £100 or £200.[40]

The visitation procedure ensured that the bishops could look to this source of income only once in three years, but they did have as a further resort some right to claim general support from their clergy in the form of a loan or benevolence. Those who attempted to raise these imposts seem to have been following the earlier precedents set by the charitable subsidies paid to the archbishops of Canterbury and probably to other prelates as well. Indeed, Overton described the grant that he asked of his clergy as a charitable subsidy. The dean and chapter of Lichfield denied their share of the payment and challenged Overton to prove that such grants had been due to the bishops 'time out of mind'. Other prelates evidently thought that they had a right to such dues. We have already noted that Scambler asked for a benevolence from his rural deans, and Sandys certainly intended to ask the clergy of York for a grant that would yield him £800. The question is less whether these claims could be defended by precedent than whether their immediate advantages justified the legacy of ill-feeling within the church which they must have created. Bishop Wolton of Exeter thought they did not: in 1585 he was accused of raising a general grant from his clergy and failing to repay it, but he responded that he had only taken a few specific loans from friends, which were gradually being repaid. The dean and chapter of Lichfield claimed that there had been 'murmurings' in the diocese against the payments made to Overton, and, given the general levels of taxation already asked of the parish clergy, this is scarcely surprising. No amount of claiming that the bishops had a traditional right to tax their clergy could disguise the fact that they were very ill advised to do so in the new environment of Reformed Protestantism.[41]

Those bishops who had a legitimate claim to the tenths of their clergy as a result of the 1559 exchanges faced a similar problem. They needed legal sanctions to ensure that they could collect the revenue due to them, but sanctions used by prosperous bishops against poor clerics were bound to cause resentment. One of the requests that Parker and his fellows made in 1559 was 'we may have remedy by law to recover the tenths denied or delayed, as well as

40. BL, Lans. MS. 36/55. CUL, Mm/3/12, p. 383. Bodl., Tanner MS. 135/fo. 129. Houlbrooke, 'The Protestant Episcopate', in *Church and Society*, pp. 96–7.
41. BL, Lans. MS. 36/55. PRO, SP 12/112/45. BL, Lans. MS. 45/42.

when they were parcels of the revenues of the crown'. No specific provision was made in the legislation for the act of exchange, but the bishops were able to use the weapon of sequestration without any hindrance from the government. Richard Cox, perhaps aware of the vulnerability of his position, used sequestration against only five of his clergy and lost revenue as a result of his leniency. When the crown undertook the administration of Ely diocese it felt no such scruples: in 1590 there was a drive to tighten control, and twenty-three parishes had their revenues sequestered within three months. The right to collect tenths had been accorded only to Ely and Canterbury, but several other sees received the same dues from the cathedral clergy, thereby providing another reason for an increase in the traditional hostility between the close and the palace.[42]

When a prelate succeeded in overcoming his initial financial difficulties he was exposed to another problem: the possibility of attacks upon him for wealth and greed. John Scory was one of those who passed through the crisis caused by the 1559 act to a further crisis precipitated by charges that he was a usurer. In the field of money-lending such accusations were easy to make and awkward to refute. Scory, like many of his fellows, continued the pre-Reformation practice of making loans to the laity out of his reserves, but he was less discreet than others and probably did ask for interest on his money. Richard Meye, a Worcester clothier, accused the bishop of hoarding £20,000 from these activities, a charge which should not be taken too seriously in view of Meye's own status as a money-lender and an enemy of Scory's. The latter indignantly denied that he was a usurer, a fact which does not exclude the possibility that he took 10 per cent on his loans, since this was now acknowledged as a legitimate rate of interest. At the very least, he appears to have been over-zealous in his offers of financial help to his fellow men and to have reaped a reward for his pains: he died in possession of a comfortable fortune. Other prelates who lent money – Pilkington, Whitgift, Cox and Young among them – managed to avoid much calumny, though Cox was accused of taking money on his loans among the rush of complaints against him in 1575. They could not afford to expose themselves to the censoriousness of lay society, which would not have accepted a continuation of the very active lending policy pursued by some of the pre-Reformation bishops. A similar difficulty arose when accumulated wealth was employed in other ways. Any form of display

42. *Parker Correspondence*, p. 99. EDR, G/2/18, 19.

L

was liable to attract accusations of greed and ambition: even the easiest way of storing surplus income – in plate – was no longer simple. Although plate was necessary for the proper maintenance of hospitality and rank, any excess invited the argument that the church had not yet been short of enough of its surplus. The result is that very few inventories, even those of relatively wealthy men like Cox and Matthew, show elaborate collections of plate. The same problem attached to land purchases. Land naturally attracted the married bishops more readily than plate, and there are plenty of examples of purchases, but much of this land was quickly passed on to wives and children in order to avoid the charge of covetousness that might be made against the bishop himself.[43]

The full list of possible means by which an Elizabethan prelate might secure his own financial well-being and that of his bishopric is impressive. It could be argued that, despite the hostility of the laity and the demands of the crown, he had little of which to complain. Perhaps much of the complaining was intended to preempt anticipated demands as much as to protect himself against existing strain. Nevertheless, at every turn genuine constraints upon episcopal finances are also visible. The most fortunate prelates were those who still had large estates, for the best hope of improvement still came from the manors, but few of the poorer sees could do much to realise this hope. At the end of the century the ten poorest owned only seventy-six small manors, mainly in long lease. Long leases were an obvious constraint everywhere, though the means of circumventing them were more numerous and diverse than is sometimes suggested. Entrenched local interests and lay hostility towards efforts of the bishops to improve their position may have been as significant as the legacy of encumbered lands which they had received. Then many of the constraints came from within the episcopal system itself. There was the problem of life-tenure, which perhaps militated more than anything else against efficient estate management. There were the interests of episcopal families to be considered and the demands of local patronage to satisfy. Finally there was the need to appear to the world as a combination of Protestant pastor and lay and spiritual

---

43. PRO, sp 12/107/34. BL, Lans. ms. 36/26. Borthwick Inst., Chancery 1569. BL, Lans. ms. 20/73. It is probable that most of the bishops loaned money on a small scale, that is, to relatives, friends and servants, but the activities of the four men mentioned seem to have extended somewhat beyond this. For Cox's inventory see Gon. and Caius, ms. 53/30, fos. 36vff.

lord, which demanded a nice balance between a display of the affluence that supported power and the modesty suitable to the reformed preacher. It might be useful to conclude this analysis with an investigation of one aspect of the bishops' affairs that indicates very well the constraints and the possible ways in which they might be overcome – estate administration.

The control of large estates, whether lay or ecclesiastical, remained essentially traditional, even in the closing decades of the sixteenth century. The system of charge and discharge accounting was unaltered, and the same hierarchy of officials still performed their function of collecting the lord's revenue honestly. The large estates of the peerage experienced much the same inertia as did the lands of the bishops or chapters. But on lay estates there are glimmers of change from at least the 1590s onwards. Perhaps the most important innovation was the introduction of the survey, which was not merely an extended rental but which examined and valued the physical nature of the property. By the turn of the century the most up-to-date peers had some estimates of income and expenditure recorded alongside their regular information upon the accounts. Calculations of the levels of fine or rent increase needed to extract a proper return from land became more sophisticated, culminating in the preparation of tables of the valuations of leases in the early seventeenth century. Yet only a minority of the peerage took advantage of these new methods of management; for many, the customary pattern of good lordship, or muddling along, remained sufficient. If this was true of a social group which was far less inhibited than the clergy, it would be surprising to find that much was changing in the management of the episcopal estates. Honesty and success in collecting traditional revenues remained the most prized virtues of the episcopal officer, and when officials obtrude in the records it is most often because they have failed in these respects. The deficiencies of such collectors of taxes as Thimbelthorpe are merely spectacular examples of the problems that faced the bishops in organising their estates. A new bishop was usually encumbered with the men appointed by his predecessors, who owed him no loyalty and might even, in the Elizabethan age, be of a different religious persuasion. The major offices were all normally granted for life, and the only hope a new prelate could have if he was dissatisfied with his assistants was that he might be able to repurchase their patents. Even if this was possible, it would be costly: Overton, for example, was so eager to rid himself of his chancellor Dr Becon that he paid £500 for the redemption of his office.[44]

Such drastic measures were worthwhile in only a few cases, and most prelates seem to have resigned themselves to working with the men already in charge of the administration and then slowly inserting their own candidates. Their own candidates often continued to be their families and immediate dependants. Family members received a disproportionate number of the keeperships and stewardships of many sees: at Ely, for example, Cox's sons and family were made bailiffs of the city of Ely, keepers of Somersham park and of Downham and Doddington parks and guardians of Ely palace. Bishop Godwin made one of his sons collector for the diocese and his two sons-in-law bailiff of Wells liberty and understeward. His successor John Still followed this unpromising example by making one son-in-law steward and giving two of his sons a share in the receivership-general. The benefits of family support have been commented on earlier: even though there were a proportion of rapacious children and dependants among them, a bishop could normally rely on more consistent help from his own kin than from outsiders. In some cases, such as that of Still and of Thomas Cooper, the marriages of daughters seem to have been arranged with more than half an eye to the administrative talents of their future husbands. But the giving of office principally as a form of patronage and reward naturally put the welfare of the estates in hazard in some cases. The family of a prelate had no more incentive than the man himself to look to the long-term benefit of the see and was less constrained by considerations of what was good for the church at large. For those sons who aspired to the ranks of the gentry, office was important principally for the opportunities it afforded for the display of authority. This may be why men such as Cox, Sandys and Aylmer gave their children the keepership of parks and houses rather than burdensome offices such as the receivership. With a mansion and hunting park at their disposal, the children of the bishops could live the life of gentlemen before they came to acquire any property of their own.[45]

Both the traditions of landholding and the circumstances of the prelates therefore militated against any significant change in estate

44. On developments on lay estates see Stone, *Crisis of the Aristocracy*, pp. 294–324. J. Norden, *The Surveyor's Dialogue* (1738) is one of the best examples of the new approach to the estate. PRO, E 135/9/6.
45. EDR, 2/6/1. Hembry, pp. 158ff, 192ff. Redhead, 'Thomas Cooper', pp. 179ff. BL, Lans. MS. 50/34.

administration. Yet our analysis so far has suggested that the beginning of improvements was already visible in some sees before the end of the Elizabethan age. One of the few advantages that government policy towards the episcopal estates offered was that it enforced residence and trimmed away many of the outer manors, leaving the prelates an inner group upon which to concentrate. Thus the administration of most of the bishops came to resemble more closely that of the resident gentry than that of the greater peerage with their far-flung property. The regular observation of their estates may have facilitated more careful supervision of their officers and revenues. The trimming of fees and costs, which was noted earlier, must have derived from just this sort of observation, from the recognition that certain officers and positions were redundant. The bishops had one other advantage: although many of the great offices of the bishoprics had become semi-hereditary or were reserved for children who could not be expected to be active administrators, they had in practice always been fairly free to choose their closest advisers and helpers, who were not necessarily confined to a specific office. It was, of course, important for the bishop to have trustworthy men as stewards, understewards, receivers-general and surveyors, but there were a variety of ways of adapting these offices to suit the circumstances. In an extreme case, when Cox found it impossible to cooperate with his steward Lord North, and equally impossible to be rid of him, he created a new office of high bailiff of the Isle, gave it to one of his family, and removed most of the duties of the steward to it. This flexibility did not allow the bishop to overlook the web of entrenched vested interests already established in positions under him, but it did permit him to govern his estates to some extent by his own policy.[46]

There is no evidence that the bishops adopted the newest method of estate administration, the land survey, but in other respects some of them kept pace with the changes being introduced on lay estates. Record-keeping, and especially the use of the more traditional types of rentals and surveys, improved markedly in the latter half of Elizabeth's reign. In several dioceses – Hereford, Norwich, Bath and Wells, Worcester and London – episcopal officers prepared the first good 'Domesdays' that had been drawn up for a century or more. The requirement that tenants furnish a terrier of their lands became more common in leases. At London there were even the beginnings

46. PRO, SP 12/105/86. Heal, 'The Bishops of Ely', ch. 7.

of an attempt to disentangle the true value of the estates from their rental price, though in most other sees this did not happen until well into the seventeenth century. A few of the officers who assisted the prelates with these activities may be seen as part of a new breed, new not so much in their close attention to detail as in the interest in profit and loss which they reveal. William Butterfield, the under-steward of Hereford, has already been mentioned. He had a hard taskmaster in Bishop Scory, but his comments in his great survey suggest above all an administrator's concern that the bishopric should not be defrauded of its income and a professional's distaste for the confusion that surrounded the bishop's relations with his tenants. John Boys, steward to Whitgift and servant to the previous two archbishops, was another administrator who saw the need for the reassertion of the rights of the church. His status was higher than Butterfield's, and he was able to make an effective contribution to his master's cause by his speech in the Parliament of 1601. Boys was evidently trusted enough to be allowed to exercise his own initiative: he was responsible for beginning and guiding a suit that won back Longbeech woods from the queen. Such skill brought its own rewards: Boys stood high in his master's favour and was allowed the first lease of the woods he had recaptured. His ornate tomb in Canterbury cathedral also bespeaks his influence, though perhaps the fact revealed in the inscription, that he had no direct descendants, explains why so much of his energy was directed to the support of the archbishops.[47]

The best example of an episcopal servant not bound by the old conventions is Anthony Harison of Norwich, whose activities can readily be studied through his *Registrum Vagum*. Harison occupied the position of episcopal secretary, which in the early seventeenth cen-tury was to develop as one of the most important of diocesan offices. His fixed duties in relation to the estates were minimal, but his posi-tion at the centre of affairs and his keen interest in the finances of the see allowed him to draw up an unrivalled schedule of information. Harison covered the receipts of the estates, the leases of the tenants, the income from the spiritualities and the history of the property of the see since the Reformation. As a result, he was able to discover

47. It is interesting to note that Howland's library contained a book entitled 'a book of husbandry and surveying'. PRO, E 178/1703. HRO, Butterfield's Survey. Harison, *Registrum Vagum*. Hembry, pp. 198–9. WRO, CC 900/1, no. 43696. Guildhall, MS. 11927. The London survey is incorporated into the middle of a document which dates from after the Restoration. CDC, Reg. w/fo. 39v.

all the small unpaid dues, all the parcels of unleased land, all the obligations of the tenants, which were overlooked for lack of information in other sees. This was not as profitable, of course, as if the bishops had been able to maximise their income by increasing rents, yet Norwich manors were almost entirely committed on long leases, and Harison was therefore able to make a most significant contribution to the welfare of the bishops. To be well informed about property and income was a tremendous advantage for a prelate who might occupy a see for only a few years and therefore have little time to acquire personal knowledge of his estates. During the seventeenth century, and especially after the Restoration, it became common for bishops or their officers to make collections similar to Harison's, but in his own age few administrators were so far-sighted. Harison and Boys also differed from many other episcopal officers in another sense: they served several bishops with equal devotion, being more interested in the well-being of the see than in the situation of a particular prelate. This is not to say that their best efforts were not stimulated by determined prelates – Whitgift in the case of Boys and Jegon in that of Harison – but that, like the best of the pre-Reformation officers, they provided continuity and consistent care of the office regardless of the person of the bishop. This was something which others were unlikely to achieve while they continued to depend upon their families, and indeed something which would not necessarily have been congenial to those who placed the interests of their relatives alongside, or higher than, that of their ecclesiastical office.[48]

48. In addition to the printed *Registrum* Harison's activities may be studied in an extensive series of rental and commonplace books – CUL, Dd/12/43 and Mm/3/13; NRO, HAR/1–3; Bodl., Tanner MS. 228.

12

CONCLUSION

I

The range of economic possibilities still available to many of the Elizabethan bishops should make us wary of taking their lamentations to the government at face value. Poverty and indebtedness were undoubtedly the preoccupying experience of a minority of the prelates, but they have to be compared with those who lived comfortably and bequeathed their heirs a dignified place within society. There are various ways in which we might try to identify the financially successful, though none which is wholly satisfactory or conclusive as evidence. The most readily available source is the episcopal wills. By the Elizabethan period most bishops were leaving testaments behind them: fifty-one survive from the seventy-six men consecrated under Elizabeth. The limitations of wills as a guide to wealth are obvious enough. They express only the intentions of the testator, not his capacity to fulfil them. The bishops were particularly likely to be left without this capacity, as their arrears in taxation payments to the crown were often not completely identified until after their death. If a will was made some years before death, this problem could be compounded: Bishop Fletcher wrote his before he reached the see of London and entered upon the series of events which led to his disgrace and indebtedness. Even as an expression of intention the wills have their limitations for the historian wishing to calculate the value of goods left: some fail to specify goods and land in any detail; others make bequests entirely or partially in land and plate, which cannot easily be assigned a monetary value. Nevertheless, the testaments are worth consulting, both for some crude guide to the assumed value of episcopal property and for the specific comparisons that can be made between the various prelates.[1]

1. The surviving will evidence has been examined in detail for this study and has also been investigated by Professor Berlatsky in 'The Elizabethan Episcopate'. Our conclusions and statistics are very similar, though I have placed three bishops in a higher category of wealth than he. PROB, 11/87/50.

Professor Berlatsky has calculated that the monetary gifts left by the bishops totalled over £28,000; if we were able to estimate the value of land and plate, this sum might be increased to £40,000 or more. When these figures are broken down into five categories of wealth they show that more than half those prelates who left wills had some considerable possessions to leave to their dependants. The calculations from the wills can, in a few cases, be compared with the far more reliable evidence of inventories. Among the richer bishops there are inventories for Matthew Parker, Richard Cox, Thomas Cooper and Tobie Matthew. All had goods in excess of £2000 and also held lands or had already passed them to their heirs. A most interesting case is that of Archbishop Young of York. He is not usually considered one of the wealthy prelates, yet the account of his administrator reveals an inventory of goods worth £2657 and good debts of over £1000. His will betrays little of this affluence, for all his bequests amounted to only £545. At the other extreme are the lists of goods belonging to the crown debtors, few of whom left wills. Anthony Kitchin of Llandaff had only £109 with which to meet his obligations, William Bradbridge of Exeter had £173 and Marmaduke Middleton had a pathetic set of goods worth only £67 to show for his years as bishop of St David's. The comfortable estates that many of the testators bequeathed must be balanced against the relative poverty of these debtors. Among those whose wills do not survive or are not itemised in detail, only Thomas Bilson and Martin Heaton were probably wealthy. Most of the rest would merely swell the totals in the last two categories of table 12:1.[2]

Wills and inventories offer some guide to the wealth of the bishops

Table 12:1 *Estimated value of the bequests of Elizabethan bishops*

Estimated value	Number of bishops
£3000 or more	9
£1000 to £3000	15
£500 to £999	8
Under £500	10
No details or indebted	9

2. Berlatsky, 'Marriage and Family', p. 19. W. Sandys (ed.), 'An Inventory of Matthew Parker's Goods at Death', *Archaeologia*, XXX (1844), 7–30. Gonville and Caius, Coll., Cambridge, MS. 53/30, fos. 35ff. PROB, 11/83/44. Borthwick Inst., Chancery 1628, 1569. PRO, E 178/3451; E 347/14/pt 2; E 178/1703. Both Bilson and Heaton were able to purchase estates for their descendants.

at death, but there is also the question of how much they were able
to accumulate and consume in life. Some property never reached the
final testaments: it was purchased and passed on to the next generation during the life of a prelate. Thus Matthew Hutton had begun
the process of establishing his son Timothy in Yorkshire while he was
still dean of York. By the time of his father's death Timothy owned
Hagthorpe and Marske manors, the advowson of Marrick Priory and
two leases, all provided directly or indirectly from the funds which
the archbishop had accumulated. Aylmer had passed some of his
Essex lands, alleged by Bancroft to be worth £16,000, to his sons
before his death, which was fortunate in view of the demands for
tenths arrears which the crown made upon his estate. Sandys, while
protesting loudly that he never purchased lands, bought the lease
of Ormesby in Worcestershire and made it the principal seat of his
eldest son. Bilson's estates, purchased in Hampshire and Sussex during
his years as bishop of Winchester, may have been passed to his heirs
during his lifetime. Examples such as these provide no great surprise,
though they serve to stress that in some cases the gulf between rich
and poor bishops was even greater than the wills and inventories
suggest. Other rich bishops could also expend more than the monies
itemised at their death: Whitgift paid much of the cost of his charitable foundation at Croydon during his lifetime, and Tobie Matthew
was able to support his difficult son with several thousand pounds
from the sees of Durham and York.[3]

In a few cases our knowledge of the other capital sums bestowed
by the bishops may adjust our assumptions made purely from the
wills. Bishop Scambler died poor for all his trafficking in church lands,
but he may have had enough funds to purchase some property in
Norfolk for his eldest son James, and therefore not to have been
quite so abject as his will suggests. The two prelates who were rumoured to have provided so lavishly for their daughters – Robert
Horne and James Pilkington – had little incentive to conserve their
wealth until death, since they had no sons. They should therefore
probably be numbered among the relatively affluent, at least until
the time when all dowries had been paid. An extreme example of the
difference this could make to an estate comes from William Chader-

3. *VCH, Yorkshire North Riding*, I, pp. 22, 100, 102–3, 240. J. T. Cliffe, *The Yorkshire Gentry from the Reformation to the Civil War* (1969), p. 372. BL, Lans. MS. 84/81. *VCH, Hampshire*, III, p. 89; IV, p. 317. *Sussex Manors in the Feet of Fines*, ed. E. H. W. Dulkin, Sussex Rec. Soc. XX (ii) (1915), p. 136.

ton, who had only a wife and granddaughter to provide for at his death. The granddaughter should have been provided for on her marriage to the son of Sir Edwin Sandys, when her grandfather had promised a dowry of £2000 in return for a proper jointure settled on the bride. It was only because this agreement had not been fulfilled by Sir Edwin that the £2000 was included in Chaderton's estate and that he therefore ranks among the wealthy bishops. But the size of this dowry was exceptional, and only a few bishops with a bevy of daughters would have had their whole financial situation affected by the sums they had to pay for suitable marriages.[4]

The introduction of these purchases and payments made before death indicates how elusive is the concept of episcopal wealth. Once wealth is assessed as anything other than annual income, a whole range of problems emerge about capital accumulation and patterns of consumption. While one prelate might conserve all his extra income and ruthlessly exploit his position to build up capital, another might feel obliged to spend any surplus in lavish hospitality. Sir John Wynn, a contemporary and friend of some of the Elizabethan bishops of Wales, reveals this problem in his comments on his acquaintances. Richard Vaughan, he claimed, died poor, not because of his frequent promotions but because he 'respected a good name more than wealth'. Similarly, Richard Davies, bishop of St David's, 'kept an exceeding great post' and died poor, 'having never had regard to riches'. Even so, in Davies's case poverty was only relative, for he had lands in Carmarthen and a substantial flock of sheep to leave to his family. Henry Rowland of Bangor was apparently unusual among the Welsh bishops in being able to finance a generous household and help his family and the poor. Wynn registered some surprise that he had discharged all the obligations of a good bishop, 'yet died rich'. Wynn's views reinforce the point that it is not sufficient to be reasonably well informed upon the estates which the prelates thought they possessed at death: this needs to be combined with a knowledge of their behaviour during life. Only when a bishop could neither live in the style expected by his contemporaries nor accumulated land and money can it safely be said that he suffered from a chronic lack of resources. Once again the inadequacy of the records does not make it easy to be sure of the precise numbers involved, but only about a quarter of the bishops can be said definitely to have failed on these criteria.[5]

4. PROB, 11/84/50; 11/111/47.
5. Sir John Wynn, *History of the Gwydir Family* (1827), pp. 102-6.

Wealth is anyway a relative concept. The archbishops of Canterbury, who still consorted with the greatest peers in the realm, were expected to leave estates worth some thousands of pounds, even if no longer as substantial as those of the lay nobility. The Welsh bishops, on the other hand, were now mainly natives of the principality and had as their associates the gentlemen of their own area. These gentlemen had estates that were more modest than those of the greater gentry in England, so the resources of the prelates and the capital that they accumulated could also afford to be modest. Seen in these terms, the financial achievement of William Blethin, bishop of Llandaff, who left lands and leases and a substantial flock of sheep, is greater than that of Edmund Grindal, whose legacies in cash and plate cannot have been worth much more than £1500. Wealth is also relative in the sense that the Elizabethan bishops lived through seventy years of continuous inflation and that the capital which they accumulated towards the end of that period therefore had to have a higher monetary value in order to yield the same benefits. John Jewel left bequests which amounted to the fairly modest sum of £666 in 1571, which places him in the third category of table 12:1. If the Phelps-Brown price index is used to estimate the money equivalent of this amount, had Jewel died in the second decade of the seventeenth century the figure would approximately double to around £1300. This would place Jewel in the second category for wealth and make his estate comparable with that of men such as Godfrey Goldsborough.[6]

Table 12:2 *Range of wealth of the Elizabethan bishops at death*

	Rich	Middling	Poor/indebted	Unknown
1559–80	5%	25%	45%	25%
1581–1603	14%	35%	35%	16%
Post-1603	32%	41%	5%	22%

Inflation and the need to counteract its effects may provide a part of the explanation for the pattern of wealth at death shown in table 12:2. Here the categories of wealth have been divided even more crudely than in the preceding list – into rich prelates, holding more

6. PROB, 11/77/42. Grindal, *Remains*, pp. 458–63. Phelps-Brown and Hopkins, 'Seven Centuries of the Price of Consumables', p. 312. PROB, 11/53/43; 11/104/65.

than £3000; those of middling wealth, ranging down to about £500; and the poor and indebted. The last group do not include those such as Aylmer and Horne who were found to owe money to the crown at death but had substantial estates which they had already given away. The major shift away from poverty and indebtedness and towards affluence which is shown in the last line of the table seems too marked to be explained by inflation alone. It indicates a genuine improvement in the wealth and comfort of the early Jacobean episcopate. The first Elizabethan generation suffered many of the problems generated by the upheaval of the mid-Tudor period. They often found their sees neglected and their officials demoralised, their own experience of administration was very limited, and the exiles among them had had little opportunity to accumulate wealth before coming to their bishoprics. Although they were not moved rapidly from see to see, a number did experience at least one change during this period and therefore had to pay two sets of first-fruits. The group who died in the latter half of Elizabeth's reign were less affected by the atmosphere of crisis inherited from the Reformation, but once again a number had the dubious benefit of being moved from one living to another. Twenty-eight bishops were moved or appointed in the 1590s, a sharp contrast with the subsequent decade, when only eight of the Elizabethans were moved or promoted. Since heavy charges for first-fruits and the other burdens of coming to a new bishopric made it difficult for even the best-endowed and most prudent prelate to save much income, the relative stability of the early Jacobean years must be a major explanation for the greater affluence observed in the table.[7]

Yet the figures for the post-1603 period also lead us back to the efforts of the bishops discussed in the last chapter. Men such as Still, Matthew and Whitgift did not merely wait upon events, upon changing political or economic circumstances, to improve their situation. They adopted a very positive attitude to estate-management and sought to rule their lands once again with something of the authority of their Catholic predecessors. They were often helped by the falling-

7. On the greater security of the bishops under James see Hill, pp. 33–4. The rapid changes in the English sees during the 1590s might suggest a positive government policy of maximising first-fruits. However, there is no clear evidence that this was any more than a response to high mortality and the development of a more systematic policy of promotion from less important to more important bishoprics. See Whitgift's letter to Hutton, *Correspondence of Hutton*, pp. 93–5.

in of the first of the long leases made in the mid-Tudor years and by
the consequent opportunity to take fines as some compensation for
the loss of the true value of their estates. These improvements in
turn were encouraged by the greater stability of the episcopal order.
In certain ways the late decades of Elizabeth's reign witnessed an
increase in lay attempts to profit from the lands of the prelates,
attempts which Elizabeth was willing to condone as a cheap and
effective form of patronage. But, paradoxically, the same decades
marked a turning-point in the crown's view of the episcopate and
were the years that finally demonstrated that the episcopate would
survive in its traditional form. The struggle against puritanism,
especially in its presbyterian form, brought together the crown and
the hierarchy of the church in an effective alliance. Thus, while the
bishops' hold on particular lands might still be assailed, the order as a
whole was offered greater security and stability as the century wore
towards its end. It was this security which James I made explicit and
extended to the territorial possessions of the church when, in 1604,
legislation forbade the bishops to alienate lands to the crown.[8]

II

We may therefore conclude that a majority of the members of the
late-Tudor episcopate continued to live in some style, despite the
crises to which the order was subject. Yet no amendment of the
gloomy picture traditionally painted of the Elizabethan bench should
be allowed to obscure the fundamental contrast which it presented
with that of the early sixteenth century. The comparison can most
clearly be expressed visually in the difference between the distribution
of manors shown in fig. 2 and that presented in fig. 1 in the second
chapter of this book. Impressive clusters of land still remain, especially in Durham and around Winchester, Worcester and Hereford.
But elsewhere very little of the proud concentrations of land survive.
The losses are particularly obvious in London and the Home Counties
and include the great inns of the capital, which are not shown on the
map. They also include many of the wealthiest estates: those which
remain commanded not only less income but fewer men and tenants
than the lost lands. Income figures confirm this picture of loss,
though they are less dramatic than the evidence of the disappearance

---

8. 1 James I, c. 3. See Hill as above for some discussion of the context and con-
    sequences of the act.

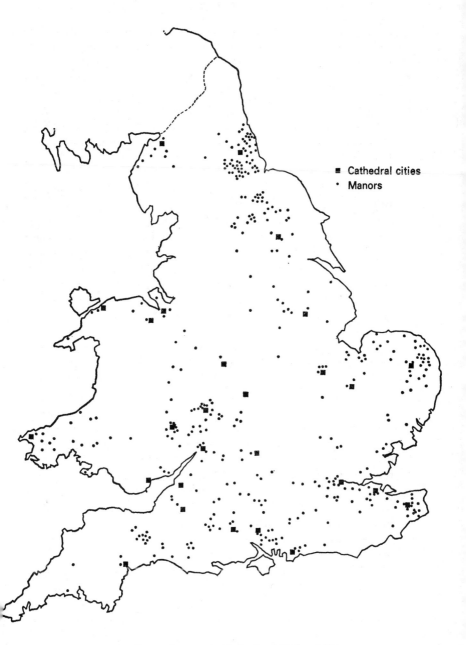

Fig. 2 *Episcopal manors in England and Wales, 1603*

of territory. After the improvement in some sees in the last years of the sixteenth century, gross receipts may have reached almost £28,000, a figure larger than the gross receipts from the temporalities before the Reformation. However, it must be stressed that these are not purely temporal revenues: in 1603 the spiritualities, including the rectories, produced at least one-third of the income of the bishops. These miscellaneous receipts might do much to fill the void left by the loss of manors, but they could never provide the prelates with that command over man and acres that had been so integral a part of their old power.[9]

Hooker argued that it was not the absolute but the relative impoverishment of the episcopate that made them vulnerable and earned them the contempt of some of their peers. Their failure to increase their incomes to counteract the effects of inflation certainly set them apart from some of the rest of the landed classes, who by the end of the century, were able to take advantage of the rising value of land. The leading bishops could no longer rival the great court nobility in their lavish hospitality and their great programmes of building. It is significant that, despite the modest revival we have noted in the fortunes of some bishops, as a group they scarcely participated at all in the great rebuilding undertaken throughout landed society between the 1580s and the 1630s. Their access to sources of revenue outside their sees was virtually cut off by the changing pattern of politics after the Reformation. Yet even in relative terms the prelates may not always have suffered more than their lay contemporaries. The nobility were experiencing economic difficulties at the end of the century and were not in command of the vast fortunes once casually assumed to be theirs. In 1602 fourteen peers certainly had rental incomes in excess of £3660, but the largest group of twenty-four peers had rentals of only between £900 and £1799, comparable with those of the middle ranks of the episcopate. Laity and clergy alike had encountered difficulties in compensating for the sharp movement of prices in the last years of the century, and both suffered from some of the inflexibility and rigidity of landed income.[10]

The main contrast lay in the possibilities that were open to each group. Late Elizabethan England was now dominated politically and

9. See apps. I and II below for income estimates and the number of manors in 1603. Six manors have been omitted from fig. 2 because of doubts about their precise location.

10. P. Hembry, 'Episcopal Palaces', in *Wealth and Power in Tudor England*, pp. 162–3. Stone, *Crisis of the Aristocracy*, p. 760.

socially by the lay élite, and it was the peerage and those gentry with access to the court who had the greatest opportunities to repair their fortunes. The situation of the bishops was inevitably more complex than that of the lay peers. They could not subsist by financial success alone; indeed, they were discouraged by the attitudes of society from achieving too great a measure of wealth. Since their spiritual functions still set them apart from the rest of the political nation, they were inevitably judged by different criteria. Two potentially contradictory models of behaviour were considered appropriate to their station: they should be hospitable, live in a style suited to the dignity of their office and ensure that their descendants were provided for. They should also behave as men of God and reformed pastors, using their wealth for the benefit of the church, aiding learning and the poor and exercising restraint and modesty in their dress and mode of living. In a society where the bishops were often intensely disliked for enforcing an unattractive ecclesiastical policy, it was never difficult to find arguments to suggest that they had failed to fulfil all these obligations. The failure to be charitable, associated with too close a concentration upon the family, provided the easiest theme of attack. As we have seen, the bishops really were vulnerable to the charge that they bestowed far too high a proportion of their resources upon their families and too little upon general works of charity.[11]

The problem was that there was as little consensus among the bishops as among the laity upon what their role in society should be. Their attitudes followed closely the general changes in ecclesiastical views which are associated with Elizabeth's reign. For the generation of Jewel, Parker and Cox the episcopate was merely the most appropriate instrument for ensuring order and due obedience within the church. Wealth and some secular authority might be necessary as a means to guarantee this due order, but there was no agreement even to this. Jewel and Parkhurst represented a 'minimalist' view of wealth and secular involvement; that there should only be the commitment to help the faith, not the resources for ostentation and the display of power. But this attitude was always a minority one: the combination of an abiding respect for order and degree with the very natural ambitions of the prelates led to a stress upon those visible signs of power – land and wealth. Since their most vociferous opponents attacked both their spiritual authority and their secular power, it

11. See Hill, ch. 2.

was easy for the bishops to retaliate in kind and charge that the puritans threatened the political order and were motivated principally by greed and ambition. But throughout the main part of the queen's reign their theoretical justification of their position was weak and especially vulnerable in the face of pressures from the crown intself. The beginnings of a turning-point came in the 1590s, when Bilson and Bancroft argued that episcopacy was more than a useful accident, that it had the same status as the only true system of church government that the presbyterians claimed for their ideas of organisation. It was not until after the Elizabethan age that the full force of the 'Arminian' claim was brought to bear upon the church wealth, but it did provide an obvious support for the efforts which the bishops made to resist lay incursions into their lands and to persuade the crown to accept a responsibility for the effective preservation of what was left to the higher clergy.[12]

To end the story in 1603 is therefore merely to point to another beginning: indeed, it would in some ways be more logical to continue until the eve of the Civil War, as other studies of the wealth of the bishops have done. Yet it may be useful to see the late sixteenth century not as a prelude to the political breakdown of half a century later but rather as a time when many of the tensions created by the Reformation were resolved in an atmosphere of comparative stability. If an epilogue is necessary, it should perhaps be sought in the post-Restoration world, when the bishops, shorn of much of the independent political power which they had attempted to gain under Laud, contributed to a world made safe for men of property. Those sees which had managed during the sixteenth century to preserve a reasonable part of their lands were well placed to take advantage of the new stability of this period both in politics and in economics. The consequences were becoming clear as early as 1670, when Archbishop Sheldon's secretary prepared an estimate of the value of the English bishoprics. Since the object of his survey was to prove that the prelates were not excessively wealthy and that they spent generously in charitable causes, he had no reason to assess their income at its maximum. Nevertheless, he concluded that the total annual worth of the bishoprics was around £50,000 or about £10,000 in excess of the figure that we have calculated for the end of the sixteenth cen-

12. The beginnings of this argument can be discerned in Bancroft's attack on the puritans in 'Certain Slanderous Speeches against the Church of England by the Precisions', in *Tracts Ascribed to Richard Bancroft*, ed. A. Peel (1953).

tury. Canterbury and Winchester he placed at £4000, Durham at £3000, York at £2500 and London at £2000.[13]

These figures were certainly too low as a realistic assessment of what the great sees could be expected to yield to an energetic administrator in the later seventeenth century. Canterbury, for example, might produce only around £4000 in rents, but by 1682 its total income, net of fixed costs, had reached the very substantial sum of £6075. By the same period Ely yielded over £3000 and Winchester, £5000. In these bishoprics, therefore, the prelates were compensating for the effects of inflation upon their income in the previous century and establishing for themselves a very comfortable financial position, even if they still did not rival the greatest fortunes of the laity. Yet there was still great diversity between bishoprics. Hereford was in the 1670s claimed to be worth only £900, taking one year with another, and so was only yielding about £200 more than it had done a century and a half earlier. The formal rental of Exeter for the same period suggests that income had remained fixed at much the same level as that established after the devastation of its lands under Edward VI. Even here, however, there may have been more elasticity of income than meets the eye, for while the rental put the total income of the see at £584, it was noted that, in the first two years of any episcopate, the incumbent could hope to derive £1000 per annum from the Cornish estates alone. Moreover, the years after the Restoration were a marked contrast with those of Elizabeth in that the bishops no longer fell into debt so regularly nor complained of their poverty quite so vociferously as once they had done. The pressure seems to have been lifted even from the poorer among them.[14]

In these new circumstances some bishops were even able to give their gracious attention to the continuing problem of poverty among the lower clergy. Archbishop Sharp unilaterally decided to reserve the prebends within his gift to support deserving incumbents within his own diocese. Eventually, a national palliative was found in the establishment of Queen Anne's Bounty for the benefit of the poorest parochial clergy. This was a move in the direction urged both by the reformers of the sixteenth century and by Laud before the Civil War, but it occurred in a very different world and had fewer implications for the social structure. It made the lesser ministers neither fearless

13. On the post-Restoration state of the church see I. Green, *The Re-Establishment of the Church of England* (Oxford 1978). Bodl., Tanner MS. 141, fo. 98.
14. Bodl., Tanner MS. 127, fos. 69–70; Tanner MS. 147, fo. 79; Add. MS. C 300, fo. 107.

preachers untroubled by the pressures for conformity from crown and bishops nor the equals of the gentry and patrons able to defend the interests of the church. In the circumstances of the age of Queen Anne it was merely a gesture to ensure greater stability, a charitable gift from the growing treasury of the state.[15]

The vantage-point of the Restoration era serves to highlight both the successes and the failures of the Tudor bishops in society. The Reformation had presented a sharp challenge to the traditional organisation of the church, and from the Continent had come several alternative models of structure and discipline. The reformed churches shared a conviction that the wealth formerly held by only a few clerics should be redistributed for the advantage of all parishes and for the encouragement of that learning that was so necessary for a biblio-centric faith. It was the failure of the Tudor bishops that they never accepted this idea, although for at least three generations they shared fully the theology and intellectual concerns of Geneva, Zurich and Strassburg. Individual members of the bench, such as Hooper, Coverdale, Ponet and Parkhurst, did subscribe to the same values as their continental brethren, but even they usually strove alone and did not urge upon the lay rulers the need to undertake a full revision of the economic arrangements of the church. The reasons for the failure and silence of even the most convinced reformers are clear enough: no Tudor government desired changes of the sort that had been relatively easy in the city-states of Germany and Switzerland. The bishops remained a necessary part of the organisation of church and state, and their wealth, if it was to be redeployed, should be used to the advantage of the government rather than to make the clergy more articulate or the populace possibly less conformist. So the vision of a learned clergy, of a church ministry which was well financed with episcopal revenues and which cooperated in the endeavour to save souls, became the property of the opponents of the bishops by the end of the sixteenth century. No prelate thereafter was willing to accept that such a church could or should be achieved at the expense of their order.[16]

The failure of the bishops was, therefore, a failure to urge social revolution. It is easy to accept the voice of their critics, the voice of

15. There is no adequate study of the economic consequences of Queen Anne's Bounty, though its later workings are discussed in G. Best, *Temporal Pillars* (1964).
16. Hill, p. 40. Despite this insight, Hill too often accepts the puritan arguments and evidence at face value.

the puritan conscience, as an indictment of their behaviour, because, as one writer on the subject remarked, 'history has gone that way'. The puritans have on their side not only the advantages of moral purity that always accrue to an opposition party, but the historian's knowledge of the disastrous policies of the 1630s and the consequent collapse of the church. But in the contest of the sixteenth century we should perhaps attach more weight to the achievements of the bishops than to their failure to commit economic suicide. The Elizabethans did fulfil many of the conventional expectations of the crown and the laity at a time of considerable difficulty. They did contribute something to the maintenance of that order, degree and social harmony that were far more important to most of the political nation than writers obsessed with parliamentary disputes are prepared to allow. They did endeavour to offer hospitality, to cooperate in ruling the shires and to behave with that social dignity that was felt to be compatible with their rank. This was especially true of their leaders, the archbishops of York and Canterbury: only Sandys at York deviated from a pattern of dignified and restrained behaviour that sought to fulfil the secular obligations of a prelate. In economic affairs the bishops, or at least a leading group among them, learned the hard lessons of the Edwardian years – that financial loss to their order rarely meant a gain for the rest of the church or for charitable purposes. They therefore made efforts to prevent the property of the church from falling into the hands of the laity, efforts which met with only modest success but which prepared the way for a change of policy under James I. Most important of all, the leadership of the church did not allow the difficulties of their secular position or of their relations with the laity to undermine their efforts to reform and strengthen the church. We have already noted that economic problems occupied an indefensibly large proportion of some prelates' time, to the general disadvantage of the church, but this must be contrasted with the spiritual endeavours of men such as Pilkington, Grindal, Hutton, Whitgift and Horne. They did not deny the world but were primarily concerned with the furtherance of their own visions of the well-being of the church. It may be that a new history of the Elizabethan church is needed to do justice to those concerns.

The failures of the Tudor prelates as a whole were perhaps more the responsibility of successive monarchs and their advisers than of the men themselves. Both the choice of ecclesiastical policy and the selection of the clerics to implement it lay with the crown after the

Reformation. It chose to perpetuate a traditional system of church government, more traditional than that maintained in any other country which broke away from Rome. The choice was sound enough for a dynasty which sought by every means to strengthen its political authority: the episcopate was a natural ally in the enforcement of religious discipline and formed part of that neat symmetry of church and state over which the monarch could claim to preside. But symmetrical as the hierarchies of church and state might appear, the circumstances of the sixteenth century, and the crown's intervention, served to unbalance them. The nobility and gentry were not directly dependent upon royal goodwill as the bishops were: their support was essential to good rulership, and the crown needed to conciliate as well as dominate its leading subjects. The bishops might be consulted, but ultimately they could be controlled by the Supreme Head of the church: their material and spiritual well-being were at his or her disposal. When a conflict of interests arose it was easy to sacrifice those of the church to those of the laity, especially in financial affairs, where no major principle of rulership appeared to be at stake. In other words, the crown was not prepared to accept the full consequences of its retention of the ecclesiastical hierarchy, which should have been the indifferent protection of both its lay and clerical subjects. Nor would it reduce the clerical leaders to the level of preaching superintendents, a solution favoured by some moderate puritans which would probably have commended itself to the two greatest Tudor statesmen, Thomas Cromwell and William Cecil. Instead the prelates were left with the inheritance of uncertainty and instability, which has been such a prominent theme in this book.[17]

Yet even laying the problems of the bishops at the feet of the crown is an insufficient solution. Much of their difficulty sprang, rather, from a wider shift in European society, from the winning of spiritual initiative by the laity. Even the support of the crown in the early seventeenth century was not enough to retrieve for the English clergy the almost unquestioned authority in matters spiritual which they had enjoyed a century earlier. The laity now demanded a share in that priesthood of all believers which Luther had preached and no longer readily accepted the old structures of discipline and power. The bishops were a stumbling-block to the gentry's attempts to

17. On the general issue of the crown's authority within the church see Cross, *The Royal Supremacy in the Elizabethan Church*.

pursue their own version of spiritual truth. Only after a revolution had decisively demonstrated the limits of the church's authority could the problem of episcopal power and wealth be regarded dispassionately. Meanwhile, the Tudor bishops struggled as best they could to offer spiritual leadership in a cold climate. Their efforts should perhaps compel our sympathy, if not our unstinted praise.

Appendix I

ESTIMATES OF THE ANNUAL RENTAL AND SPIRITUAL INCOME OF EPISCOPAL SEES IN ENGLAND AND WALES, 1535–1603

Year	Temporalities	Spiritualities	Total
1535	£26,100	£3450	£29,550
1547 (Jan.)	£24,900	£5100	£30,000
1553 (July)	£15,800	£6700	£22,500
1558 (Nov.)	£21,600	£6700	£28,300
1603 (March)	£17,200	£9800	£27,000

Notes: The diocese of Man is excluded from all the calculations.

From 1547 onwards the figures include the new bishoprics established by Henry VIII in the early 1540s. Estimates of the value of spiritual jurisdiction are drawn entirely from the *Valor Ecclesiasticus*. The change in value of the spiritualities reflects an increase in the number of rectories, tithes and tenths given to the bishops.

The 1553 figure includes the £2000 which the government proposed to restore to the sees of Durham and Newcastle, though these revenues were actually in the hands of the crown on the death of Edward.

Appendix II

THE NUMBER OF MANORS HELD BY THE ENGLISH AND WELSH BISHOPS, 1500–1603

The area marked with a query under 1553 indicates the manors of the see of Durham held by the crown at Edward VI's death. It is not clear how many of these would have reverted to the new bishoprics of Durham and Newcastle under the 1553 legislation.

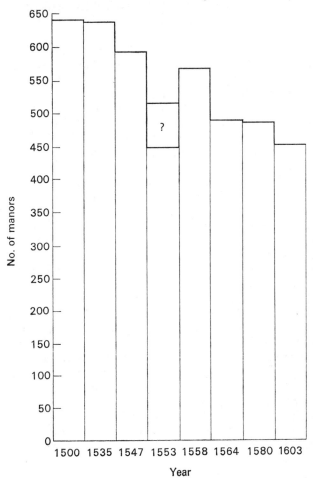

Appendix III

CHARITABLE BEQUESTS AND FOUNDATIONS
OF THE ENGLISH BISHOPS,
1488–1536

Bequests made in wills for the care of the soul are excluded, except in cases where there is an asterisk after the entry.

Where sums of money are included, they derive either from wills or from the estimates of W. K. Jordan.

Peter Courtenay, bishop of Exeter and Winchester: *ob.* 1492
> Built the north tower of Exeter Cathedral and the tower of Honiton church

Robert Morton, bishop of Worcester; *ob.* 1497
> Gift to All Souls College, Oxford, £10*

John Morton, archbishop of Canterbury; *ob.* 1500
> Built Morton's Leam to drain fenlands. Left exhibitions at Oxford and Cambridge worth £133. Left 1000 marks to poor*

John Alcock, bishop of Ely; *ob.* 1500
> Founder of Jesus College, Cambridge. Gave to the rebuilding of Great St Mary's Church, Cambridge, and the priory church at Little Malvern. Enlarged the collegiate church of Westbury. Benefactor of Peterhouse, Cambridge. Founder of Free Grammar School at Hull, which he endowed with lands worth *c.* £400

Thomas Jane, bishop of Norwich; *ob.* 1500
> Benefactor of New College, Oxford, and St Mary's Church, Oxford

Thomas Rotheram, archbishop of York; *ob.* 1500
> Completed the building of the Cambridge Schools. Gave to the rebuilding of Great St Mary's. Bequests to King's College, Cambridge – £100 at death as well as money to the chapel in lifetime. Benefactor of Lincoln College, Oxford, where he increased the fellowships from seven to twelve and gave *c.* £400. Founded College and Grammar School of Jesus, Rotheram, endowed with a yearly income from land of £91. Total charitable gifts estimated at £2460

Thomas Langton, bishop of Winchester; *ob.* 1500
> Founder of informal grammar school at Winchester. Remitted debt of £362 to Winchester Cathedral. Bequests to Great St Mary's

of £10 and Pembroke Hall, Cambridge, of £40. Established six scholarships at Queen's College, Oxford

Henry Deane, archbishop of Canterbury; *ob.* 1503
Reconstructed the choir of Bangor Cathedral

Edward Story, bishop of Chichester; *ob.* 1502
Founder of prebendal free school in Chichester. Builder of Chichester Market Cross. Left tenements to maintain these buildings. Granted two farms in Cambridgeshire to Pembroke Hall

Oliver King, bishop of Bath and Wells; *ob.* 1503
Rebuilt Bath Abbey. Left plate to the use of Wells Cathedral

John Arundel, bishop of Exeter; *ob.* 1504
Left tenements in Exeter to the dean and chapter

Richard Redman, bishop of Ely; *ob.* 1505
Rebuilt St Asaph's Cathedral. Bequest to Ely Cathedral of 100 marks

Thomas Savage, archbishop of York; *ob.* 1507
Plans to found Macclesfield College never fully matured

Christopher Bainbridge, archbishop of York; *ob.* 1514
Endowed Queen's College, Oxford, with manors worth £200

William Smith, bishop of Lincoln; *ob.* 1514
Co-founder of Brasenose College, Oxford. Endowed Lincoln College with two manors and Oriel College with fellowships worth £300. Founder of grammar school at Banbury and co-founder of two other Leicester schools and one at Farnworth. Gave £100 to the rebuilding of St John's Hospital, Banbury

James Stanley, bishop of Ely; *ob.* 1515
Built chapel of the collegiate church, Manchester.

Richard Mayhew, bishop of Hereford; *ob.* 1516
Gave £30 to poor scholars and 100 marks to repair of public highways

Edmund Birkhead, bishop of St Asaph; *ob.* 1518
Donated part of the costs of the rebuilding of Wrexham church.

Hugh Oldham, bishop of Exeter; *ob.* 1519
Benefactor of Corpus Christi College, Oxford; alleged to have given 6000 marks. Endowed Brasenose. Founder of Manchester Grammar School; paid £218 for buildings there

John Penny, bishop of Carlisle; *ob.* 1520
Founder of grammar school at St Margaret's, Leicester. Paid for building at Leicester Abbey

Richard Fitzjames, bishop of London; *ob.* 1522
Benefactor of Merton College, Oxford, and St Mary's Church. Founder of grammar school at Bruton, Somerset

Edward Vaughan, bishop of St David's; *ob.* 1522
Gave to rebuilding at St David's

Thomas Ruthal, bishop of Durham; *ob.* 1523
> Repaired great bridge over the Tyne at Newcastle. May have founded grammar school at Cirencester

Edmund Audley, bishop of Salisbury; *ob.* 1524
> Gave 200 marks to Chichele chest at Oxford. Paid for the restoration of the old House of Congregation, Oxford. Bequest to Lincoln College of £400

Richard Foxe, bishop of Winchester; *ob.* 1528
> Founder of Corpus Christi College, Oxford. Benefactor of Pembroke College. Paid for rebuilding at Winchester Cathedral and the abbey church of Netley. Founder of grammar schools at Taunton and Grantham

Thomas Wolsey, archbishop of York; *ob.* 1530
> Founder of Cardinal's College, Oxford, and a grammar school at Ipswich

Geoffrey Blythe, bishop of Coventry and Lichfield; *ob.* 1531
> Built houses for the Lichfield Cathedral choristers. Benefactor of King's Hall, Cambridge, and King's College

William Warham, archbishop of Canterbury; *ob.* 1532
> Donated lands in Hampshire to New College in 1510 and again in 1520. Donated lands in Hampshire to Winchester College

Thomas Skevington, bishop of Bangor; *ob.* 1533
> Built tower and nave of Bangor Cathedral

Nicholas West, bishop of Ely; *ob.* 1533
> Gave £13. 6s. 8d. for repair of fenland causeways in addition to substantial sums given in times of flood. Bequests to King's College

John Fisher, bishop of Rochester; *ob.* 1535
> Rebuilt Rochester bridge. Co-founder of St John's College, Cambridge; donated four fellowships and two scholarships and total gifts of £1128. Co-founder of Christ's College, Cambridge; gifts to college of £43

Henry Standish, bishop of St Asaph; *ob.* 1535
> Bequest of £40 to pave the choir of St Asaph's. Exhibition for Oxford worth £40. Bequest of £16. 13s. 4d. for highway repair and of £100 to various friaries*

Charles Booth, bishop of Hereford; *ob.* 1535
> Bequest of three London houses to Pembroke Hall

Richard Nix, bishop of Norwich; *ob.* 1536
> Rebuilt transept roofs at Norwich. Bequests of three fellowships to Trinity Hall, Cambridge – approximate value £400

Robert Sherburne, bishop of Chichester; *ob.* 1536
> Donated lands worth over £100 per annum to Chichester Cathedral

Notes: There are no details upon the charitable activities of thirteen other bishops who died between 1488 and 1536. In only two of these cases does a will survive.

W. K. Jordan estimated that it cost approximately £400 to found a grammar school and endow it with sufficient annual income and adequate buildings.

DEMESNE LEASE LENGTHS FOR EIGHT EPISCOPAL SEES: HENRY VII TO THE DEATH OF MARY TUDOR

A. A weighted average, by rental values

Dioceses: Winchester, Ely, York, Hereford, Lincoln, London, Salisbury, Worcester

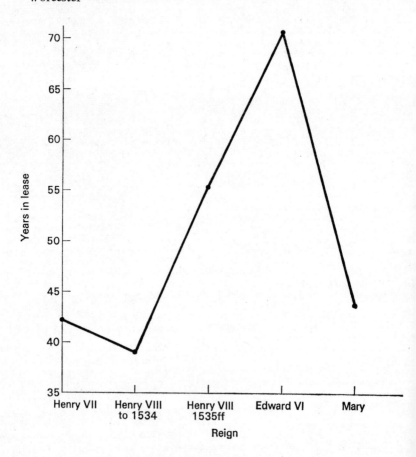

B. An unweighted average of lease lengths by diocese

Note: No reading has been given for dioceses that have fewer than five leases recorded for a particular reign.

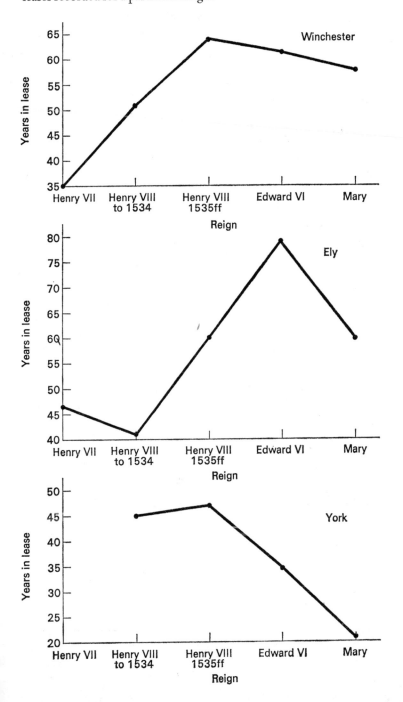

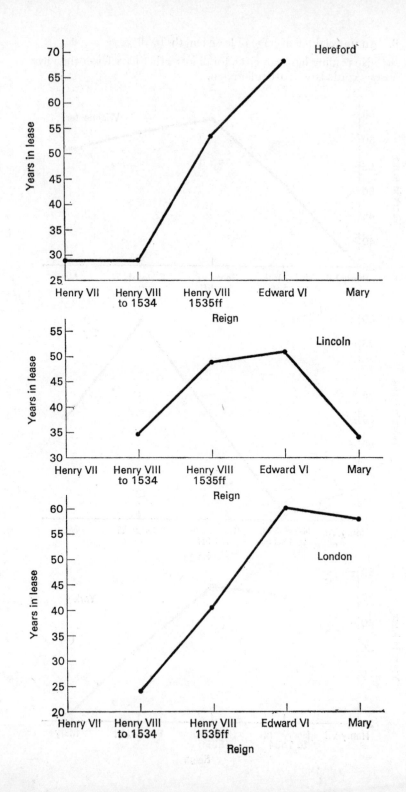

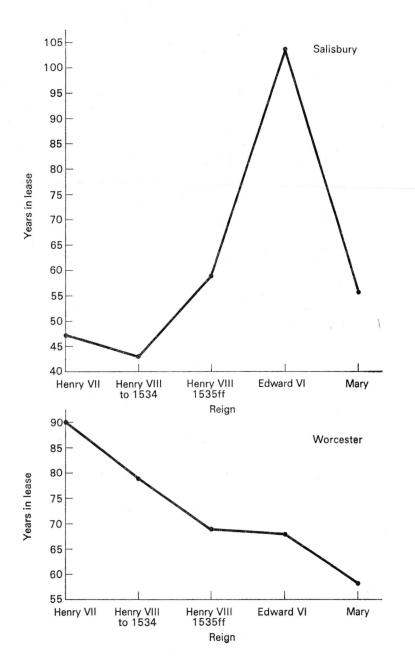

Appendix V

LEASES GRANTED TO THE CROWN UNDER THE PROVISIONS OF 1 ELIZABETH c. 19

Note: Leases which include a long reversionary period are marked with an asterisk.

See	Manor or rectory	Year of grant	Duration of lease	Beneficiary
Canterbury	Boughton	1573	40 years*	Richard Wendesley, esq., of Derbys. Later passed to John Parker
	Blackburn R.	1573	40 years*	Richard Wendesley
	Combe	1583	80 years*	Alex. Fysher, gent.
York	Mount St John, Felskirk and Kirby	1584	70 years*	N.A.
	Gisborne, Shotton and Ormesby	1584	70 years*	N.A.
Durham	Norham fisheries	1577	100 years	N.A.
	Darlington mills	1578	40 years	N.A.
	Leake R.	1578	50 years	N.A.
	Chester-le-Street	1578	50 years	N.A.
	Gateshead and Whickham	1578	99 years	Thomas Sutton. Later to Newcastle Corporation
	Bp Middleham Park	1581	80 years	George Frevile, esq.
	Byers Green	1581	80 years	Ibid.
	Middridge	1582	80 years	Richard Franklin
	Wolsingham Park	1582	80 years	Roger Gifford, royal physician. Then to John Barnes
	Quarrington Grange	1582	80 years	N.A.
	Sowerby Grange	1582	80 years	N.A.
	Hoveton, Yorks.	1584	90 years	John Gate, esq.

Diocese	Property	Year	Term	Grantee
	Coundon Grange	1585	70 years	John Stanhope, esq.
	Morton Grange	1585	70 years	N.A.
	Messuages in Stanhope Park	1585	70 years	N.A.
	Howdenshire pasture	1585	70 years	N.A.
	Crayke, Wheelhall and other lands	1586	80 years	Francis Walsingham
	Tunstall and other lands	1604	80 years	Dudley Carleton. Then to Tobie Matthew, jun.
Winchester	Alresford	1571	60 years	Richard Norton, queen's servant
	Esher	1578	In perpetuity	Lord Howard
	Ecchinswell	1581	80 years	Henry Wallop, kt
	Meon	1581	81 years	N.A.
	Lands in Wilts.	1581	61 years	John Stockman, esq.
	Brightwell	1583	79 years	N.A.
	Sutton	1583	50 years	Walter Hickman, gent.
	Harwell	1584	50 years	John Horsey, esq.
	Overton Warren	1585	40 years	N.A.
Ely	Droxford, Beauworth, Hambledon and other lands worth 2000 marsk	1596	N.A.	Francis Carew, kt
London	Littlebury, Balsham and Hadstock	1579	79 years*	Thos Wilson. Then to Thos Sutton
	Much Dunmow R.	1581	40 years	Thos Dannet
	Wickham and Paddington	1587	76 years	Retained by crown. Later released to Bp Fletcher
Salisbury	Bp's Stortford	1596	21 years*	Edward Denny, kt
	Old Palace, London	1597	90 years	N.A.
	Bp Lavington	1572	70 years*	Burghley. Then to Mr Dantesey
	Monkton Farleigh and Keyhaven	1575	80 years*	Thos Smith, kt
	Burton, Holmes and Upcerne	N.A.	N.A.	N.A.
	Sherborne	1592	N.A.	Walter Raleigh, kt
Worcester	Hallow Park	1581	51 years	N.A.
	Tredington	1588	90 years	Roger Lopes, M.D.
	Blockley Park	1592	90 years	N.A.

See	Manor or rectory	Year of grant	Duration of lease	Beneficiary
Lincoln	Clee R. and Mumby R.	1588	70 years	Edward Carey, esq.
Bath and Wells	Wivelscombe	1585	99 years	George Bond, esq.
	Lands in Banwell	1590	120 years	Thos Gorges, esq., of the privy chamber
Coventry and Lichfield	Bugby R.	1573	60 years*	Chris. Hatton, kt
	Pightsley R.	1582	51 years*	Francis Nichols, gent.
	Lichfield	N.A.	In perpetuity	Lichfield Corporation
	Belgrave R.	1583	50 years	Lisle Cave
	Eccleshall	1584	50 years	N.A.
	Sawtry	1594	N.A.	Thos Stanhope, kt
Norwich	61 manors and rectories	1588	80 years	Thos Heneage, kt
Chichester	Amberley Castle	1588	50 years	N.A.
Exeter	Crediton	1595	In perpetuity	Wm Killegrew
Carlisle	Horncastle	1578	N.A.	Edw. Clinton, earl of Lincoln
Rochester	Dartford	1569	79 years*	Thos Asteley, groom of the privy chamber
Chester	Bolton R. and Clapham R.	1587	46 years*	Henry, Lord Compton
Peterborough	Peterborough rents	1581	60 years	N.A.
	Eye	1601	70 years	William Hake. Then to William Dove
Gloucester	Maisemore	1568	99 years	Cecil. Then to cousin

SELECT BIBLIOGRAPHY

What follows is not intended as an exhaustive bibliographical guide but as an aid to pursuing those printed primary and secondary works listed more than once in the footnotes. It also offers a list of recent secondary works published in the area relevant to this volume. Books were published in London unless otherwise stated.

PRINTED SOURCES

Primary

Acts of the Dean and Chapter of the Cathedral Church of Chichester, 1472–1544, The, ed. W. D. Peckham (Sussex Record Soc. LII) (1951–2)

Alcock, J. *Gallicantus in Sinodo apud Bernwell* (1498?)

Aylmer, J. *An Harborowe for Faithfull and Trewe Subjects* (Strassburg 1559)

Batho, G. R. (ed.). *The Household Papers of Henry Percy, 9th Earl of Northumberland, 1564–1632* (Camden Soc., 3rd ser., XCIII) (1962)

Becon, T. *Early Writings*, ed. J. Ayre (Parker Soc.) (Cambridge, 1843)

Brewer, J. S., Gairdner, J. and Brodie, R. H. (eds.). *Letters and Papers Foreign and Domestic of the Reign of Henry VIII*. 21 vols. (1862–1932)

Brinkelow, H. *The Complaynt of Roderick Mors*, ed. J. M. Cowper (EETS, extra ser., XXII) (1874)

Bruce, J. and Perowne, T. T. (eds.). *The Correspondence of Matthew Parker* (Parker Soc.) (Cambridge 1853)

Calendar of the Patent Rolls

Calendar of State Papers Domestic

Calendar of State Papers Foreign

Calendar of State Papers Venetian

Chapter Acts of the Cathedral Church of St. Mary of Lincoln, ed. R. E. Cole, 3 vols. (Lincoln Record Soc. XII, XIII, XV) (1915, 1917, 1923)

Clay, T. *Brief and Necessary Tables* (1622)

Coke, D. *Institutes of the Laws of England*, 4 pts (1797)

Collection of Original Letters from the Bishops to the Privy Council, A, ed. M. Bateson (Camden Soc., Misc., IX) (1893)

Correspondence of Dr. Matthew Hutton, ed. J. Raine (Surtees Soc. XVII) (1843)

Cranmer, T. *Remains*, ed. H. Jenkyns, 4 vols. (Oxford 1833)

Dudley, E. *The Tree of Commonwealth*, ed. D. M. Brodie (Cambridge 1948)

Fish, S. *A Supplication for the Beggars*, ed. J. M. Cowper (EETS, extra ser., XIII) (1871)

Fisher, J. *English Works*, ed. J. E. B. Mayor (EETS, extra ser., XXVII) (1876)

Foxe, J. *Acts and Monuments*, ed. S. R. Cattley and G. Townshend. 8 vols. (1837–41)

Godwin, F. *A Catalogue of the Bishops of England* (1601)

Gorham, G. C. (ed.). *Gleanings of a Few Scattered Ears during the Reformation* (1857)

Grindal, E. *Remains*, ed. W. Nicholson (Parker Soc.) (Cambridge 1843)

Harington, J. *Nugae Antiquae*, ed. T. Park. 2 vols. (1804)

Harison, A. *Registrum Vagum*, ed. T. F. Barton. 2 vols. (Norfolk Record Soc. XXXII, XXXIII) (1963–4)

Harpsfield, N. *Historia Anglicana Ecclesiastica* (1622)

Harrison, W. *A Description of England*, ed. G. Edelen (New York 1968)

Historiae Dunelmensis Scriptores Tres, ed. J. Raine (Surtees Soc. IX) (1839)

Historical Manuscript Commission Reports
  De L'Isle and Dudley, vol. II (no. 77)
  Salisbury MSS., vols. II, V–XII (no. 9)
  Wells, vol. II (no. 12)

Hooker, R. *Of the Laws of Ecclesiastical Polity*. 8 vols. (1888)

Hooper, J. *Early Writings*, ed. S. Carr (Parker Soc.) (Cambridge 1843)

Howden, M. P. (ed.). *Register of Richard Foxe, Bishop of Durham, 1494–1501* (Surtees Soc. CXLVII) (1932)

Illustrations of British History, ed. E. Lodge. 3 vols. (1838)

Itinerary of John Leland in or about the Years 1535–1543, The, ed. L. T. Smith. 5 vols. (1907–10)

Jewel, J. *Works*, ed. J. Ayre. 4 vols. (Parker Soc.) (Cambridge 1845–50)

Kershaw, I. (ed.). *Bolton Priory Rentals and Ministers' Accounts, 1473–1539* (Yorkshire Archaeological Soc. Record Ser. CXXXII) (1970)

Kitchin, G. W. and Madge, F. T. (eds.). *Documents relating to the Foundation of the Chapter of Winchester* (Hampshire Record Soc. I) (1889)

Langland, W. *Piers the Ploughman*, ed. J. F. Goodrich (1968)

Latimer, H. *Remains*, ed. G. E. Corrie. 2 vols. (Parker Soc.) (Cambridge 1844)

Letter Book of John Parkhurst, The, ed. R. Houlbrooke (Norfolk Record Soc. XLIII) (1974–5)

Letters and Papers Illustrative of the Reigns of Richard III and Henry VII, ed. J. Gairdner. 2 vols. (1861–3)

Letters of Richard Fox, 1486–1527, The, ed. P. S. and H. M. Allen (Oxford 1928)

Letters of Stephen Gardiner, ed. J. A. Muller (Cambridge 1933)

Letters of Thomas Wood, Puritan, 1566–1577, ed. P. Collinson (*BIHR* special supp. no. 5, 1960)

Literary Remains of King Edward VI, ed. J. G. Nichols. 2 vols. (Roxburghe Club)(1857)

Lyndwood, W. *Provinciale seu constitutiones Anglie* (Oxford 1679)

Machyn, Henry. *Diary*, ed. J. G. Nichols (Camden Soc. XLII) (1848)

Marprelate Tracts, The, ed. W. Pierce (1911)

Narratives of the Days of the Reformation, ed. J. G. Nichols (Camden Soc. LXXVII)(1859)

Norden, J. *The Surveyor's Dialogue* (1738)

Notebook of John Penry, The, ed. A. Peel (Camden Soc., 3rd ser., LXVII)(1944)

Original Letters Relative to the English Reformation, ed. H. Robinson. 2 vols. (Parker Soc.)(Cambridge 1846–7)

Parsons, R. *Memorial for the Reformation of England* (1824)

Paule, G. *The Life of the Most Reverend Prelate J. Whitgift* (1612)

Peck, F. (ed.). *Desiderata Curiosa: or A Collection of Divers Scarce and Curious Pieces relating Chiefly to Matters of English History*. 2 vols. (1732–5)

Peterborough Local Administration, ed. W. T. Mellows (Northamptonshire Record Soc. XIII)(1941)

Pilkington, J. *Works*, ed. J. Scholefield (Parker Soc.) (Cambridge 1842)

Purvis, J. S. (ed.). *Select Sixteenth Century Causes in Tithe* (Yorkshire Archaeological Soc. CXIV)(1949)

Raines, F. R. (ed.). *Notitia Cestriensis: Historical Notes of the Diocese of Chester* (Chetham Soc. VIII)(1845)

Registrum Caroli Bothe, ed. A. T. Bannister (Cantilupe Soc.) (1921)

Registrum Ricardi Mayhew, ed. A. T. Bannister (Cantilupe Soc.) (1920)

Ridley, N. *Works*, ed. H. Christmas (Parker Soc.) (Cambridge 1841)

St German, C. *A Treatise concerning the Division between the Spirituality and Temporality* (1532?)

Sandys, E. *The Sermons of Archbishop Sandys*, ed. J. Ayre (Parker Soc.) (Cambridge 1842)

Sandys, W. (ed.). 'An Inventory of Matthew Parker's Goods at Death', *Archaeologia* XXX (1844)

Second Parte of a Register, The, ed. A. Peel. 2 vols. (Cambridge 1915)

Thompson, A. H. (ed.). *Statutes of the Cathedral Church of Durham* (Surtees Soc. CXLIII)(1929)

Townshend, H. *Historical Collections* (1680)

Turner, W. *The Hunting of the Romish Wolf* (Basel 1554? 1555?)

Tytler, P. (ed.). *England under the Reigns of Edward VI and Mary*. 2 vols. (1839)

Valor Ecclesiasticus, ed. J. Caley and J. Hunter. 6 vols. (1810–34)

Vowell, J., alias Hooker. *A Catalog of the Bishops of Exeter* (1584)

Walsingham, T. *Historia Anglicana*, ed. H. T. Riley. 2 vols. (1864)

Wilkins, D. (ed.). *Concilia Magnae Britanniae*. 4 vols. (Oxford 1761)

Williams, J. F. and Cozens-Hardy, B. (eds.). *Extracts from the Two Earliest Minute Books of the Dean and Chapter of Norwich, 1566–1649* (Norfolk Record Soc. XXIV)(1954)

Wilson, T. *The State of England, Anno Domini 1600* (Camden Soc., Misc., XVI (3rd ser., LII)) (1936)

Wycliffe, J. *De Civile Dominio*, ed. R. L. Lane Poole (1885)
Opera Minora, ed. J. Loserth (1913)

Wynn, J. *History of the Gwydir Family* (1827)

Zurich Letters, The, ed. H. Robinson. 2 vols. (Parker Soc.) (Cambridge 1842–5)

Secondary

Agrarian History of England and Wales, The, vol. IV: *1500–1640*, ed. J. Thirsk (Cambridge 1967)

Aston, M. *Thomas Arundel* (Oxford 1967)

Bean, J. M. *The Estates of the Percy Family, 1416–1537* (Oxford 1958)

Beer, B. L. *Northumberland: The Political Career of John Dudley* (1973)

Berlatsky, J. A. 'Thomas Bentham and the Plight of the Early Elizabethan Bishops', *Historical Magazine of the Protestant Episcopal Church* XLIII (1974)
'Marriage and Family in a Tudor Elite', *Journal of Family History* III (1978)

Blench, J. *Preaching in England in the Late Fifteenth and Sixteenth Centuries* (Oxford 1964)

Bossy, J. *The English Catholic Community, 1570–1850* (1975)

Bowker, M. *The Secular Clergy in the Diocese of Lincoln, 1495–1520* (Cambridge 1967)
'The Commons' Supplication against the Ordinaries in the Light of Some Archidiaconal Accounts', *TRHS*, 5th ser., XXI (1971)

Burnet, G. *History of the Reformation*, ed. N. Pocock. 7 vols. (Oxford 1865)

Bush, M. L. *The Government Policy of Protector Somerset* (1975)

Carsten, F. L. *Princes and Parliaments in Germany* (Oxford 1959)

Chambers, D. S. *Cardinal Bainbridge in the Court of Rome, 1509–1514* (1965)

Church and Society in England: Henry VIII to James I, ed. F. Heal and M. R. O'Day (1977)

Continuity and Change: Personnel and Administration of the Church in England, 1500–1640, ed. M. R. O'Day and F. Heal (Leicester 1976)

Cooper, C. H. *Annals of Cambridge*. 5 vols. (Cambridge 1842–1908)

Cornwall, J. 'The Early Tudor Gentry', *EcHR*, 2nd ser., XVII (1965)

Cross, C. *The Royal Supremacy in the Elizabethan Church* (1969)
'Economic Problems of the See of York: Decline and Recovery in the Sixteenth Century', *Agricultural History Review*, supp., XVIII (1970)
Church and People, 1450–1660 (1976)

Dickens, A. G. *Robert Holgate, Archbishop of York* (St Anthony's Hall) (York 1955)
The English Reformation (1964; Fontana edn 1967)

Dietz, F. C. *English Government Finance, 1485–1558* (Urbana, Ill. 1920)

Du Boulay, F. 'Archbishop Cranmer and the Canterbury Temporalities', *EHR* LXVII (1952)

'The Quarrel between the Carmelite Friars and the Secular Clergy of London, 1464–1458', *JEH* VI (1955)

'A Rentier Economy in the Later Middle Ages: The Archbishopric of Canterbury', *EcHR*, 2nd ser., XVI (1964)

The Lordship of Canterbury (1966)

Dunkley, E. H. *The Reformation in Denmark* (1948)

Dyer, C. 'A Redistribution of Incomes in Fifteenth-Century England', *Past and Present* XXXIX (1968)

Elton, G. R. 'Parliamentary Drafts, 1529–40', *BIHR* XXV (1952)

Reform and Renewal: Thomas Cromwell and the Common Weal (Cambridge 1973)

Fuller, T. *Church History of Britain*, ed. J. S. Brewer. 6 vols. (Oxford 1845)

Gilchrist, J. *The Church and Economic Activity in the Middle Ages* (1969)

Goring, C. 'The General Proscription of 1522', *EHR* LXXXVI (1971)

Green, I. *The Re-Establishment of the Church of England, 1660–63* (Oxford 1978)

Haigh, C. *The Last Days of the Lancashire Monasteries and the Pilgrimage of Grace* (Manchester 1969)

Reformation and Resistance in Tudor Lancashire (Cambridge 1975)

Hassell-Smith, A. *County and Court: Government and Politics in Norfolk, 1558–1603* (Oxford 1974)

Haugaard, W. *Elizabeth and the English Reformation* (Cambridge 1968)

Heal, F. 'The Bishops and the Act of Exchange of 1559', *HJ* XVII (1974)

'Henry VIII and the Wealth of the English Episcopate', *Archiv für Reformationsgeschichte* LXVI (1975)

Hembry, P. *The Bishops of Bath and Wells, 1530–1640* (1967)

Heylyn, P. *Ecclesia Restaurata: or The History of the Reformation of the Church of England*, ed. J. C. Robertson (Cambridge 1849)

Examen Historicum (1659)

Hill, C. *Economic Problems of the Church from Archbishop Whitgift to the Long Parliament* (Oxford 1956)

Hoak, D. *The King's Council under Edward VI* (Cambridge 1976)

Hoskins, W. G. *The Age of Plunder* (1976)

Howell, M. *Regalian Right in Medieval England* (Oxford 1962)

Hughes, P. *The Reformation in England*, 3 vols. (1951–4)

Hutton, E. *The Franciscans in England, 1224–1538* (1926)

James, M. R. *Family, Lineage and Civil Society* (Oxford 1974)

Jones, N. L. 'Profiting from Religious Reform: The Land Rush of 1559', *HJ* XXII (1979)

Jordan, W. K. *The Charities of Rural England* (1961)

Edward VI: The Young King (1968)

Edward VI: The Threshold of Power (1970)

Kennett, White. *The Case of Impropriations Truly Stated* (1704)

Kitching, C. J. 'The Quest for Concealed Lands in the Reign of Elizabeth I', *TRHS*, 5th ser., xxiv (1974)

Lansdell, H. *The Sacred Tenth* (1906)

Lapsley, G. T. *The County Palatine of Durham* (New York 1900)

Loades, D. M. *The Oxford Martyrs* (1970)

   'The Last Years of Cuthbert Tunstall, 1547–1559', *Durham Univ. Journal* LXVI (1973–4)

Lunt, W. J. *Financial Relations between England and the Papacy, 1317–1534* (Cambridge, Mass. 1962)

MacCaffrey, W. *Exeter, 1540–1640* (Cambridge, Mass. 1958)

Manning, R. B. *Religion and Society in Elizabethan Sussex* (Leicester 1969)

Miller, E. *The Abbey and Bishopric of Ely* (Cambridge 1951)

Miller, H. 'Subsidy Assessments of the Peerage in the Sixteenth Century', *BIHR* xxviii (1955)

Morgan, W. T. 'Two cases concerning Dilapidations to Episcopal Property in the Diocese of St. David's', *Nat. Library of Wales Journal* vii (1951–2)

Muller, J. A. *Stephen Gardiner and the Tudor Reaction* (1926)

Mumford, A. A. *Hugh Oldham* (1936)

Neale, J. E. *Elizabeth I and her Parliaments*, 2 vols. (1953)

Nef, J. *The Rise of the British Coal Industry*, 2 vols. (1932)

O'Day, M. R. 'Thomas Bentham: A Case Study of the Problems of the Early Elizabethan Episcopate', *JEH* xxiii (1972)

   'Cumulative Debt: The Bishops of Coventry and Lichfield and their Economic Problems', *Midland History* iii (1975)

Palmer, W. M. 'Enclosure at Ely, Downham and Littleport, 1548', *Trans. of the Cambridgeshire and Huntingdonshire Archaeological Soc.* v (1930–7)

Phelps-Brown, E. H. and Hopkins, S. 'Seven Centuries of the Prices of Consumables', *Economica* xcii (n.s. xxiii) (1956)

Plucknett, T. F. T. *Legislation of Edward I* (Oxford 1949)

Pogson, R. 'Revival and Reform in Mary Tudor's Church: A Question of Money', *JEH* xxvi (1975)

Pollard, A. F. *Wolsey*, ed. G. R. Elton (1965)

Powell, K. 'The Beginnings of Protestantism in Gloucestershire', *Trans. of the Bristol and Gloucestershire Archaeological Soc.* xc (1972)

Report from the Select Committee on Church Leases. 2 vols. (1837–8)

Roberts, M. *The Early Vasas* (1968)

Rogers, J. E. Thorold. *A History of Agriculture and Prices in England.* 7 vols. (Oxford 1866–1902)

Ross, C. and Pugh, T. B. 'Materials for the Study of Baronial Incomes in Fifteenth-Century England', *EcHR*, 2nd ser., vi (1953)

Savine, A. 'English Monasteries on the Eve of the Dissolution', in *Oxford Studies in Social History*, vol. i, ed. P. Vinogradoff (Oxford 1909)

Scarisbrick, J. J. 'Clerical Taxation in England, 1485–1547', *JEH* xi (1960)
  Henry VIII (1968)
Schenk, W. *Reginald Pole, Cardinal of England* (1950)
Simpson, A. *The Wealth of the Gentry, 1540–1640* (Cambridge 1961)
Smith, L. B. *Tudor Prelates and Politics* (Princeton, N.J. 1953)
  Henry VIII: The Mask of Royalty (1971)
Smith, R. B. *Land and Politics in the England of Henry VIII* (Oxford 1970)
Spelman, H. *History and Fate of Sacrilege* (1853)
Stone, L. 'The Political Programme of Thomas Cromwell', *BIHR* xxiv (1951)
  The Crisis of the Aristocracy, 1558–1641 (Oxford 1967)
Storey, R. L. *Thomas Langley and the Bishopric of Durham, 1406–1537* (1961)
Strype, J. *Ecclesiastical Memorials Relating chiefly to Religion . . .* 3 vols. (Oxford 1820–40)
  Annals of the Reformation. 4 vols. (Oxford 1820–40)
  The Life and Acts of the Most Reverend Father in God, John Whitgift. 3 vols. (Oxford 1822)
  Memorials of the Most Reverend Father in God, Thomas Cranmer. 2 vols. (Oxford 1840)
Sturge, C. *Cuthbert Tunstal* (1938)
Venables, E. *Episcopal Palaces* (1895)
Victoria County Histories of England
Wealth and Power in Tudor England, ed. E. W. Ives, J. J. Scarisbrick and R. J. Knecht (1978)
White, F. O. *Lives of the Elizabethan Bishops* (1898)
Wilkie, W. *The Cardinal Protectors of England* (Cambridge 1974)
Willan, T. S. 'The Parliamentary Surveys of the North Riding of Yorkshire', *Yorkshire Archaeological Soc. Journal* xxxi (1954)
Williams, G. 'Richard Davies, Bishop of St. David's, 1561–81', *Trans. of the Hon. Soc. of Cymmrodorion* (1948)
Willis, Browne. *A Survey of the Cathedrals.* 3 vols. (1742)
Wolffe, B. P. *The Crown Lands, 1461–1536* (1970)
Workman, H. B. *John Wyclif: A Study of the English Medieval Church* (Oxford 1926)
Youings, J. *The Dissolution of the Monasteries* (1972)

UNPUBLISHED THESES

Berlatsky, J. A. 'The Social Structure of the Elizabethan Episcopate', Northwestern University Ph.D. (1970)
Daeley, J. I. 'The Episcopal Administration of Matthew Parker, Archbishop of Canterbury, 1559–75', University of London Ph.D. (1967)

Heal, F. 'The Bishops of Ely and their Diocese during the Reformation', University of Cambridge Ph.D. (1972)

Horton, P. 'Administrative, Social and Economic Structure of the Durham Bishopric Estates, 1500–1640', University of Durham M.Litt. (1975)

Houlbrooke, R. 'Church Courts and People in the Diocese of Norwich, 1519–70', University of Oxford D.Phil. (1969)

Jones, N. L. 'Faith by Statute: The Politics of Religion in the Parliament of 1559', University of Cambridge Ph.D. (1977)

Lander, S. J. 'The Diocese of Chichester, 1508–58: Episcopal Reform under Robert Sherburne and its Aftermath', University of Cambridge Ph.D. (1974)

Marcombe, D. 'The Dean and Chapter of Durham, 1558–1603', University of Durham Ph.D. (1973)

Redhead, J. V. 'Thomas Cooper and the Elizabethan Church', University of Newcastle M.Litt. (1975)

Scarisbrick, J. J. 'The Conservative Episcopate in England, 1529–35', University of Cambridge Ph.D. (1956)

INDEX

Abington family, 36; John, 275
Acle, Norfolk, 260
adiaphora, concept of, 237–8
Alcock, John, bishop of Ely, 35, 66, 97
Aldingbourne, Sussex, manor of, 40
Aldington Park, Kent, 40
Aldrich, Robert, bishop of Carlisle, 148
alien priories, 11
Allerton, Yorks., manor of, 259, 270
Alley, William, bishop of Exeter, 249
almoner: episcopal, 76, 96; royal, 249, 278
Alresford, Hants., manor of, 24
Andrewes, Lancelot, bishop of Winchester, 256
annuities, 80–1, 188, 207, 231, 255–6, 275–6
anticlericalism, 101–2, 215
appropriated rectories, 29, 54–5, 62, 114, 118, 123–4, 131, 183, 205, 271, 283, 301
Arches, Court of, 300
Arminianism, 19, 142, 322
arrears, 46, 51, 60, 82, 192, 194, 275
Arundel, Thomas, archbishop of Canterbury, 14, 78
Ashwell, Herts., rectory of, 200
At Mere, William, steward of Norwich, 37
Auckland, Bishop, Durham, manor of, 40–1, 88, 145, 292
Auckland, Durham, bailiwick of, 46
auditors, episcopal, 36, 41, 43–5, 53, 81
Audley, Edmund, bishop of Salisbury, 25, 30, 38, 48, 61, 174
Audley, Thomas, 114
Augmentations, Court of, 112
Austin friars, 11
Aylmer, John, bishop of London, 216, 230, 241–2, 246, 251, 253, 259, 260, 274, 280, 287–8, 290, 292, 295, 297, 300–2, 308, 314, 317; his son John, 251

Babington, Gervase, bishop of Exeter, 250
bailiffs, 44, 50, 52, 81; accounts of, 50–2, 60

Bainbridge, Christopher, cardinal and archbishop of York, 43, 66
Balsham, Cambs., manor of, 231
Banbury, Oxon., manor of, 132
Bancroft, Richard, archbishop of Canterbury, 212, 219, 222, 237, 250, 274, 314, 322
Bangor, bishopric of, 21, 42, 108, 279; bishops of, 71, 94, 197; dean and chapter of, 108
Banwell, Somerset, manor of, 24, 32, 158, 231
Barlow, Jerome, 101
Barlow, William, bishop of Bath and Wells, 115–16, 132–3, 136, 140, 164, 171, 176, 198–9, 219
Barnes, Richard, bishop of Durham, 230–1, 255, 275, 283, 285, 288, 292, 295; his brother, 230
Barnes, Robert, 172
Barons, William, bishop of London, 93
bartons or granges, 24
Bath and Wells, bishopric of, 37, 42, 44, 57, 130, 132–3, 137, 143, 146, 148, 185, 223, 273–4, 277, 282, 286, 293, 308–9; bishops of, 32, 94, 112, 295
Baynes, Ralph, bishop of Coventry and Lichfield, 298
Beale, Robert, clerk of the privy council, 216
Beauchamp, Lord, 113
Beaufort, Lady Margaret, 97
Becon, Thomas, 7
Becon, Thomas, chancellor of Coventry and Lichfield, 254, 308
Bedfordshire, 23
Bekesbourne, Kent, manor of, 260, 292
Bellysis, Richard, 47
Bentham, Thomas, bishop of Coventry and Lichfield, 253, 260–1, 263, 290, 292, 298
Berkeley, Gilbert, bishop of Bath and Wells, 231, 257, 274, 292
Berlatsky, Joel, 242, 247, 313